Name: Takeshi Konomi

Top 5 Favorite Songs

1. Hikaru Utada, "Time Limit"

2. Yasuyuki Okamura, "Seinen 14-sai"

3. L'Arc~en~Ciel, "Peaces"

4. Kenji Hayashida, "Sora, Kumo, Hoshi, Tsuki"

5. B'z "Deep Kiss"

WITHDRAWN

About Takeshi Konomi

Takeshi Konomi exploded onto the manga scene with the incredible **THE PRINCE OF TENNIS**. His refined art style and sleek character designs proved popular with **Weekly Shonen Jump** readers, and propelled him to become the No. 1 sports manga artist. The incredibly original and fascinating male and female characters quickly won over readers, even those who wouldn't normally read such a comic. The manga and its spin-off anime series went on to become huge hits and generate mountains of merchandise.

THE PRINCE OF TENNIS
VOL. 8
SHONEN JUMP Manga Edition

STORY AND ART BY
TAKESHI KONOMI

English Adaptation/Gerard Jones
Translation/Joe Yamazaki
Touch-up Art & Lettering/Andy Ristaino
Cover & Interior Design/Terry Bennett
Editor/Michelle Pangilinan

Printed in the U.S.A.

Published by VIZ Media, LLC
P.O. Box 77010
San Francisco, CA 94107

10 9 8 7 6 5 4 3 2
First printing, June 2005
Second printing, July 2015

PARENTAL ADVISORY
THE PRINCE OF TENNIS
is rated A for All Ages. It is
recommended for any age
group.
ratings.viz.com

RATED
A
FOR
ALL AGES

THE WORLD'S
MOST POPULAR MANGA

SHONEN
JUMP

www.viz.com

www.shonenjump.com

SHONEN JUMP Manga

Vol. 8
Change the Script!

Story & Art by
Takeshi Konomi

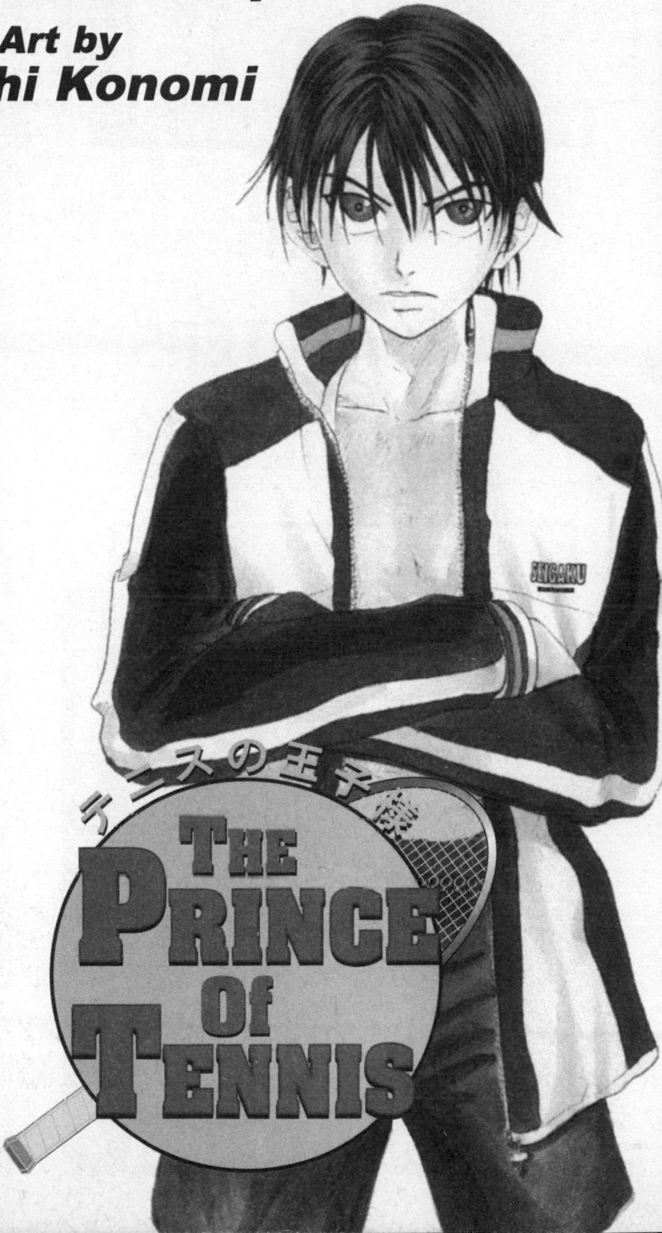
SEIGAKU
THE PRINCE OF TENNIS

THE PRINCE OF TENNIS

Kunimitsu Tezuka

Seishun Academy Tennis Team Captain (9th Grade)

Shuichiro Oishi

Seishun Academy Tennis Team Alternate Captain (9th Grade)

Shusuke Fuji

Seishun Academy Tennis Team (9th Grade)

STORY & CHARACTERS

VOLUME 1 ▸ 8

Ryoma Echizen

Seishun Academy Tennis Team (7th Grade)

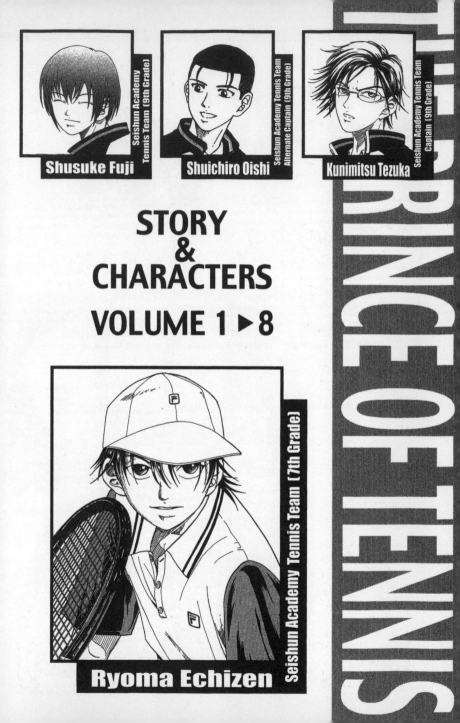

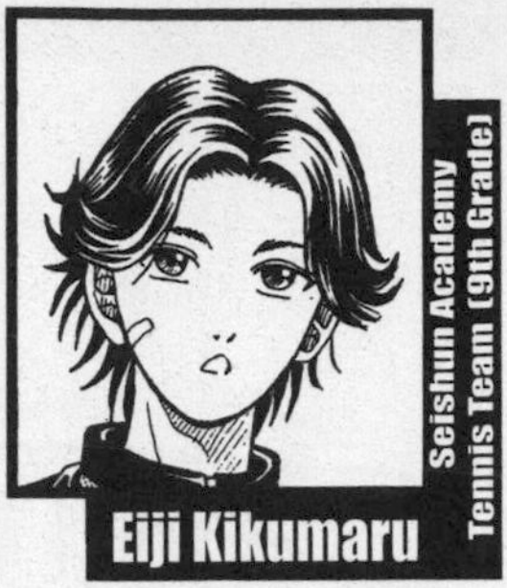
Eiji Kikumaru
Seishun Academy Tennis Team (9th Grade)

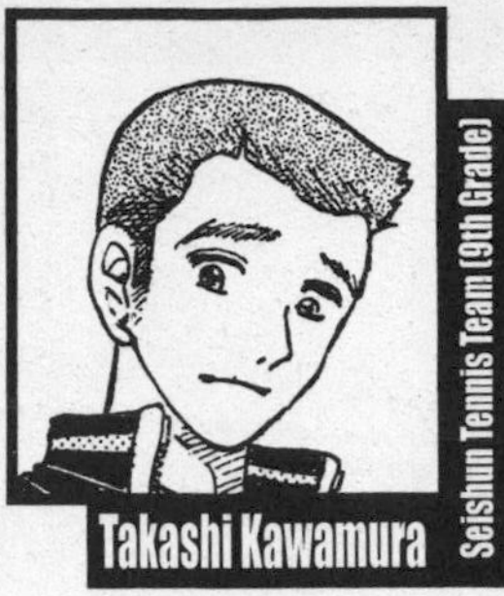
Takashi Kawamura
Seishun Tennis Team (9th Grade)

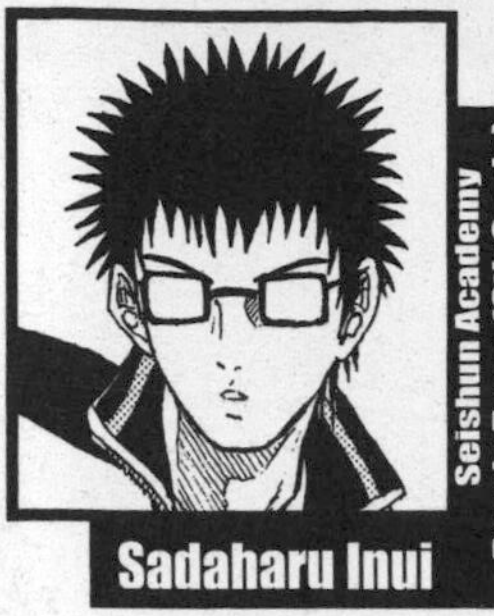
Sadaharu Inui
Seishun Academy Tennis Team (9th Grade)

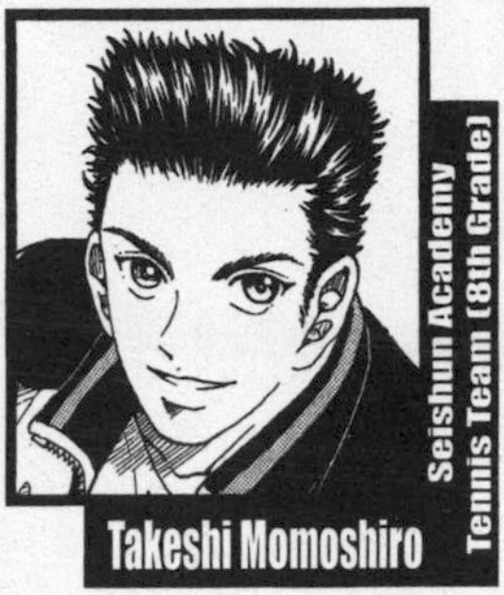
Takeshi Momoshiro
Seishun Academy Tennis Team (8th Grade)

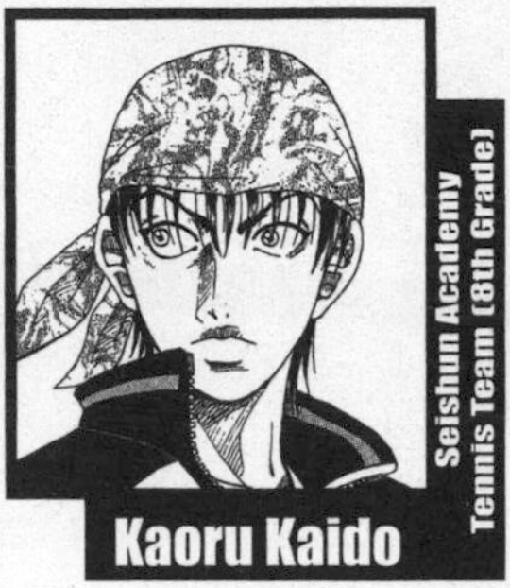
Kaoru Kaido
Seishun Academy Tennis Team (8th Grade)

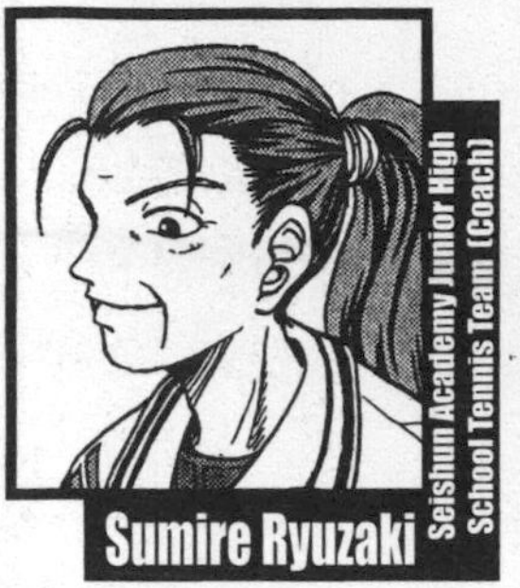
Sumire Ryuzaki
Seishun Academy Junior High School Tennis Team (Coach)

Ryoma Echizen, a tennis prodigy and winner of four U.S. Junior tournaments, has returned to Japan and enrolled at Seishun Academy Junior High. To everyone's astonishment, he becomes a starter in the District Preliminaries, while still in the 7th grade, and helps Seishun earn a berth in the City Tournament. Seishun advances easily until they meet St. Rudolph Academy, where the manager, Hajime, has researched them exhaustively. Suddenly they find themselves faced with a much tougher struggle than they ever anticipated!

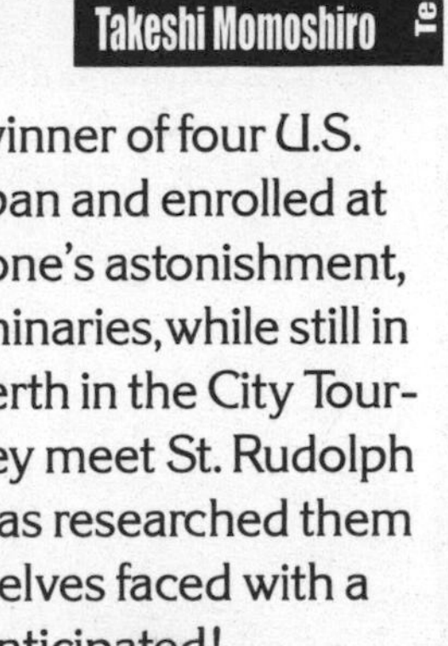
Sakuno Ryuzaki
Seishun Academy Tennis Team (7th Grade)

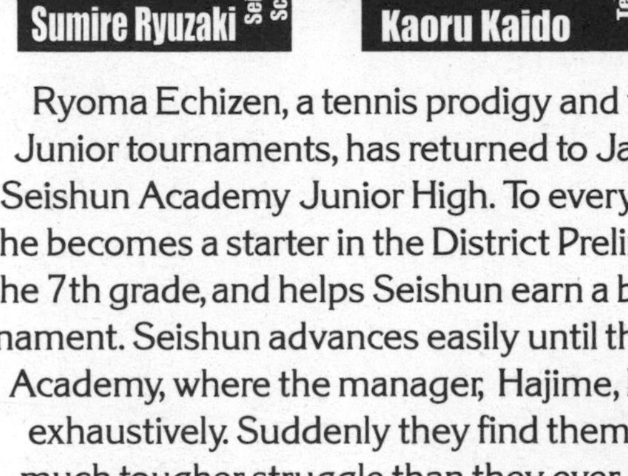
Kachiro
Horio
Katsuo
Seishun Academy Tennis Team (7th Grade)

 CONTENTS

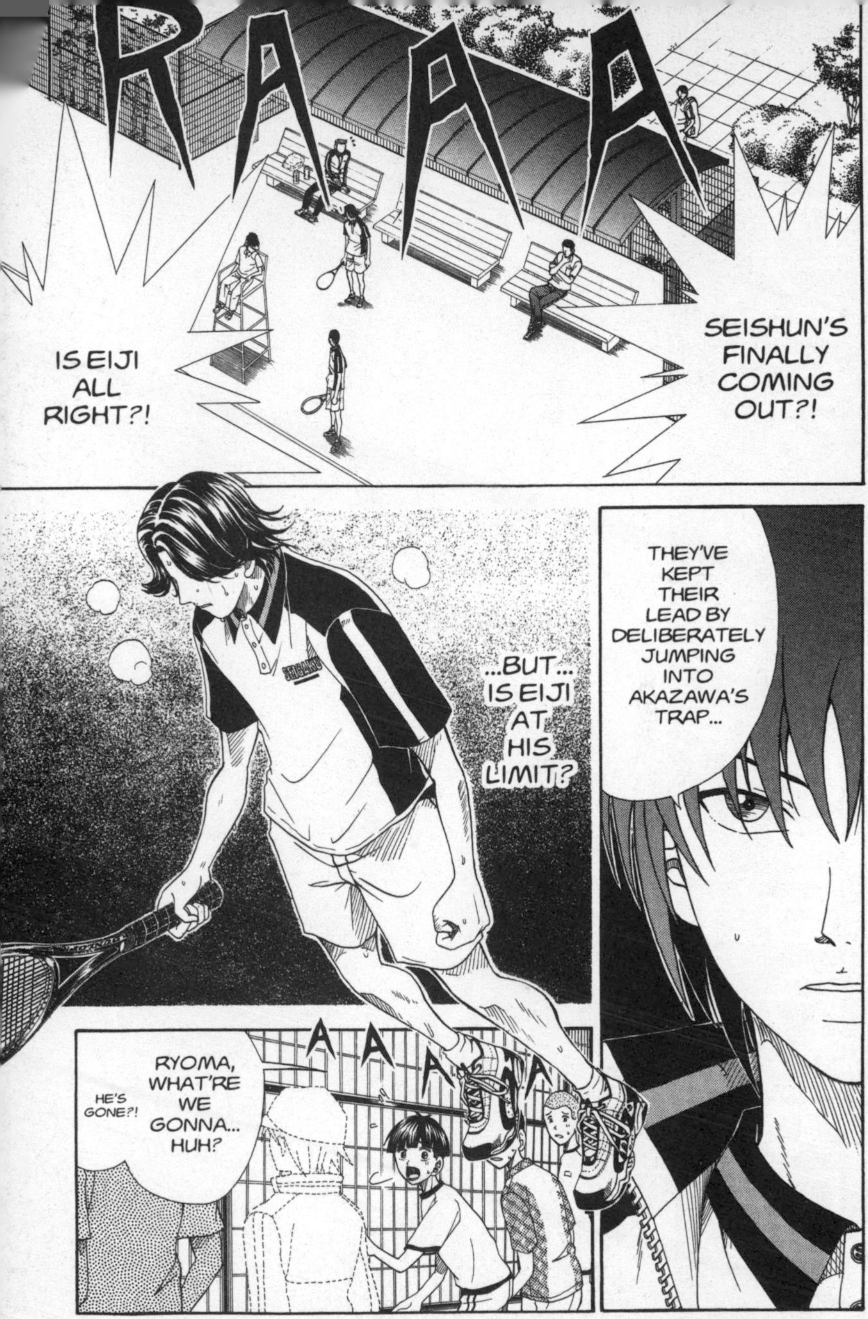
RAAA
SEISHUN'S FINALLY COMING OUT?!
IS EIJI ALL RIGHT?!
THEY'VE KEPT THEIR LEAD BY DELIBERATELY JUMPING INTO AKAZAWA'S TRAP...
...BUT... IS EIJI AT HIS LIMIT?
AAAA
RYOMA, WHAT'RE WE GONNA... HUH?
HE'S GONE?!

GENIUS 61: TRUMP CARD

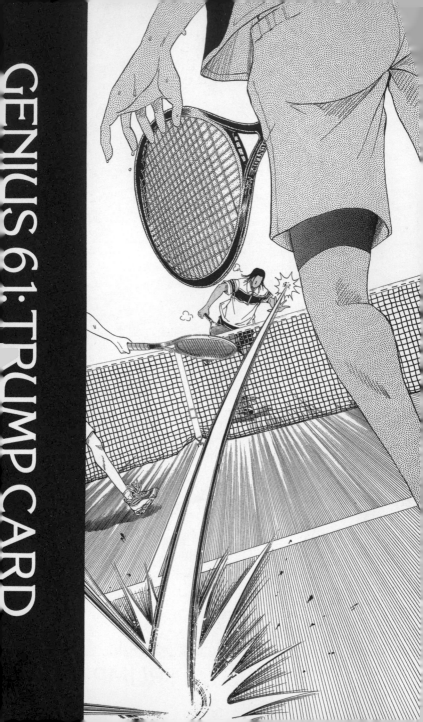

GENIUS 61: TRUMP CARD

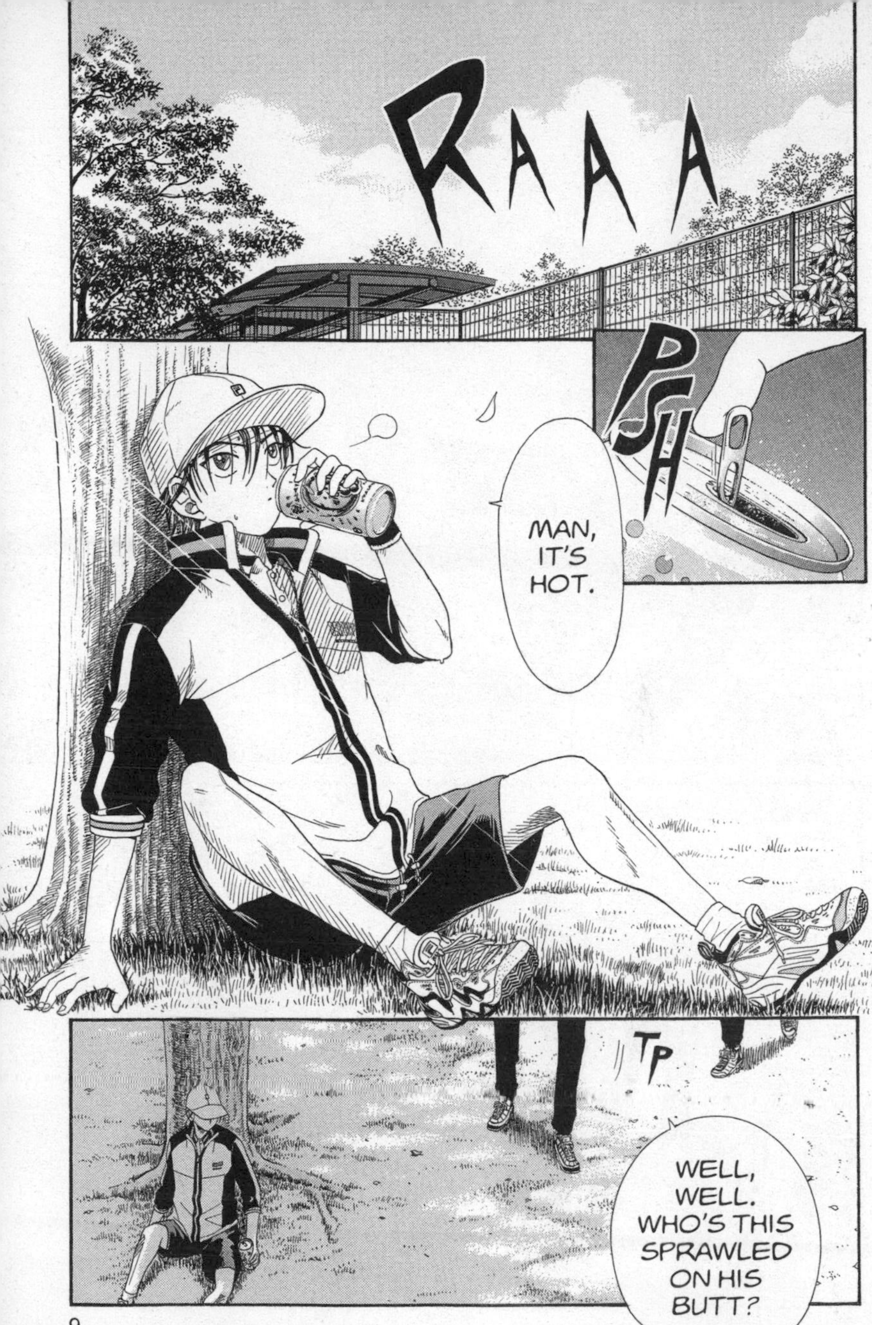
RAAA
PSH!
MAN, IT'S HOT.
TP
WELL, WELL. WHO'S THIS SPRAWLED ON HIS BUTT?

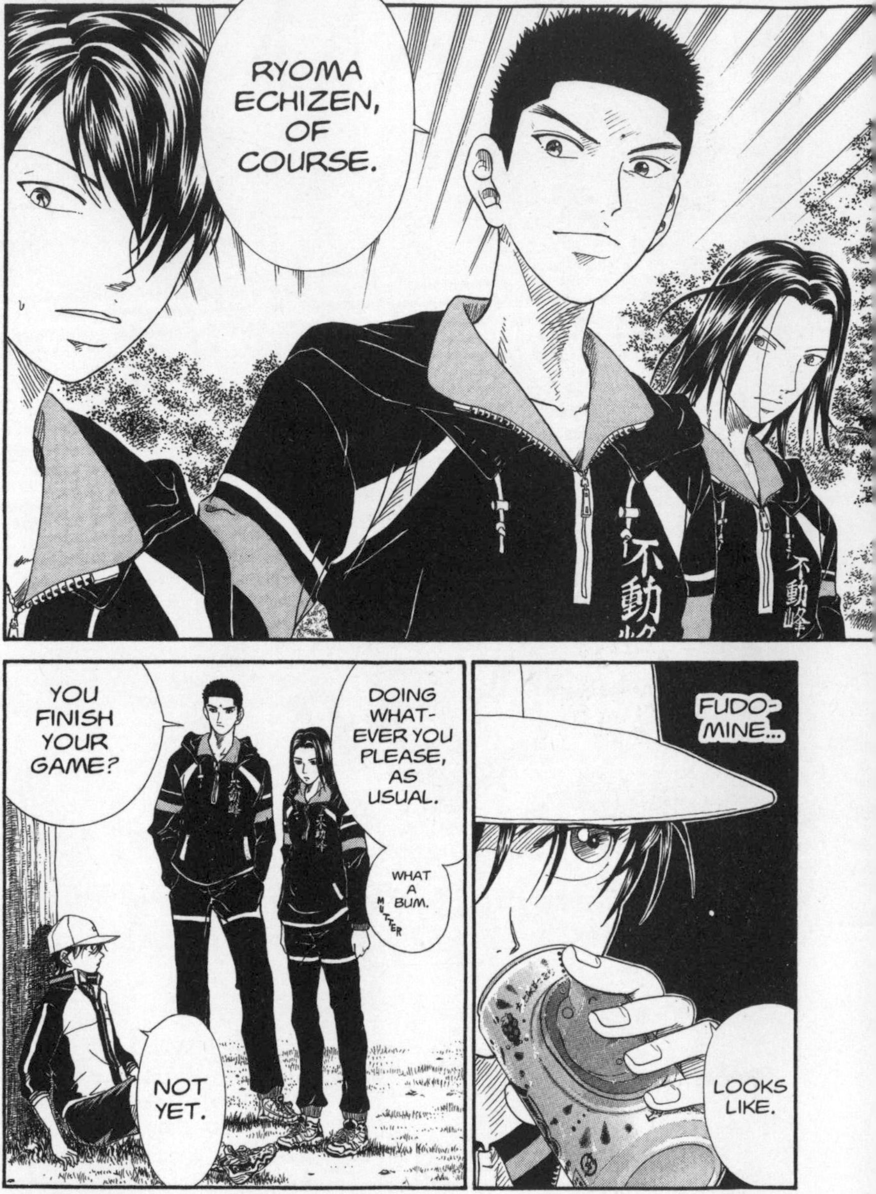
RYOMA ECHIZEN, OF COURSE.
FUDO-MINE...
LOOKS LIKE.
DOING WHATEVER YOU PLEASE, AS USUAL.
YOU FINISH YOUR GAME?
WHAT A BUM.
MUTTER
NOT YET.

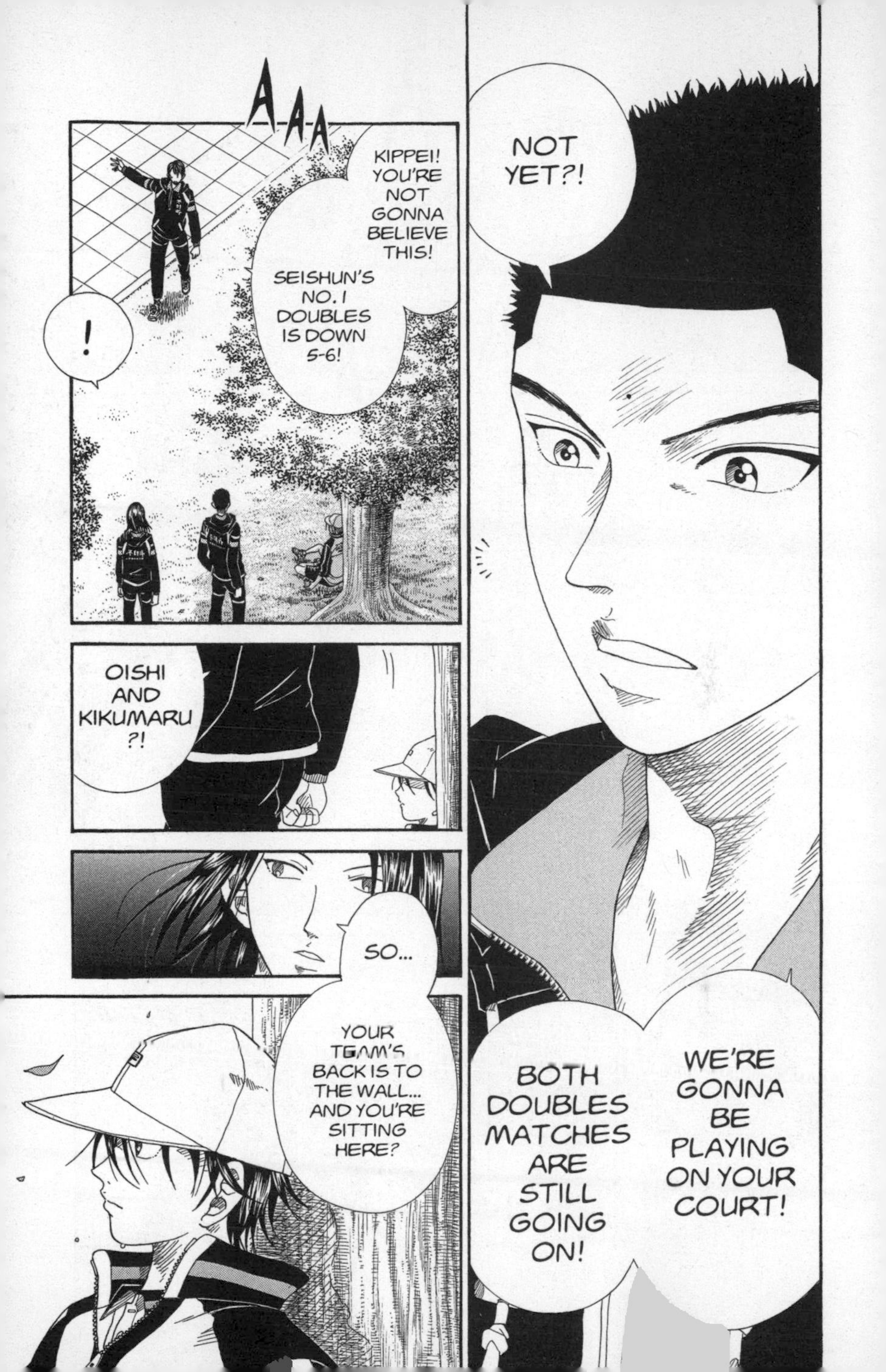
AAA
KIPPEI! YOU'RE NOT GONNA BELIEVE THIS!
SEISHUN'S NO. 1 DOUBLES IS DOWN 5-6!
!
OISHI AND KIKUMARU ?!
SO...
YOUR TEAM'S BACK IS TO THE WALL... AND YOU'RE SITTING HERE?
NOT YET?!
BOTH DOUBLES MATCHES ARE STILL GOING ON!
WE'RE GONNA BE PLAYING ON YOUR COURT!

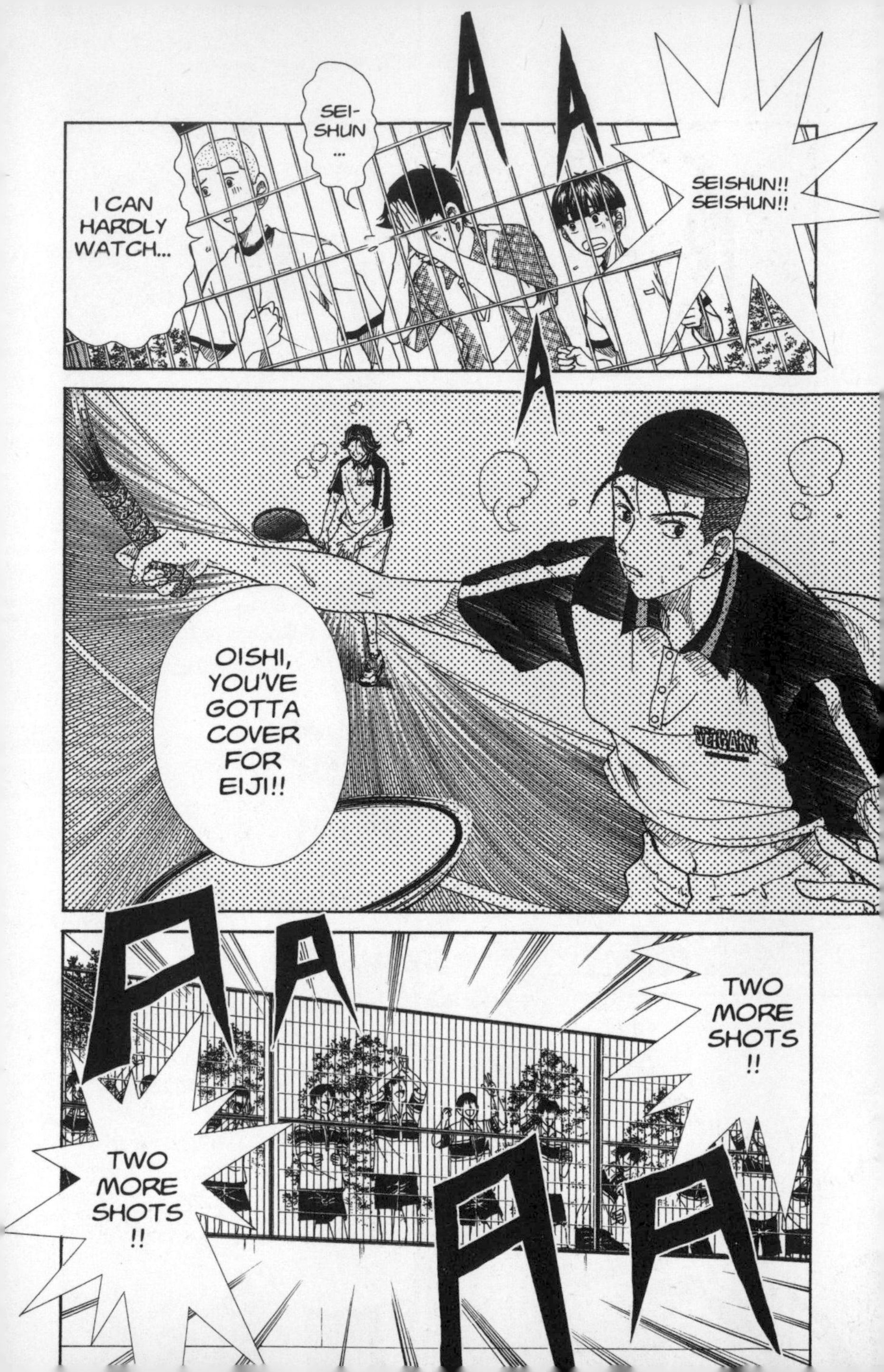
SEISHUN!! SEISHUN!!
SEI-SHUN ...
I CAN HARDLY WATCH...
OISHI, YOU'VE GOTTA COVER FOR EIJI!!
TWO MORE SHOTS !!
TWO MORE SHOTS !!

READ THIS WAY

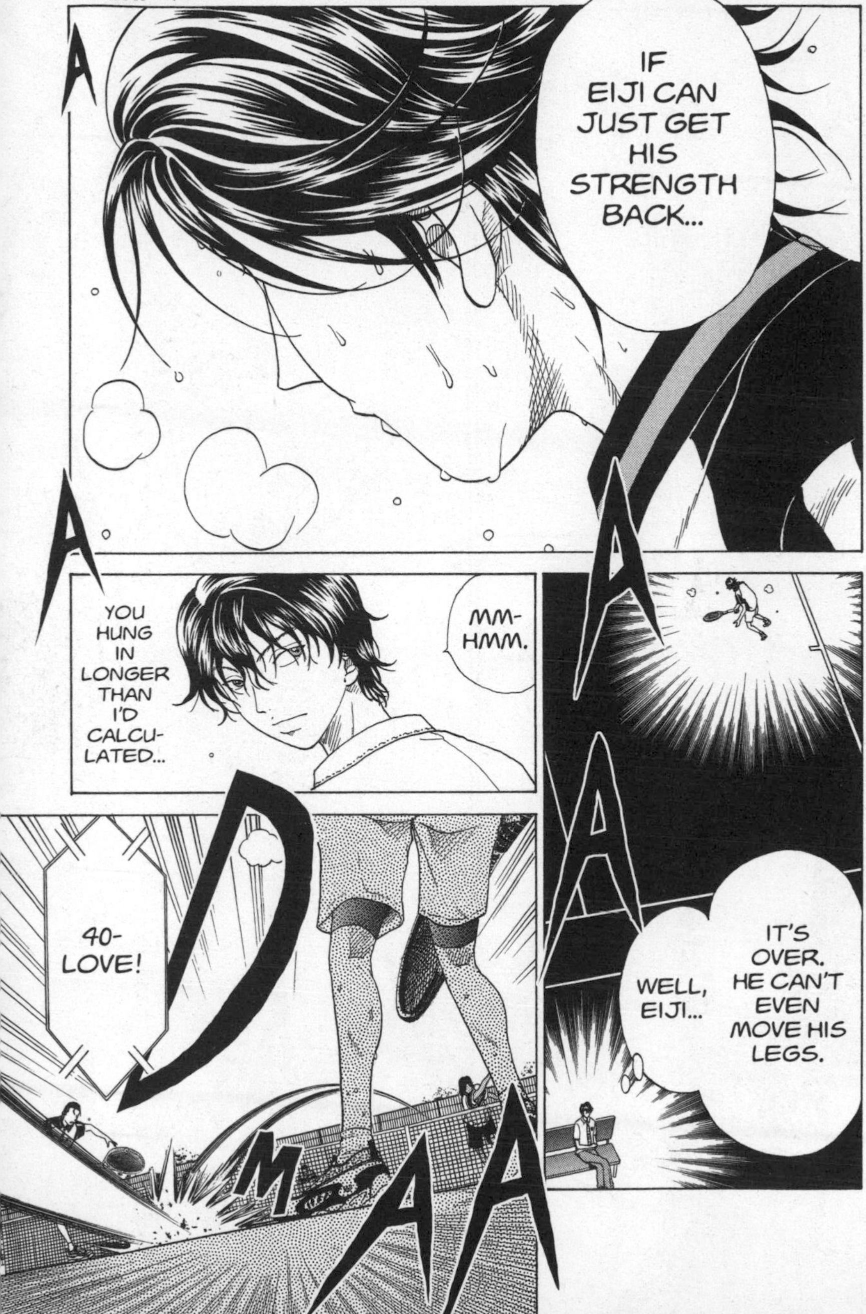
IF EIJI CAN JUST GET HIS STRENGTH BACK...
WELL, EIJI...
IT'S OVER. HE CAN'T EVEN MOVE HIS LEGS.
MM-HMM.
YOU HUNG IN LONGER THAN I'D CALCU-LATED...
40-LOVE!

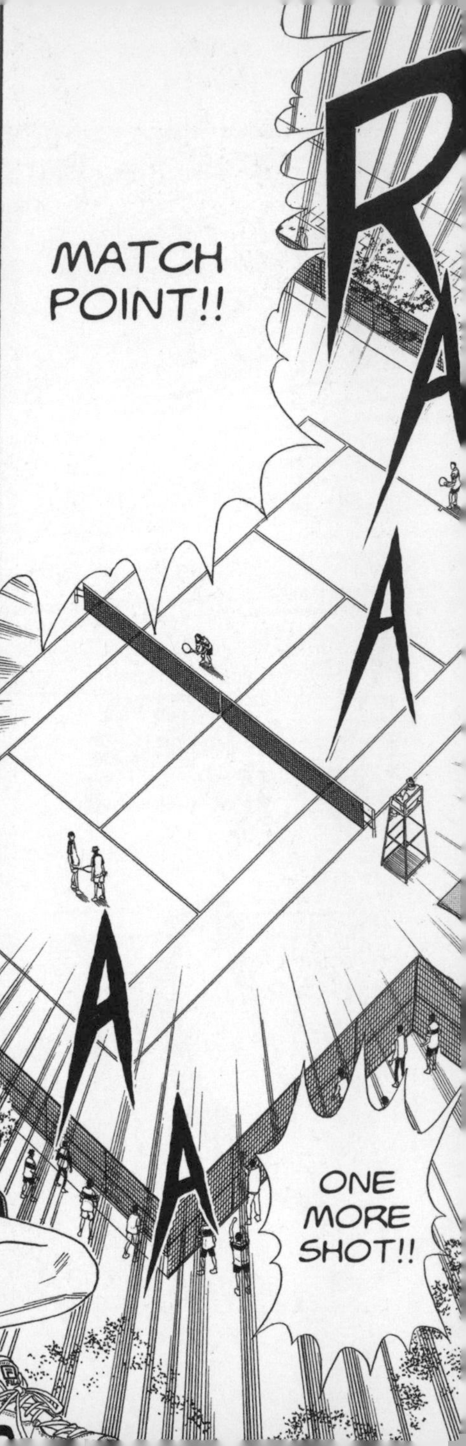
RAAAA
MATCH POINT!!
ONE MORE SHOT!!

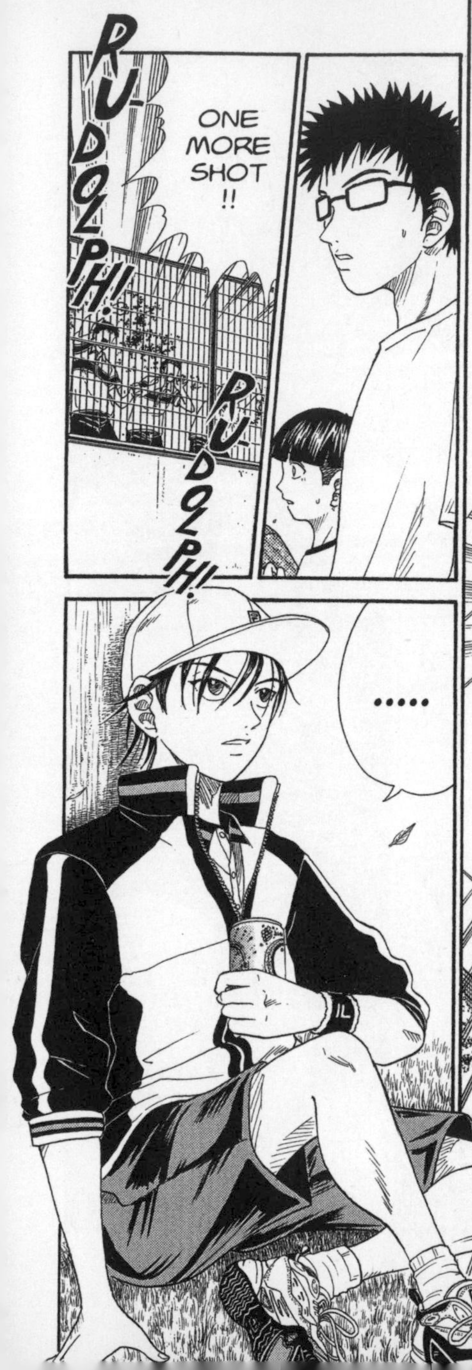
RU-RUDOLPH!
ONE MORE SHOT !!
RU-RUDOLPH!
.....

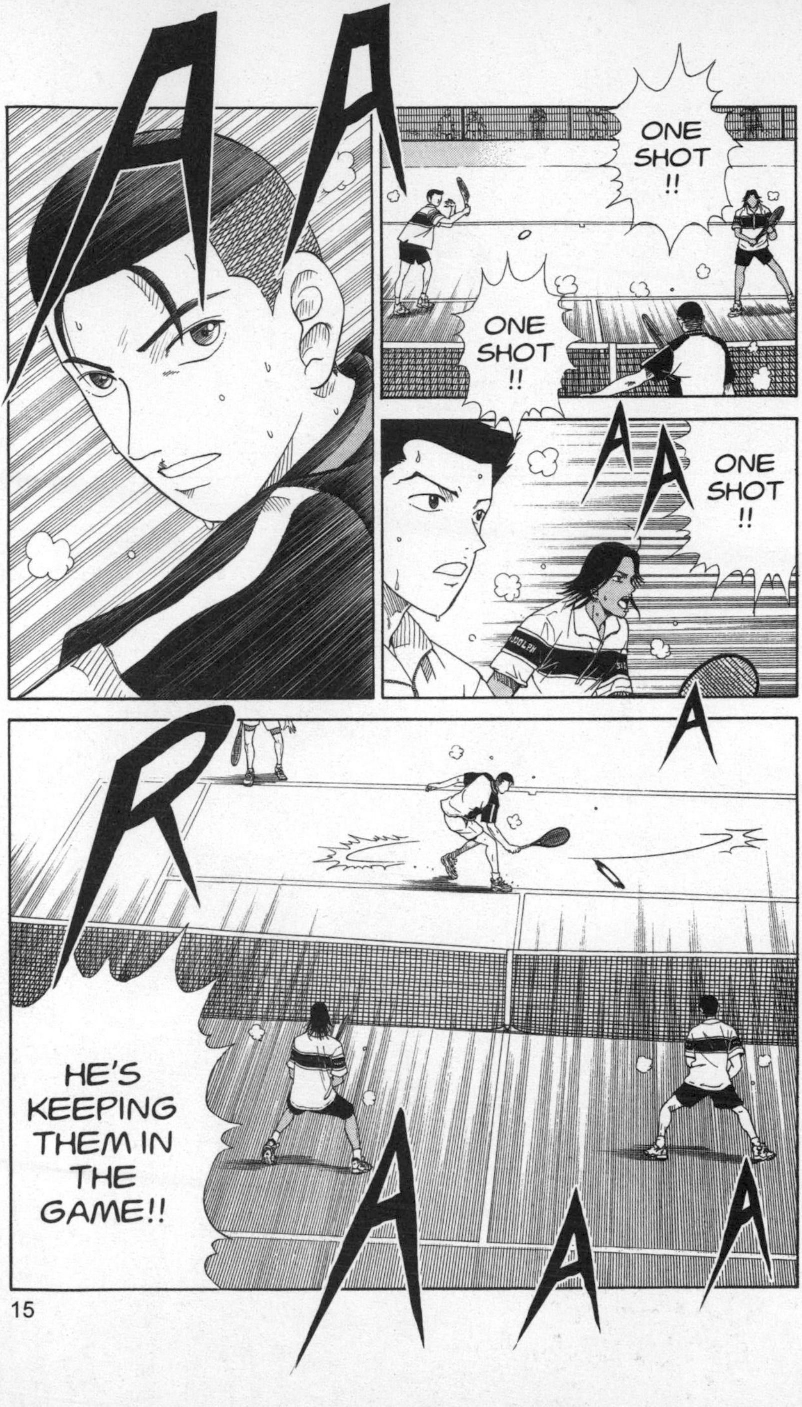
ONE SHOT !!
ONE SHOT !!
ONE SHOT !!
AA
AA
R
A
AAA
HE'S KEEPING THEM IN THE GAME!!

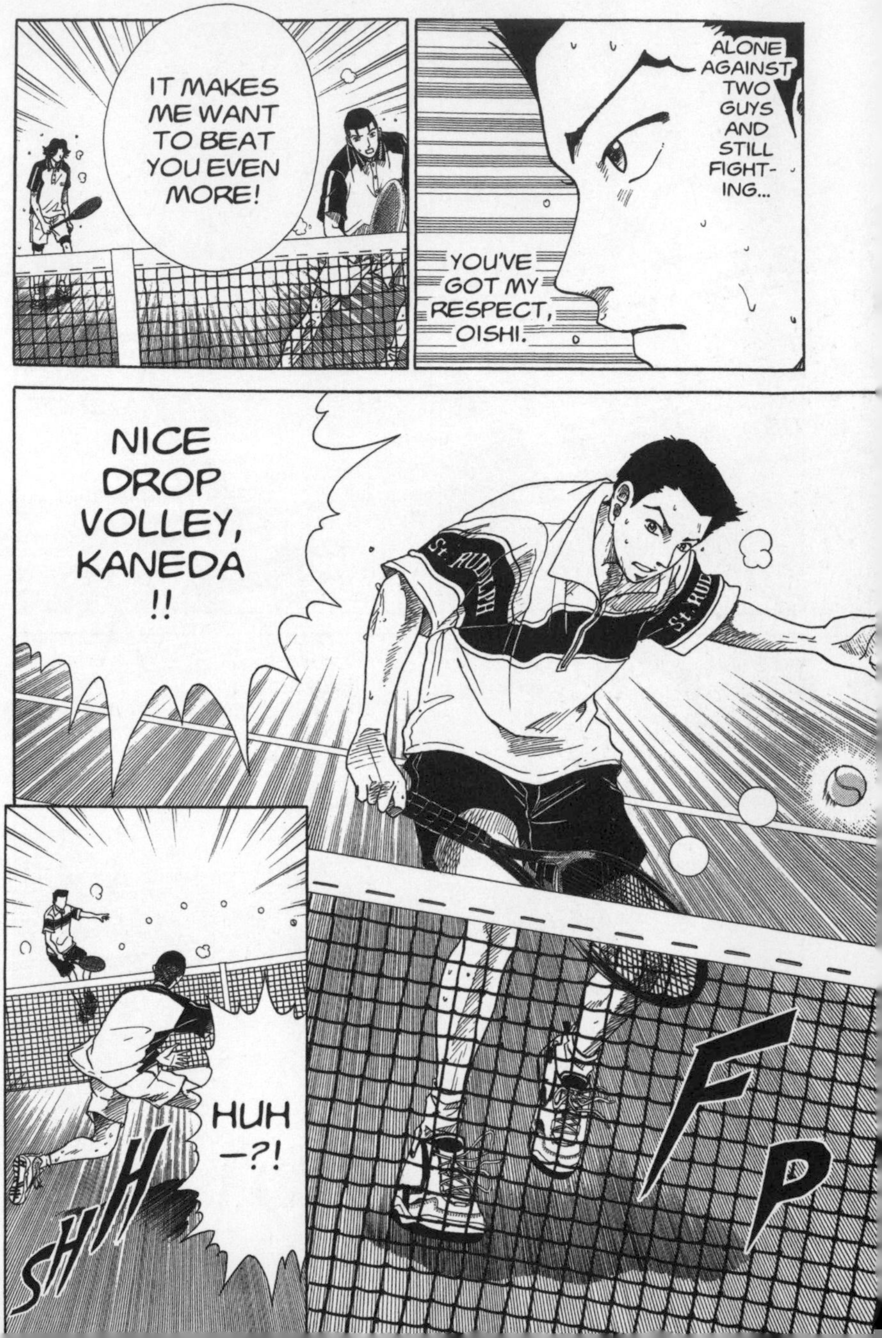
ALONE AGAINST TWO GUYS AND STILL FIGHT-ING...
YOU'VE GOT MY RESPECT, OISHI.
IT MAKES ME WANT TO BEAT YOU EVEN MORE!
NICE DROP VOLLEY, KANEDA!!
FP
HUH—?!
SHH

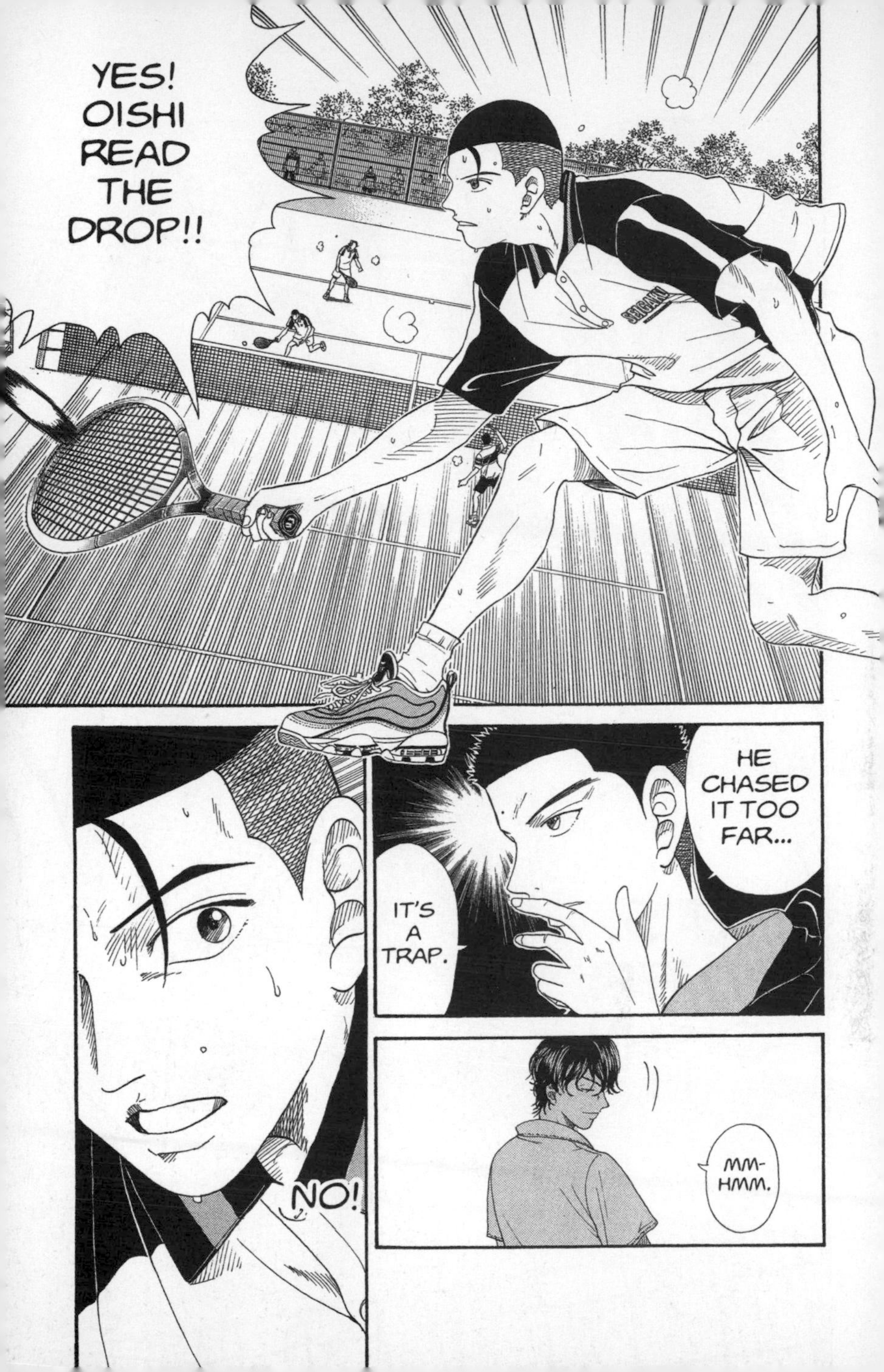
YES! OISHI READ THE DROP!!
HE CHASED IT TOO FAR...
IT'S A TRAP.
MM-HMM.
NO!

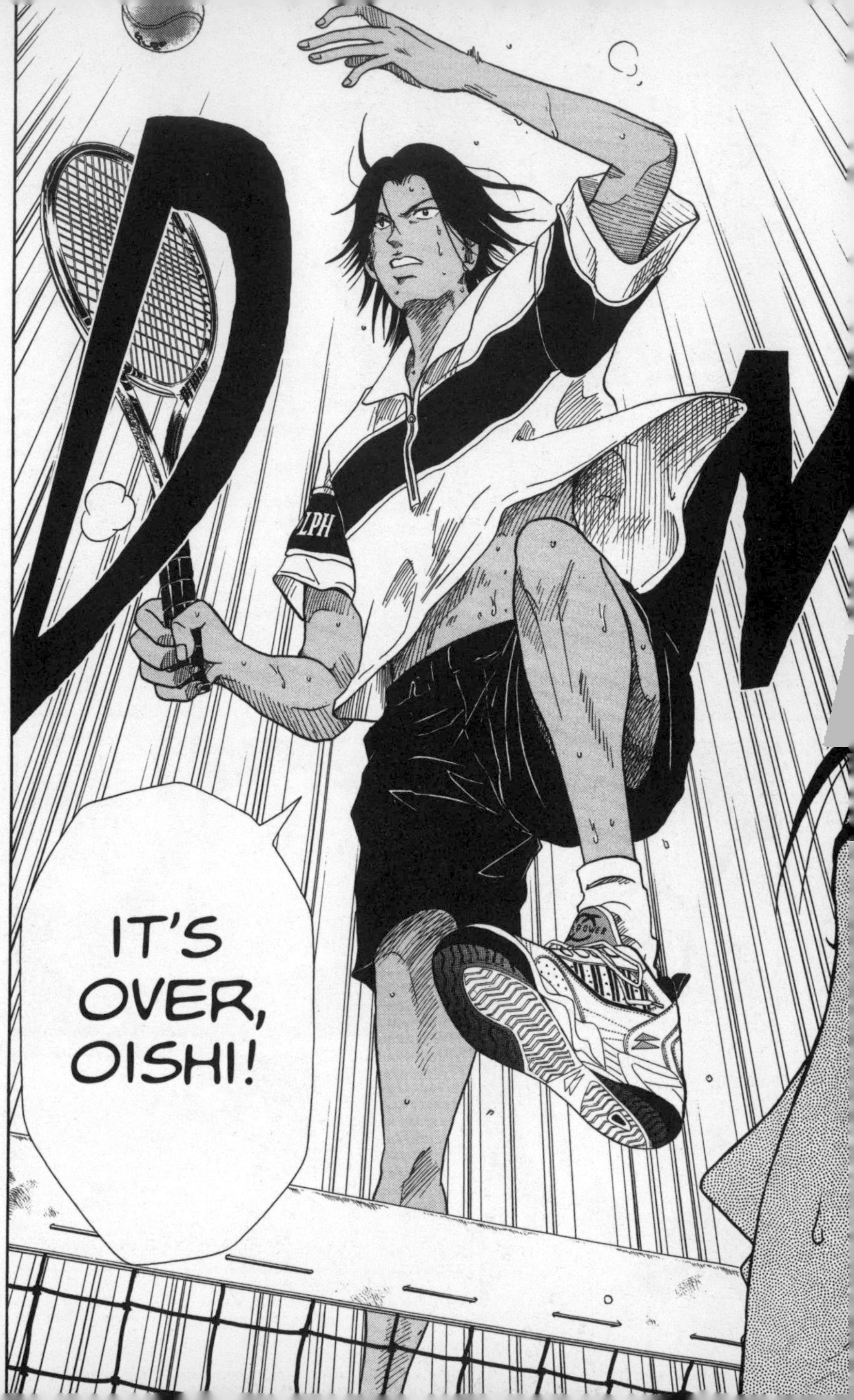
IT'S OVER, OISHI!

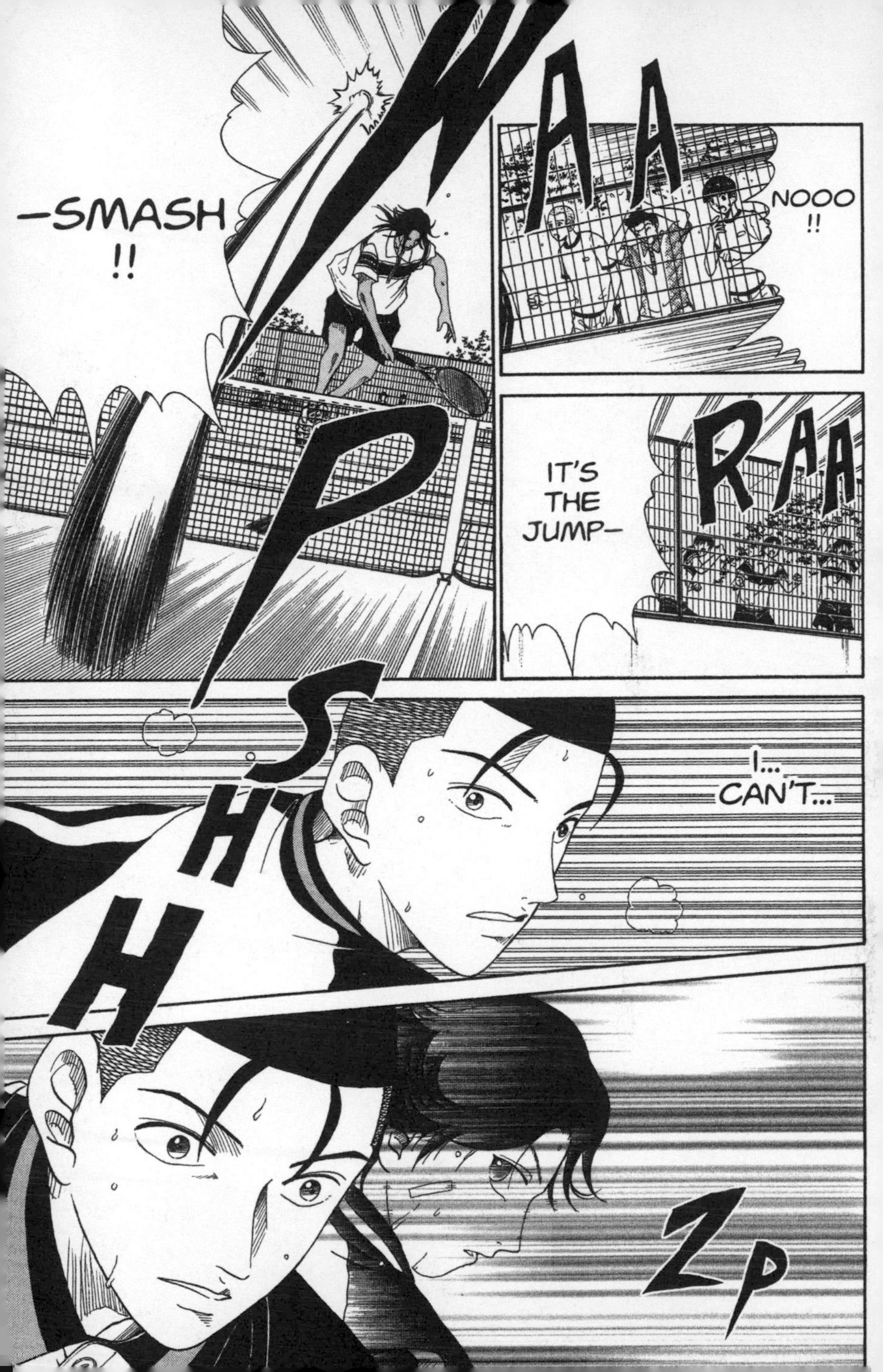

WAA
NOOO !!
RAA
IT'S THE JUMP-
-SMASH !!
I... CAN'T...
ZP

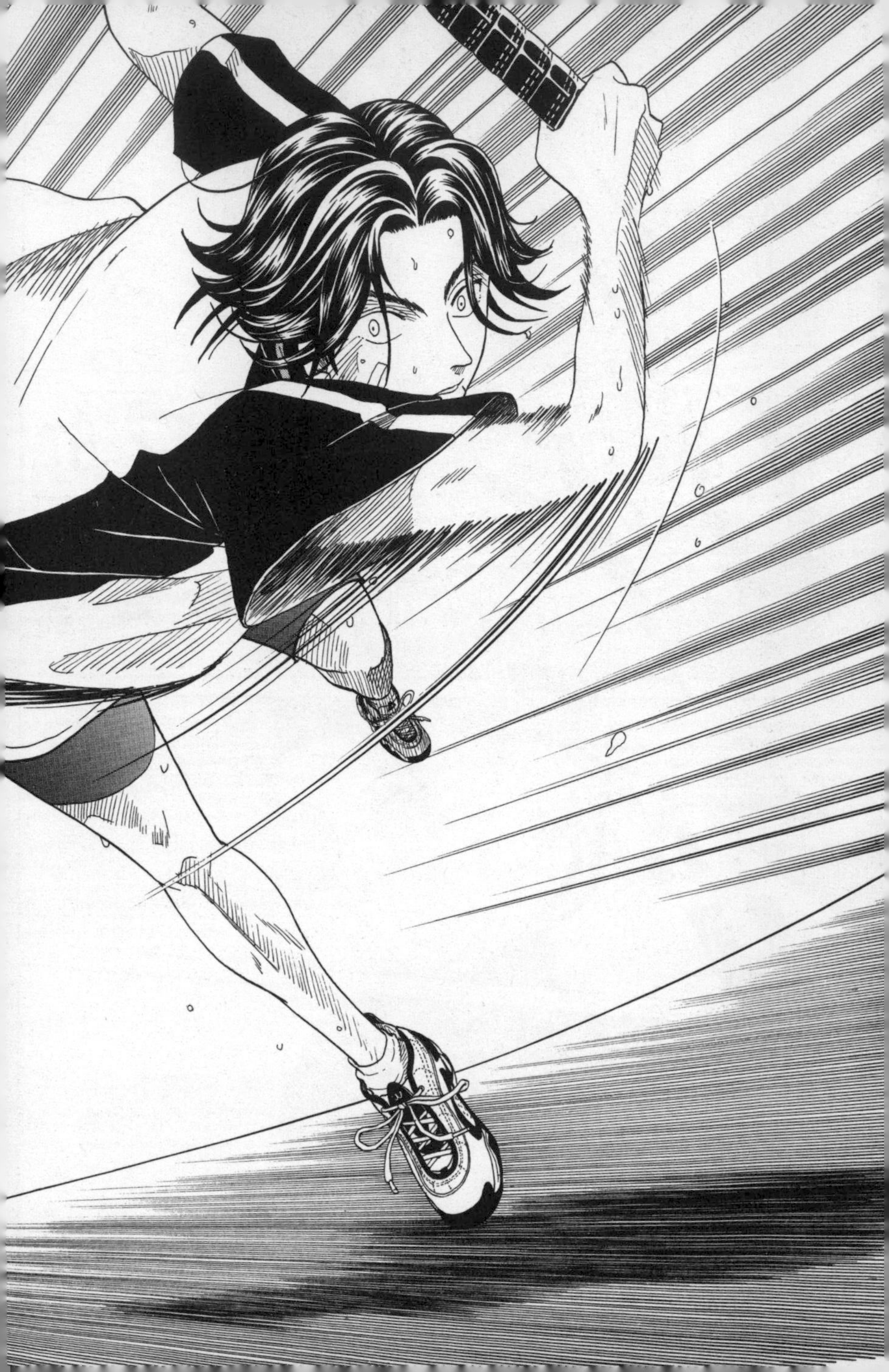

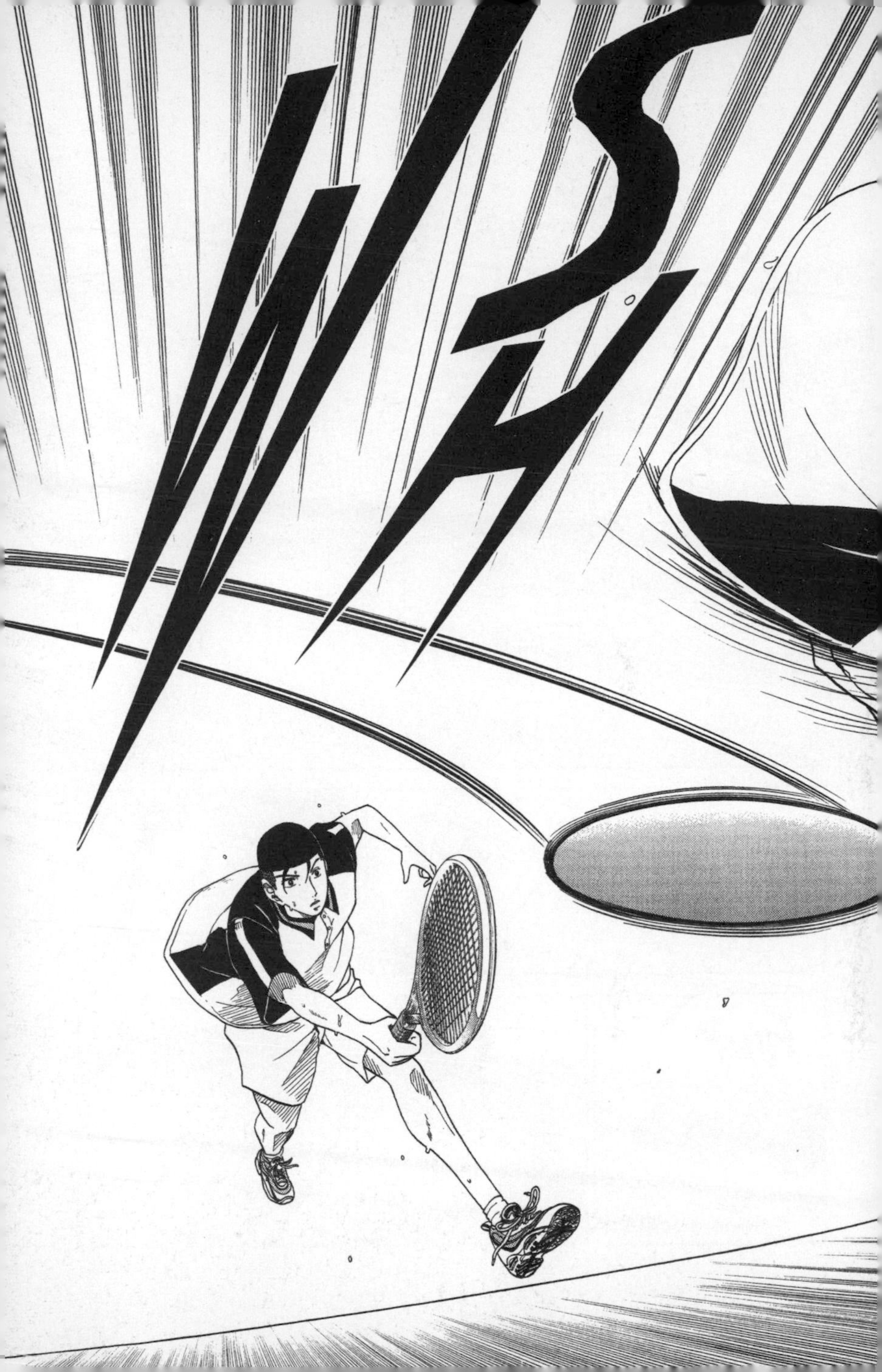
WHS

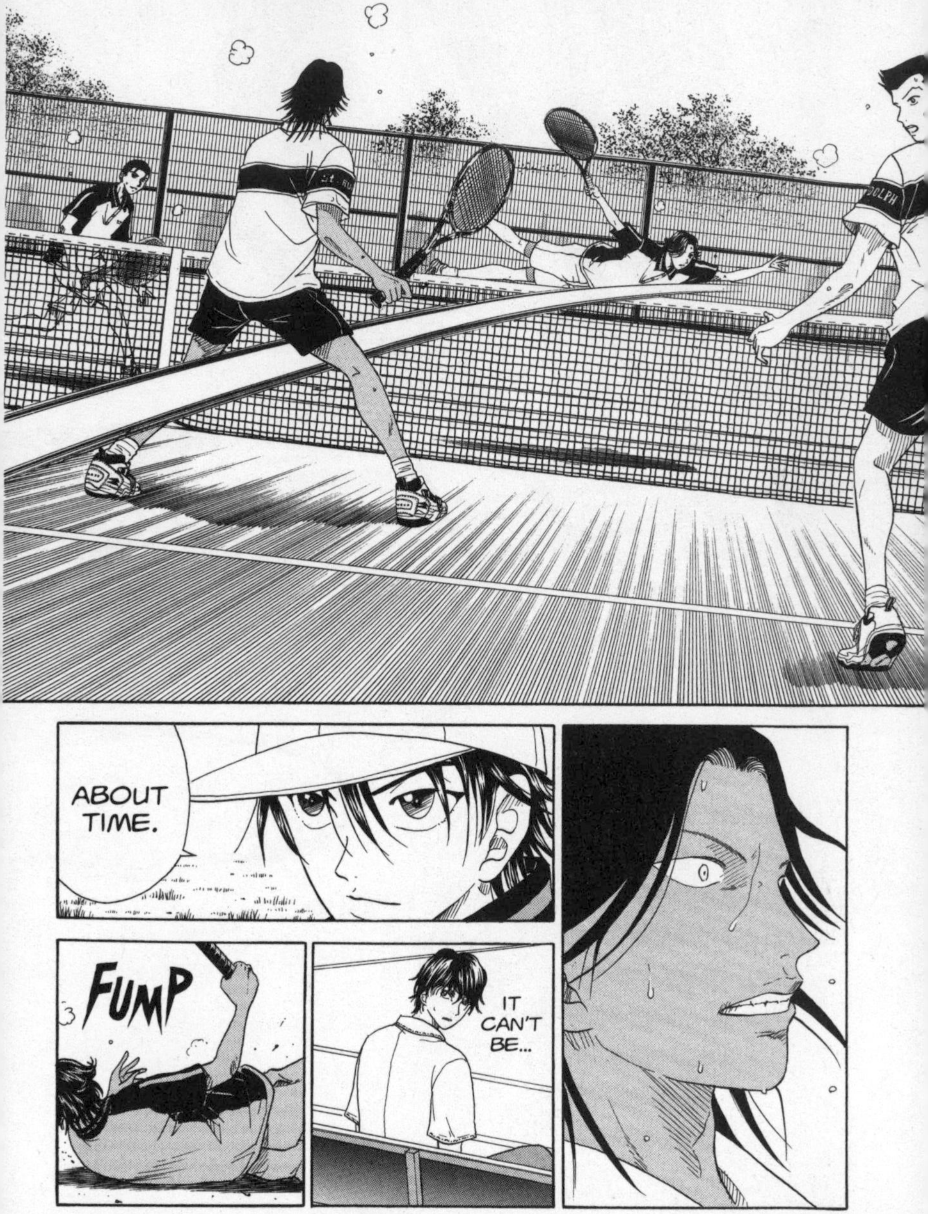
ABOUT TIME.
IT CAN'T BE...
FUMP

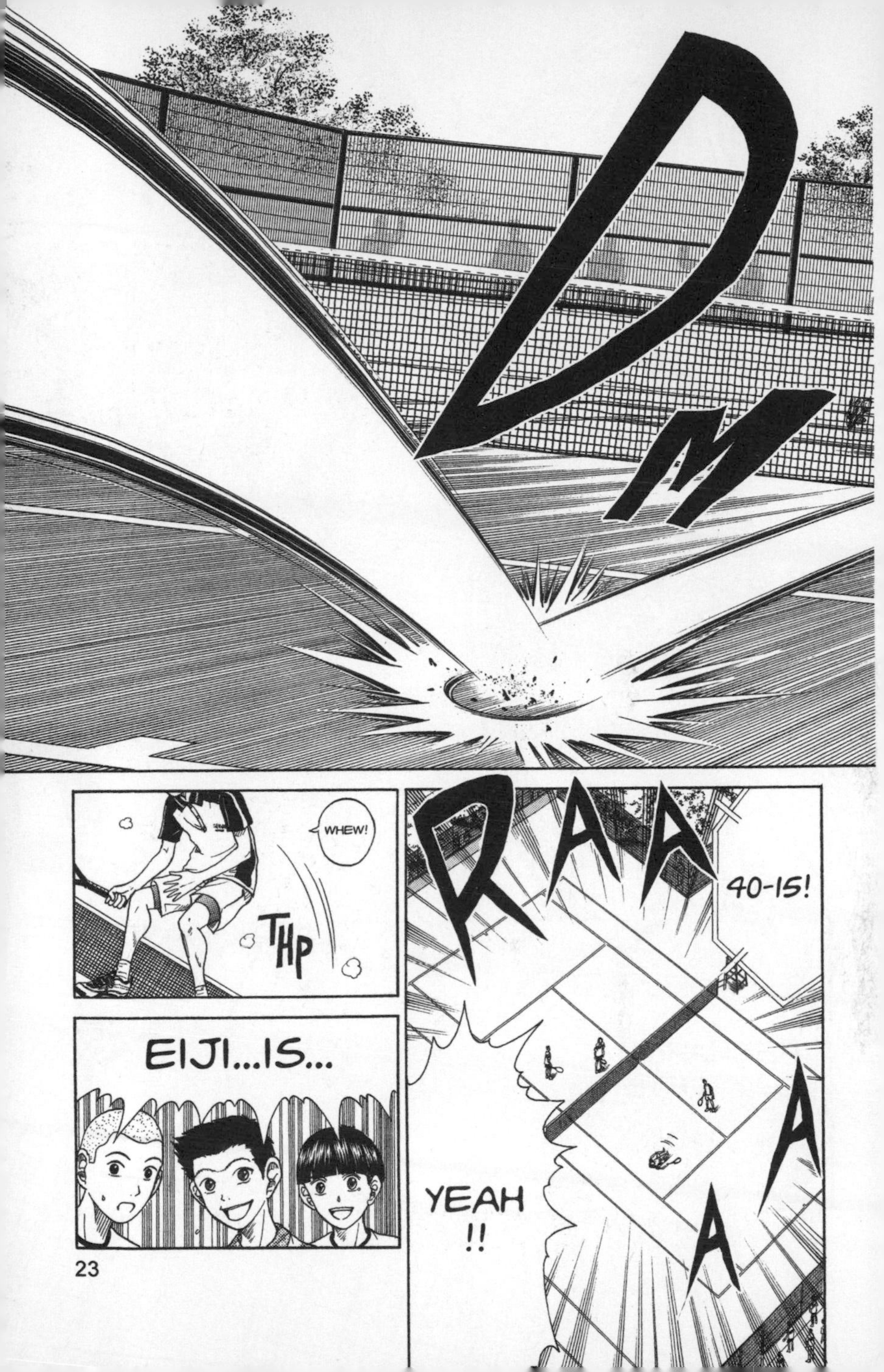
DM
RAAAA
40-15!
YEAH!!
WHEW!
THP
EIJI...IS...

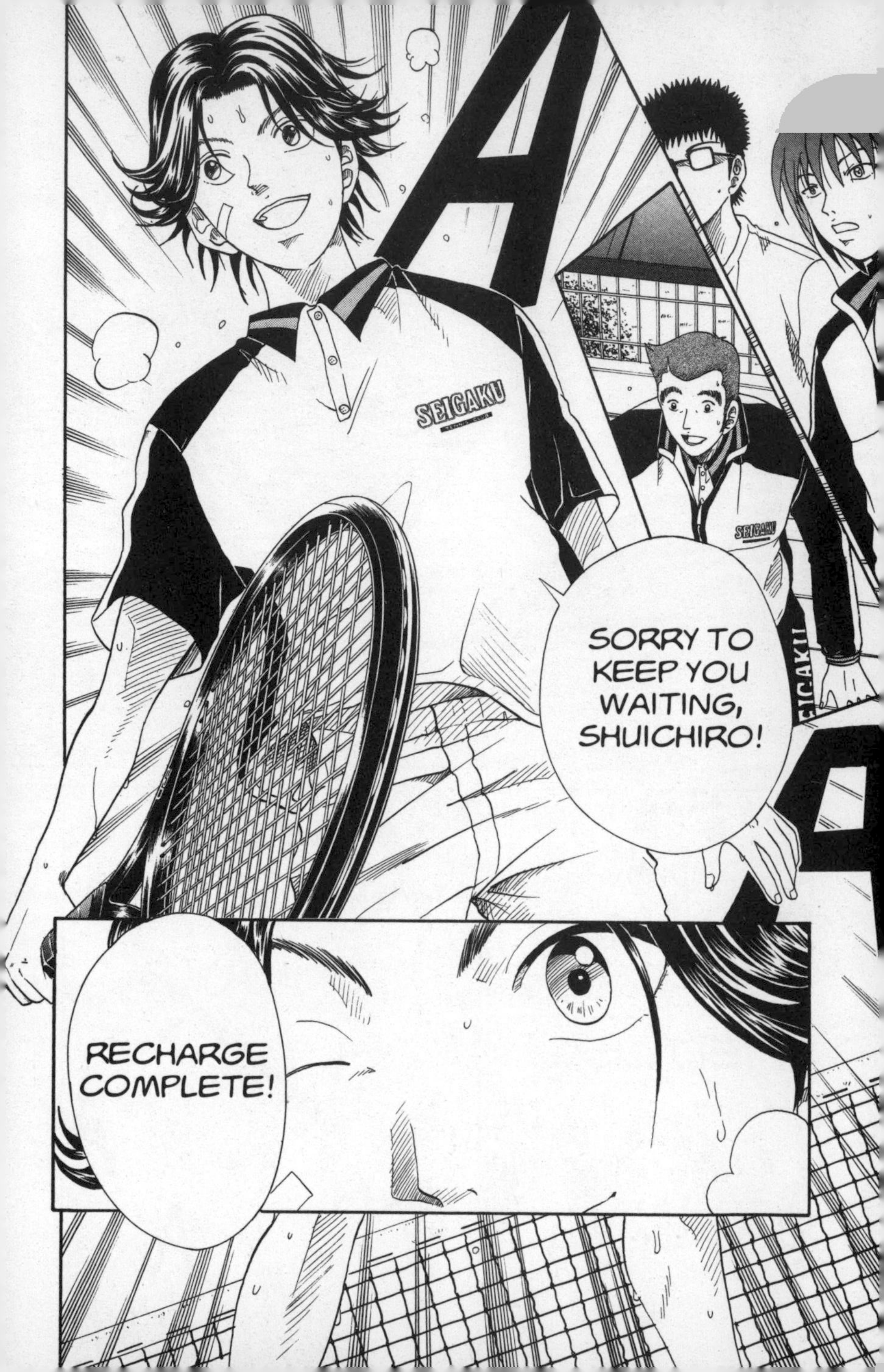
SORRY TO KEEP YOU WAITING, SHUICHIRO!
RECHARGE COMPLETE!

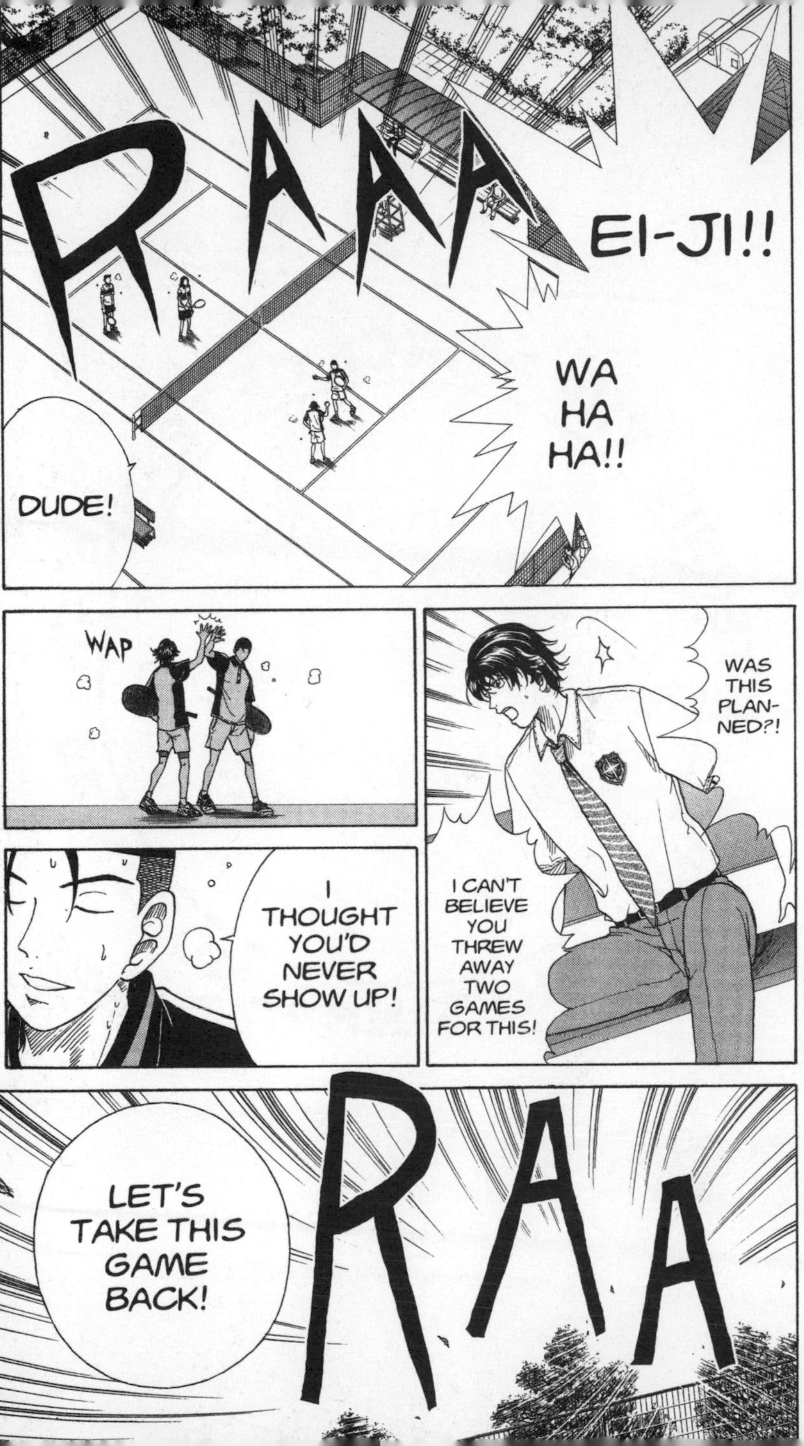
EI-JI!!
WA HA HA!!
RAAA
DUDE!
WAS THIS PLAN-NED?!
I CAN'T BELIEVE YOU THREW AWAY TWO GAMES FOR THIS!
WAP
I THOUGHT YOU'D NEVER SHOW UP!
RAA
LET'S TAKE THIS GAME BACK!

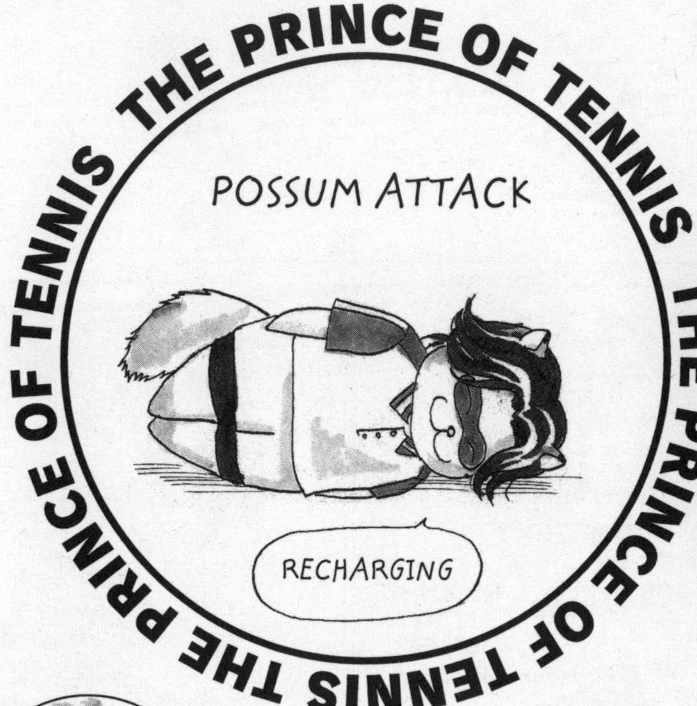
THE PRINCE OF TENNIS THE PRINCE OF TENNIS THE PRINCE OF TENNIS
POSSUM ATTACK
RECHARGING

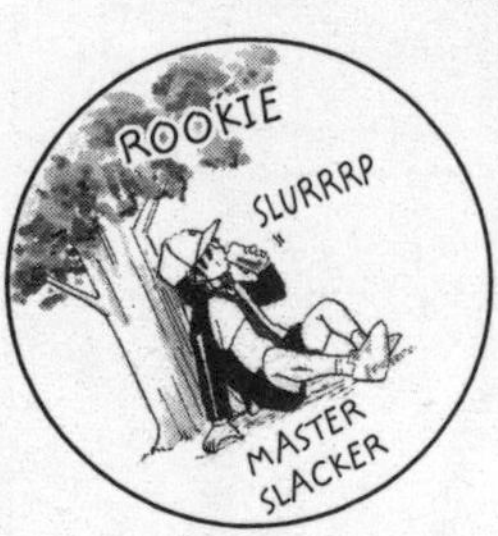
ROOKIE
SLURRRP
MASTER SLACKER

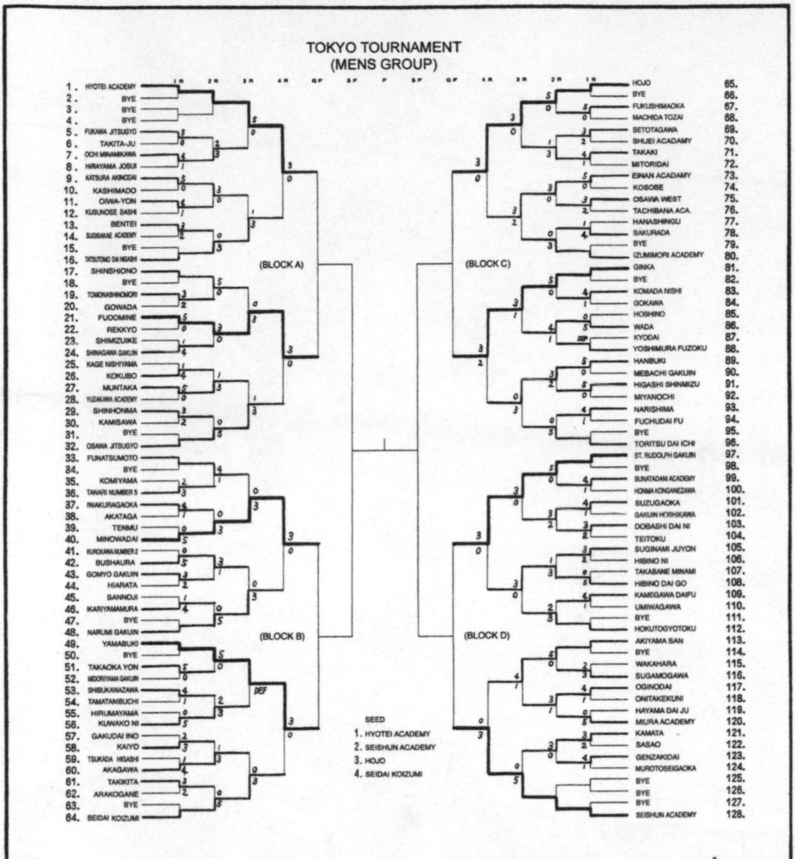
TOKYO TOURNAMENT
(MENS GROUP)
1. HYOTEI ACADEMY
2. BYE
3. BYE
4. BYE
5. FUKAWA JITSUGYO
6. TAKITA-JU
7. OCHI MINAMIKAWA
8. HIRAYAMA JOSUI
9. KATSURA AKINODAI
10. KASHIMADO
11. OIWA-YON
12. KUSUNOSE BASHI
13. BENTEI
14. SUGISAKAE ACADEMY
15. BYE
16. TATSUTOMO DAI HIGASHI
17. SHINSHIONO
18. BYE
19. TOMONASHINOMORI
20. GOWADA
21. FUDOMINE
22. REKKYO
23. SHIMIZUIKE
24. SHINAGAWA GAKUIN
25. KAGE NISHIYAMA
26. KOKUBO
27. MUNTAKA
28. YUZAKAWA ACADEMY
29. SHINHONMA
30. KAMISAWA
31. BYE
32. OSAWA JITSUGYO
33. FUNATSUMOTO
34. BYE
35. KOMIYAMA
36. TANARI NUMBER 5
37. IWAKURAGAOKA
38. AKATAGA
39. TENMU
40. MINOWADAI
41. KUROKAWA NUMBER 2
42. BUSHAURA
43. GOMYO GAKUIN
44. HIARATA
45. SANNOJI
46. IKARIYAMAMURA
47. BYE
48. NARUMI GAKUIN
49. YAMABUKI
50. BYE
51. TAKAOKA YON
52. MIDORIYAMA GAKUIN
53. SHIBUKAWAZAWA
54. TAMATANIBUCHI
55. HIRUMAYAMA
56. KUWAKO NI
57. GAKUDAI INO
58. KAIYO
59. TSUKADA HIGASHI
60. AKAGAWA
61. TAKIKITA
62. ARAKOGANE
63. BYE
64. SEIDAI KOIZUMI
(BLOCK A)
(BLOCK B)
(BLOCK C)
(BLOCK D)
HOJO 65.
BYE 66.
FUKUSHIMAOKA 67.
MACHIDA TOZAI 68.
SETOTAGAWA 69.
SHUEI ACADAMY 70.
TAKAKI 71.
MITORIDAI 72.
EINAN ACADEMY 73.
KOSOBE 74.
OSAWA WEST 75.
TACHIBANA ACA. 76.
HANASHINGU 77.
SAKURADA 78.
BYE 79.
IZUMIMORI ACADEMY 80.
GINKA 81.
BYE 82.
KOMADA NISHI 83.
GOKAWA 84.
HOSHINO 85.
WADA 86.
KYODAI 87.
YOSHIMURA FUZOKU 88.
HANBUKI 89.
MEBACHI GAKUIN 90.
HIGASHI SHINMIZU 91.
MIYANOCHI 92.
NARISHIMA 93.
FUCHUDAI FU 94.
BYE 95.
TORITSU DAI ICHI 96.
ST. RUDOLPH GAKUIN 97.
BYE 98.
SUNATADANI ACADEMY 99.
HONMA KONGANEZAWA 100.
SUZUGAOKA 101.
GAKUIN HOSHIKAWA 102.
DOBASHI DAI NI 103.
TEITOKU 104.
SUGINAMI JUYON 105.
HIBINO NI 106.
TAKABANE MINAMI 107.
HIBINO DAI GO 108.
KAMEGAWA DAIFU 109.
UMIWAGAWA 110.
BYE 111.
HOKUTOGYOTOKU 112.
AKIYAMA SAN 113.
BYE 114.
WAKAHARA 115.
SUGAMOGAWA 116.
OGINODAI 117.
ONITAKEKUNI 118.
HAYAMA DAI JU 119.
MIURA ACADEMY 120.
KAMATA 121.
SASAO 122.
GENZAKIDAI 123.
MUROTOSEIGAOKA 124.
BYE 125.
BYE 126.
BYE 127.
SEISHUN ACADEMY 128.
SEED
1. HYOTEI ACADEMY
2. SEISHUN ACADEMY
3. HOJO
4. SEIDAI KOIZUMI

Genius 62: Deep Power

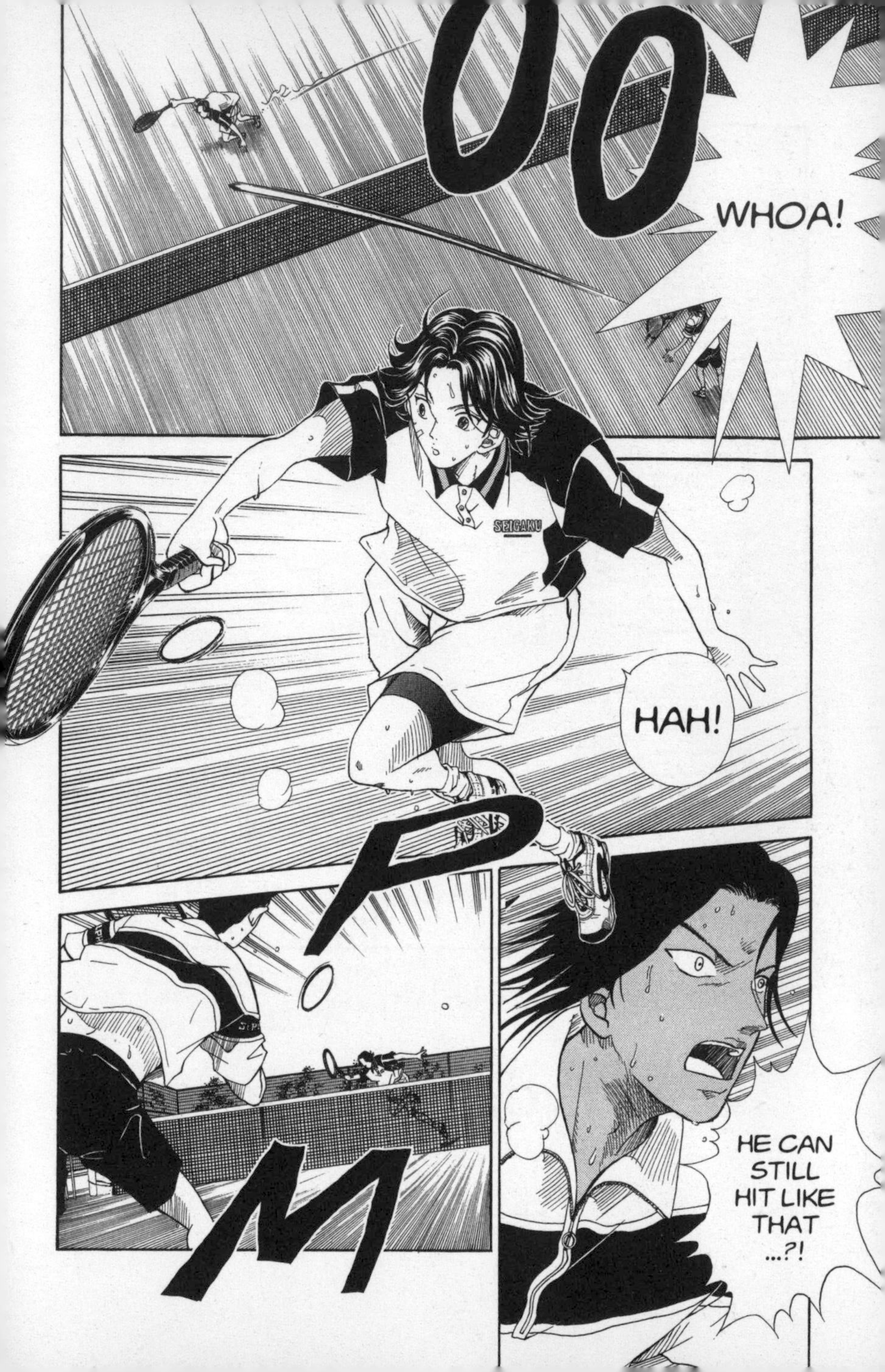
OO
WHOA!
HAH!
P
M
HE CAN STILL HIT LIKE THAT ...?!

READ THIS WAY

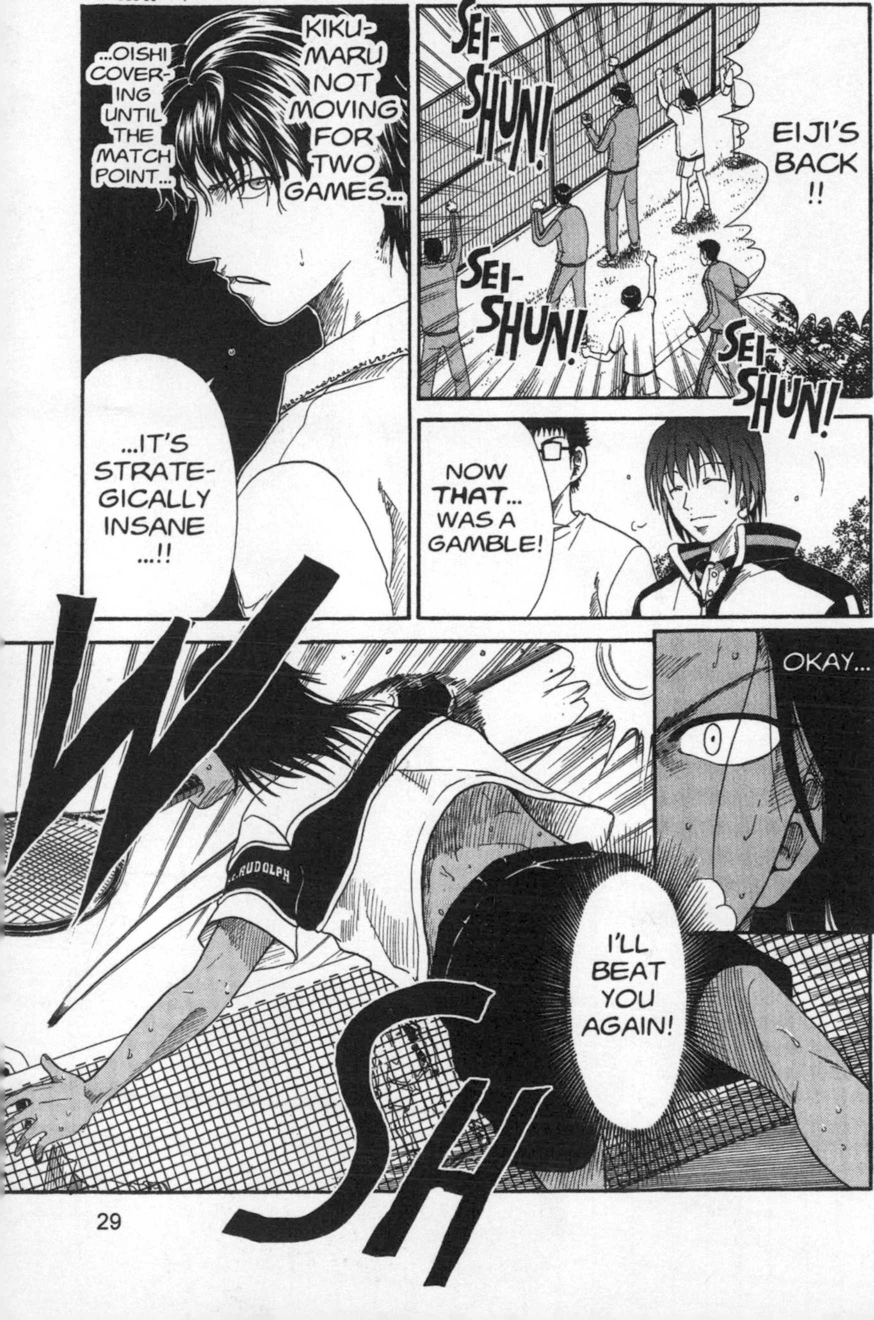
EIJI'S BACK !!
SEI-SHUN!
SEI-SHUN!
SEI-SHUN!
NOW THAT... WAS A GAMBLE!
KIKU-MARU NOT MOVING FOR TWO GAMES...
...OISHI COVERING UNTIL THE MATCH POINT...
...IT'S STRATEGICALLY INSANE ...!!
OKAY...
I'LL BEAT YOU AGAIN!
WHSH

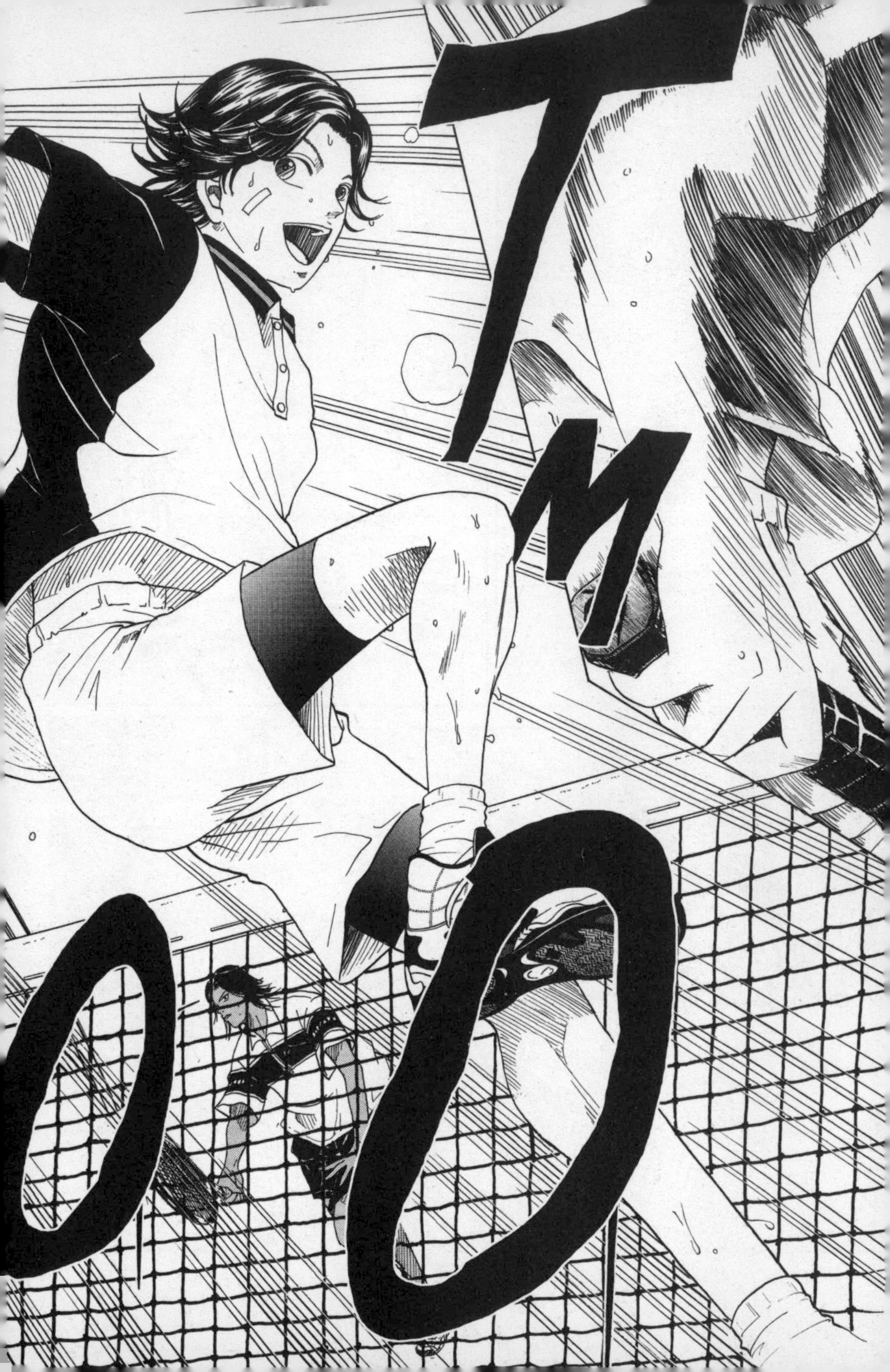

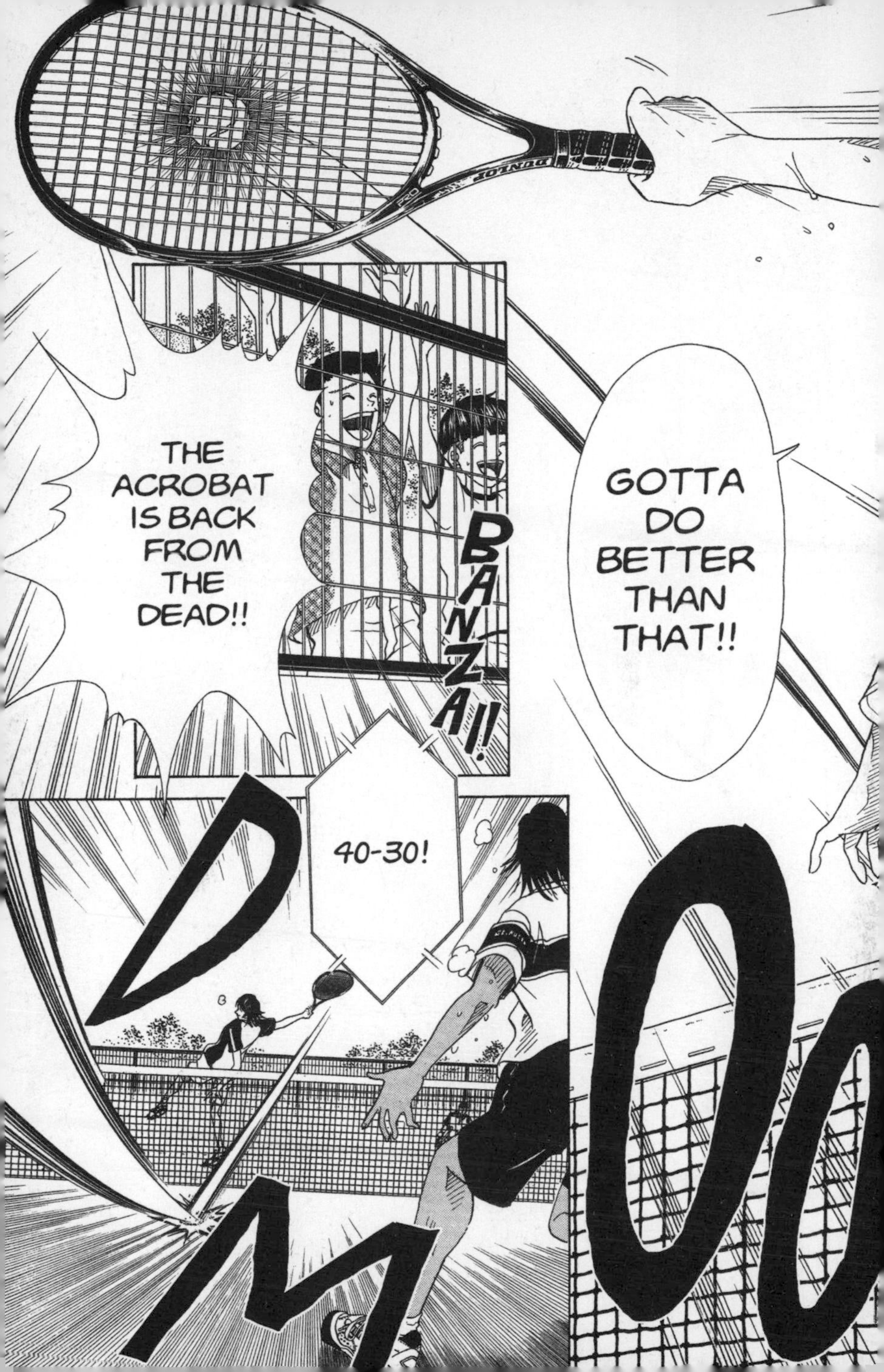
GOTTA DO BETTER THAN THAT!!
THE ACROBAT IS BACK FROM THE DEAD!!
BANZAI!
40-30!

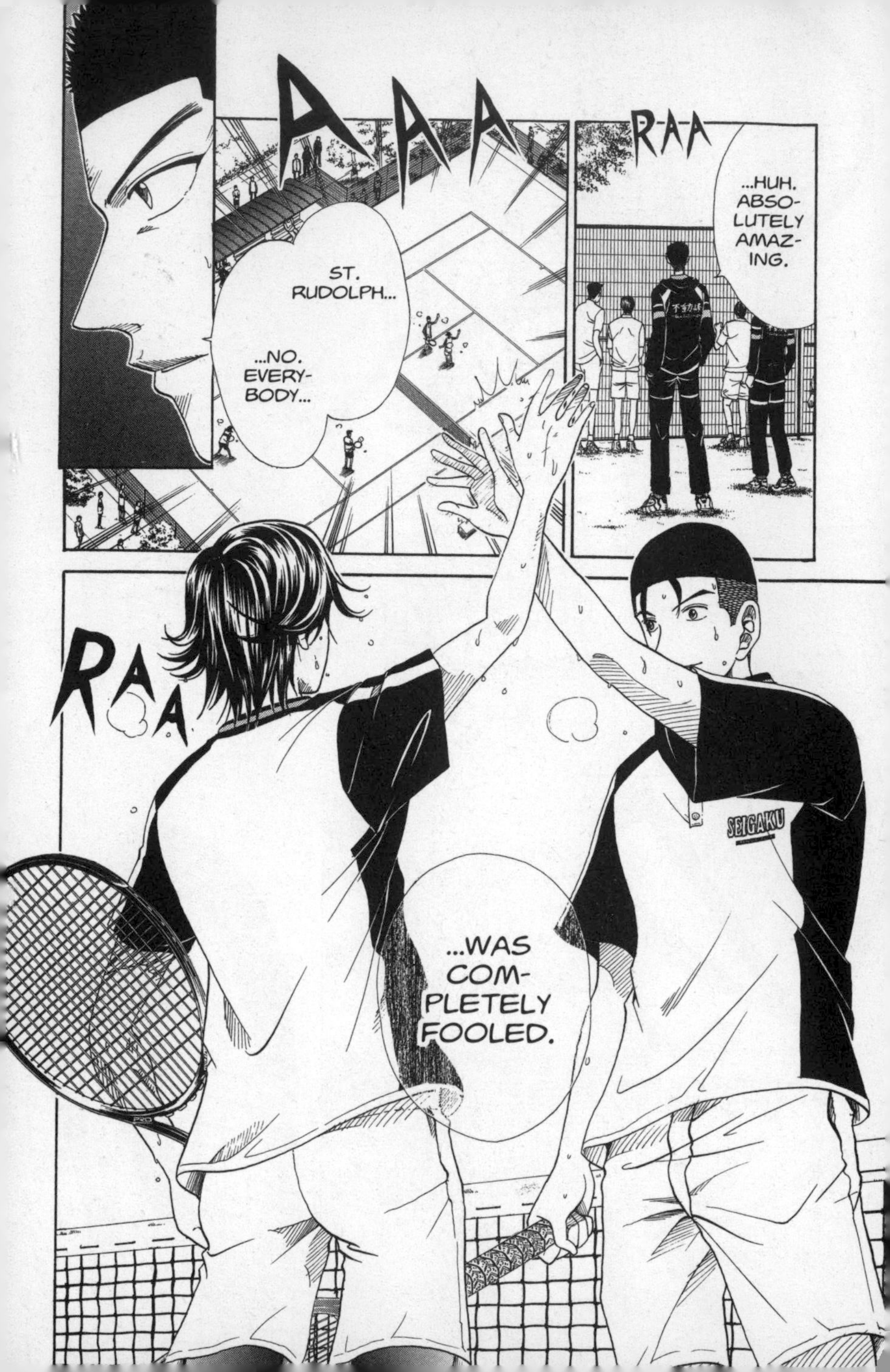
RAA
...HUH. ABSOLUTELY AMAZING.
AAA
ST. RUDOLPH...
...NO. EVERYBODY...
RAA
...WAS COMPLETELY FOOLED.

READ THIS WAY

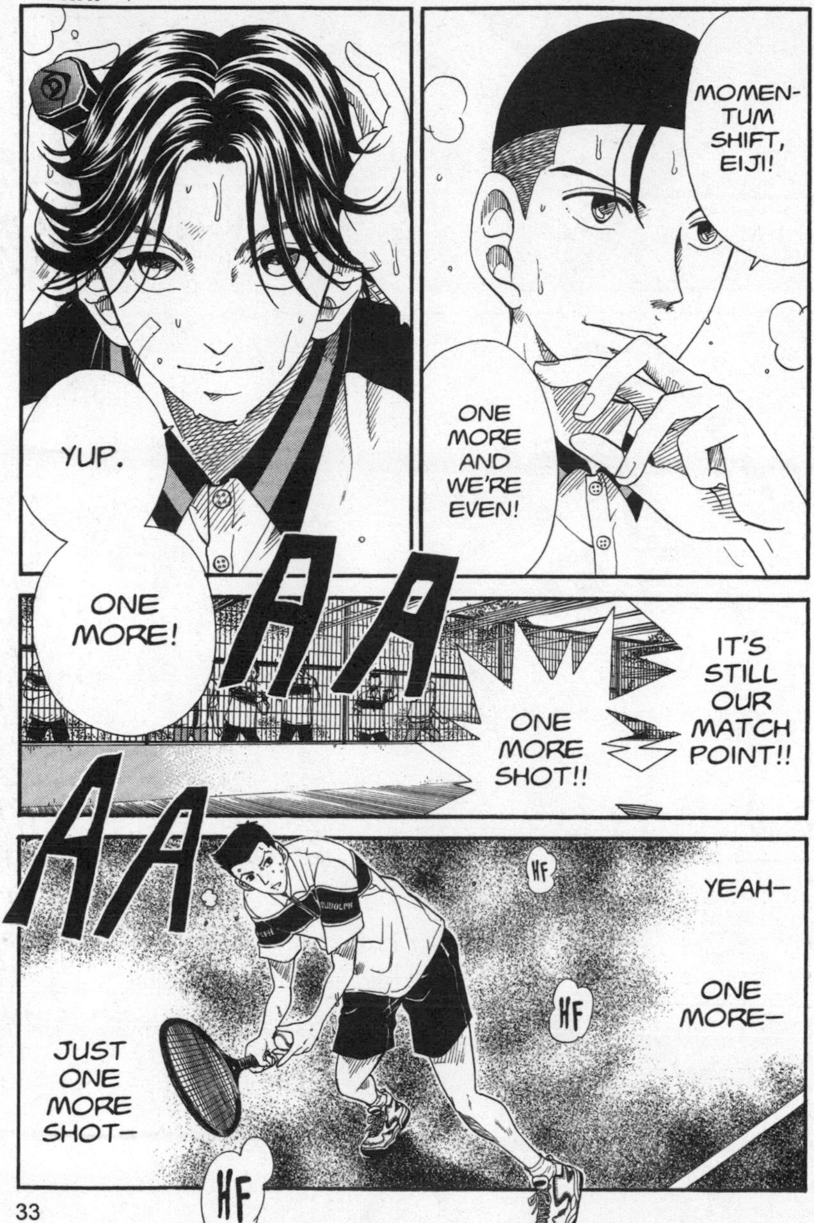
MOMEN-TUM SHIFT, EIJI!
ONE MORE AND WE'RE EVEN!
YUP.
ONE MORE!
AAAA
IT'S STILL OUR MATCH POINT!!
ONE MORE SHOT!!
YEAH—
ONE MORE—
HF
HF
JUST ONE MORE SHOT—
HF

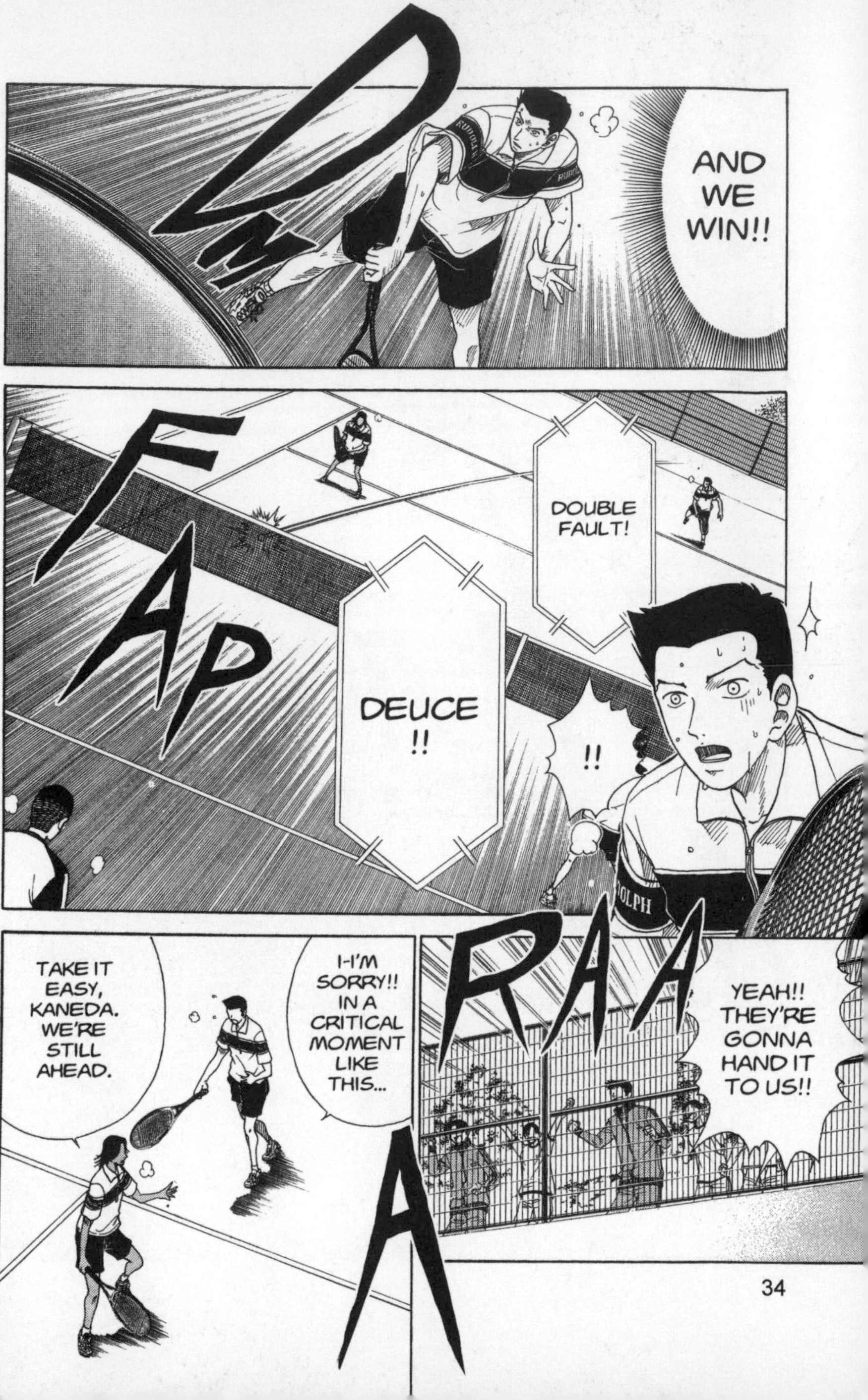
DM
AND WE WIN!!
!!
DOUBLE FAULT!
DEUCE !!
FAP
YEAH!! THEY'RE GONNA HAND IT TO US!!
RAAA
I-I'M SORRY!! IN A CRITICAL MOMENT LIKE THIS...
TAKE IT EASY, KANEDA. WE'RE STILL AHEAD.

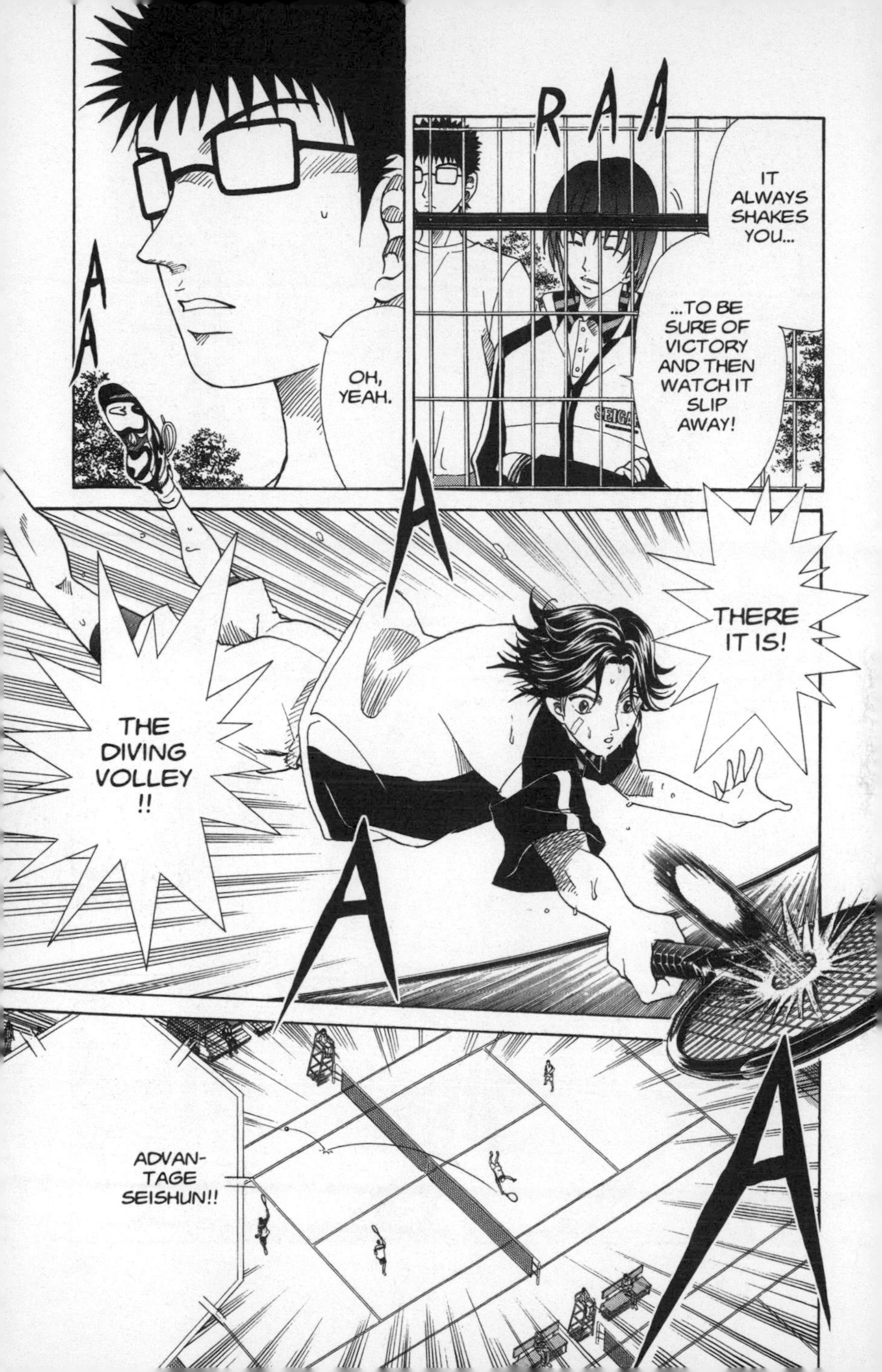
RAA
IT ALWAYS SHAKES YOU...
...TO BE SURE OF VICTORY AND THEN WATCH IT SLIP AWAY!
OH, YEAH.
AA
THERE IT IS!
A
THE DIVING VOLLEY !!
A
A
ADVAN-TAGE SEISHUN!!

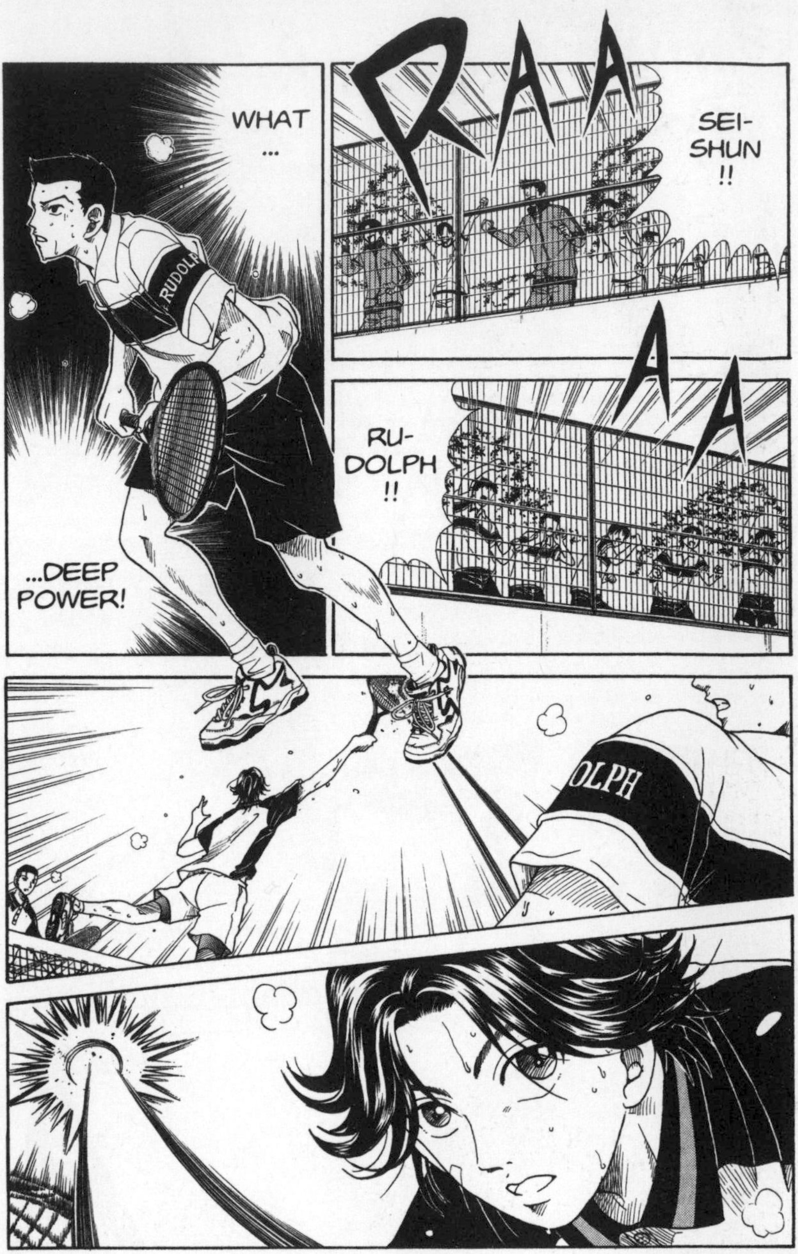
RAA
SEI-SHUN !!
AA
RU-DOLPH !!
WHAT ...
RUDOLPH
...DEEP POWER!
OLPH

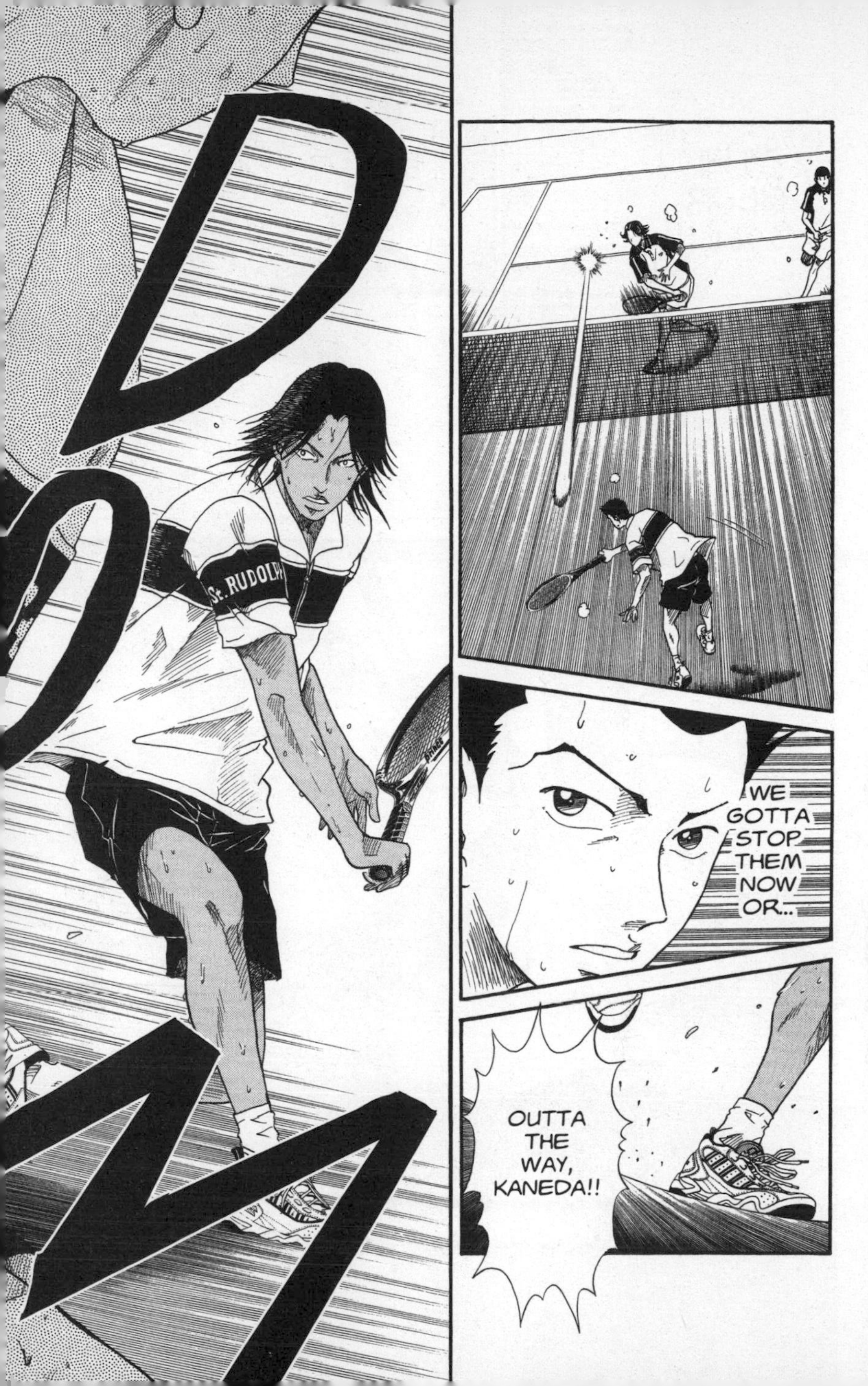
WE GOTTA STOP THEM NOW OR...
OUTTA THE WAY, KANEDA!!
DOM

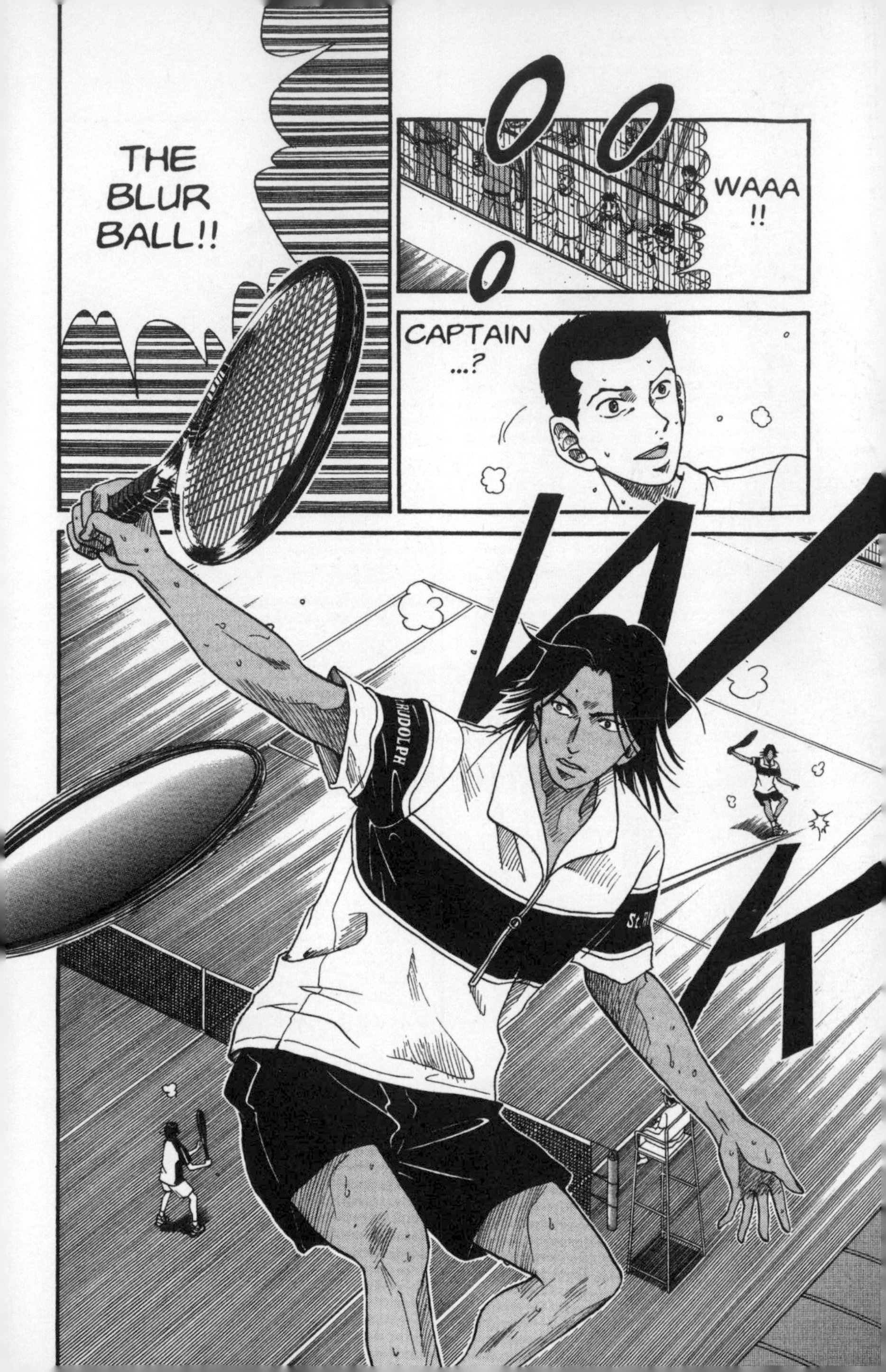
OOO
WAAA !!
CAPTAIN ...?
THE BLUR BALL!!

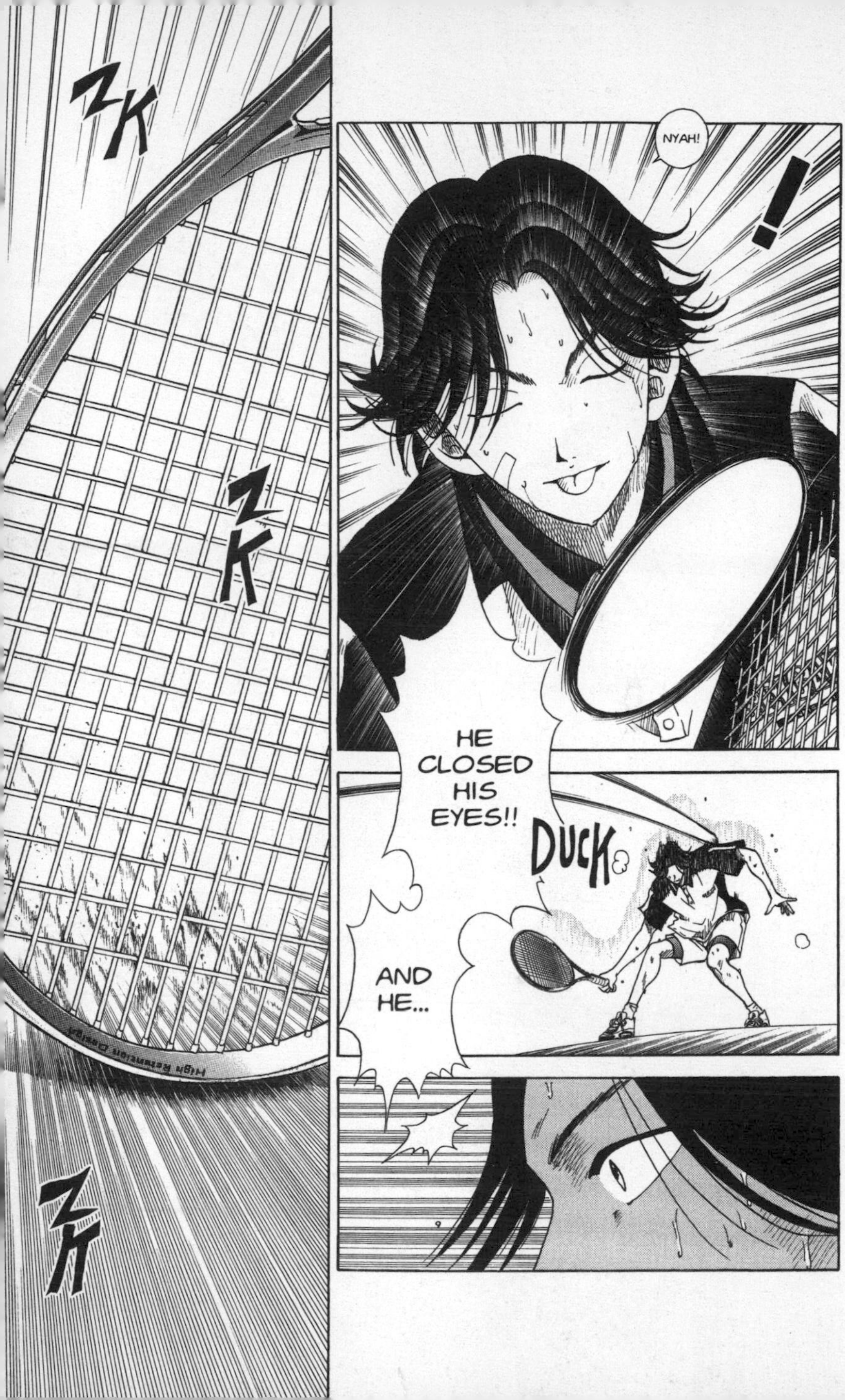
NYAH!
!
HE CLOSED HIS EYES!!
DUCK
AND HE...
ZK
ZK
ZK

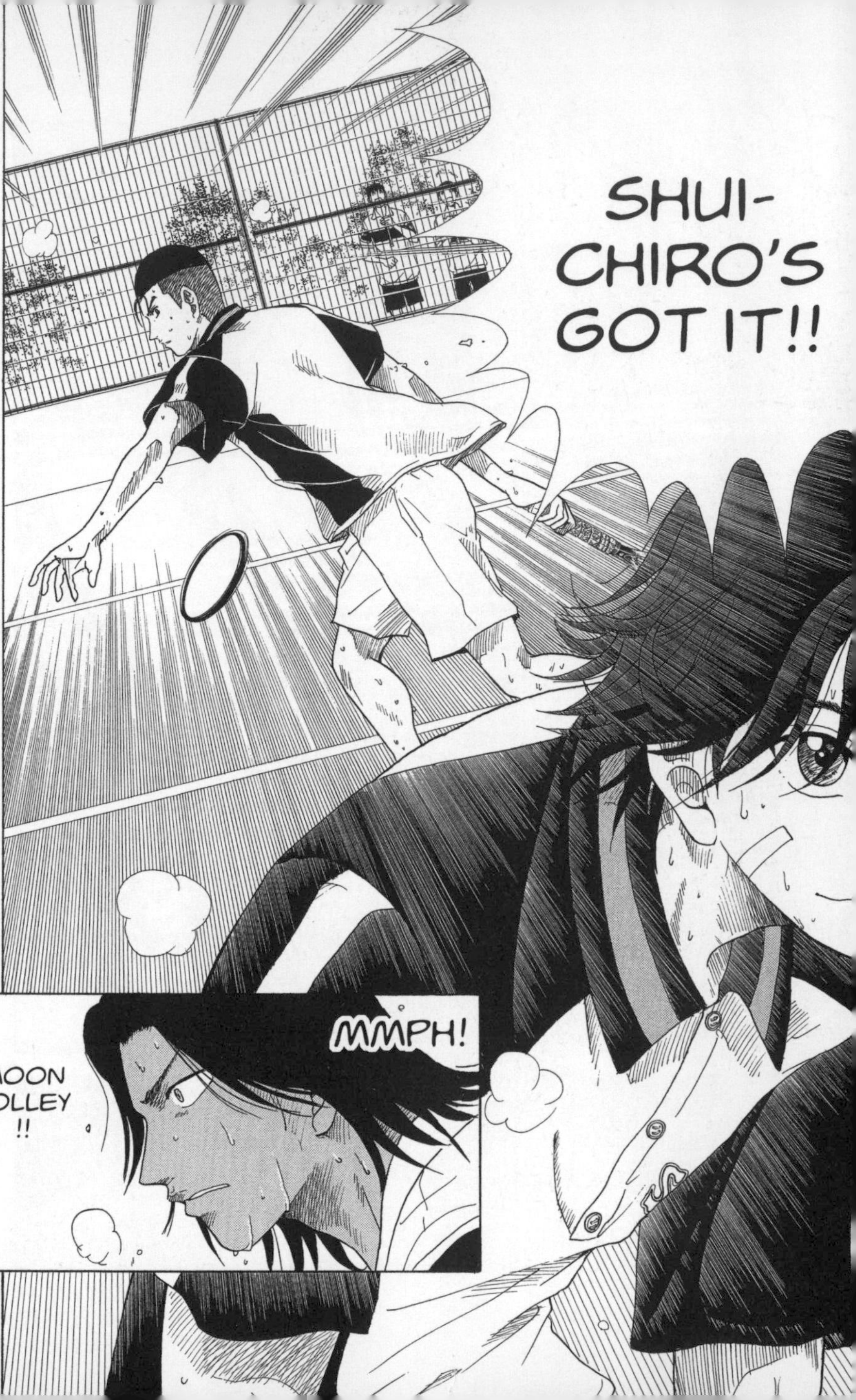
SHUI-CHIRO'S GOT IT!!
MMPH!
MOON VOLLEY !!

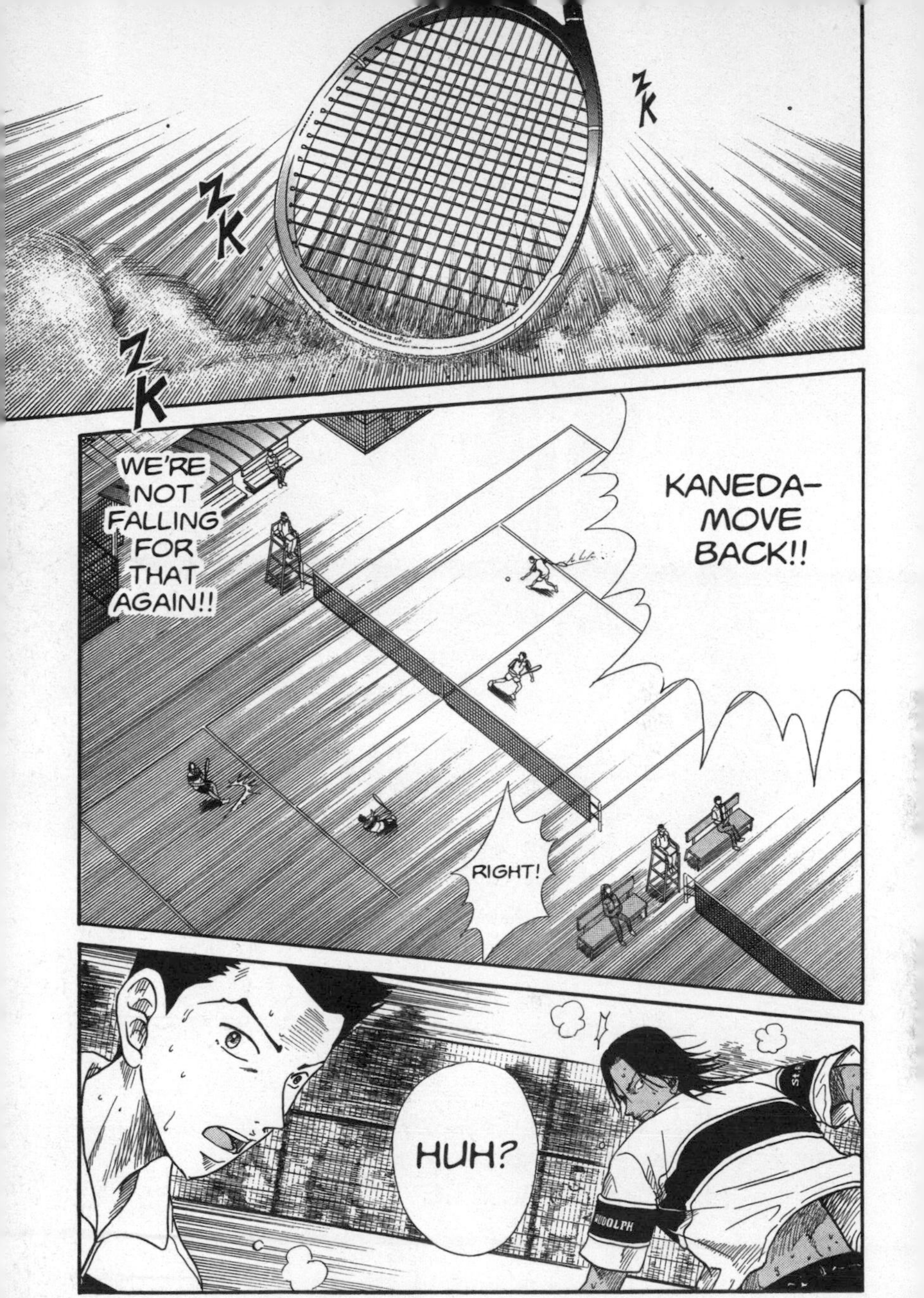
ZK
ZK
ZK
KANEDA-MOVE BACK!!
RIGHT!
WE'RE NOT FALLING FOR THAT AGAIN!!
HUH?

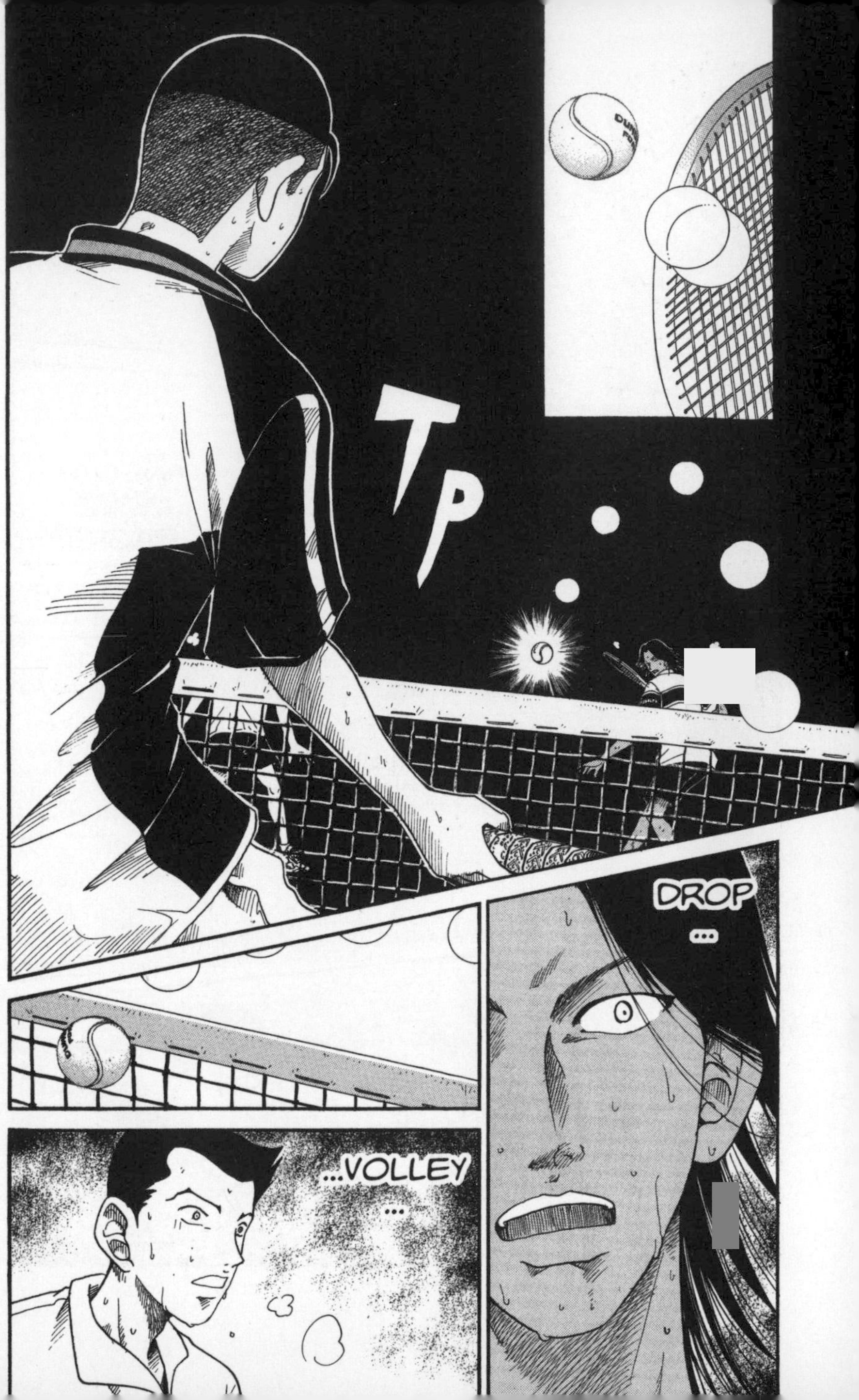
TP
DROP ...
...VOLLEY ...

READ THIS WAY

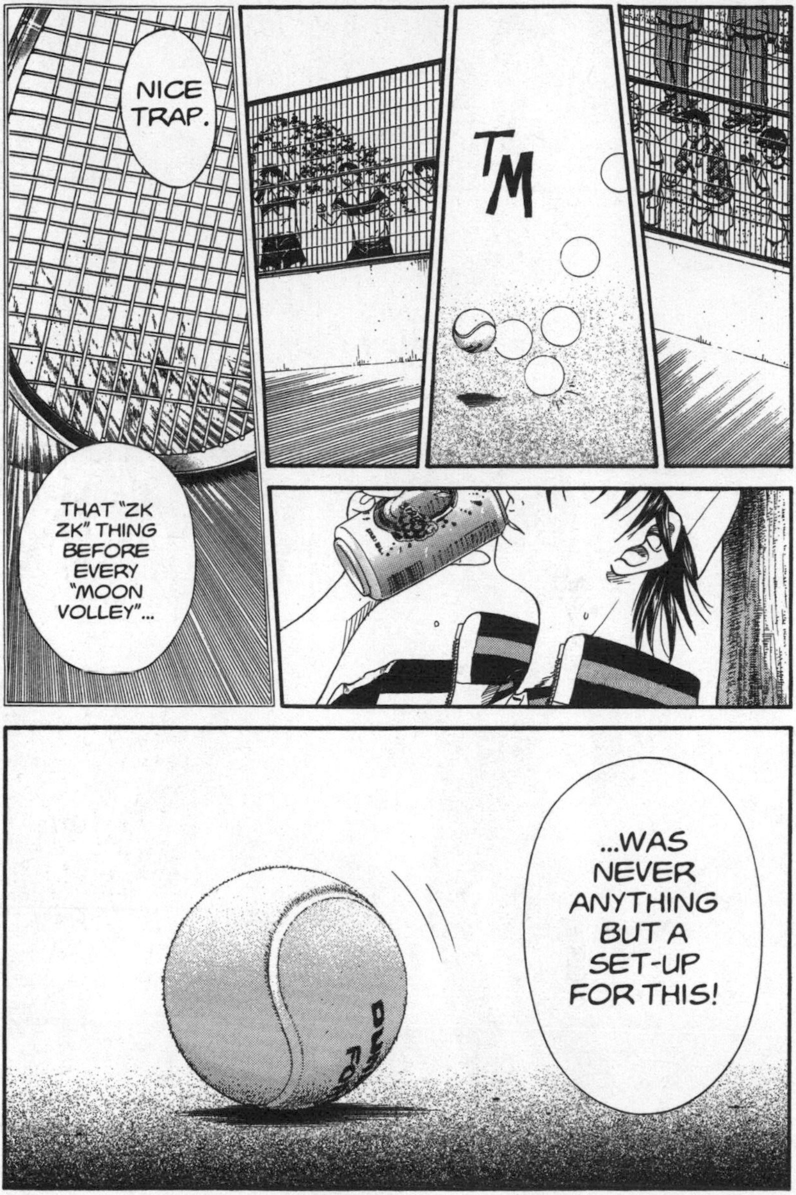
TM
NICE TRAP.
THAT "ZK ZK" THING BEFORE EVERY "MOON VOLLEY"...
...WAS NEVER ANYTHING BUT A SET-UP FOR THIS!

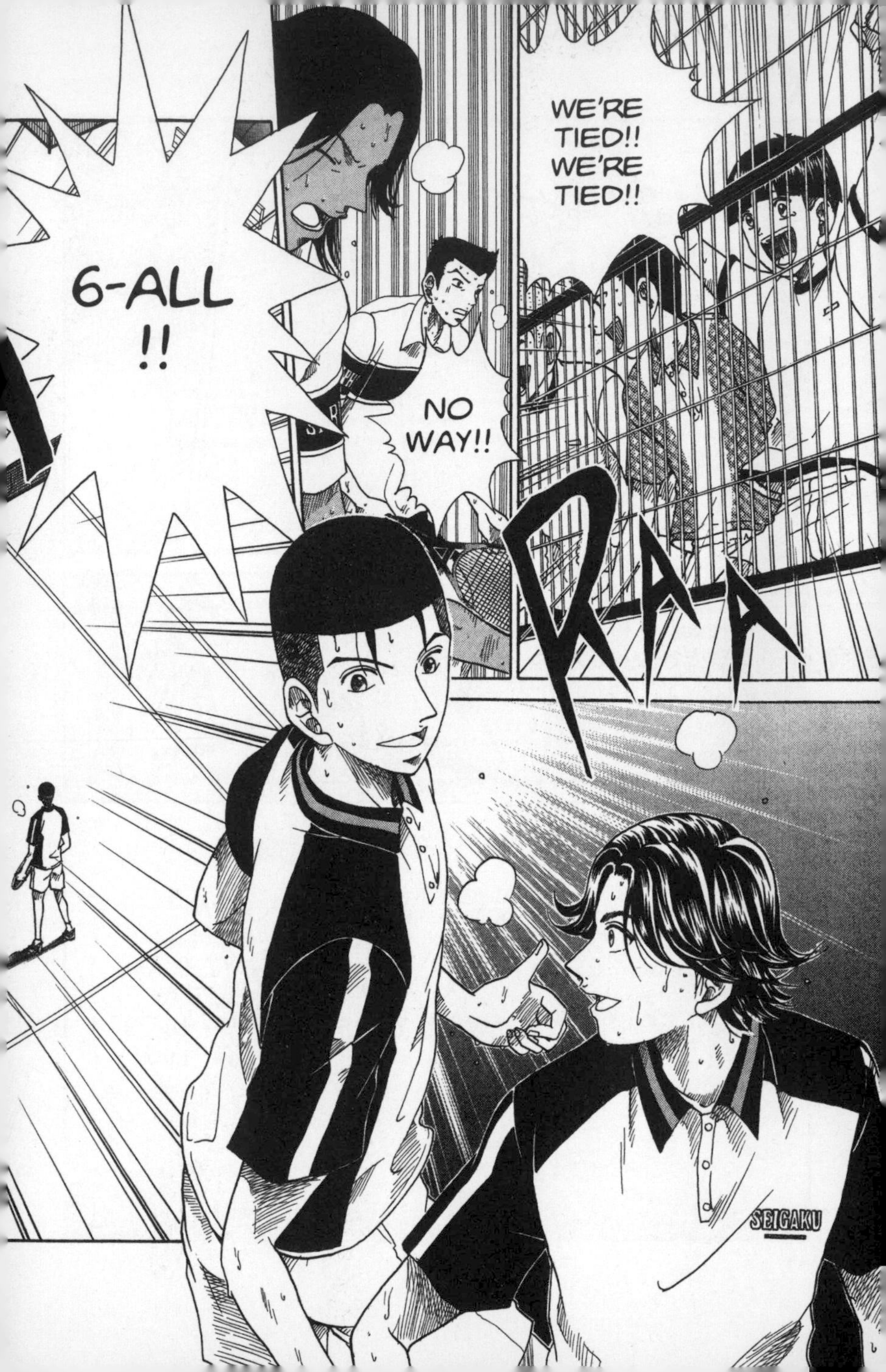
WE'RE TIED!! WE'RE TIED!!
6-ALL !!
NO WAY!!
RAA
SEIGAKU

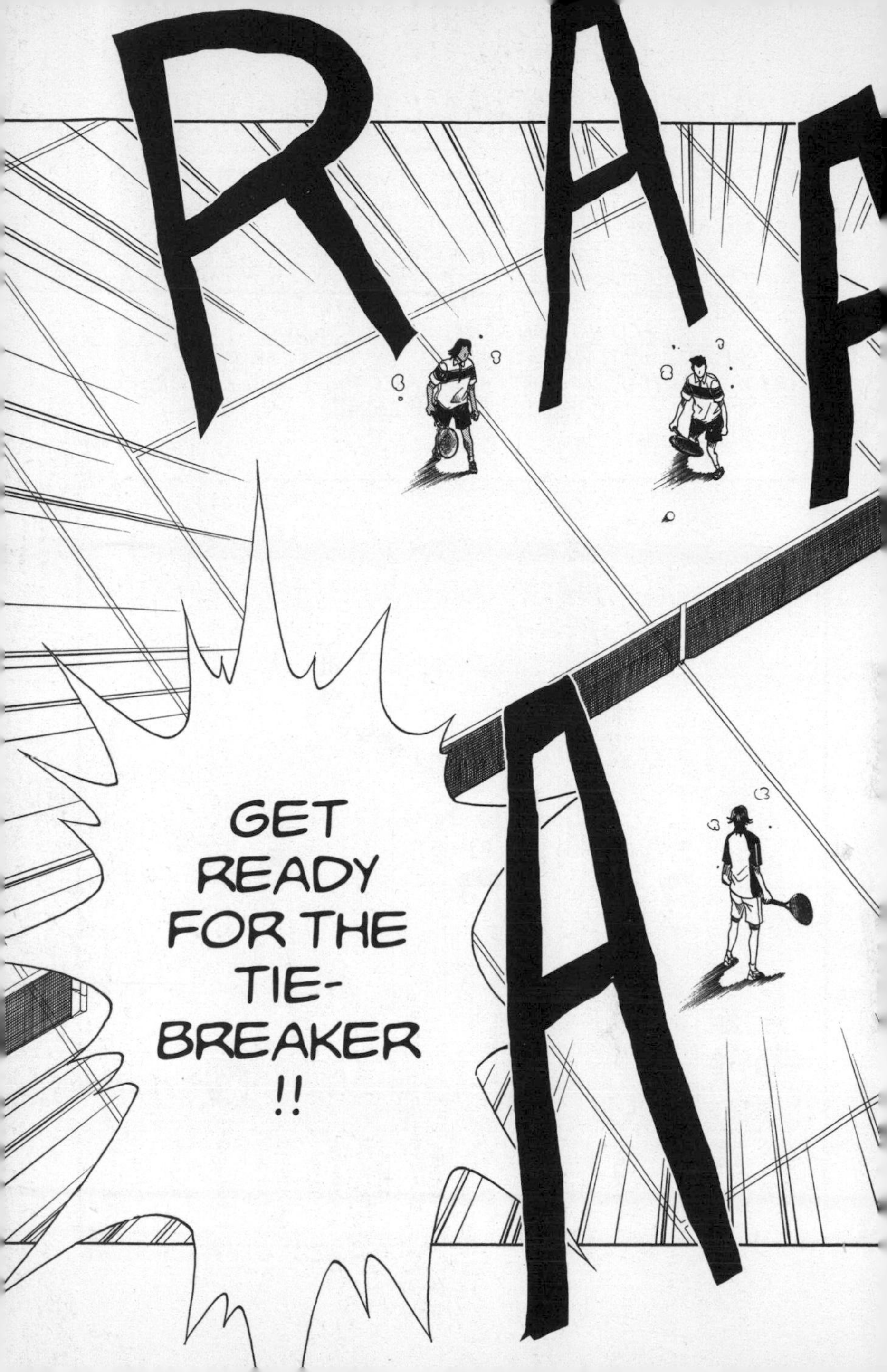
RAAAA
GET READY FOR THE TIE-BREAKER !!

VALENTINE CHOCOLATE ACQUISITION RANKING

ONCE AGAIN, WE RECEIVED OCEANS OF VALENTINE'S GIFTS FOR THE CHARACTERS. WE WERE A LITTLE OVERWHELMED BY THE COUNTLESS CARDBOARD BOXES SENT FROM THE EDITORIAL OFFICE, BUT IT WAS ALSO A GREAT ENCOURAGEMENT! THANK YOU SO MUCH!!
MOST OF YOU ATTACHED A NOTE SAYING, "PLEASE TALLY THE GIFTS AND PUBLISH THE RESULTS." SO, THIS YEAR'S VALENTINE CHOCOLATE ACQUISITION RANKING IS AS FOLLOWS—
PREDICTABLY, IT WAS A LANDSLIDE FOR ONE CHARACTER...
(BY THE WAY, IT WASN'T JUST CHOCOLATES. THERE WERE COOKIES, RICE CRACKERS, EVEN SHICHIMI!)

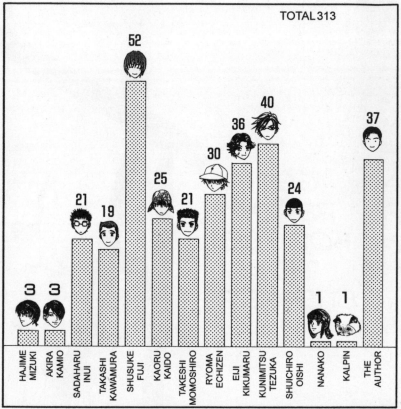

TOTAL 313

HAJIME MIZUKI 3 · AKIRA KAMIO 3 · SADAHARU INUI 21 · TAKASHI KAWAMURA 19 · SHUSUKE FUJI 52 · KAORU KAIDO 25 · TAKESHI MOMOSHIRO 21 · RYOMA ECHIZEN 30 · EIJI KIKUMARU 36 · KUNIMITSU TEZUKA 40 · SHUICHIRO OISHI 24 · NANAKO 1 · KALPIN 1 · THE AUTHOR 37

(TAKEN FROM SADAHARU INUI'S (SECRET) NOTES)

GENIUS 63: TIEBREAK

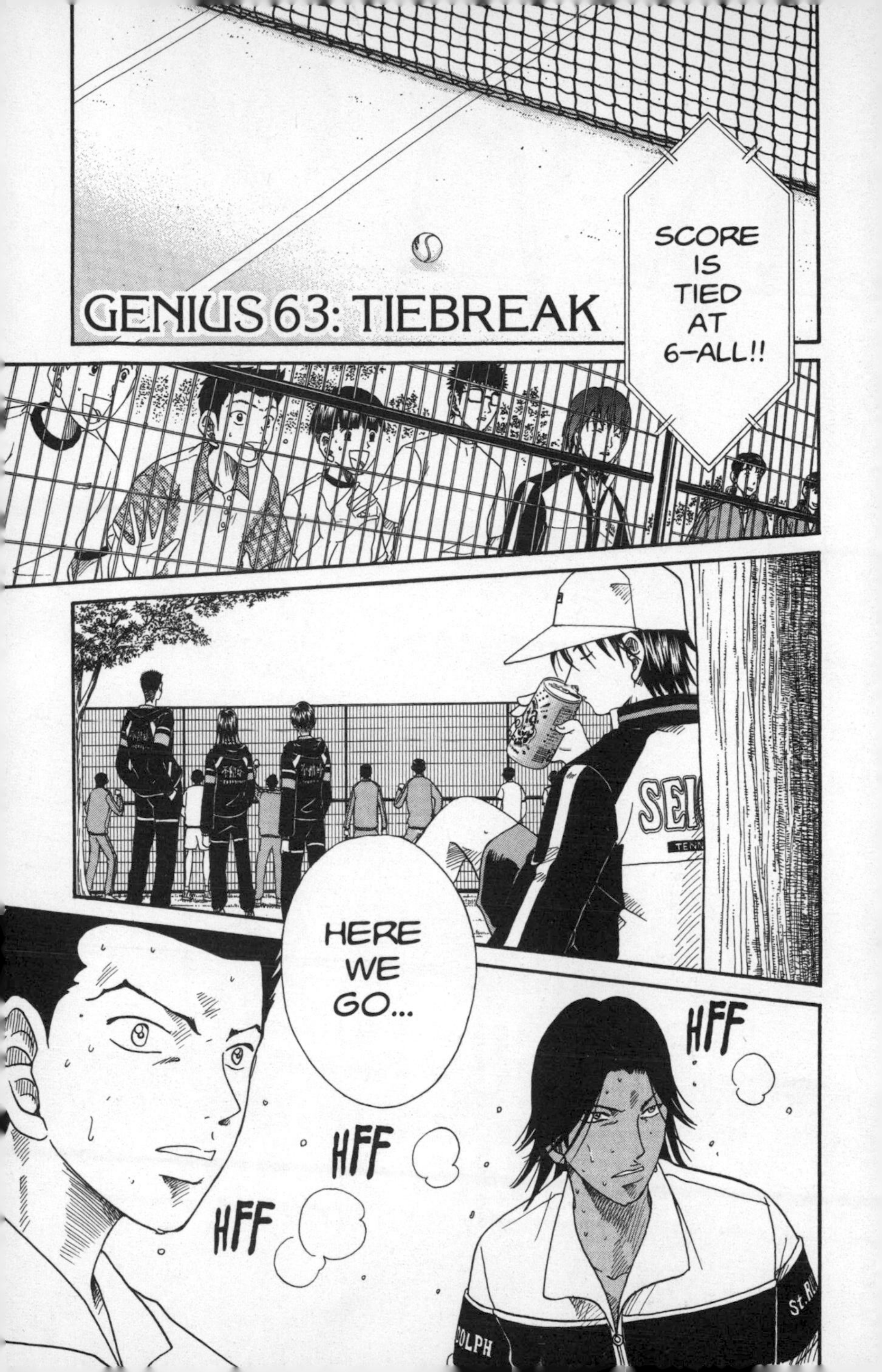
SCORE IS TIED AT 6-ALL!!
HERE WE GO...
HFF
HFF
HFF

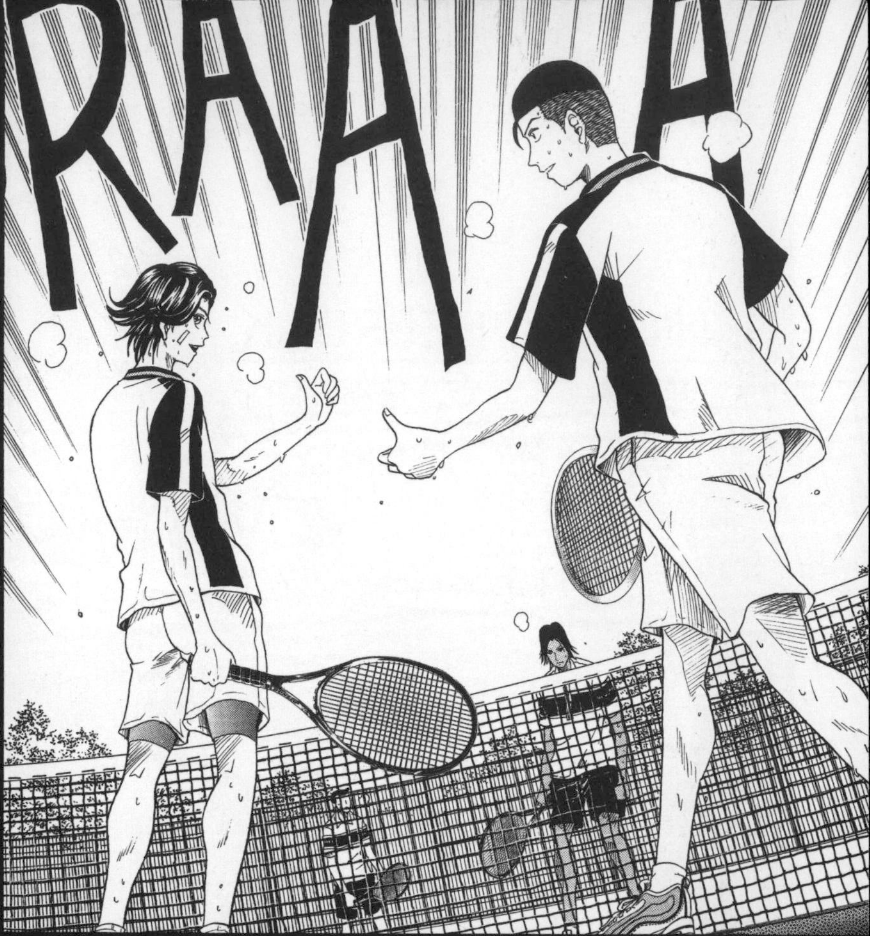
RAAA

GENIUS 63: TIEBREAK

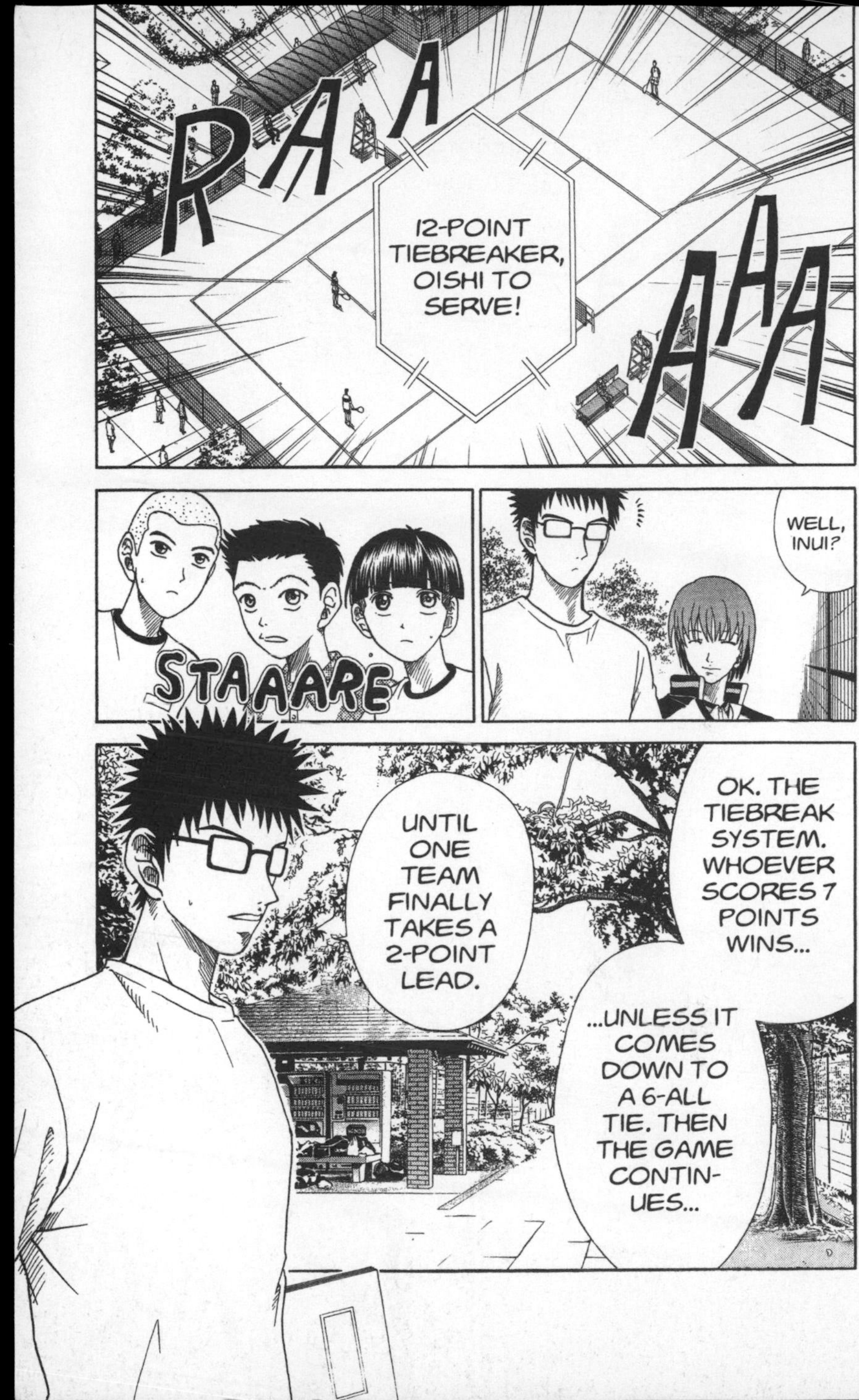
RAAA
12-POINT TIEBREAKER, OISHI TO SERVE!
AAAA
WELL, INUI?
STAAARE
OK. THE TIEBREAK SYSTEM. WHOEVER SCORES 7 POINTS WINS...
...UNLESS IT COMES DOWN TO A 6-ALL TIE. THEN THE GAME CONTIN-UES...
UNTIL ONE TEAM FINALLY TAKES A 2-POINT LEAD.

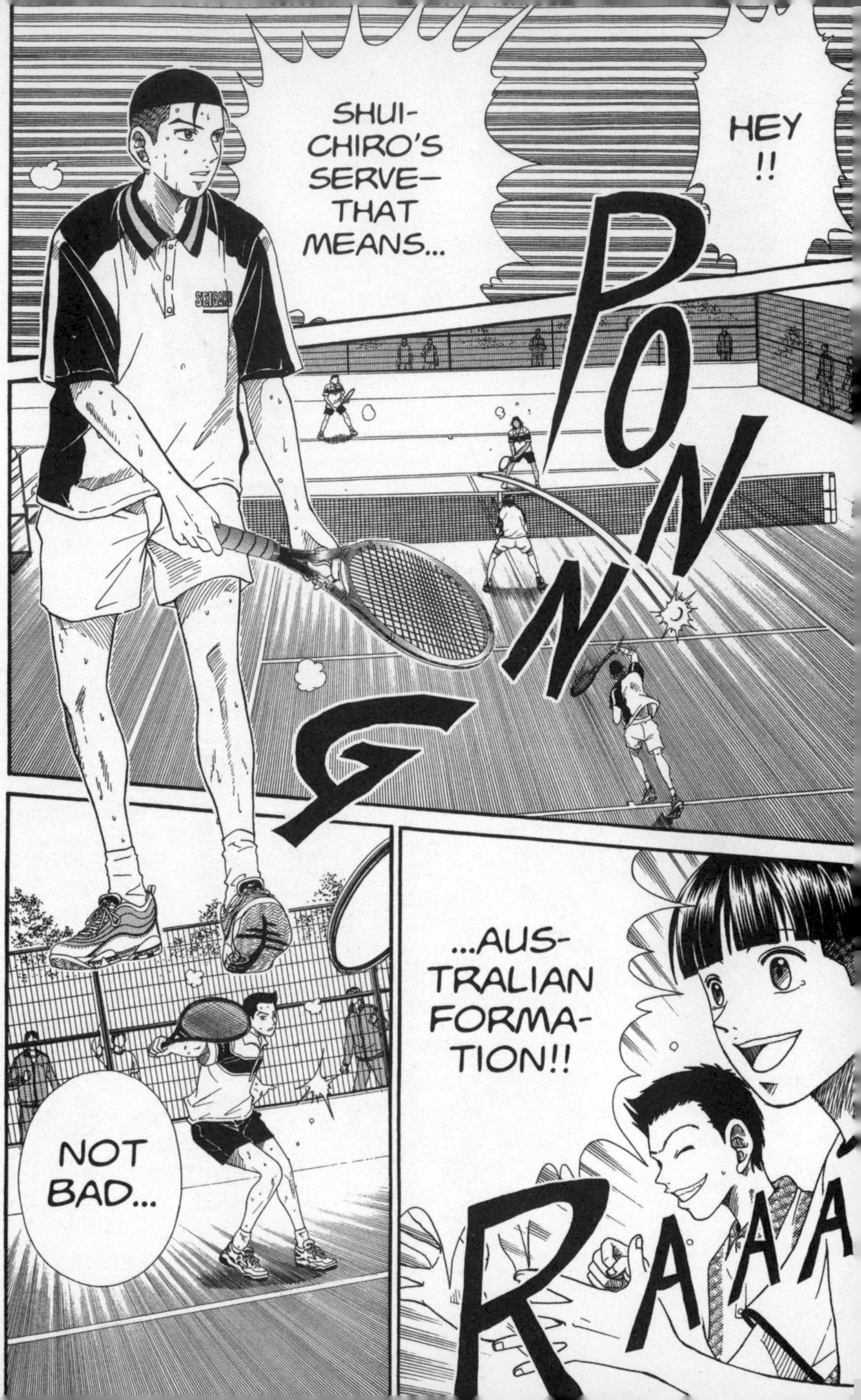
HEY !!
SHUI-CHIRO'S SERVE—THAT MEANS...
PONNG
...AUS-TRALIAN FORMA-TION!!
RAAAA
NOT BAD...

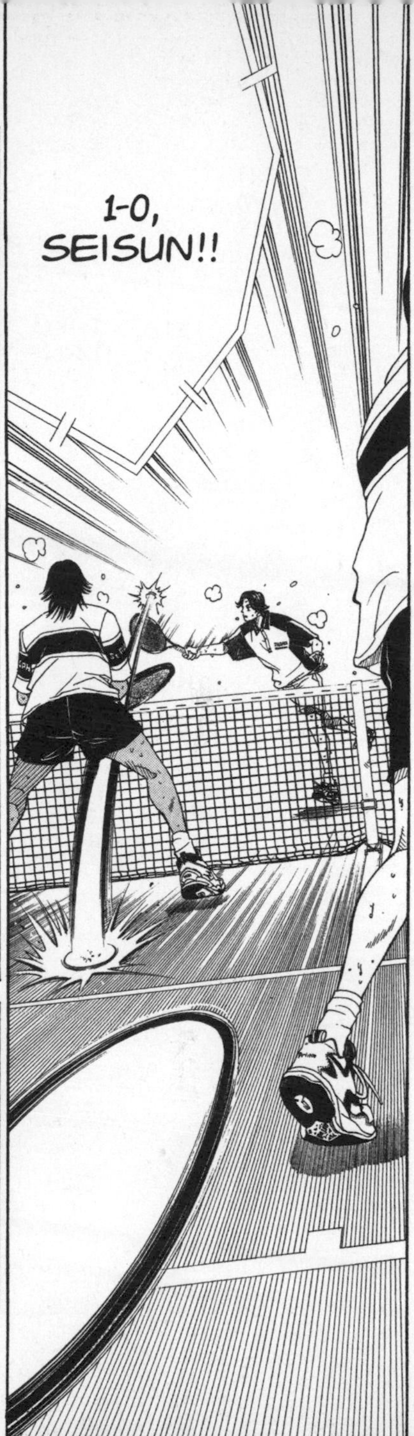
1-0, SEISUN!!

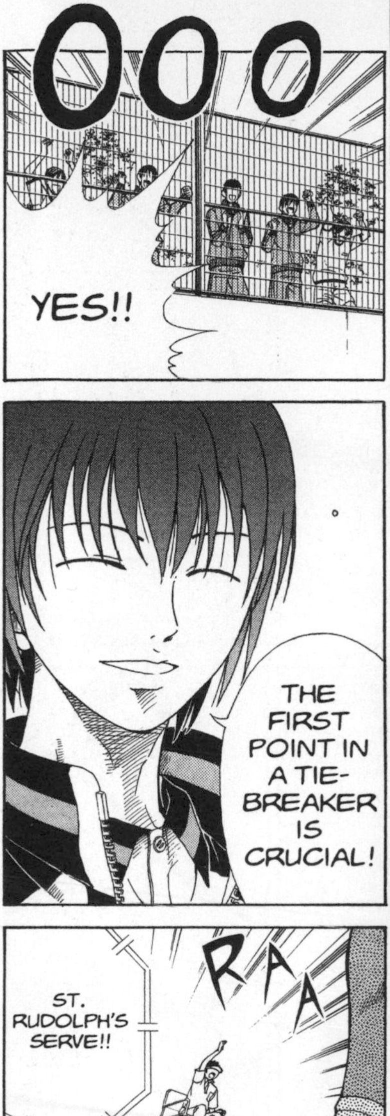
OOO
YES!!
THE FIRST POINT IN A TIE-BREAKER IS CRUCIAL!
RAA
ST. RUDOLPH'S SERVE!!

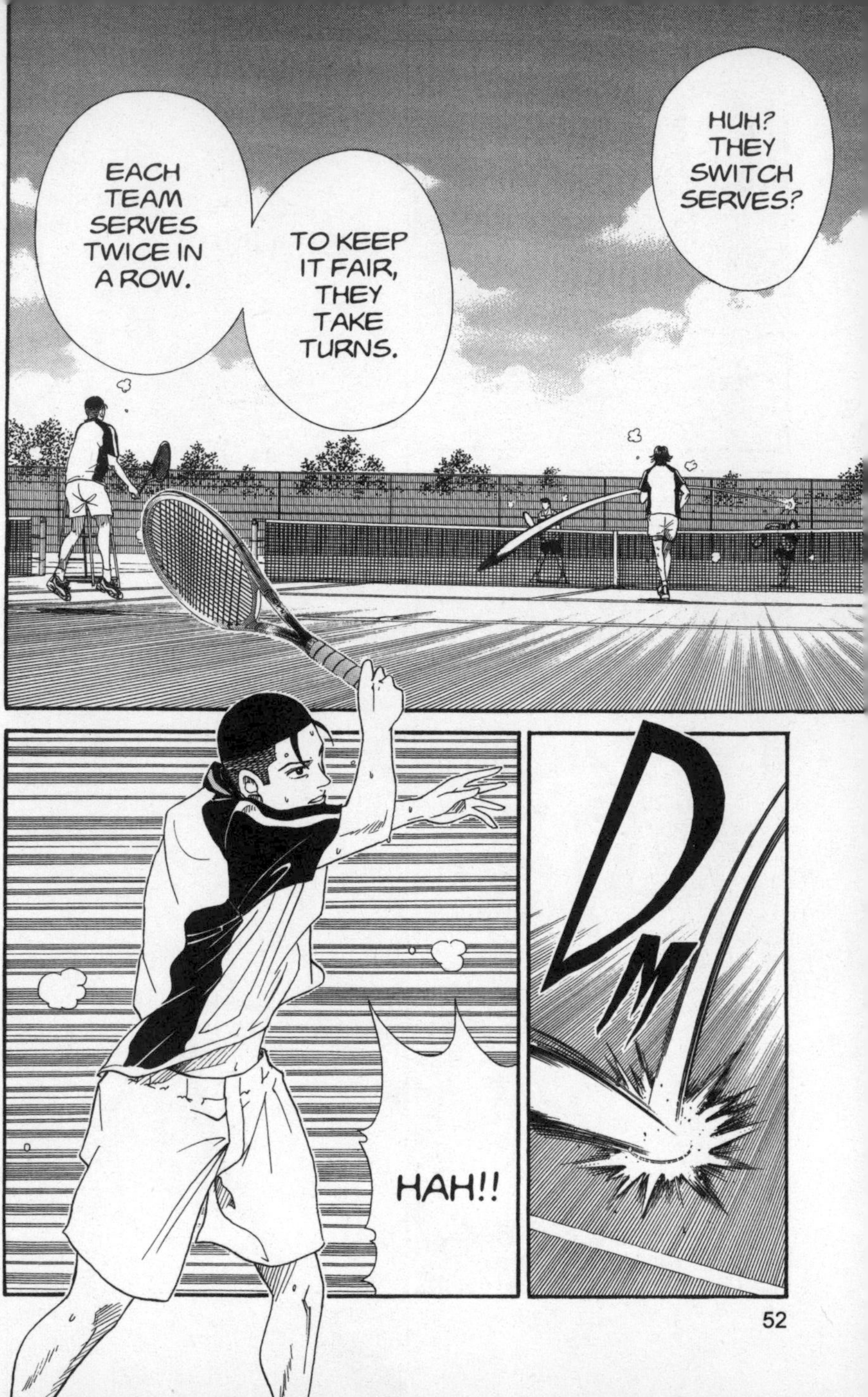
HUH? THEY SWITCH SERVES?
TO KEEP IT FAIR, THEY TAKE TURNS.
EACH TEAM SERVES TWICE IN A ROW.
DM
HAH!!

READ THIS WAY

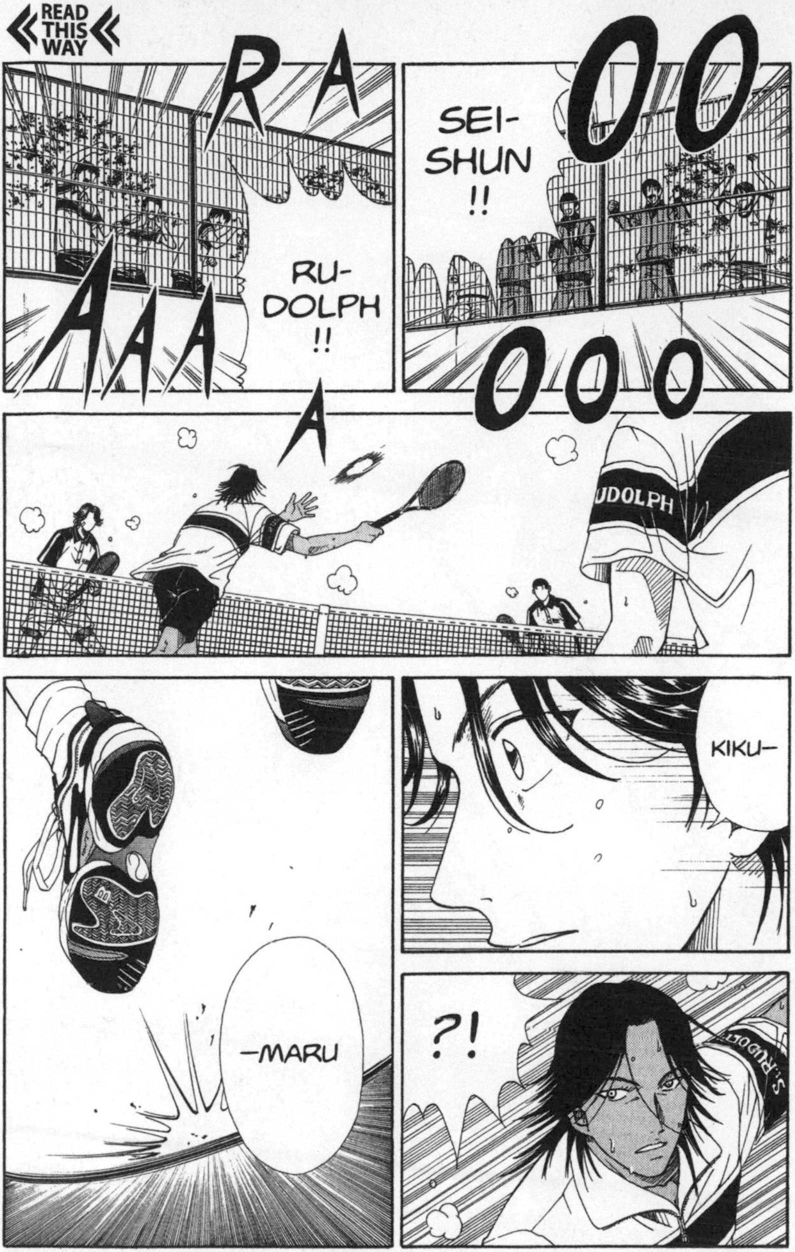

OO
SEI-SHUN!!
OOO
RA
RU-DOLPH!!
AAA
A
KIKU-
?!
-MARU

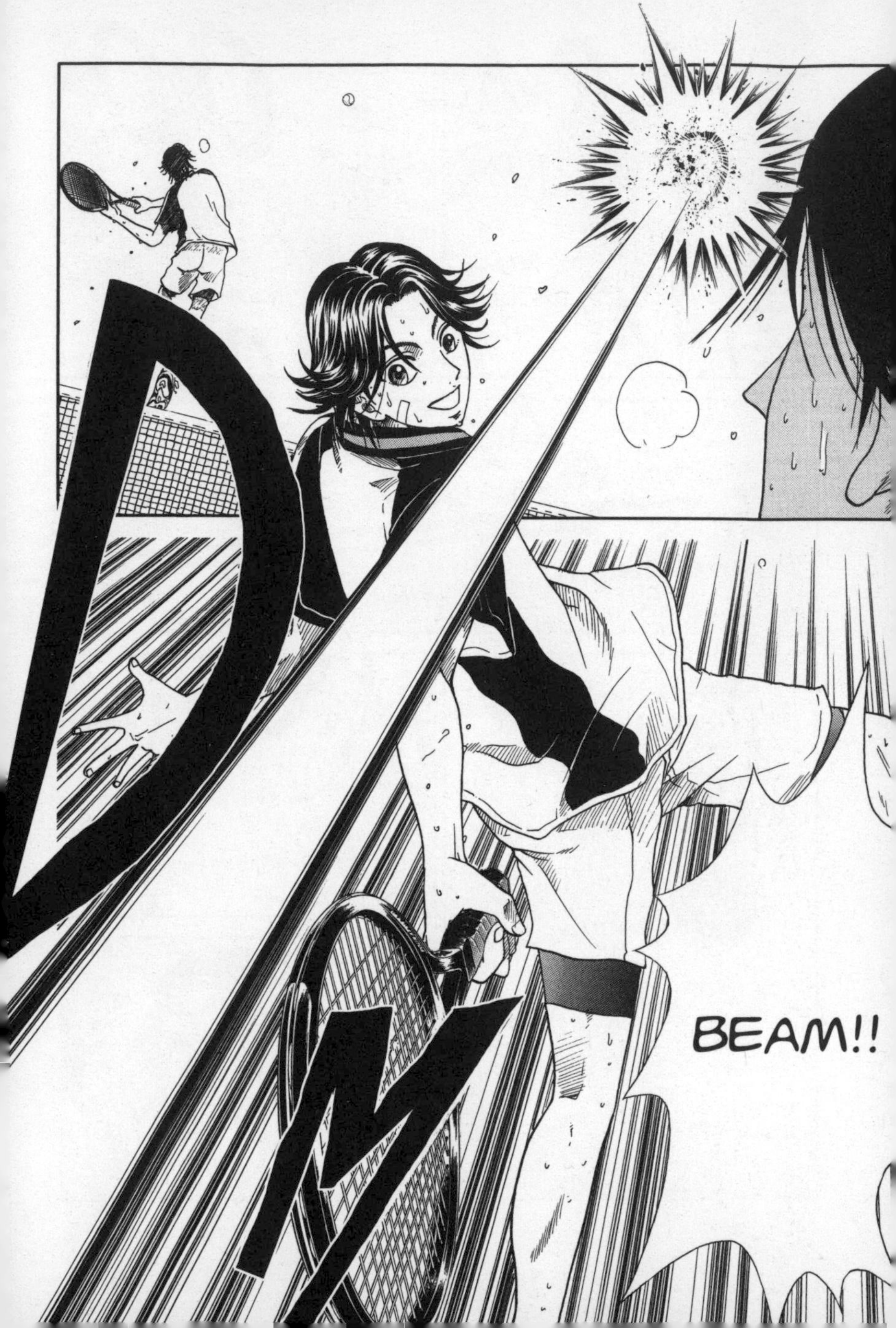
BEAM!!

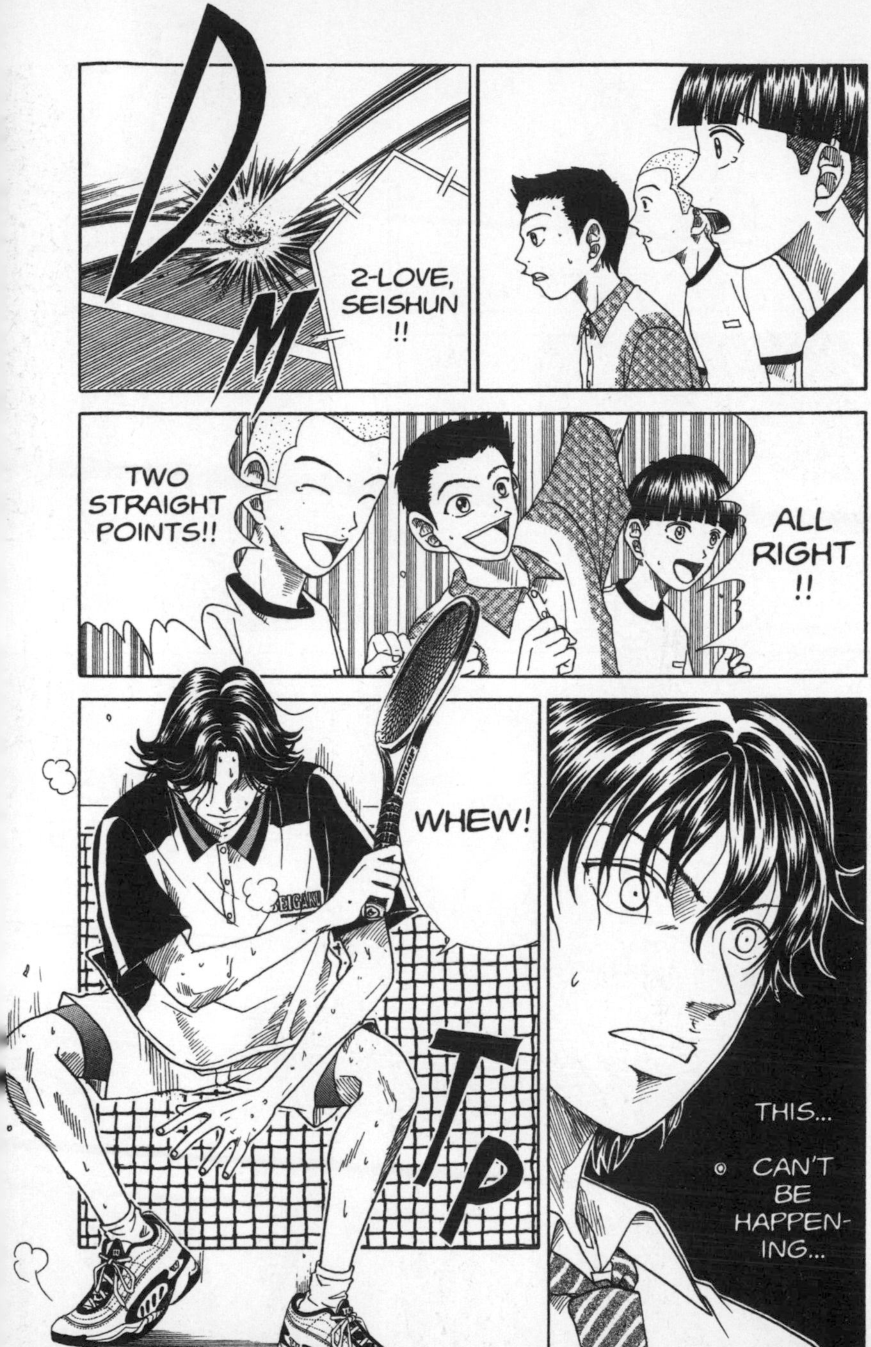
DM
2-LOVE, SEISHUN !!
ALL RIGHT !!
TWO STRAIGHT POINTS!!
THIS... CAN'T BE HAPPENING...
WHEW!
TP

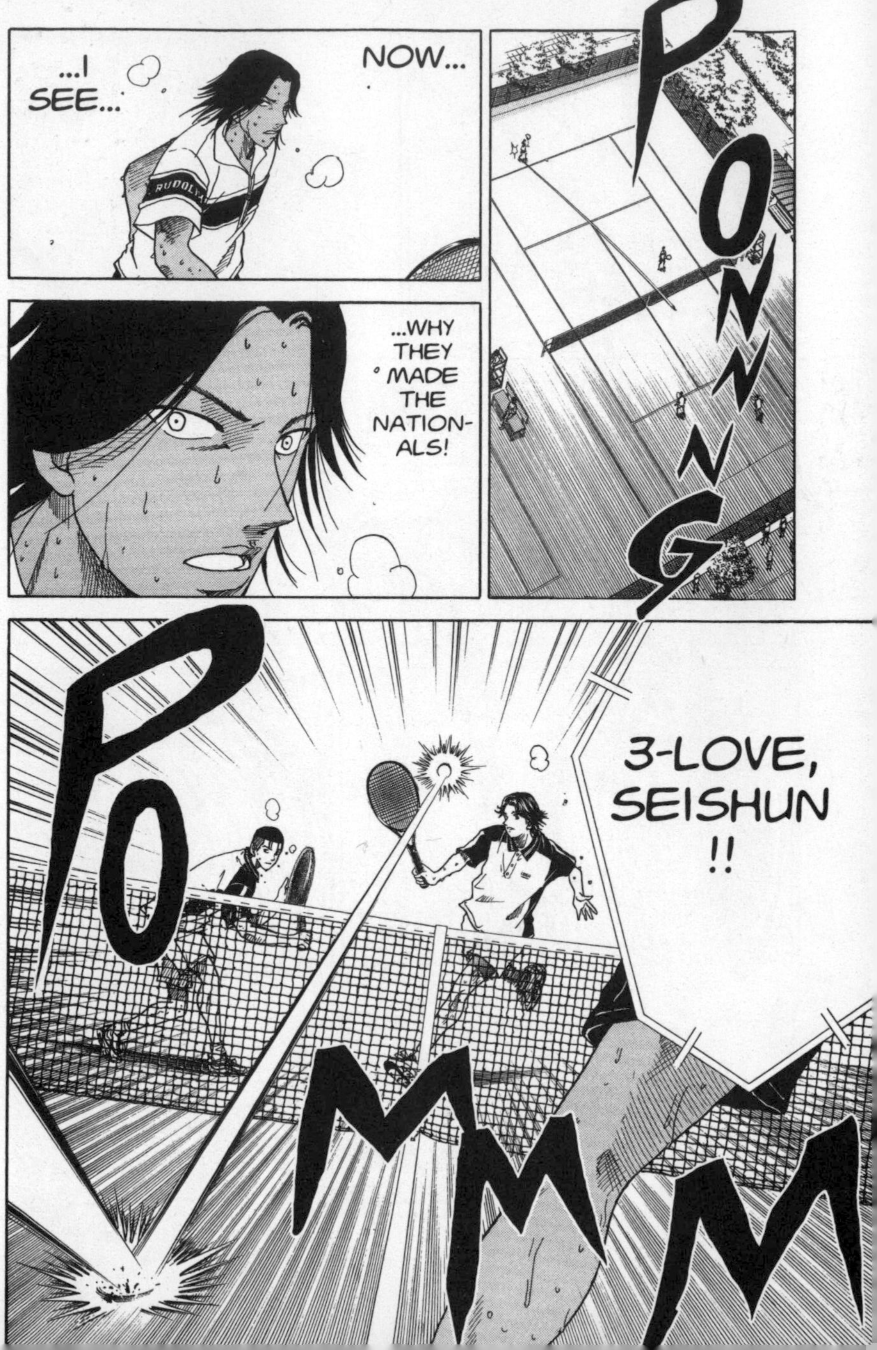
PONNNG
NOW...
...I SEE...
...WHY THEY MADE THE NATION-ALS!
3-LOVE, SEISHUN !!
POMMMM

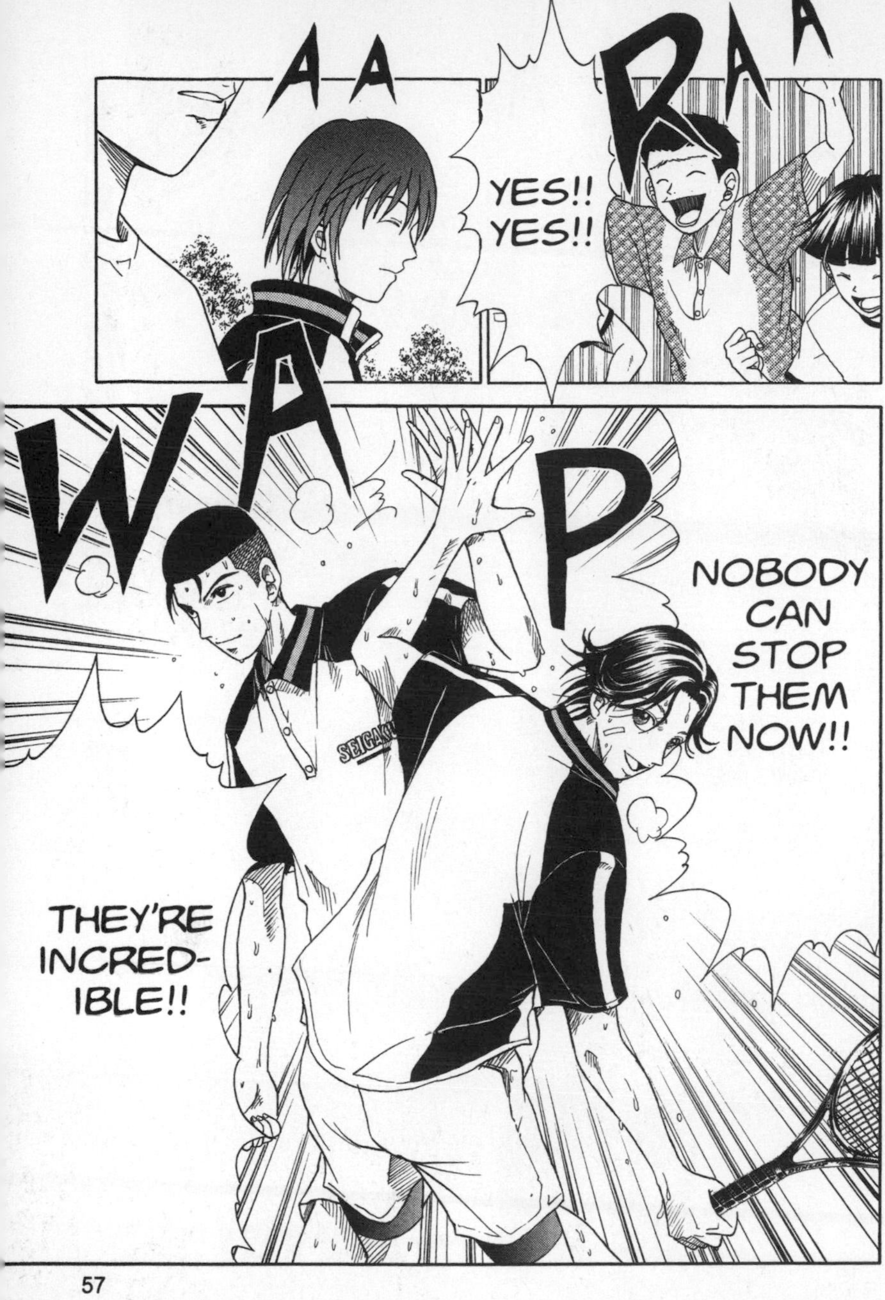
AARAA
YES!! YES!!
NOBODY CAN STOP THEM NOW!!
WAP
THEY'RE INCRED-IBLE!!

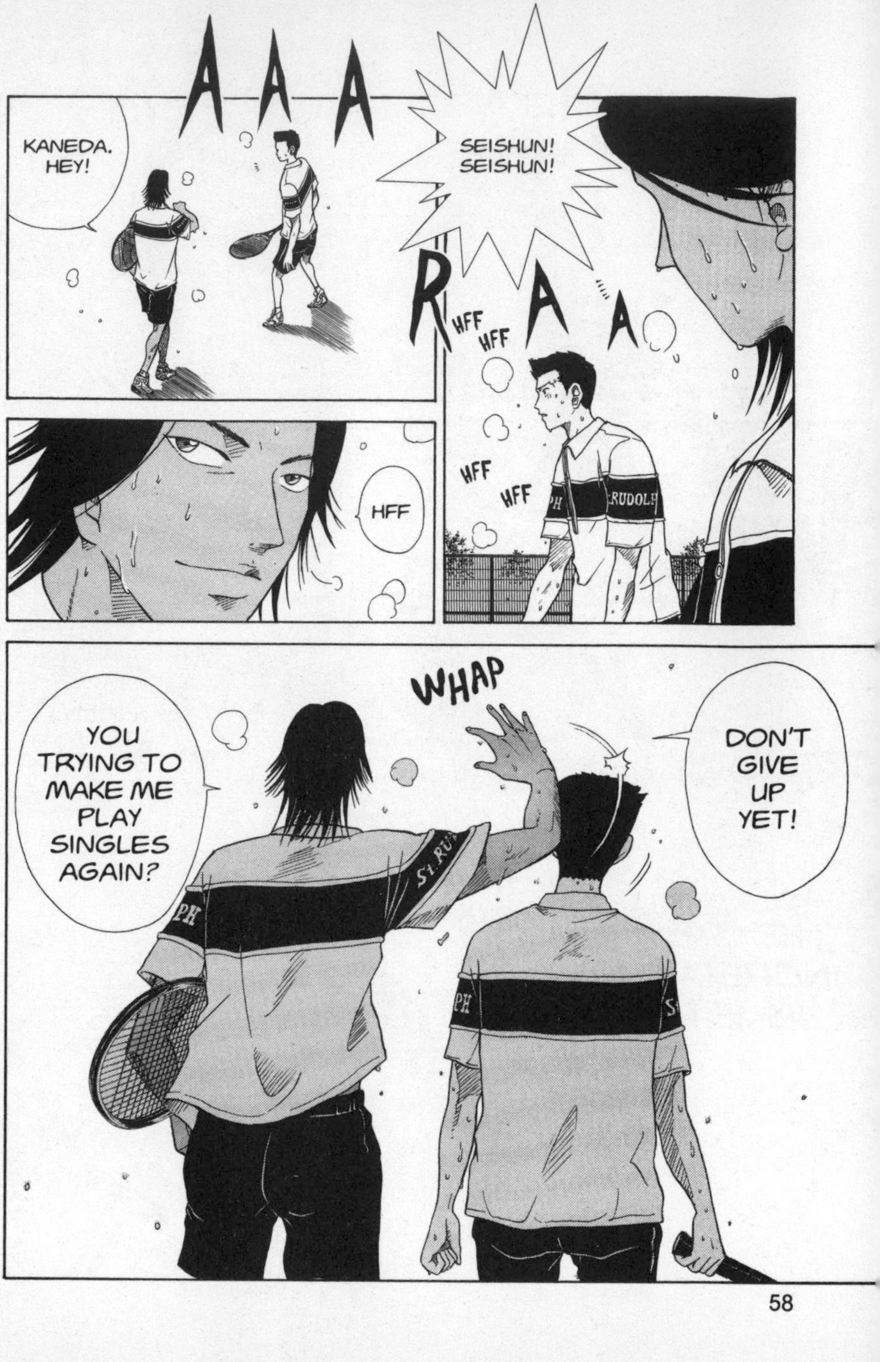

AAA
RAAA
SEISHUN! SEISHUN!
HFF HFF
HFF HFF
KANEDA. HEY!
HFF
DON'T GIVE UP YET!
WHAP
YOU TRYING TO MAKE ME PLAY SINGLES AGAIN?

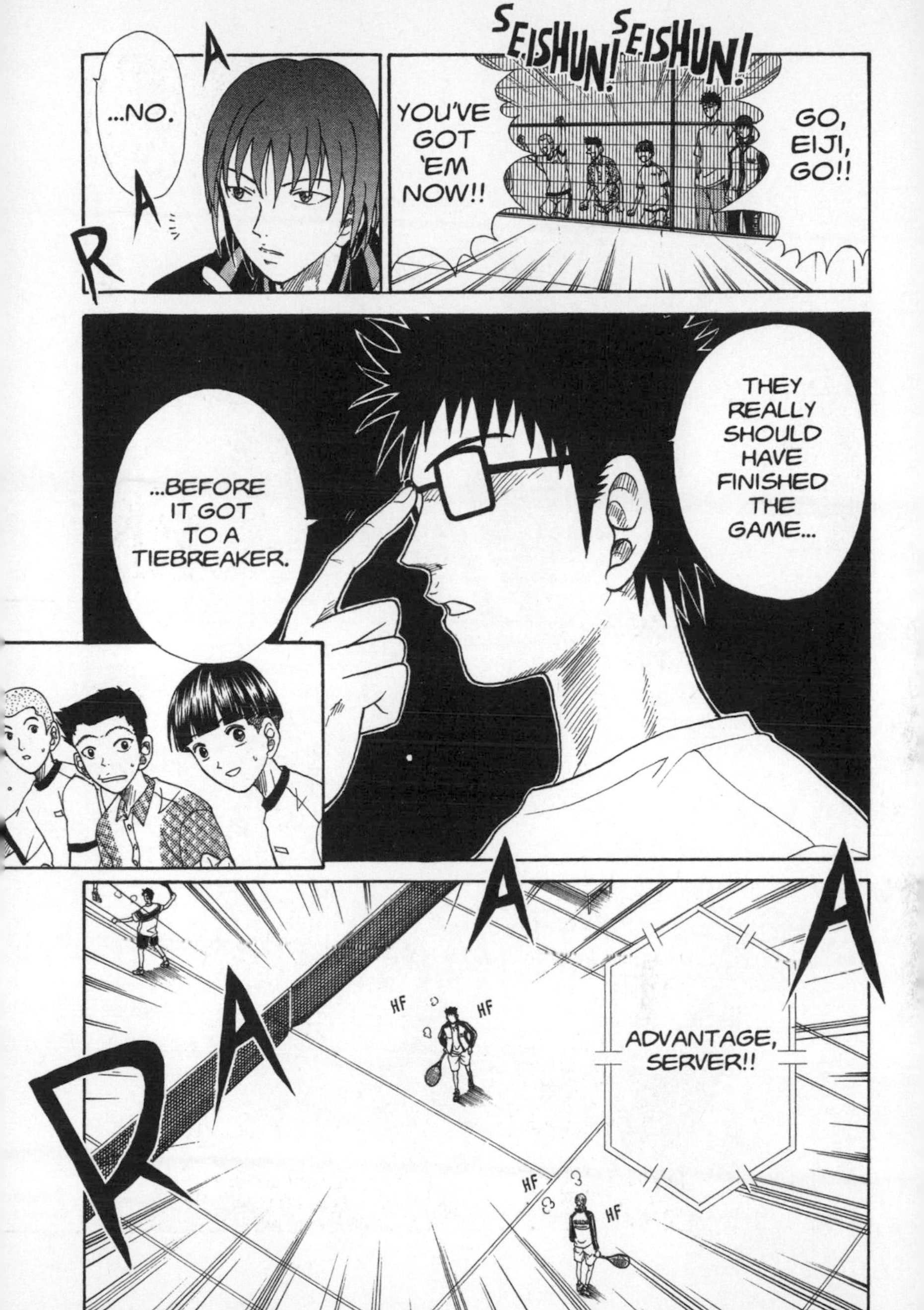
SEISHUN! SEISHUN!
GO, EIJI, GO!!
YOU'VE GOT 'EM NOW!!
RAA
...NO.
THEY REALLY SHOULD HAVE FINISHED THE GAME...
...BEFORE IT GOT TO A TIEBREAKER.
RAA
ADVANTAGE, SERVER!!
HF HF
HF HF

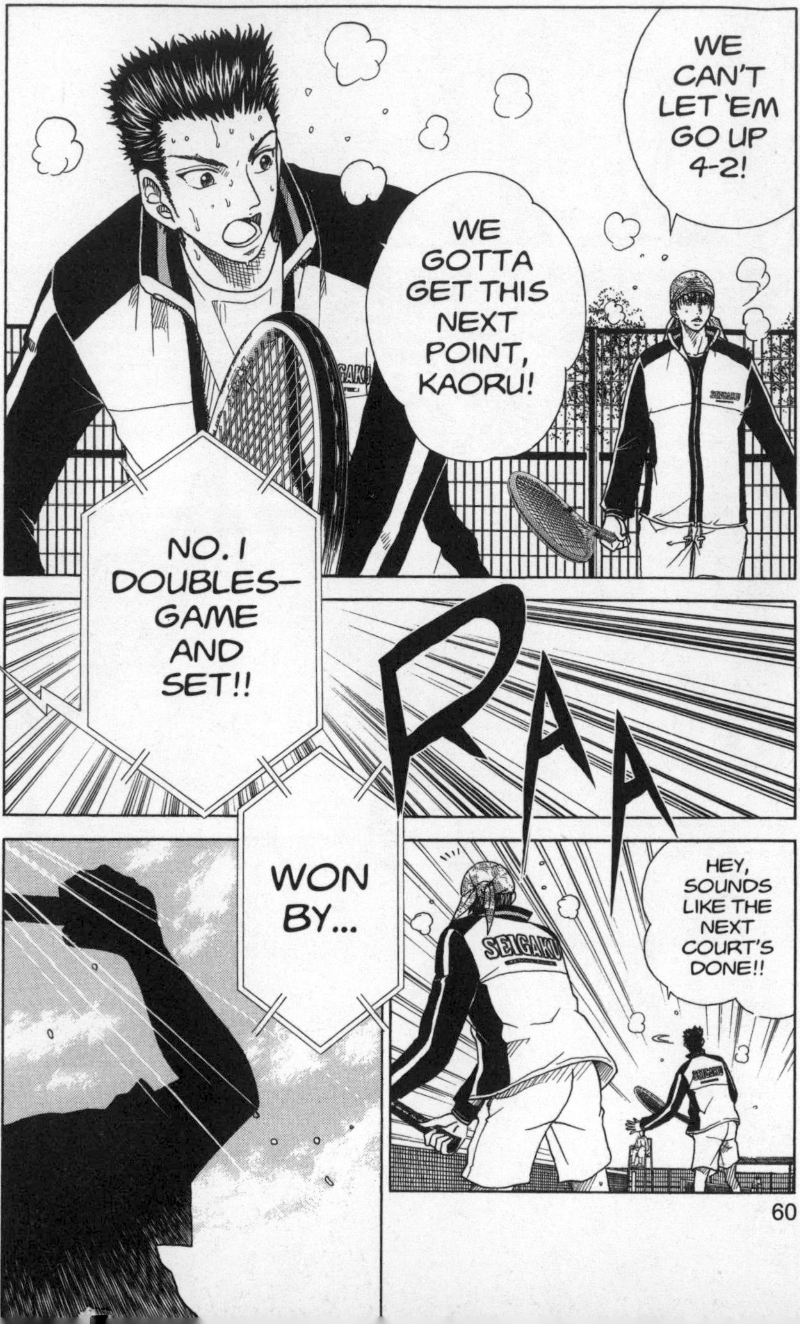
WE CAN'T LET 'EM GO UP 4-2!
WE GOTTA GET THIS NEXT POINT, KAORU!
RAA
NO. 1 DOUBLES-GAME AND SET!!
HEY, SOUNDS LIKE THE NEXT COURT'S DONE!!
WON BY...

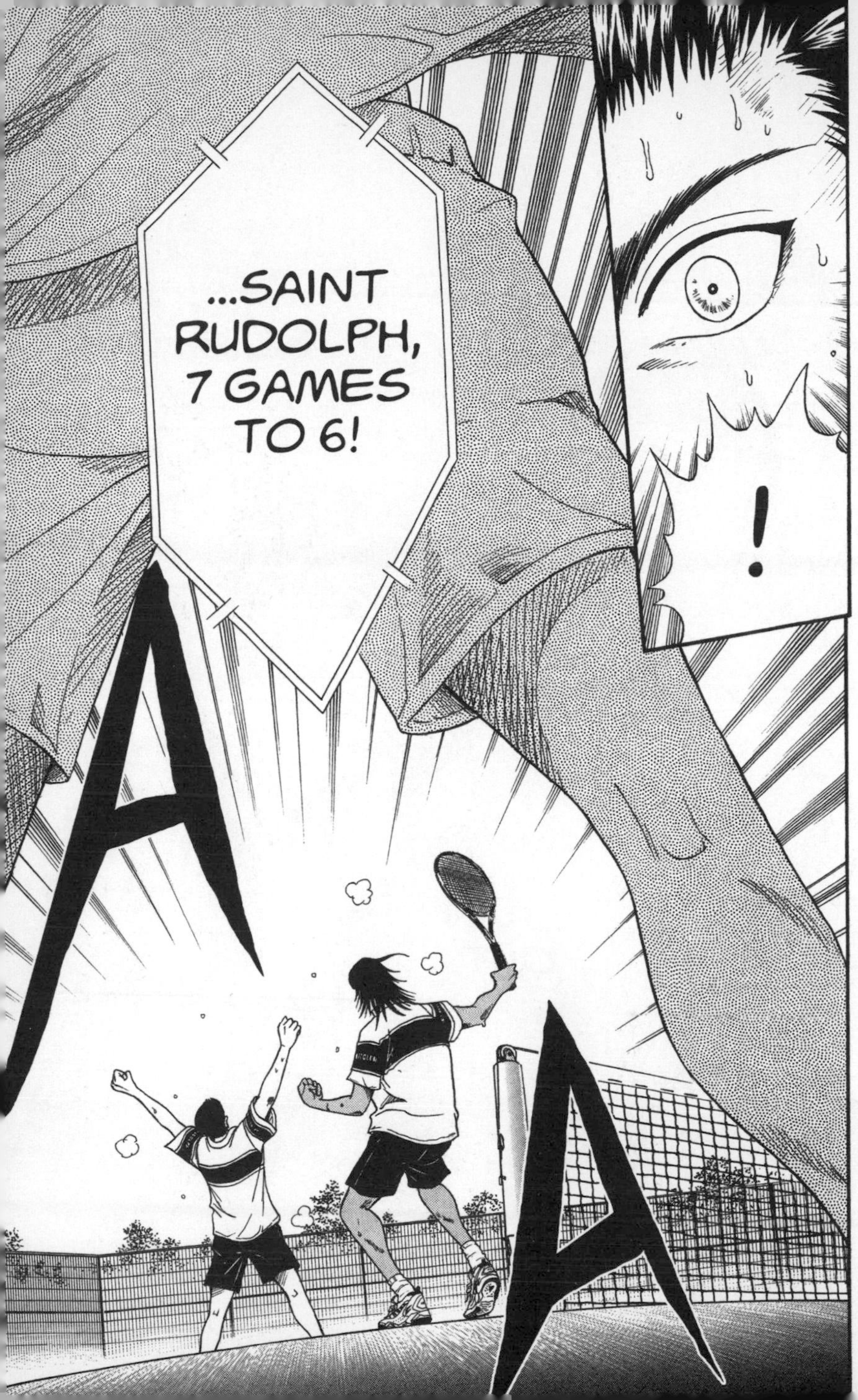
...SAINT RUDOLPH, 7 GAMES TO 6!
!

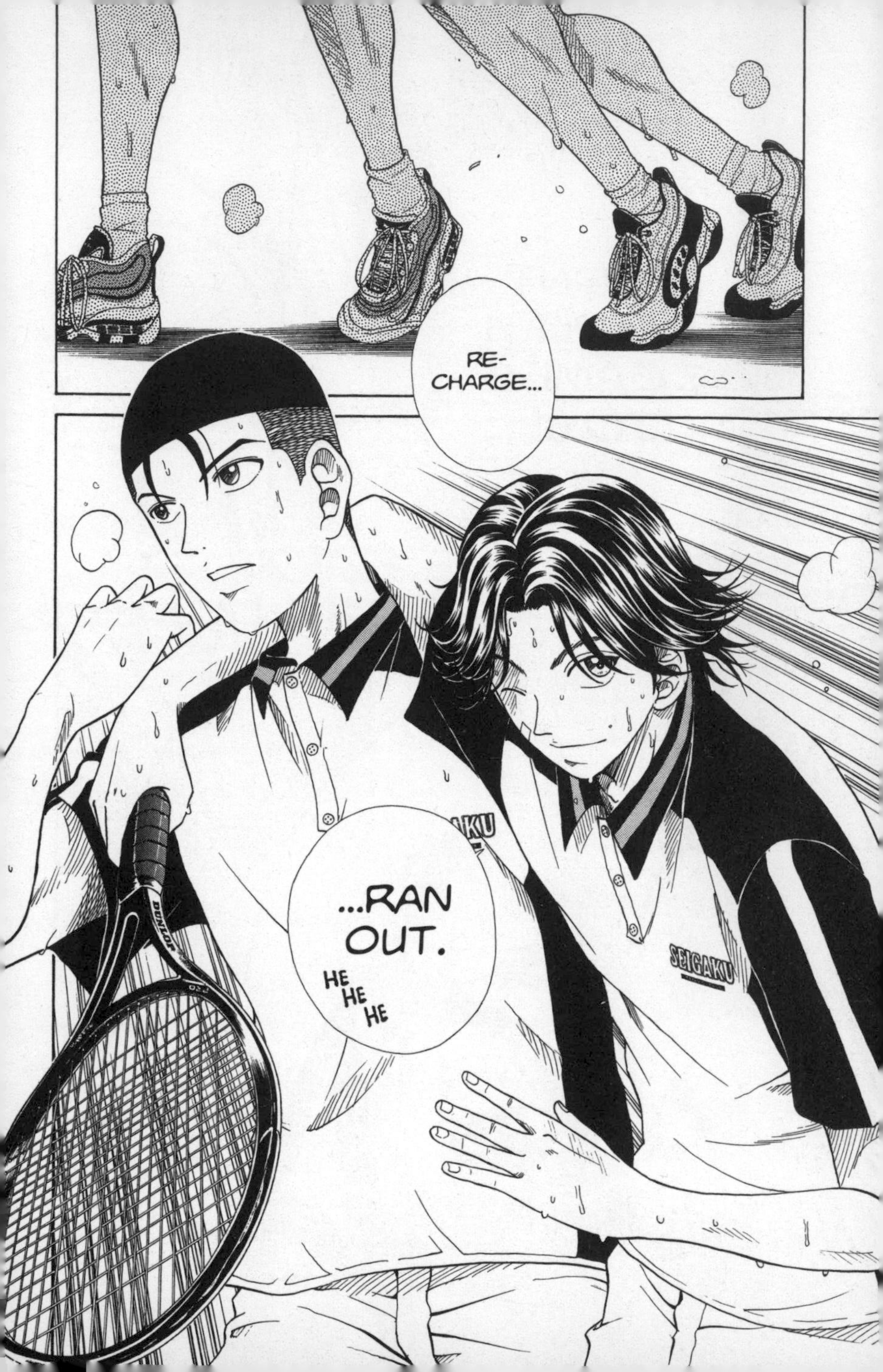
RE-CHARGE...
...RAN OUT.
HE HE HE
SEIGAKU

READ THIS WAY

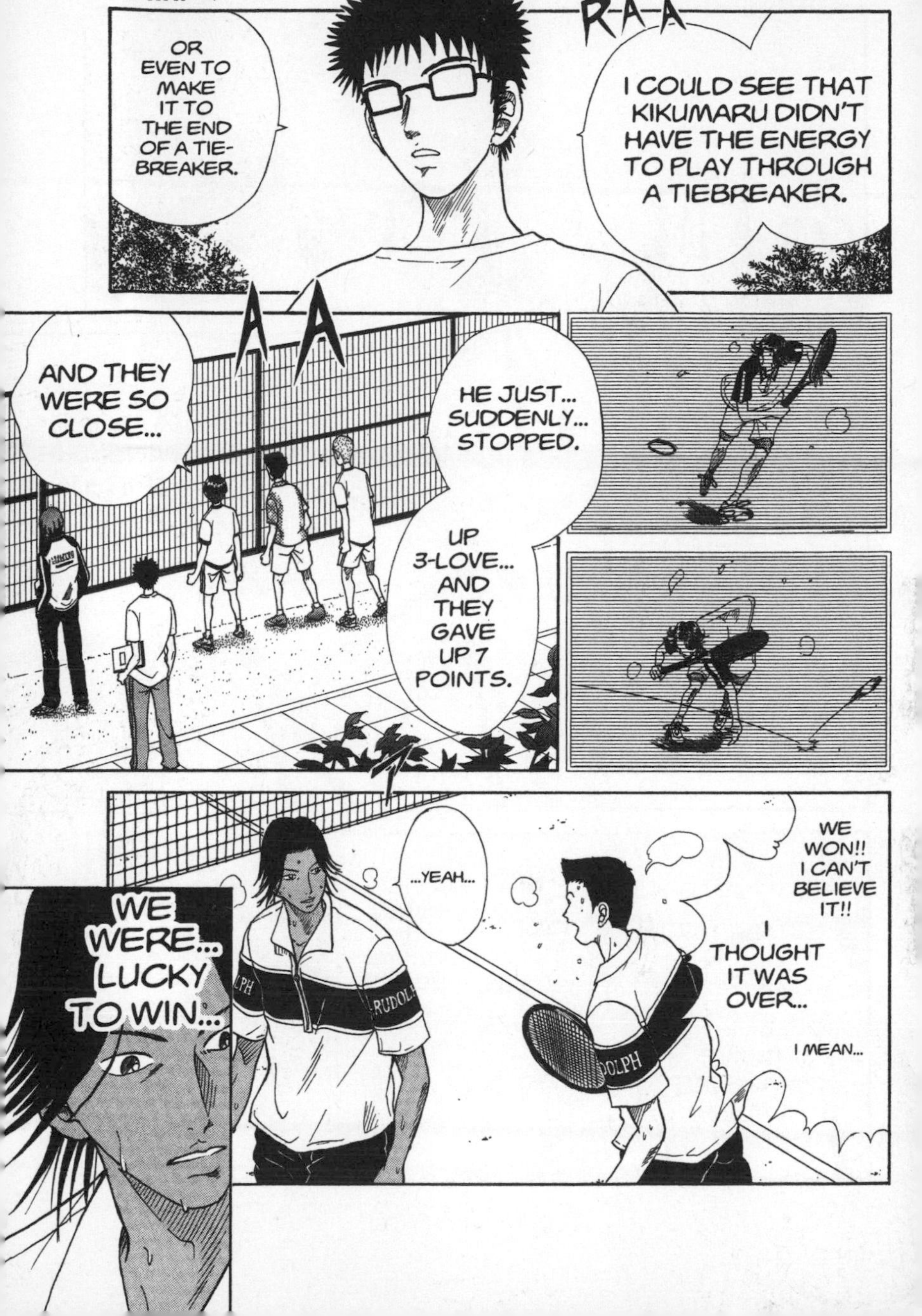
RA-A-A-A
I COULD SEE THAT KIKUMARU DIDN'T HAVE THE ENERGY TO PLAY THROUGH A TIEBREAKER.
OR EVEN TO MAKE IT TO THE END OF A TIE-BREAKER.
HE JUST... SUDDENLY... STOPPED.
UP 3-LOVE... AND THEY GAVE UP 7 POINTS.
AND THEY WERE SO CLOSE...
WE WON!! I CAN'T BELIEVE IT!!
I THOUGHT IT WAS OVER...
I MEAN...
...YEAH...
WE WERE... LUCKY TO WIN...

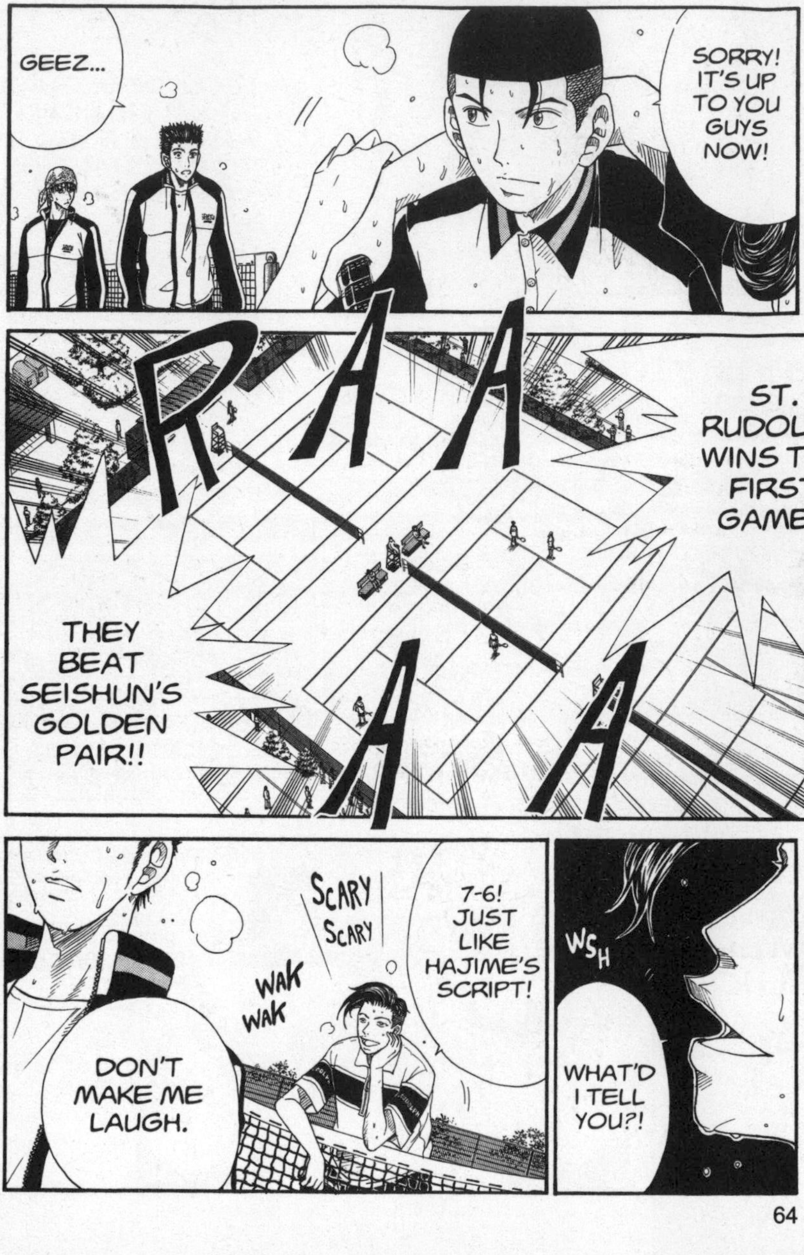
SORRY! IT'S UP TO YOU GUYS NOW!
GEEZ...
ST. RUDOLPH WINS THE FIRST GAME!!
RAAAA
THEY BEAT SEISHUN'S GOLDEN PAIR!!
WSH
WHAT'D I TELL YOU?!
7-6! JUST LIKE HAJIME'S SCRIPT!
SCARY SCARY
WAK WAK
DON'T MAKE ME LAUGH.

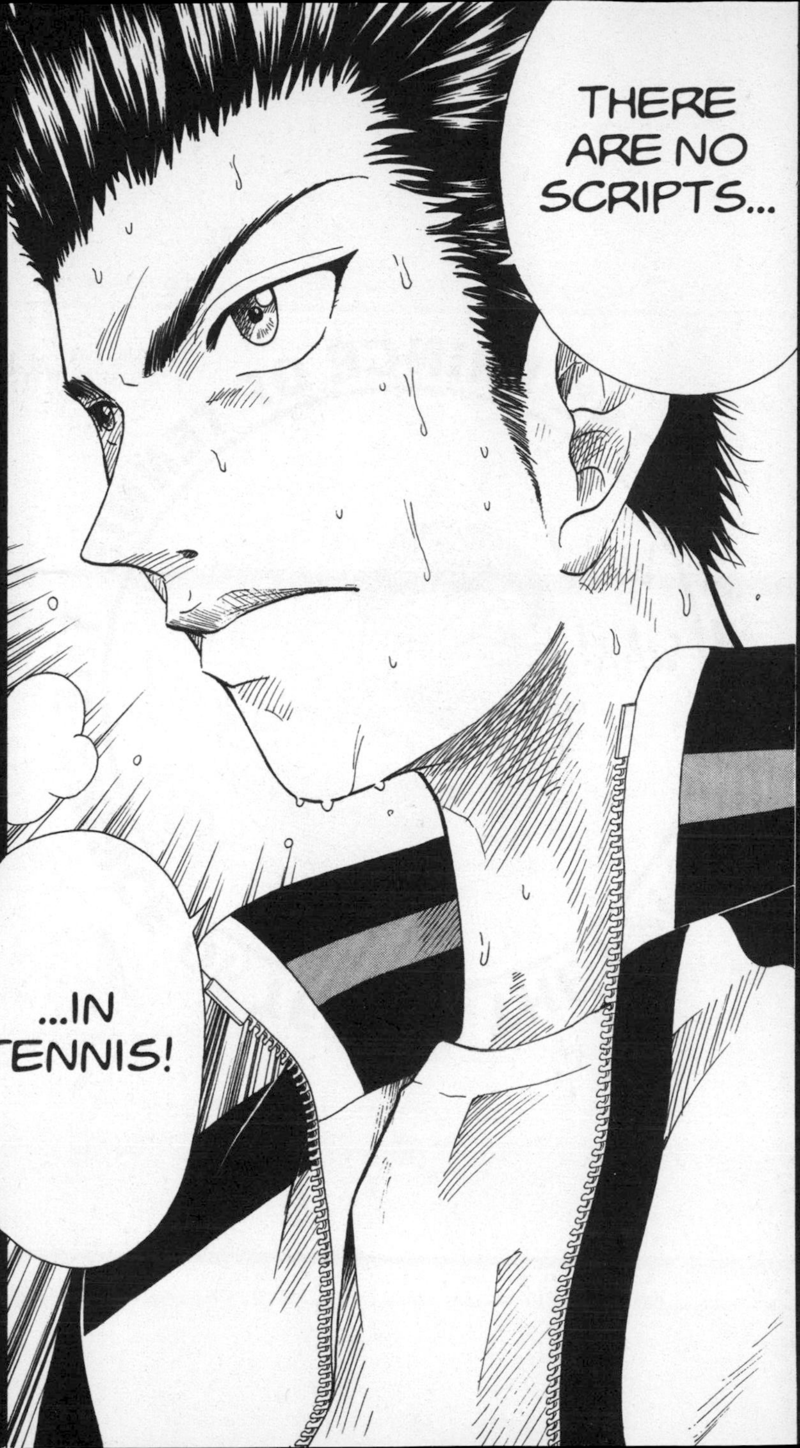
THERE ARE NO SCRIPTS...
...IN TENNIS!

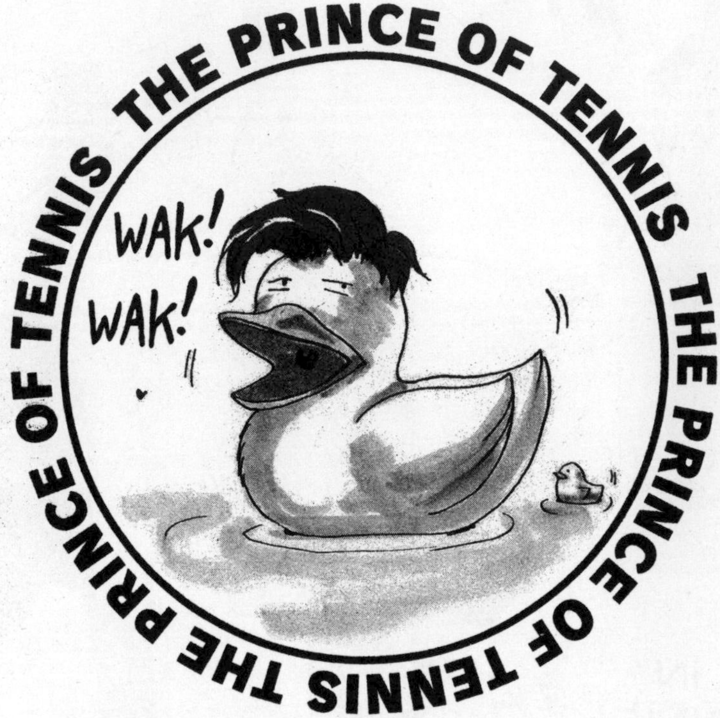
THE PRINCE OF TENNIS THE PRINCE OF TENNIS THE PRINCE OF TENNIS
WAK!
WAK!

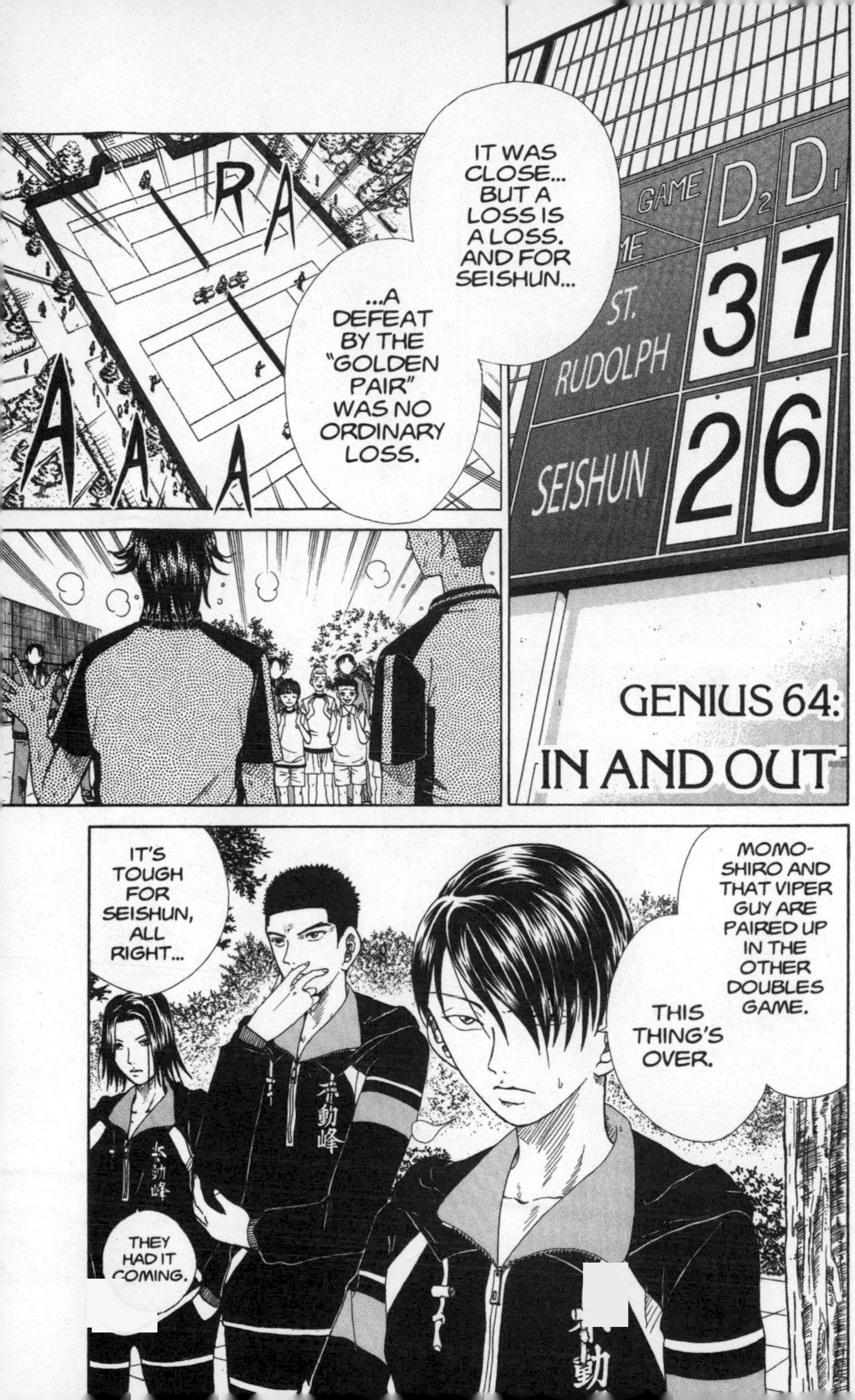
GAME
D2 D1
ST. RUDOLPH 3 7
SEISHUN 2 6
GENIUS 64:
IN AND OUT
IT WAS CLOSE... BUT A LOSS IS A LOSS. AND FOR SEISHUN...
...A DEFEAT BY THE "GOLDEN PAIR" WAS NO ORDINARY LOSS.
RA
A
A
A
MOMO-SHIRO AND THAT VIPER GUY ARE PAIRED UP IN THE OTHER DOUBLES GAME.
THIS THING'S OVER.
IT'S TOUGH FOR SEISHUN, ALL RIGHT...
THEY HAD IT COMING.

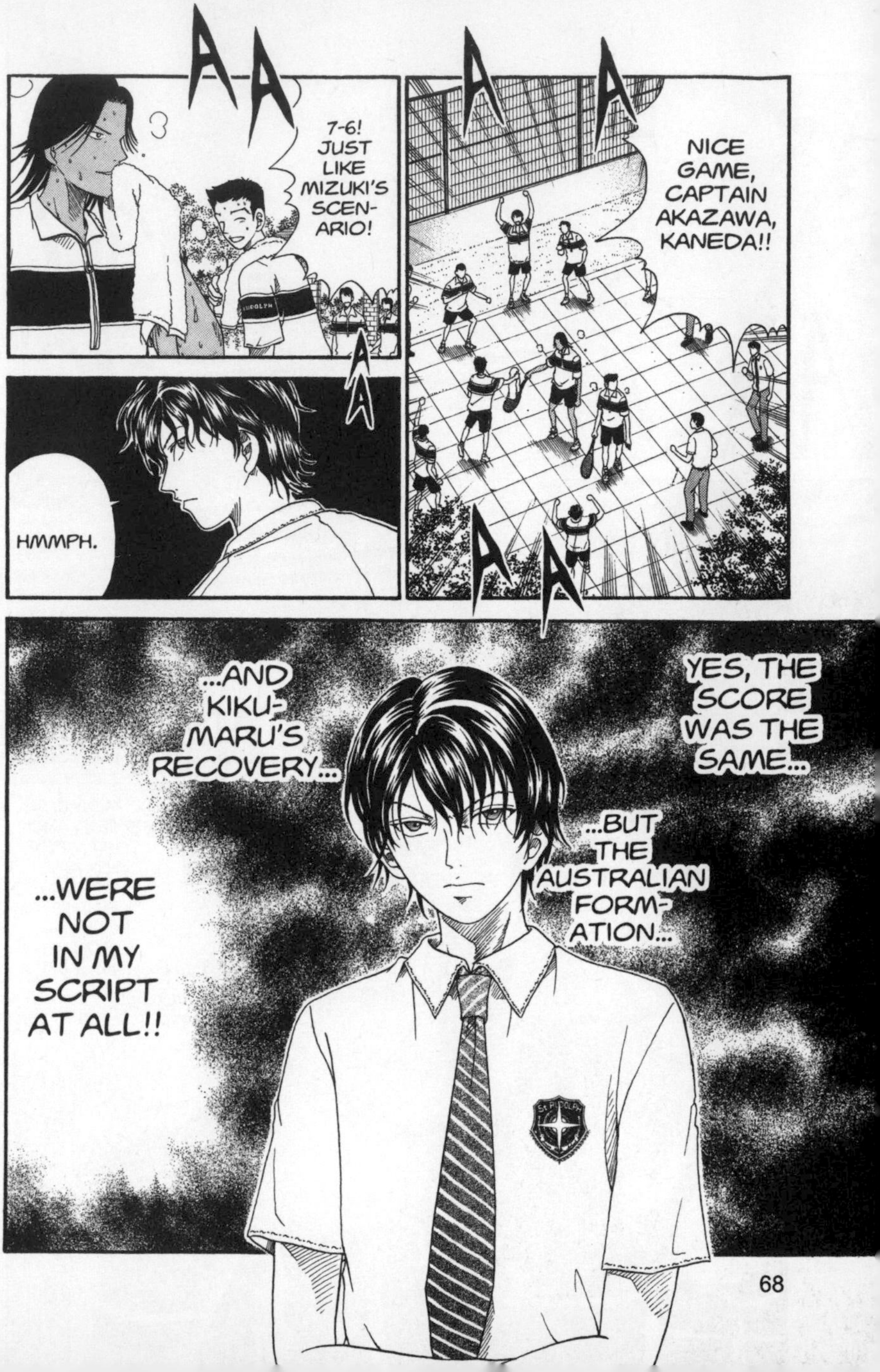
AA
NICE GAME, CAPTAIN AKAZAWA, KANEDA!!
AA
7-6! JUST LIKE MIZUKI'S SCEN-ARIO!
AA
HMMPH.
AA
YES, THE SCORE WAS THE SAME...
...BUT THE AUSTRALIAN FORM-ATION...
...AND KIKU-MARU'S RECOVERY...
...WERE NOT IN MY SCRIPT AT ALL!!

GENIUS: 64

IN AND OUT

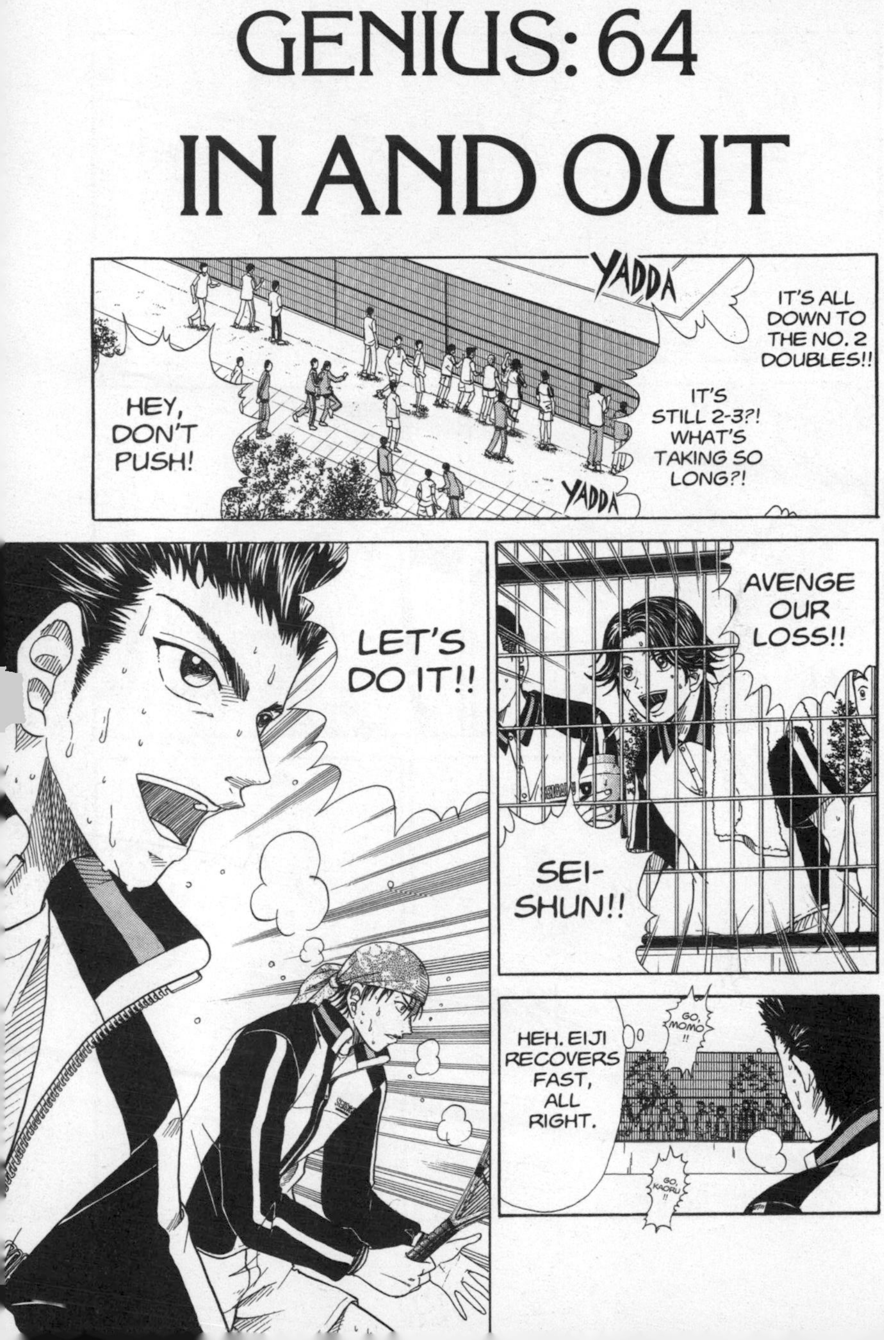

IT'S ALL DOWN TO THE NO. 2 DOUBLES!!
YADDA
IT'S STILL 2-3?! WHAT'S TAKING SO LONG?!
YADDA
HEY, DON'T PUSH!
AVENGE OUR LOSS!!
SEI-SHUN!!
GO, MOMO!!
HEH. EIJI RECOVERS FAST, ALL RIGHT.
GO, KAORU!!
LET'S DO IT!!

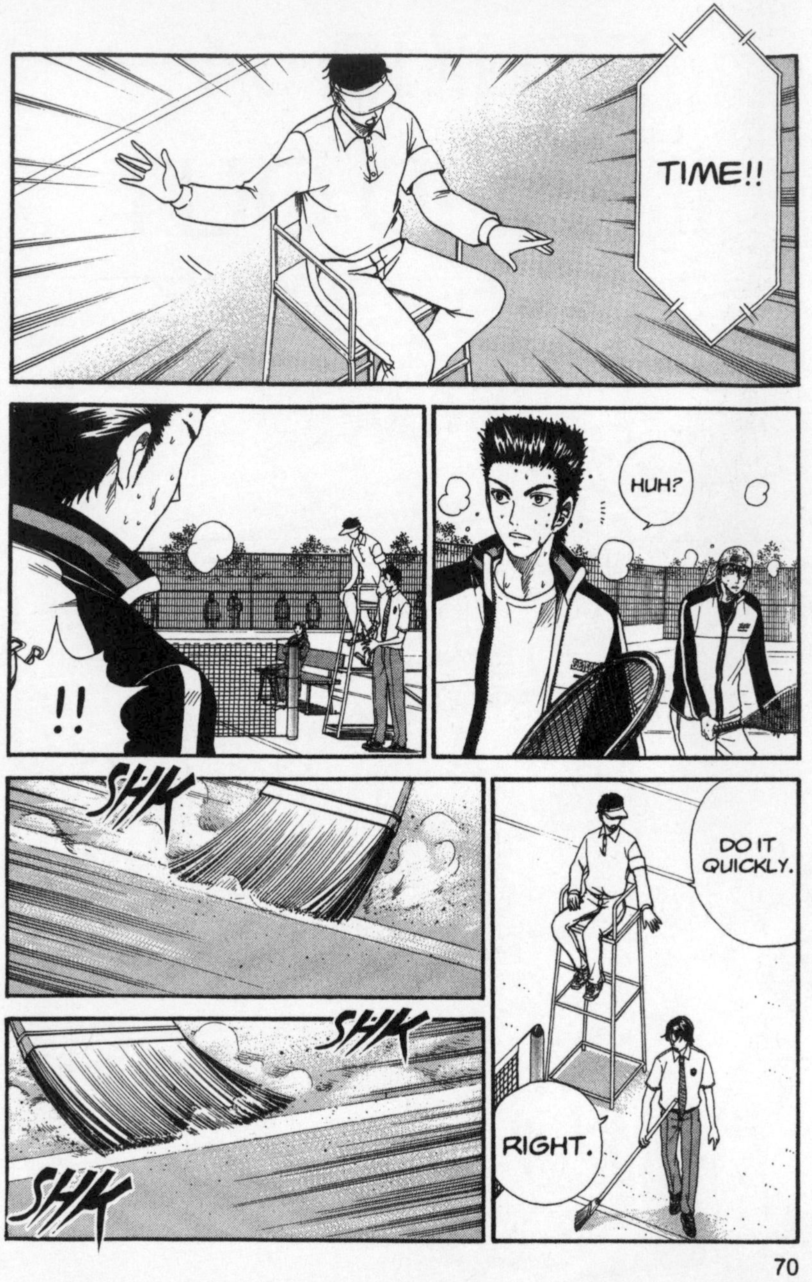
TIME!!
HUH?
!!
DO IT QUICKLY.
RIGHT.
SHK
SHK
SHK

READ THIS WAY

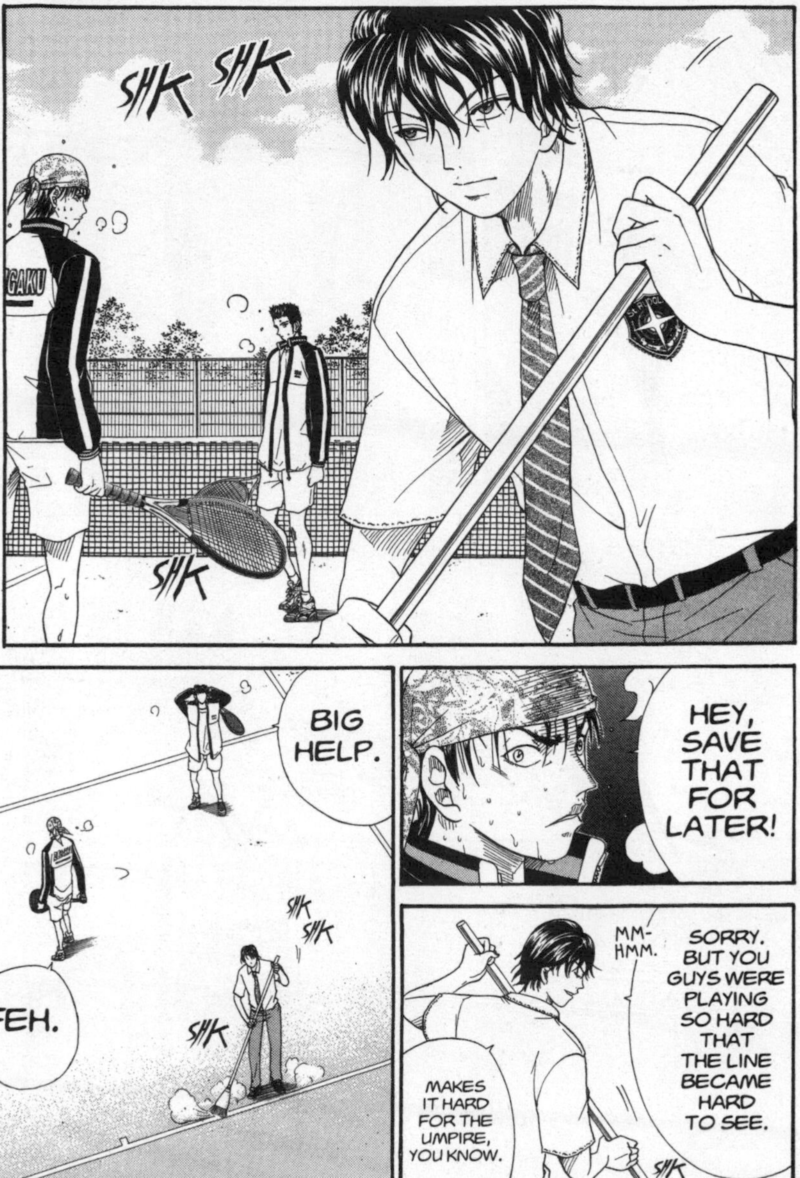
SHK SHK
SHK
HEY, SAVE THAT FOR LATER!
SORRY. BUT YOU GUYS WERE PLAYING SO HARD THAT THE LINE BECAME HARD TO SEE.
MM-HMM.
MAKES IT HARD FOR THE UMPIRE, YOU KNOW.
SHK
BIG HELP.
SHK SHK
SHK
FEH.

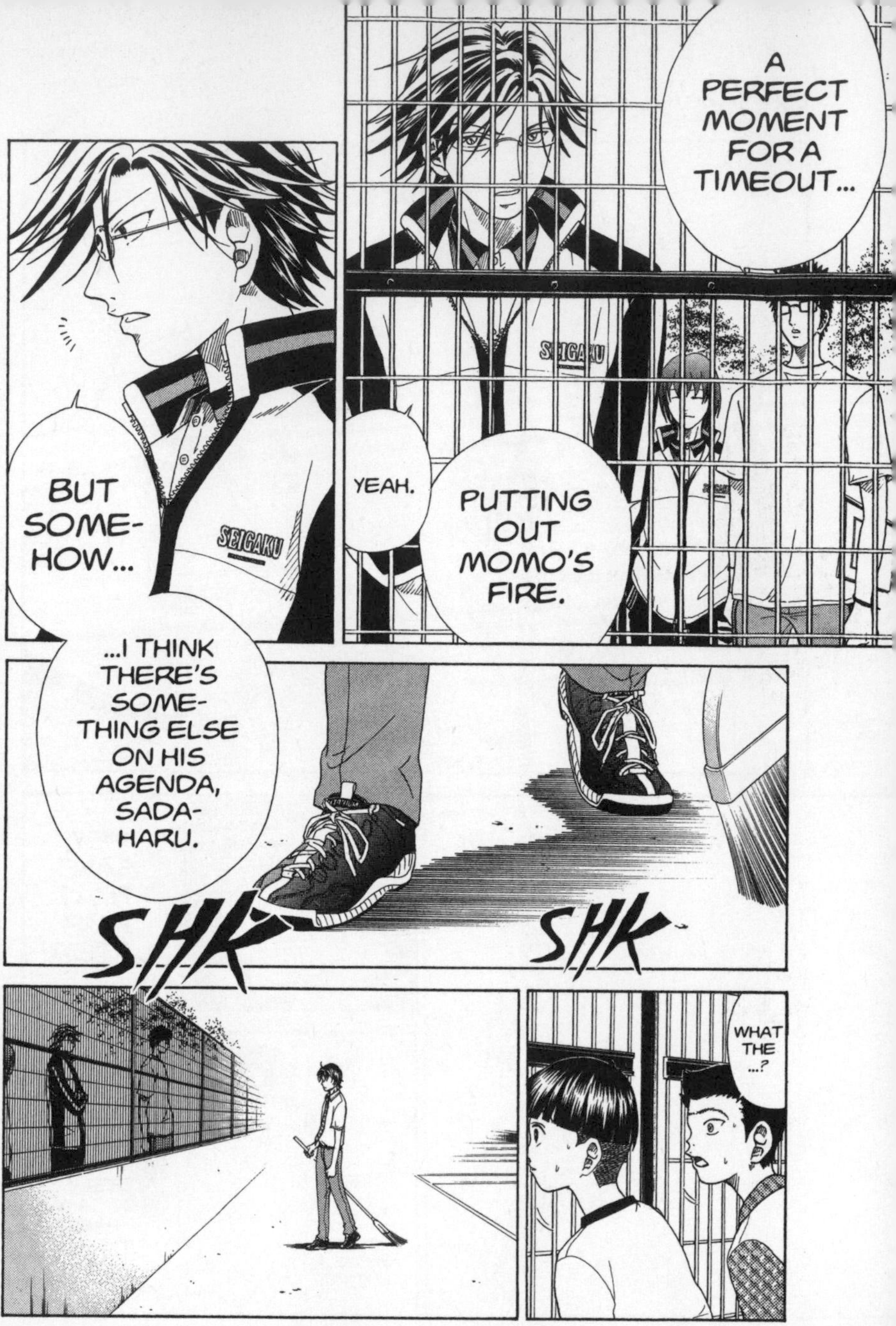
A PERFECT MOMENT FOR A TIMEOUT...
PUTTING OUT MOMO'S FIRE.
YEAH.
BUT SOMEHOW...
...I THINK THERE'S SOMETHING ELSE ON HIS AGENDA, SADAHARU.
SHK
SHK
WHAT THE ...?

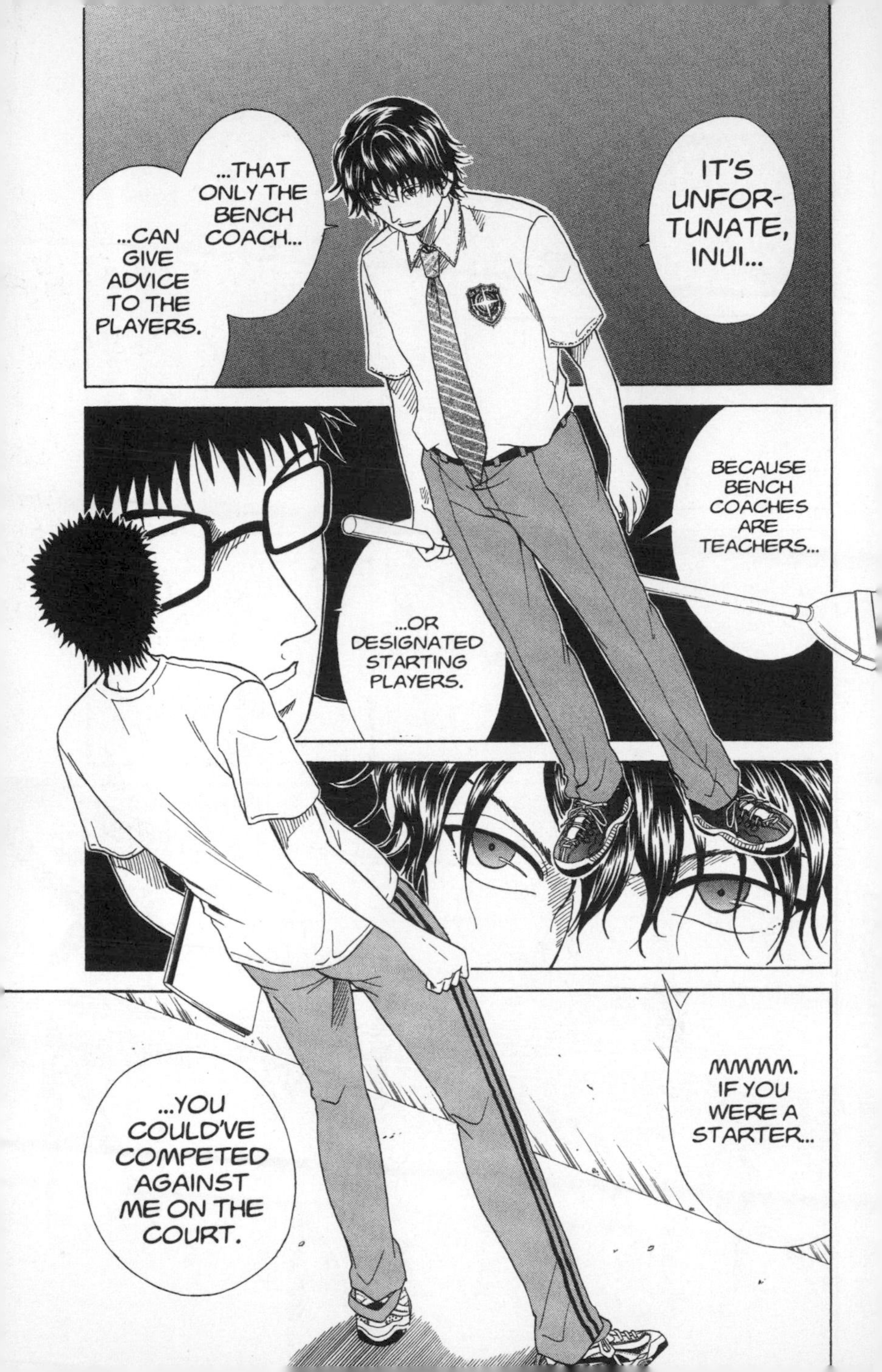
IT'S UNFOR-TUNATE, INUI...
...THAT ONLY THE BENCH COACH...
...CAN GIVE ADVICE TO THE PLAYERS.
BECAUSE BENCH COACHES ARE TEACHERS...
...OR DESIGNATED STARTING PLAYERS.
MMMM. IF YOU WERE A STARTER...
...YOU COULD'VE COMPETED AGAINST ME ON THE COURT.

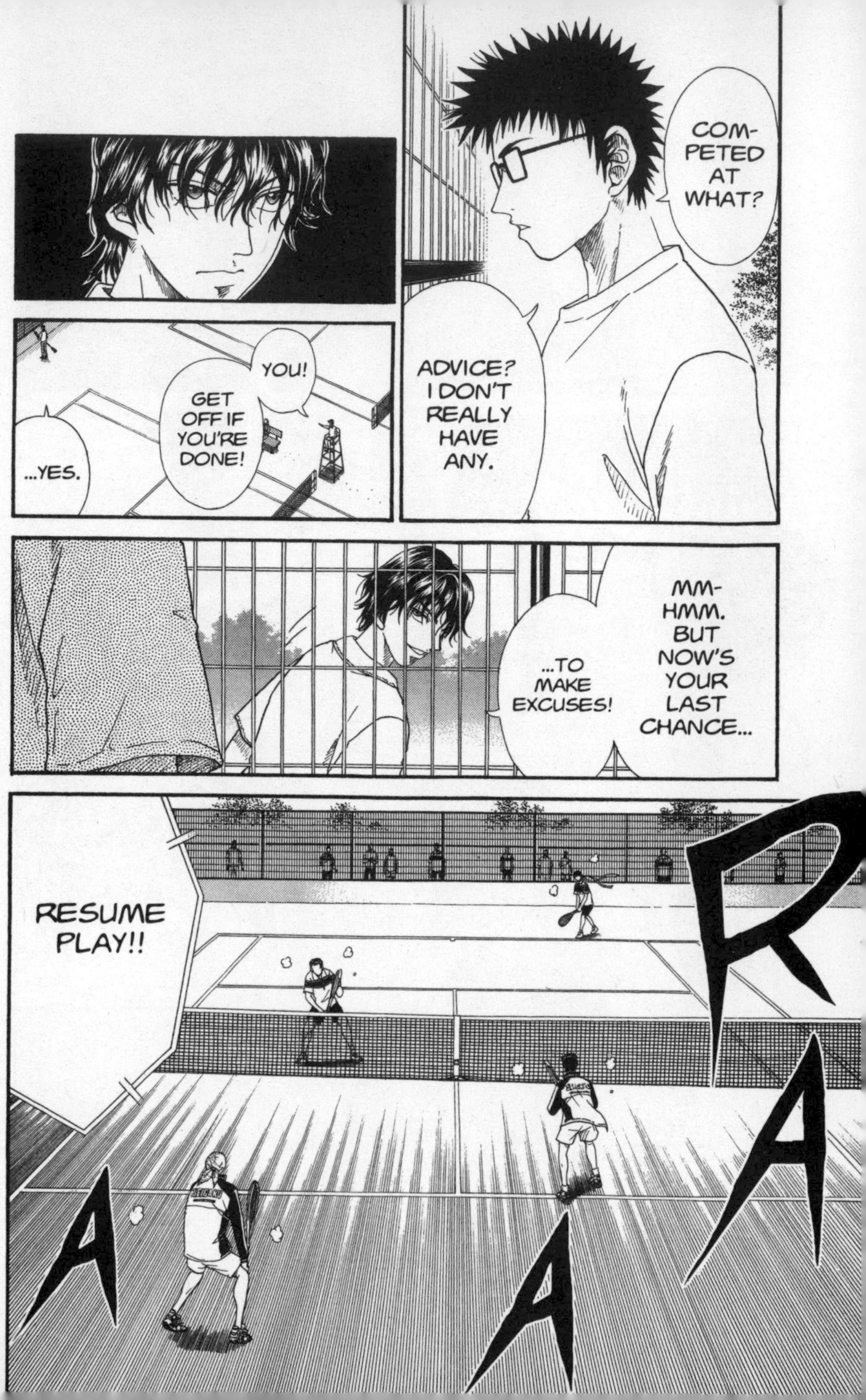
COMPETED AT WHAT?
ADVICE? I DON'T REALLY HAVE ANY.
YOU!
GET OFF IF YOU'RE DONE!
...YES.
MM-HMM. BUT NOW'S YOUR LAST CHANCE...
...TO MAKE EXCUSES!
RAAA
RESUME PLAY!!

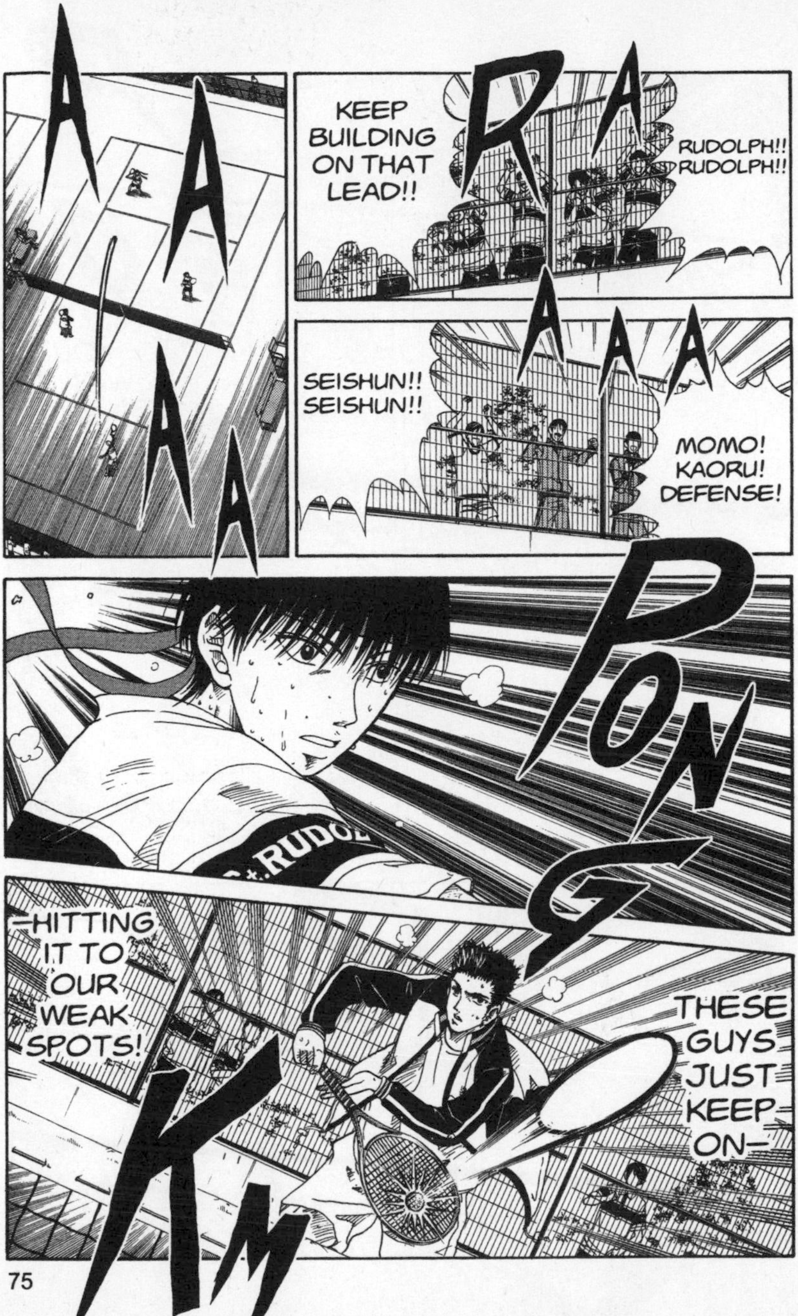
RUDOLPH!! RUDOLPH!!
KEEP BUILDING ON THAT LEAD!!
RAAAAA
SEISHUN!! SEISHUN!!
MOMO! KAORU! DEFENSE!
AAAAAA
PONG
THESE GUYS JUST KEEP ON—
—HITTING IT TO OUR WEAK SPOTS!
KM

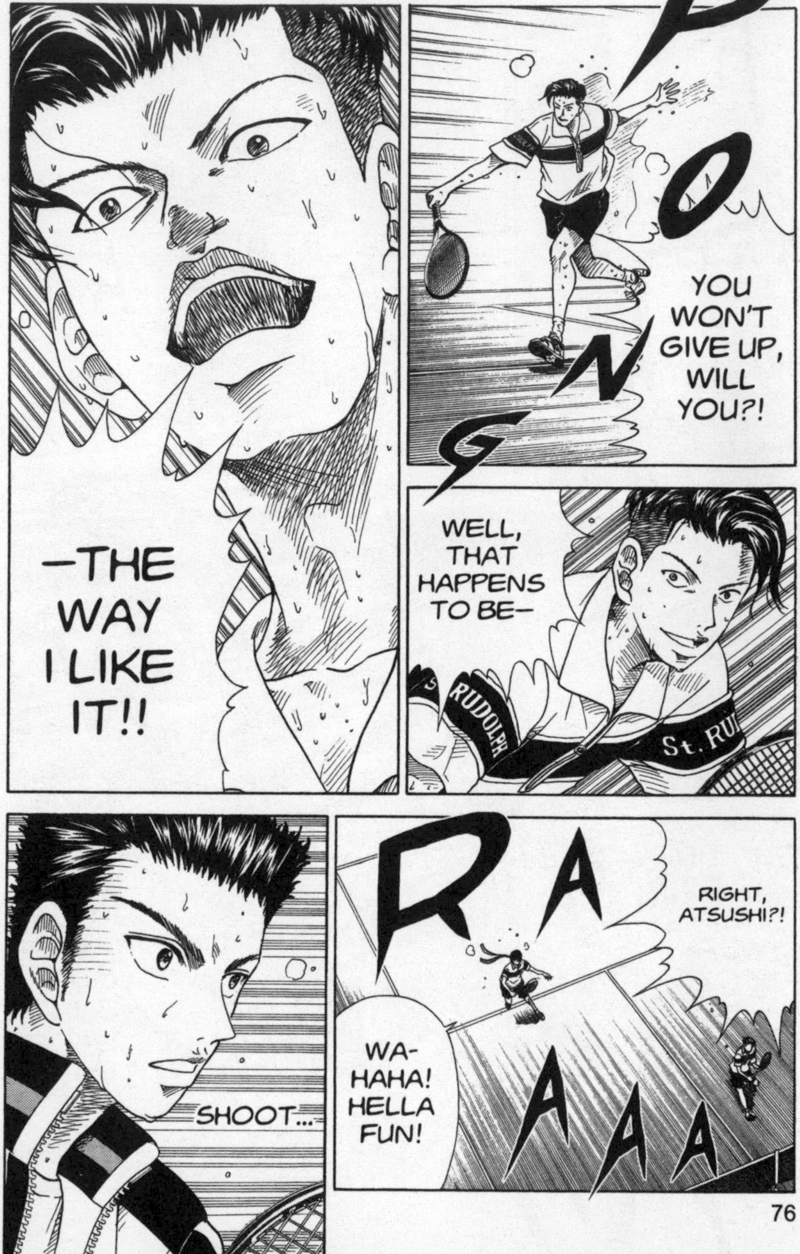
PONG
YOU WON'T GIVE UP, WILL YOU?!
WELL, THAT HAPPENS TO BE—
—THE WAY I LIKE IT!!
RAAAA
RIGHT, ATSUSHI?!
WA-HAHA! HELLA FUN!
SHOOT...

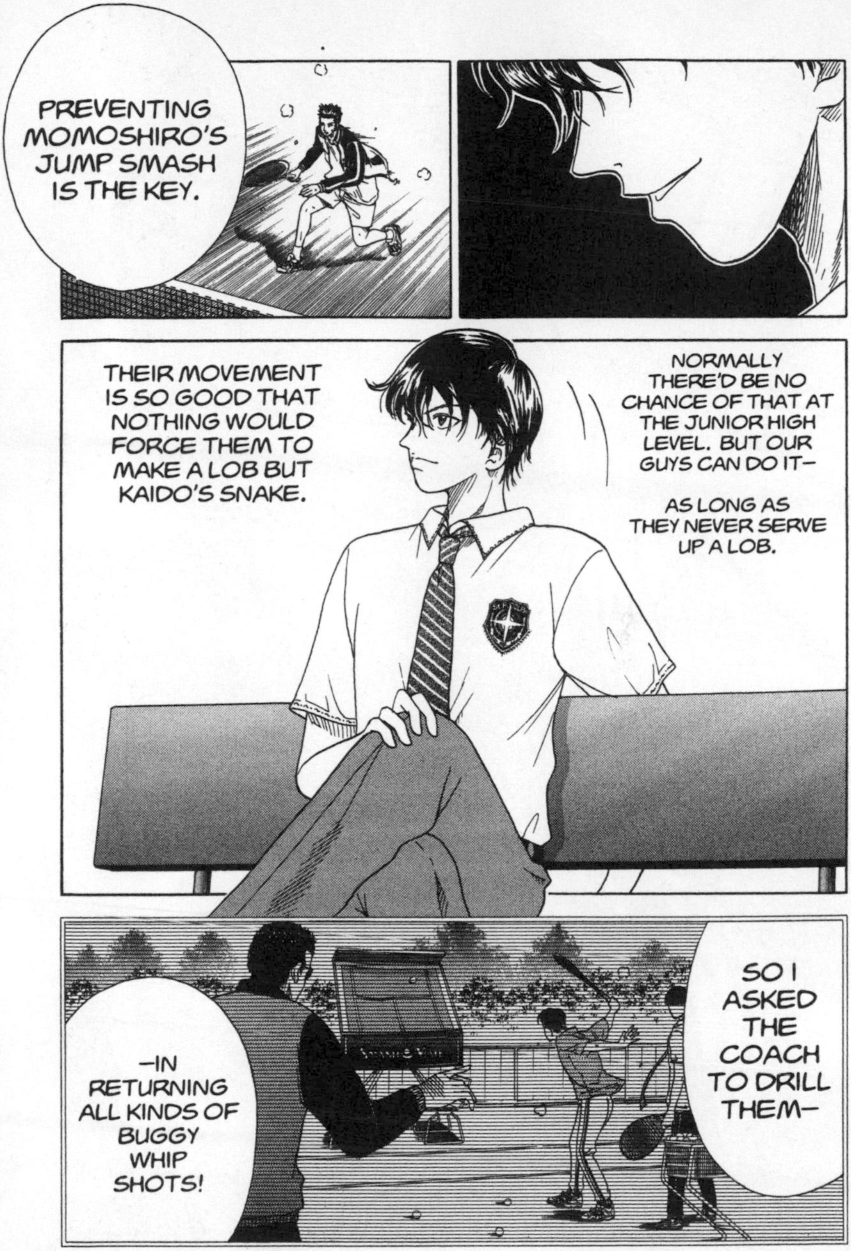
PREVENTING MOMOSHIRO'S JUMP SMASH IS THE KEY.
NORMALLY THERE'D BE NO CHANCE OF THAT AT THE JUNIOR HIGH LEVEL. BUT OUR GUYS CAN DO IT—
AS LONG AS THEY NEVER SERVE UP A LOB.
THEIR MOVEMENT IS SO GOOD THAT NOTHING WOULD FORCE THEM TO MAKE A LOB BUT KAIDO'S SNAKE.
SO I ASKED THE COACH TO DRILL THEM—
—IN RETURNING ALL KINDS OF BUGGY WHIP SHOTS!

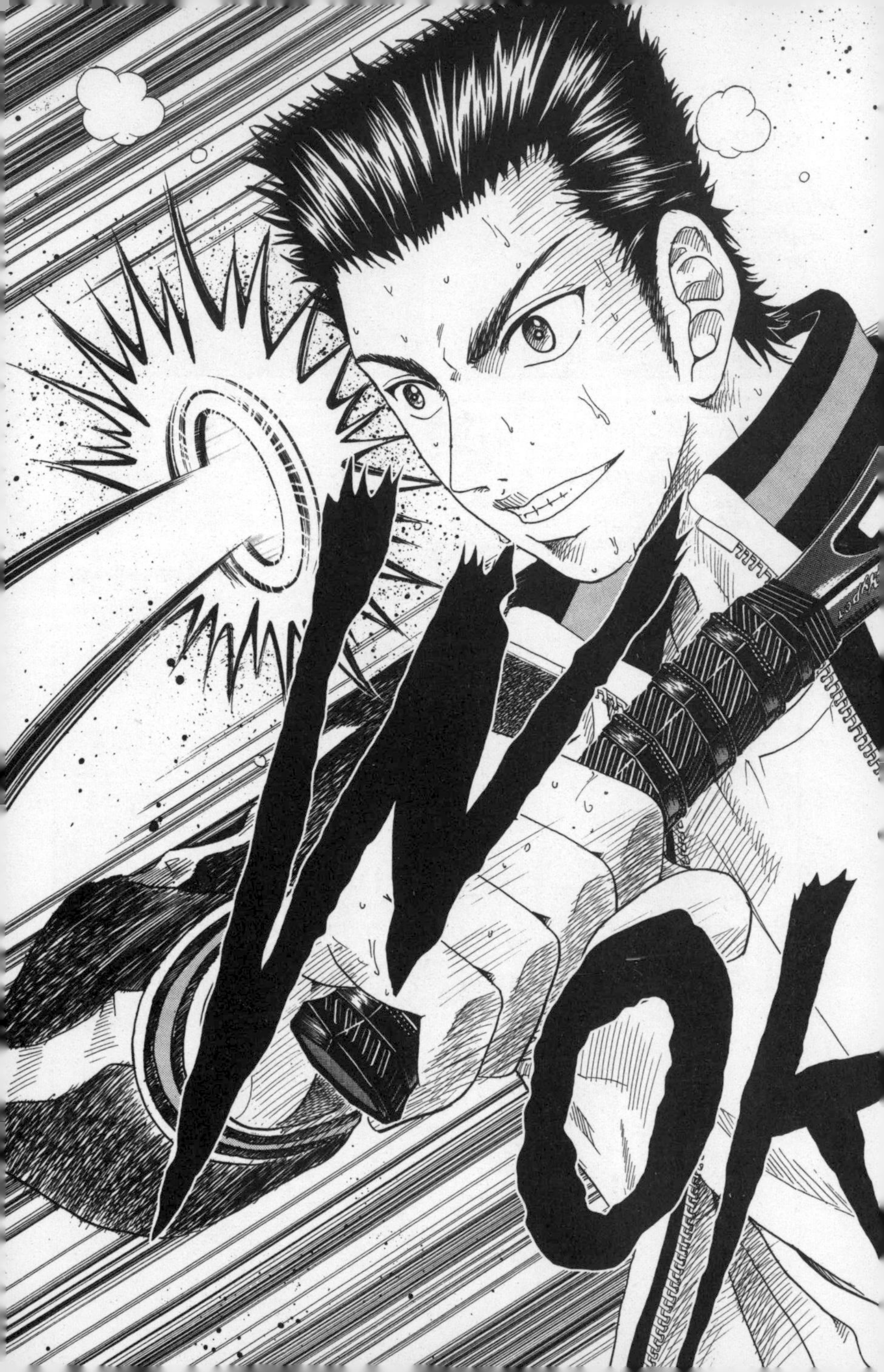
WOK

READ THIS WAY

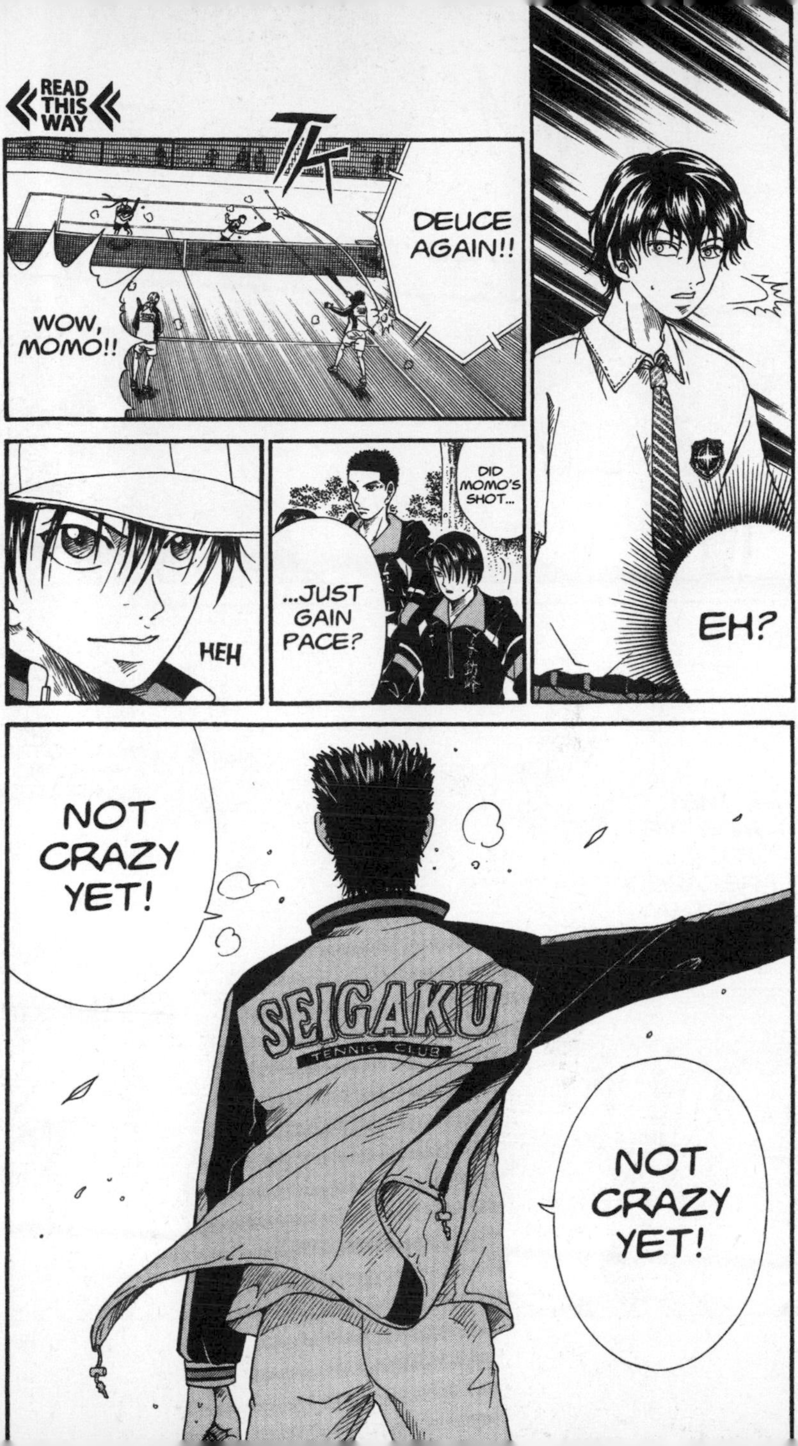
EH?
TK
DEUCE AGAIN!!
WOW, MOMO!!
DID MOMO'S SHOT...
...JUST GAIN PACE?
HEH
NOT CRAZY YET!
NOT CRAZY YET!
SEIGAKU
TENNIS CLUB

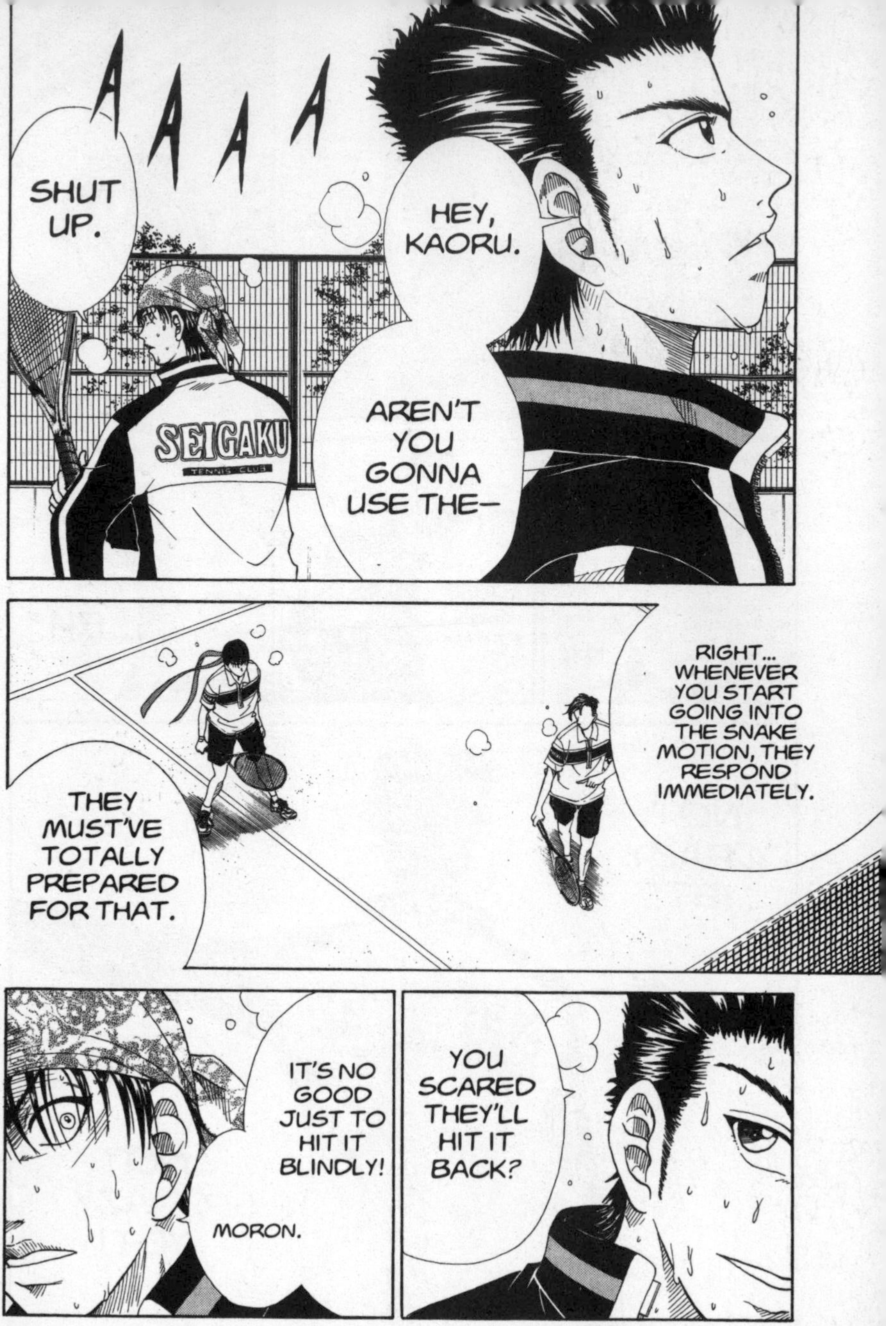
HEY, KAORU.
AREN'T YOU GONNA USE THE–
AAAA
SHUT UP.
RIGHT... WHENEVER YOU START GOING INTO THE SNAKE MOTION, THEY RESPOND IMMEDIATELY.
THEY MUST'VE TOTALLY PREPARED FOR THAT.
YOU SCARED THEY'LL HIT IT BACK?
IT'S NO GOOD JUST TO HIT IT BLINDLY!
MORON.

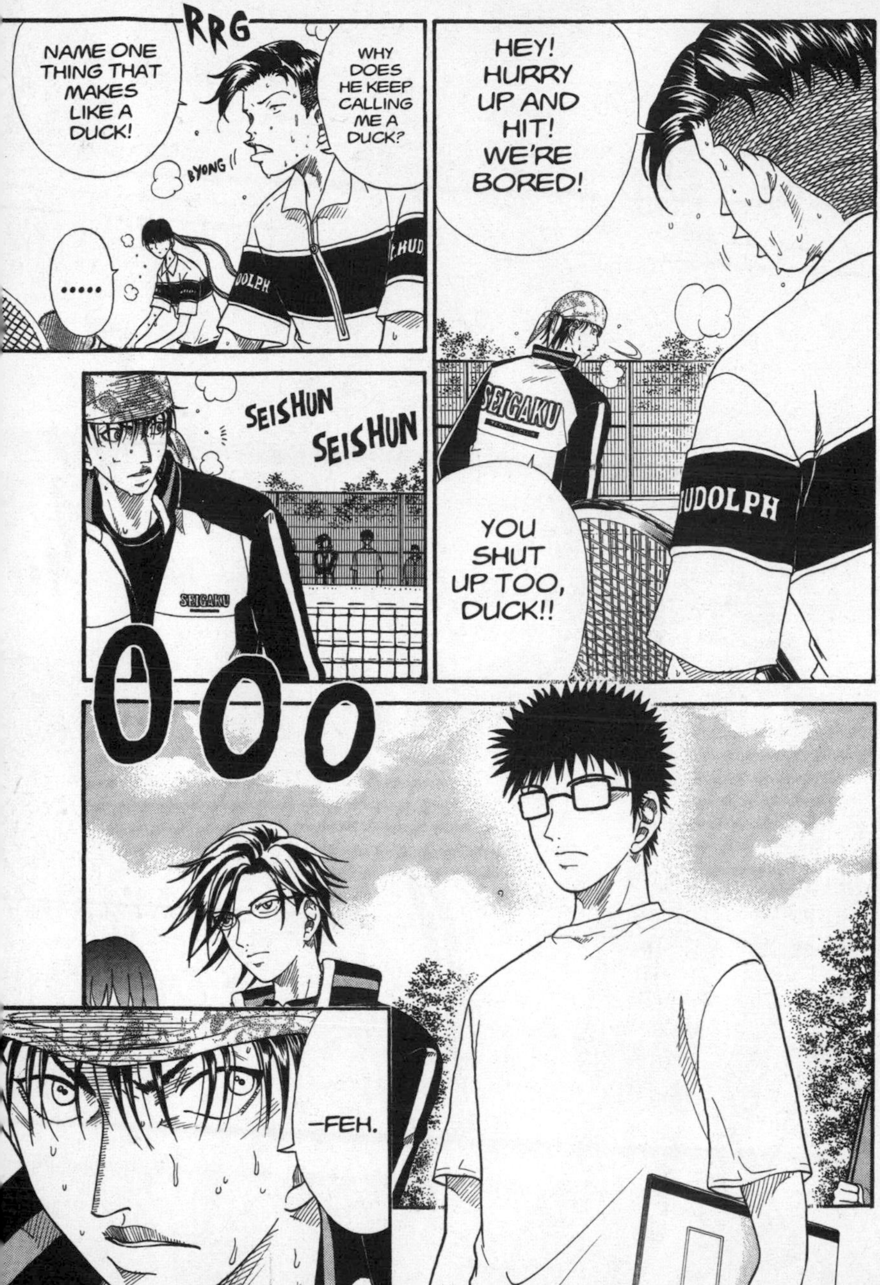
HEY! HURRY UP AND HIT! WE'RE BORED!
YOU SHUT UP TOO, DUCK!!
RRG
WHY DOES HE KEEP CALLING ME A DUCK?
NAME ONE THING THAT MAKES LIKE A DUCK!
BYONG
......
SEISHUN SEISHUN
OOO
—FEH.

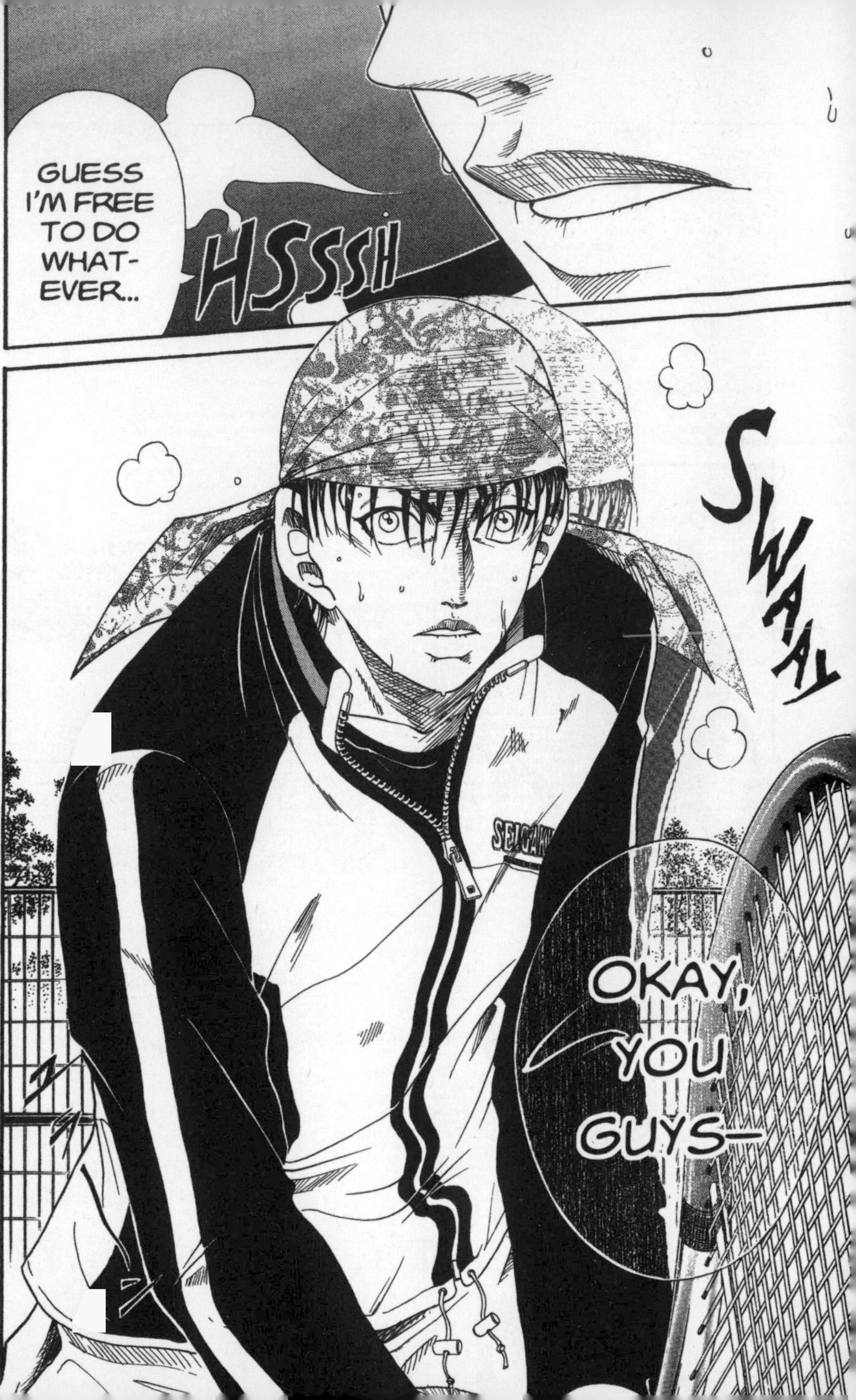
GUESS I'M FREE TO DO WHAT-EVER...
HSSSH
SWAAY
OKAY, YOU GUYS—

READ THIS WAY

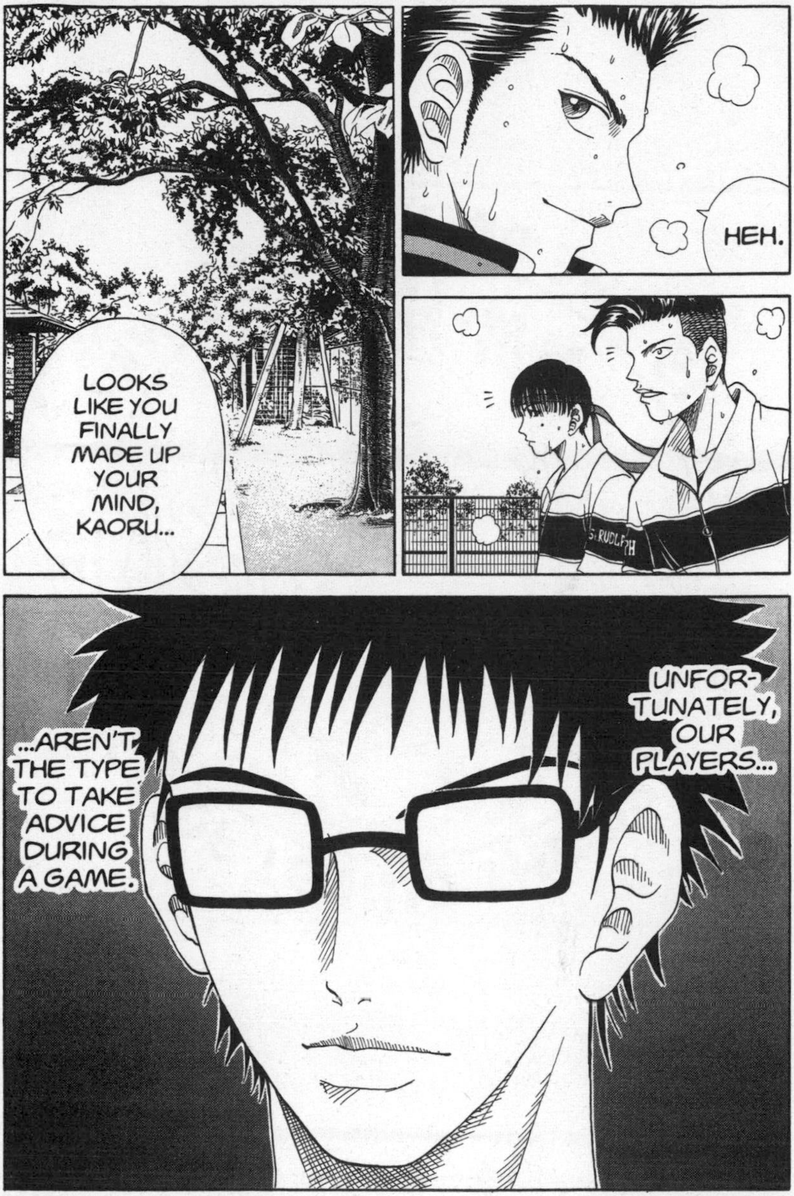
HEH.
LOOKS LIKE YOU FINALLY MADE UP YOUR MIND, KAORU...
UNFOR-TUNATELY, OUR PLAYERS...
...AREN'T THE TYPE TO TAKE ADVICE DURING A GAME.

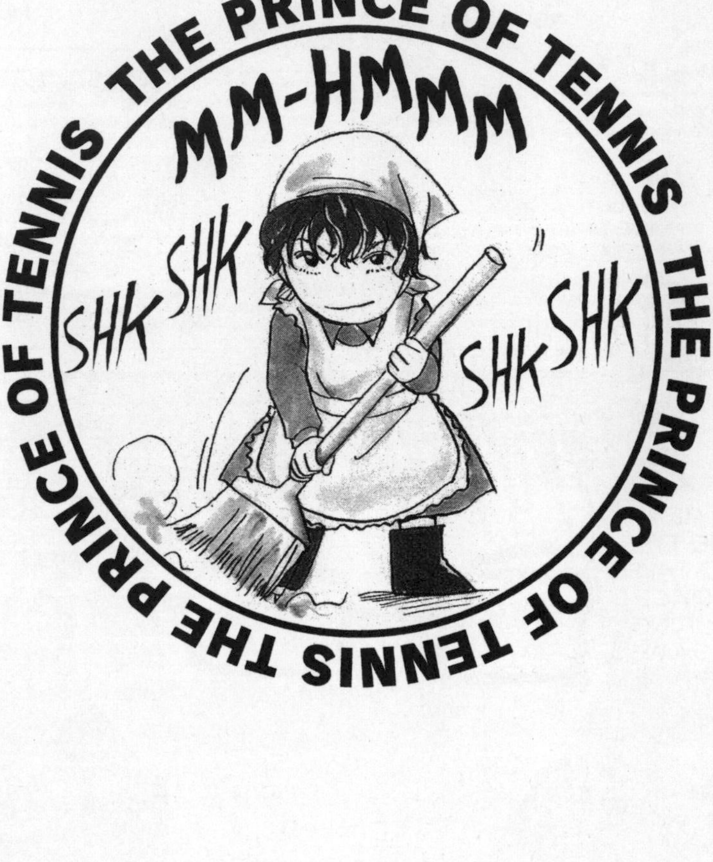
THE PRINCE OF TENNIS THE PRINCE OF TENNIS THE PRINCE OF TENNIS
MM-HMMM
SHK SHK
SHK SHK

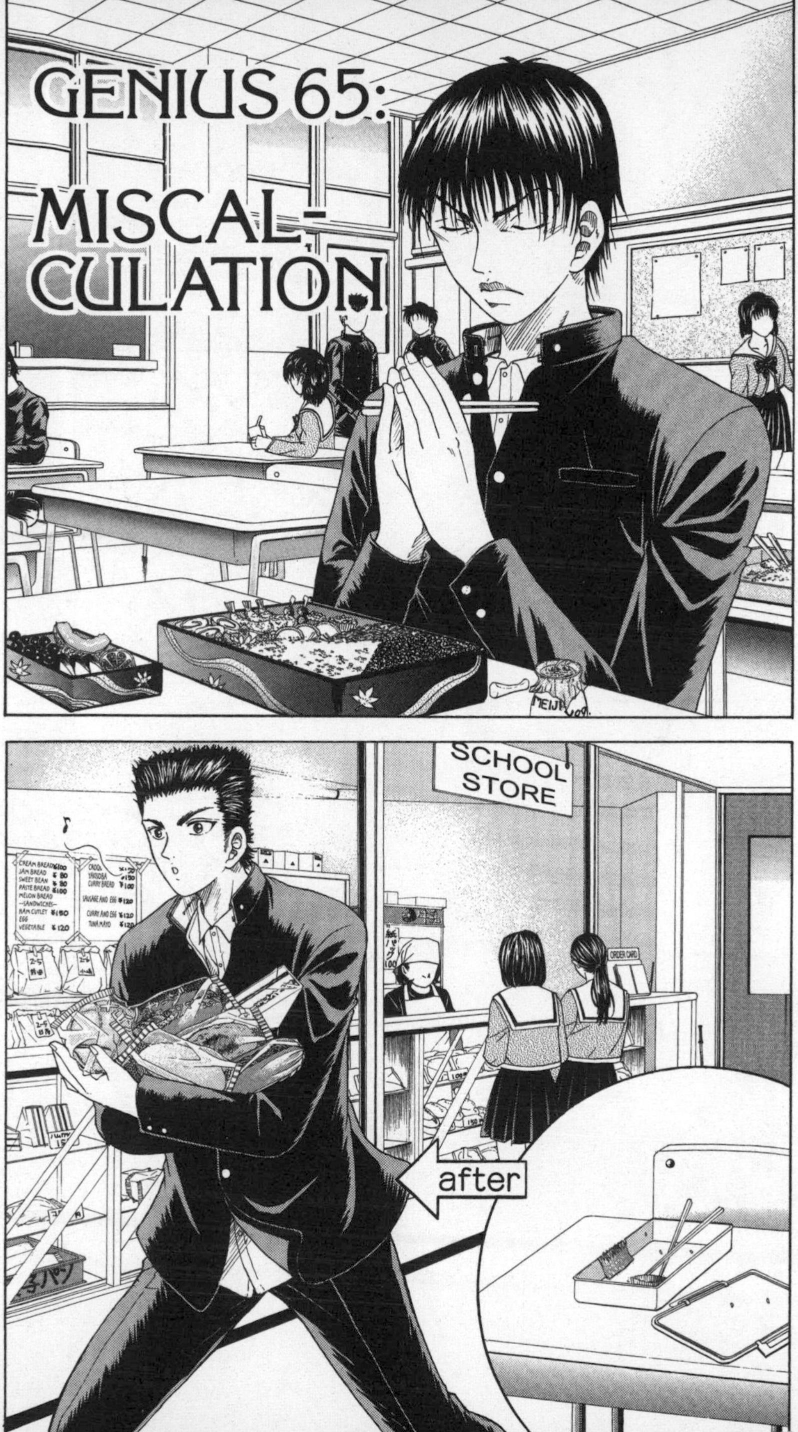
GENIUS 65:
MISCAL-
CULATION
SCHOOL STORE
after

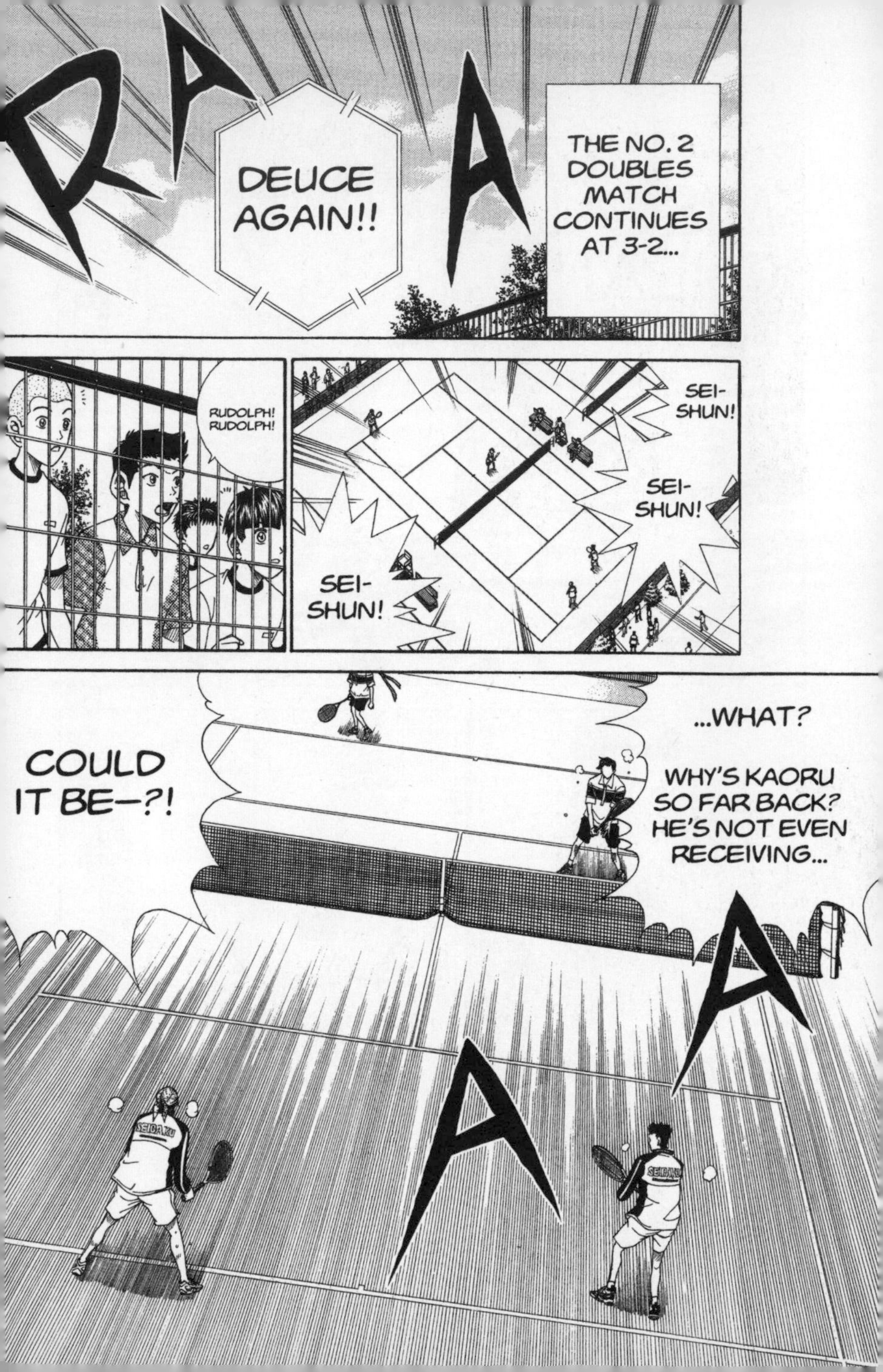
THE NO. 2 DOUBLES MATCH CONTINUES AT 3-2...
DEUCE AGAIN!!
RAA
SEI-SHUN!
SEI-SHUN!
SEI-SHUN!
RUDOLPH! RUDOLPH!
...WHAT?
WHY'S KAORU SO FAR BACK? HE'S NOT EVEN RECEIVING...
COULD IT BE—?!
AA

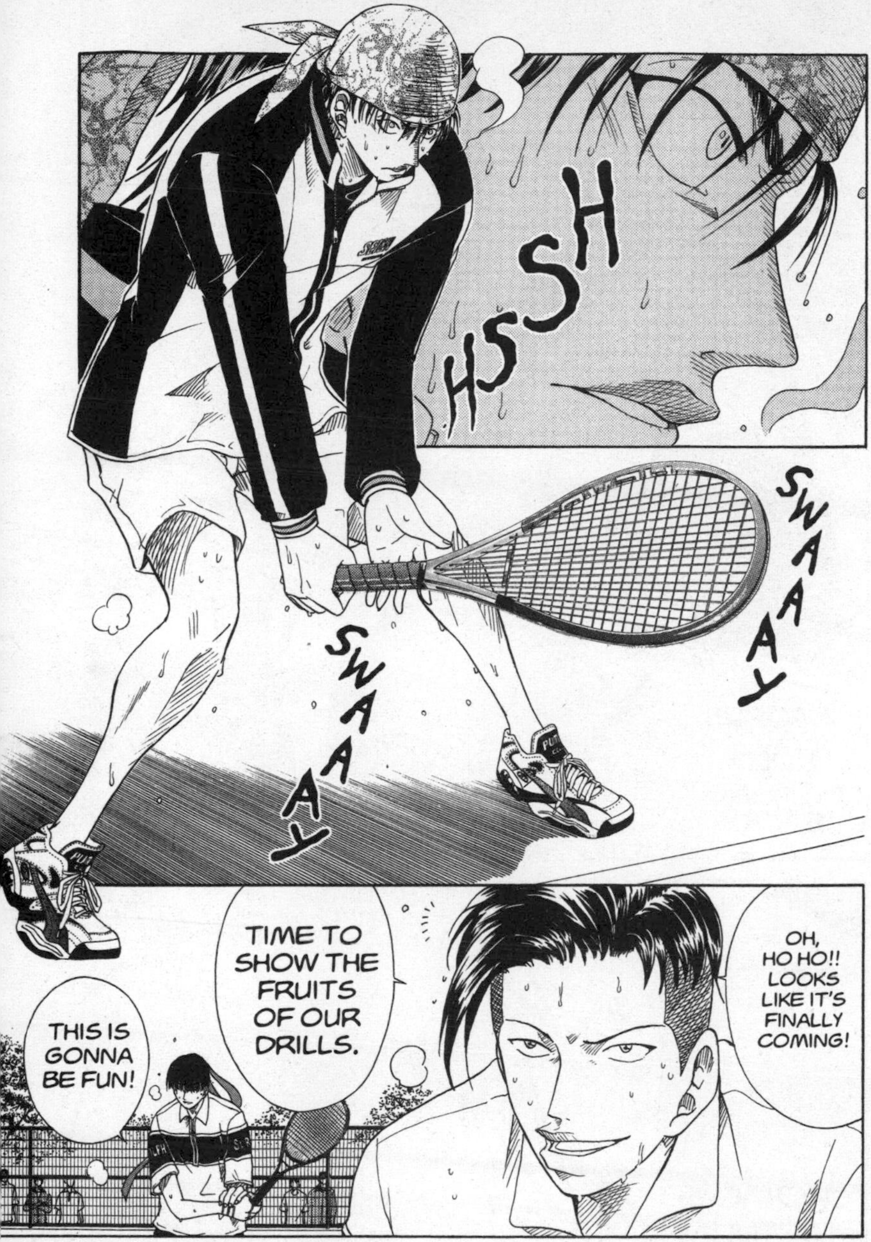
HSSH
SWAAAAY
SWAAAY
OH, HO HO!! LOOKS LIKE IT'S FINALLY COMING!
TIME TO SHOW THE FRUITS OF OUR DRILLS.
THIS IS GONNA BE FUN!

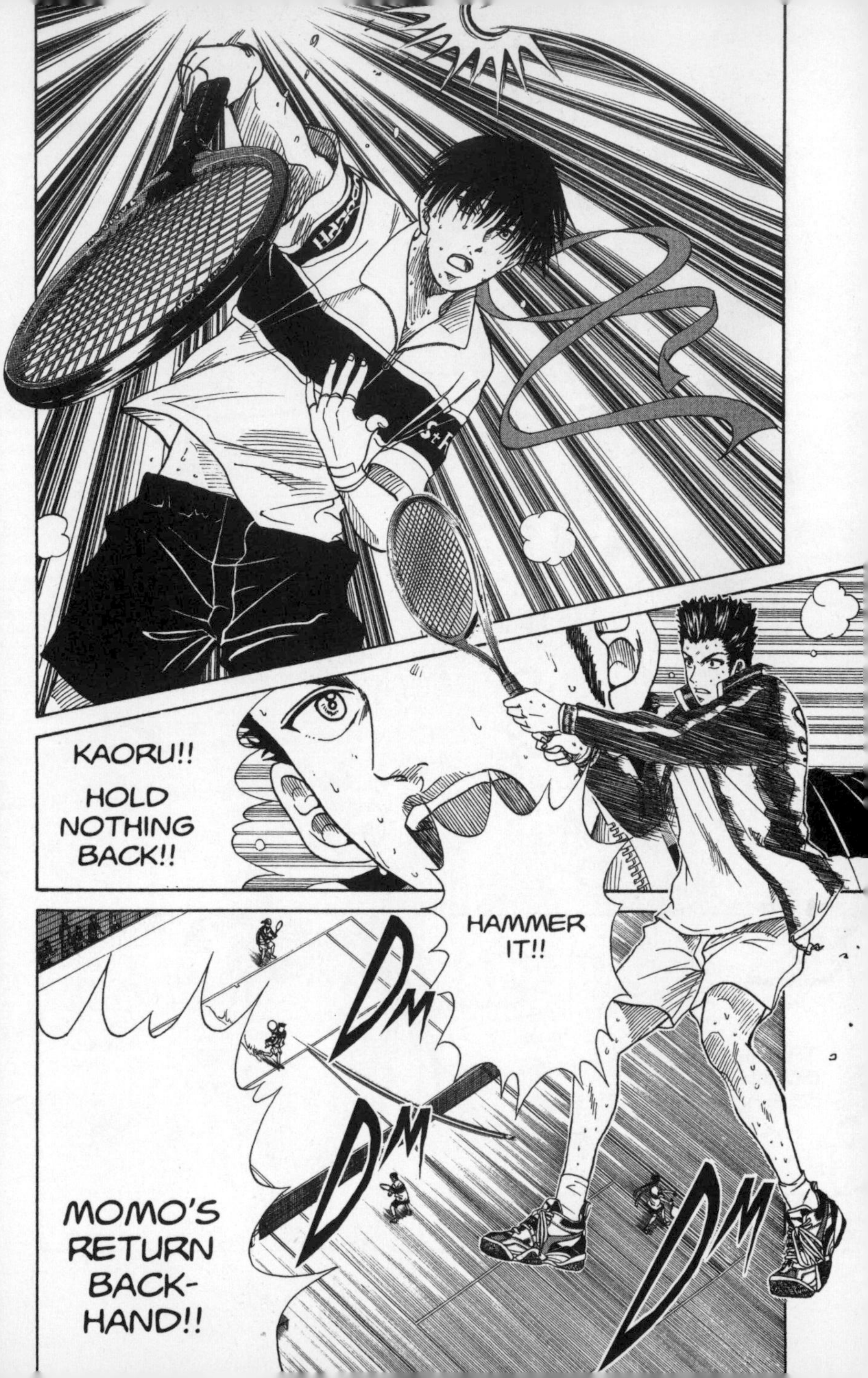
KAORU!!
HOLD NOTHING BACK!!
HAMMER IT!!
MOMO'S RETURN BACK-HAND!!

READ THIS WAY

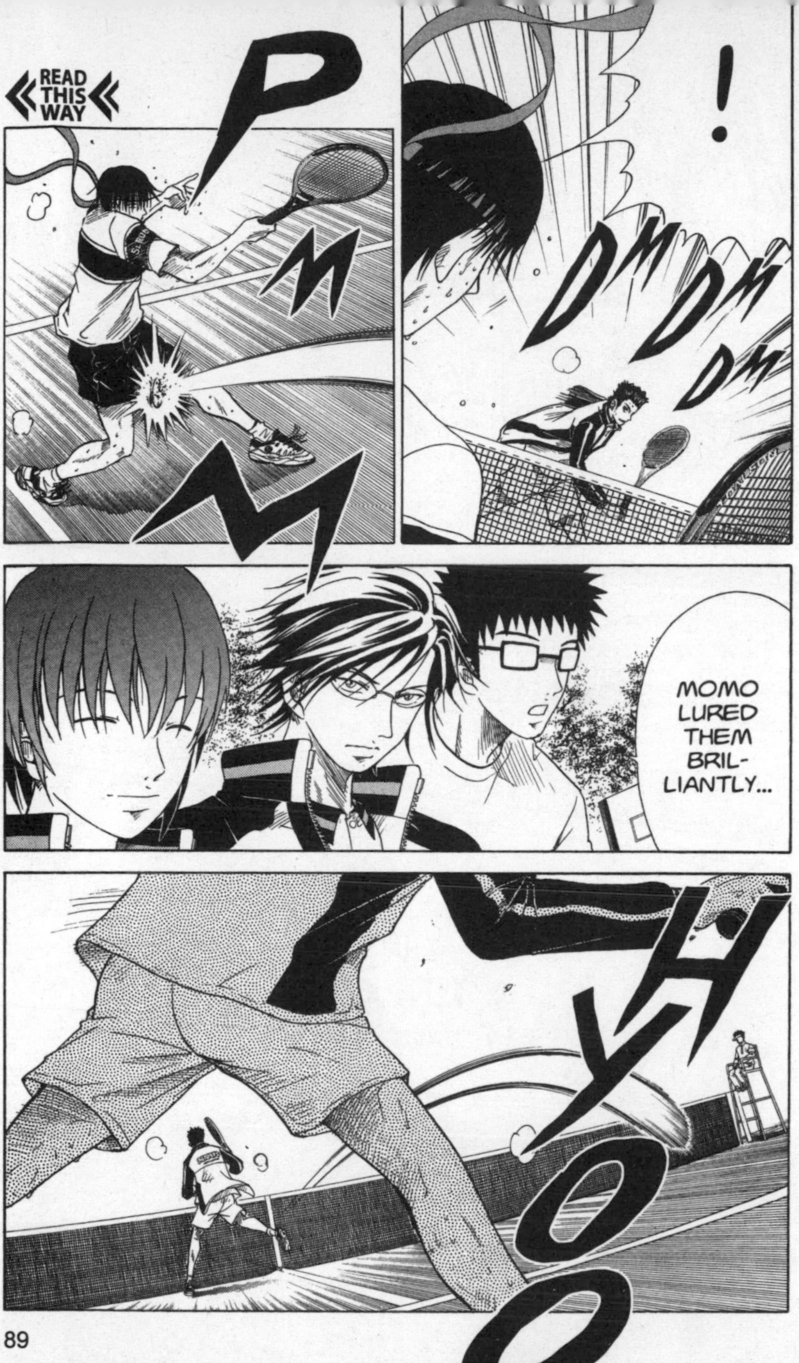
!
DMDMDM
PMM
MOMO LURED THEM BRILLIANTLY...
HYOO

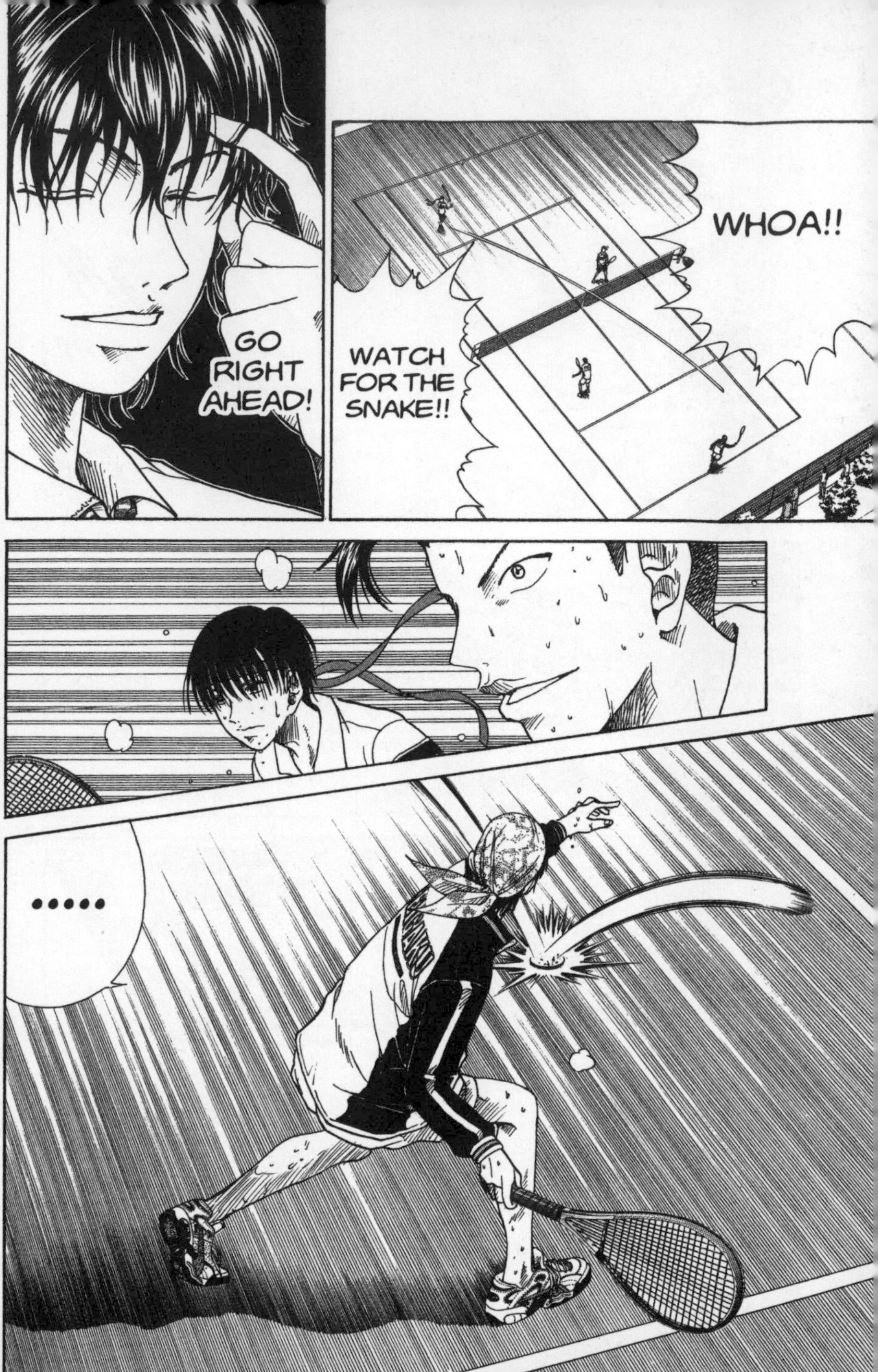
WHOA!!
WATCH FOR THE SNAKE!!
GO RIGHT AHEAD!
•••••

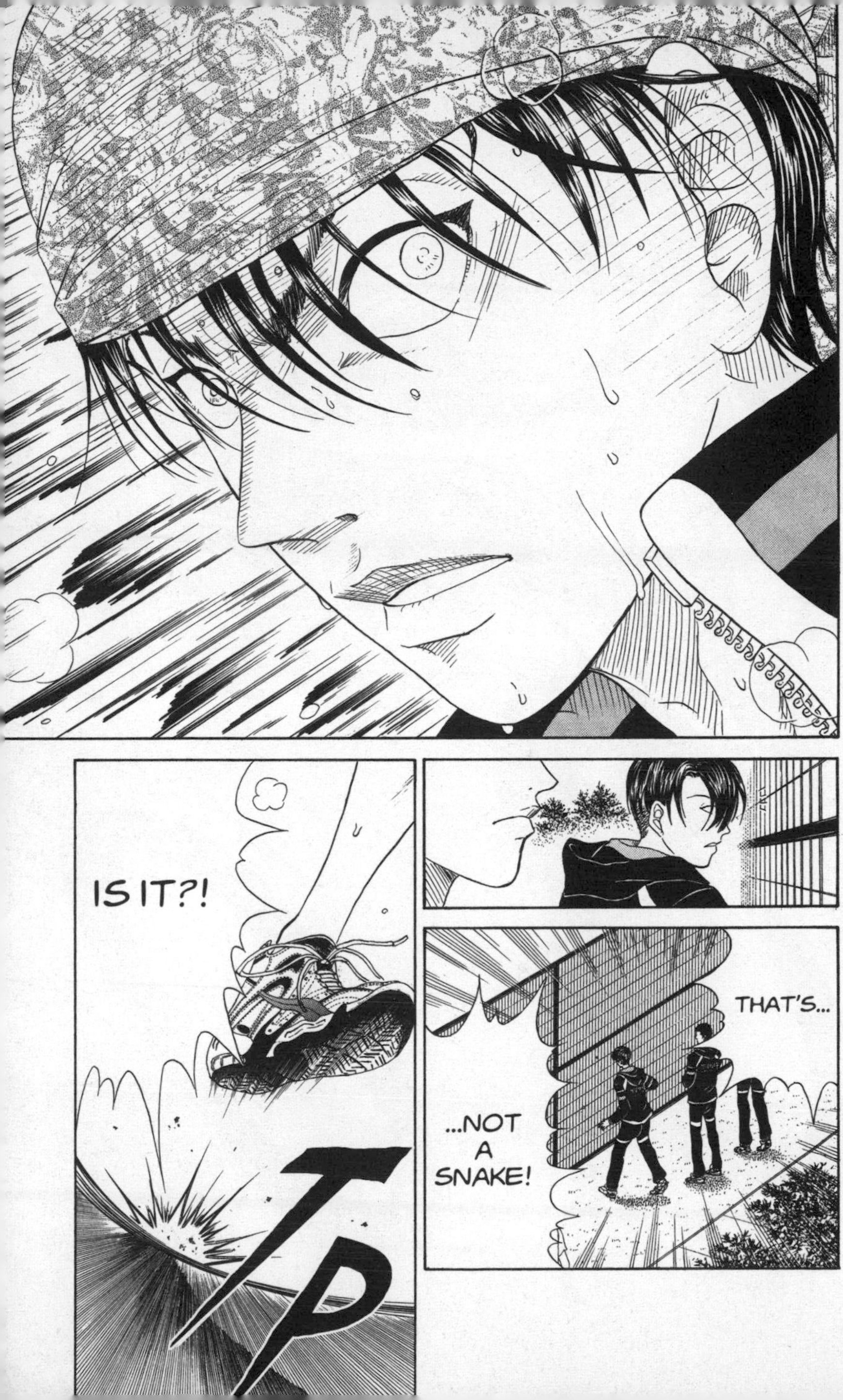
THAT'S...
...NOT A SNAKE!
IS IT?!
TP

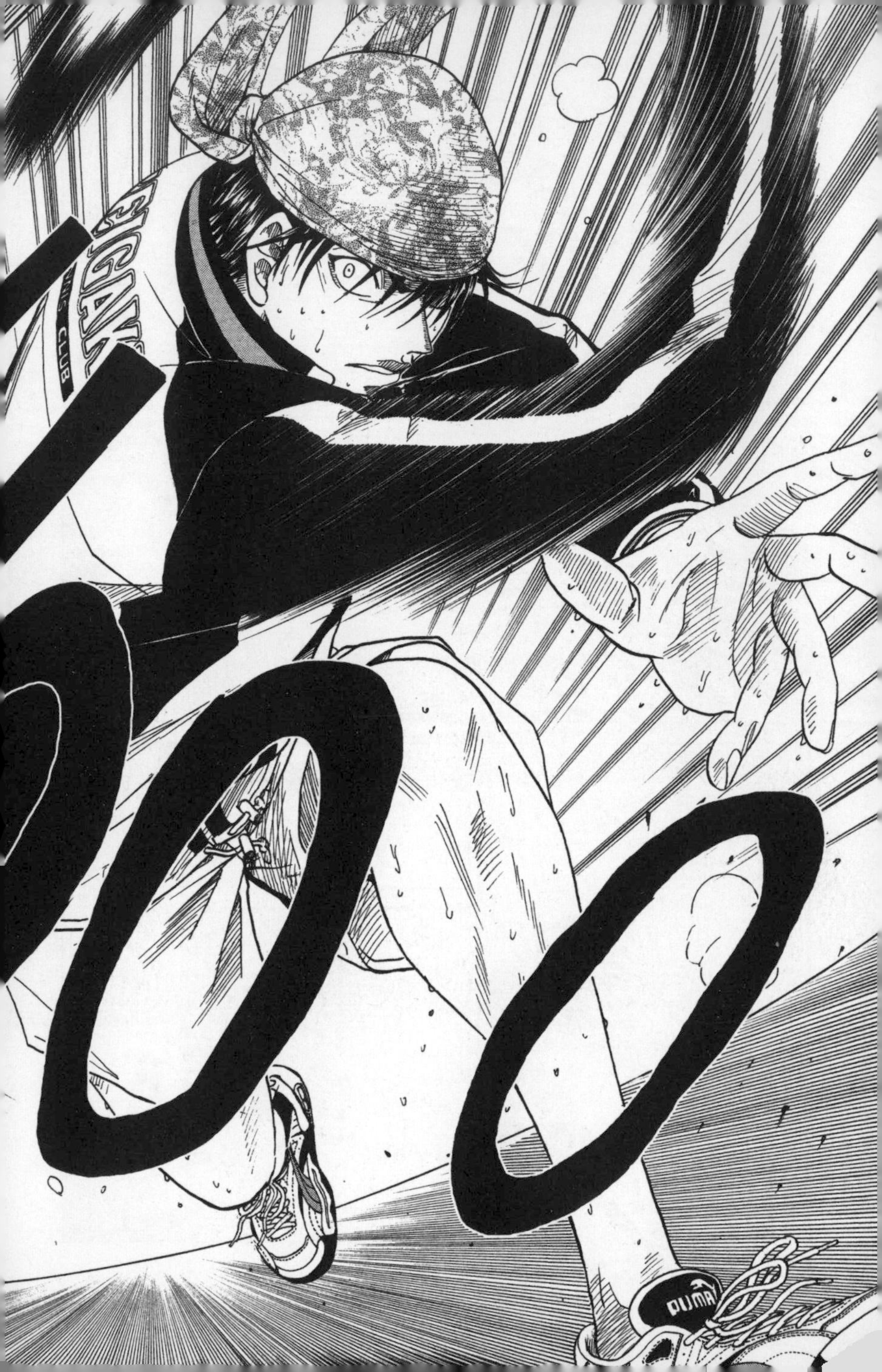
CLUB
PUMA

READ THIS WAY

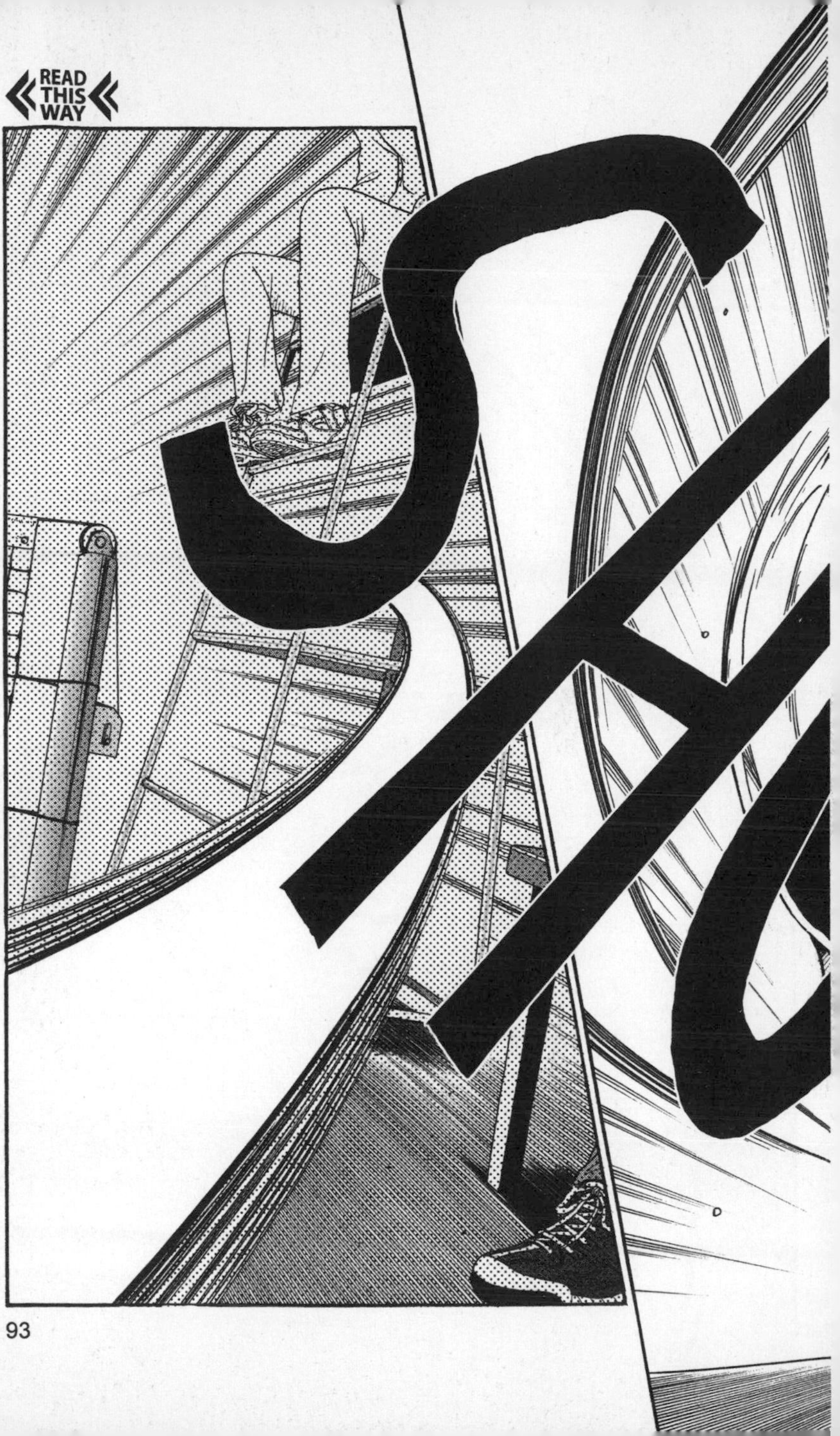
SH

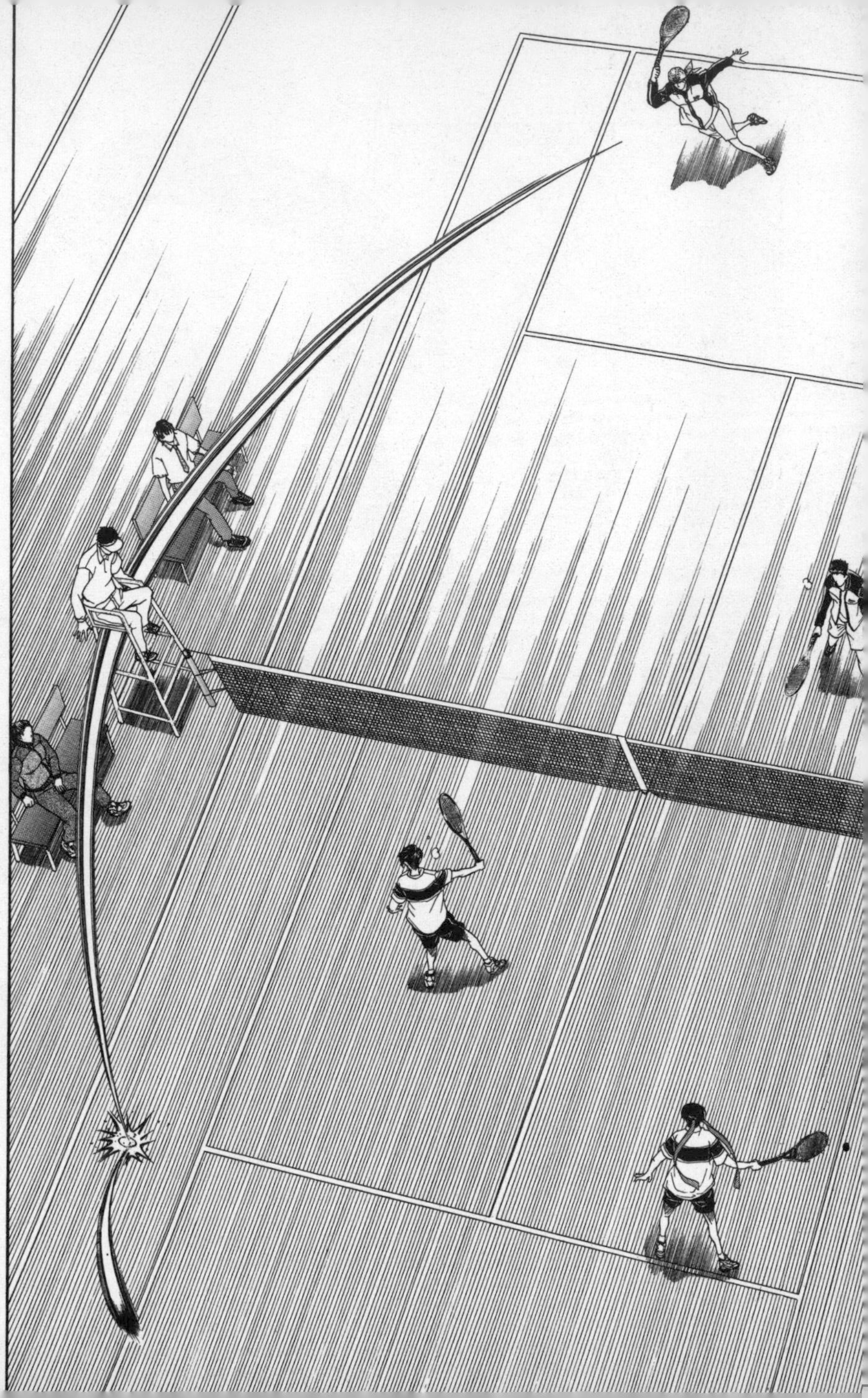

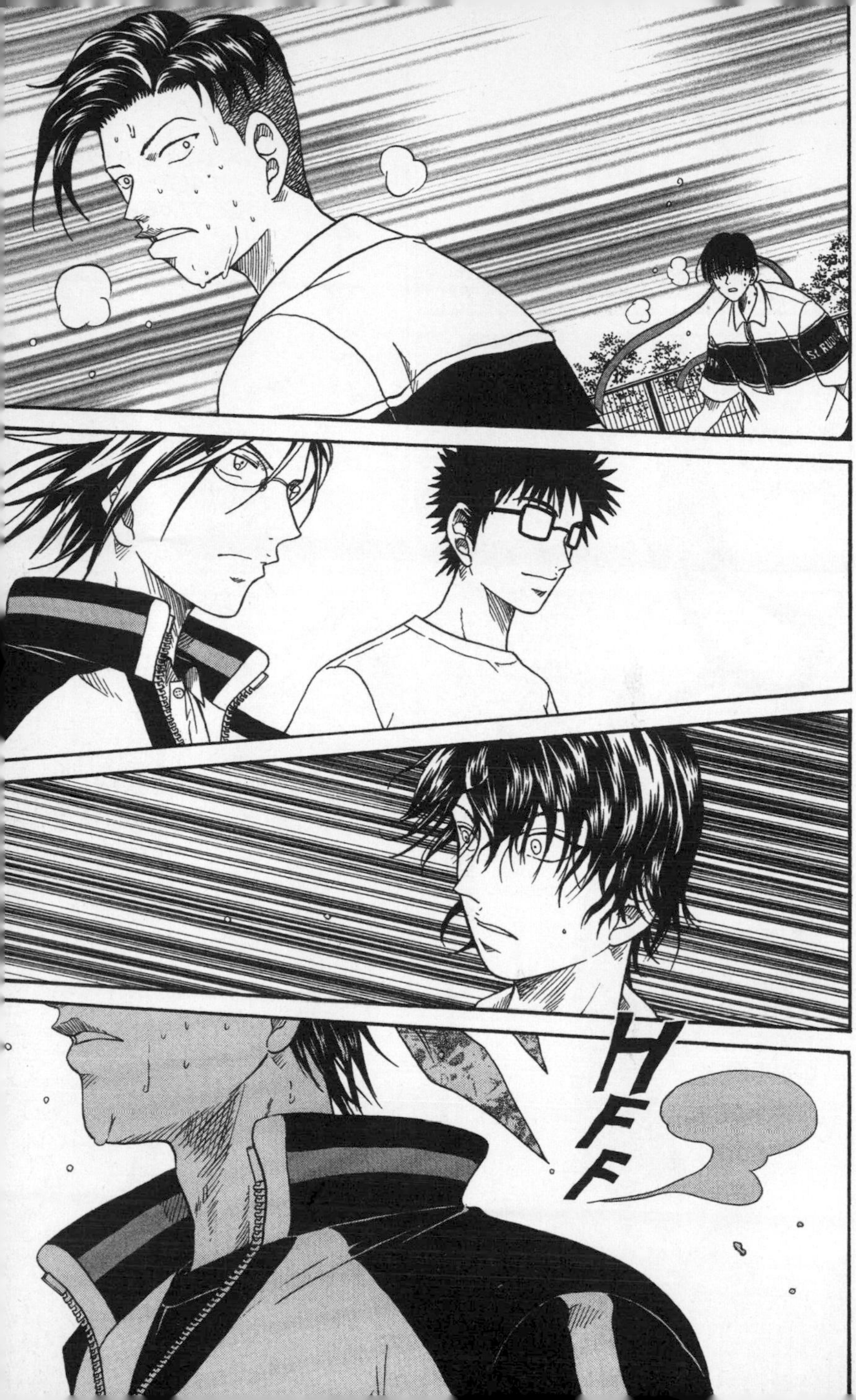
HFF

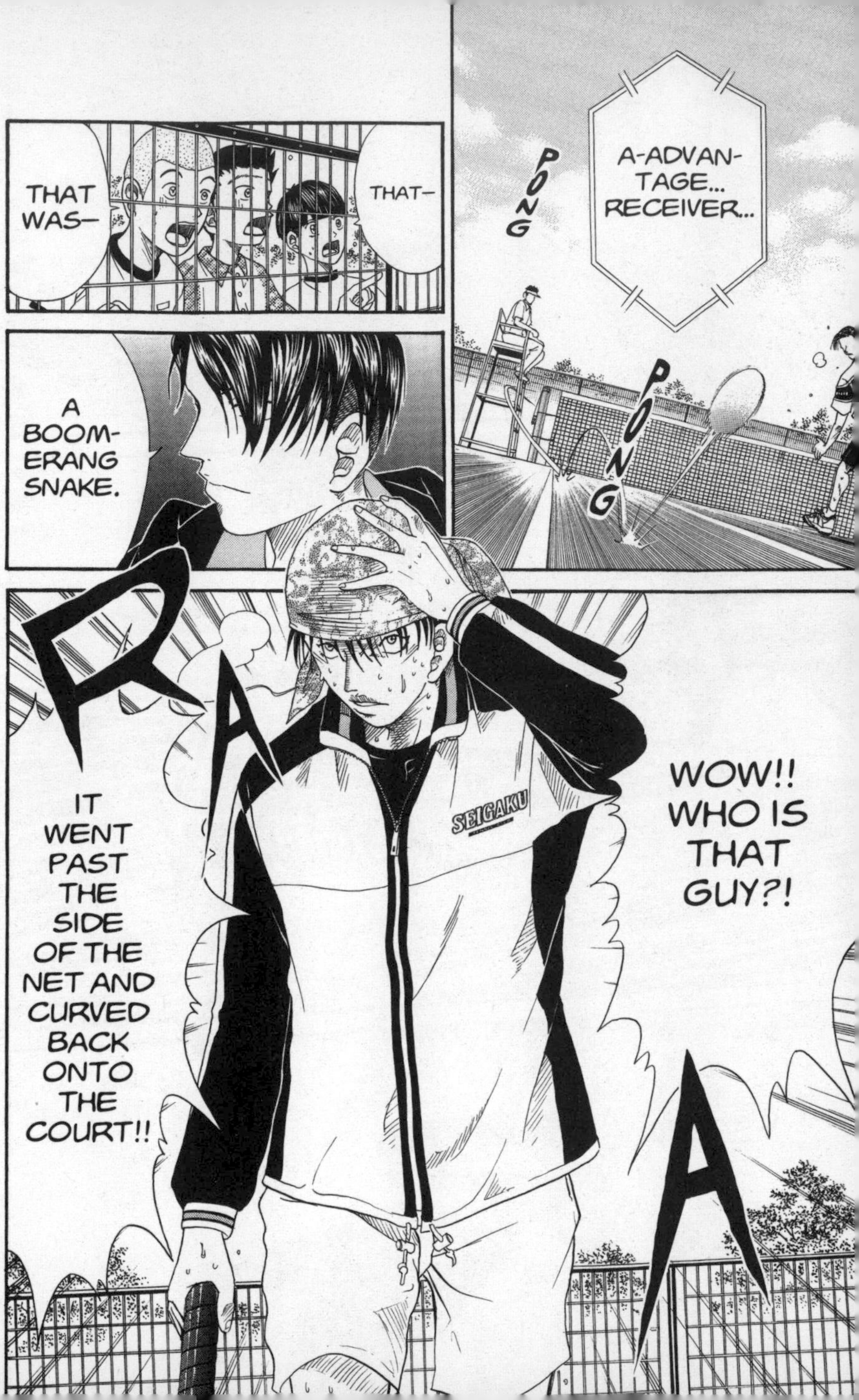
A-ADVANTAGE... RECEIVER...
PONG
PONG
THAT—
THAT WAS—
A BOOMERANG SNAKE.
WOW!! WHO IS THAT GUY?!
IT WENT PAST THE SIDE OF THE NET AND CURVED BACK ONTO THE COURT!!
RAA

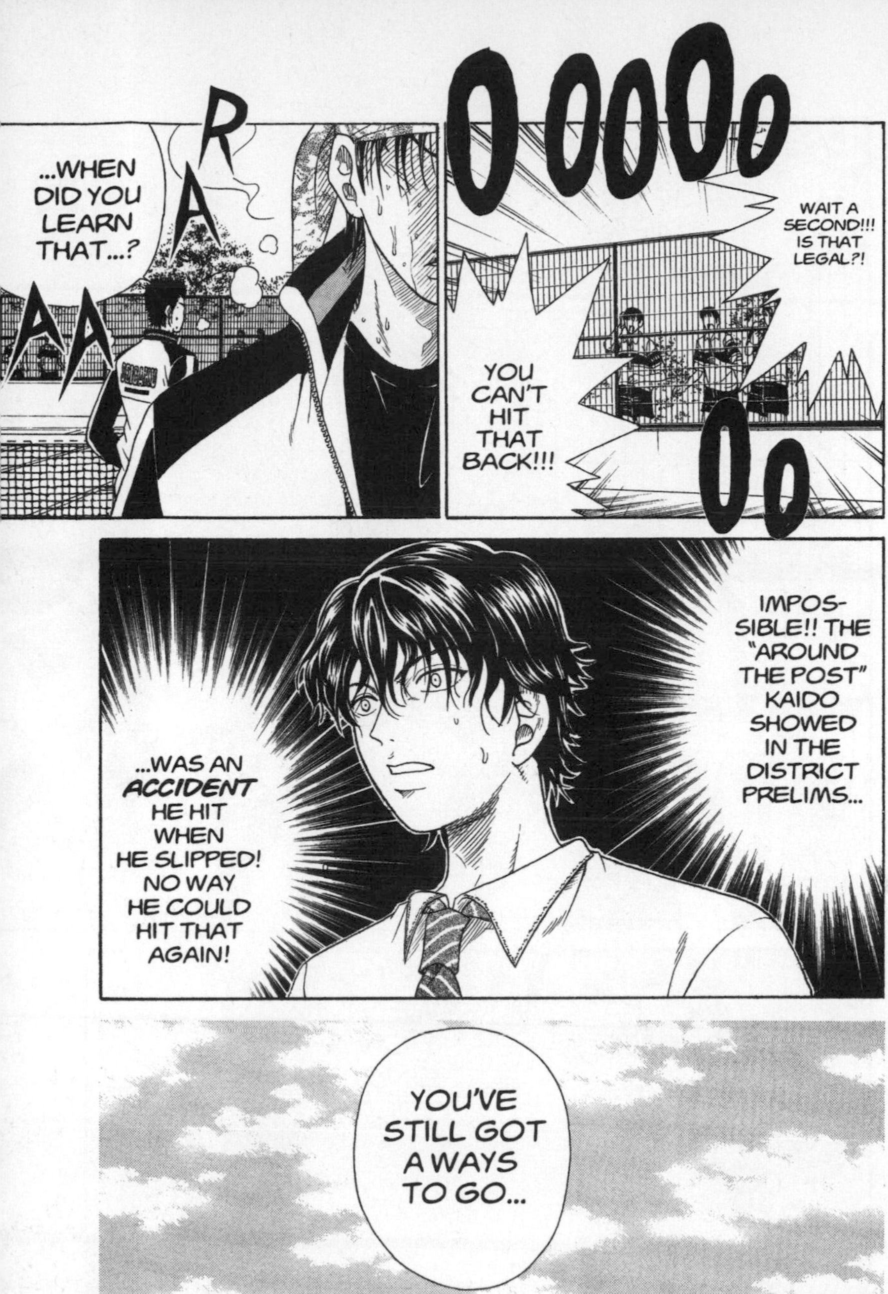
WAIT A SECOND!!! IS THAT LEGAL?!
YOU CAN'T HIT THAT BACK!!!
...WHEN DID YOU LEARN THAT...?
IMPOSSIBLE!! THE "AROUND THE POST" KAIDO SHOWED IN THE DISTRICT PRELIMS...
...WAS AN ACCIDENT HE HIT WHEN HE SLIPPED! NO WAY HE COULD HIT THAT AGAIN!
YOU'VE STILL GOT A WAYS TO GO...

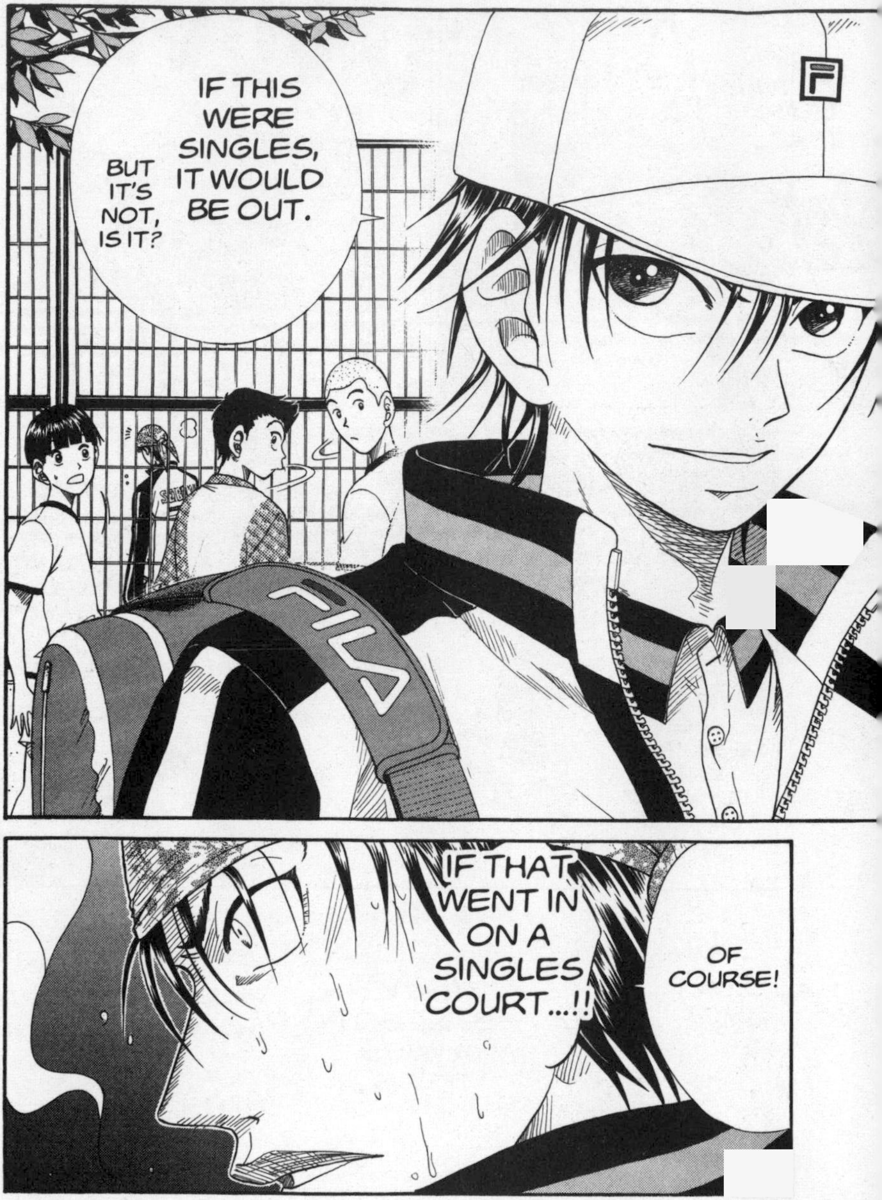
IF THIS WERE SINGLES, IT WOULD BE OUT.
BUT IT'S NOT, IS IT?
OF COURSE!
IF THAT WENT IN ON A SINGLES COURT...!!

READ THIS WAY

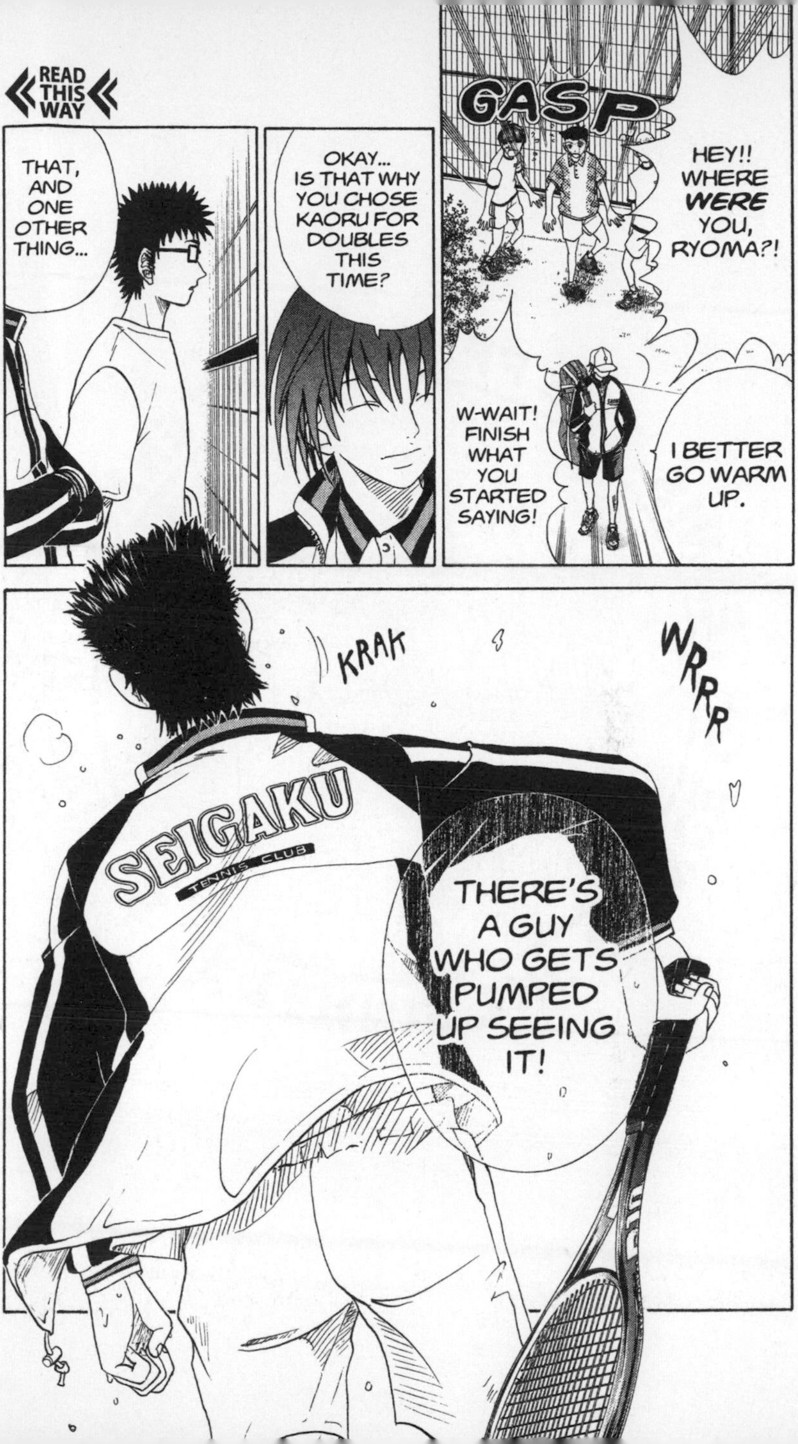
GASP
HEY!! WHERE WERE YOU, RYOMA?!
I BETTER GO WARM UP.
W-WAIT! FINISH WHAT YOU STARTED SAYING!
OKAY... IS THAT WHY YOU CHOSE KAORU FOR DOUBLES THIS TIME?
THAT, AND ONE OTHER THING...
WRRR
KRAK
SEIGAKU
TENNIS CLUB
THERE'S A GUY WHO GETS PUMPED UP SEEING IT!

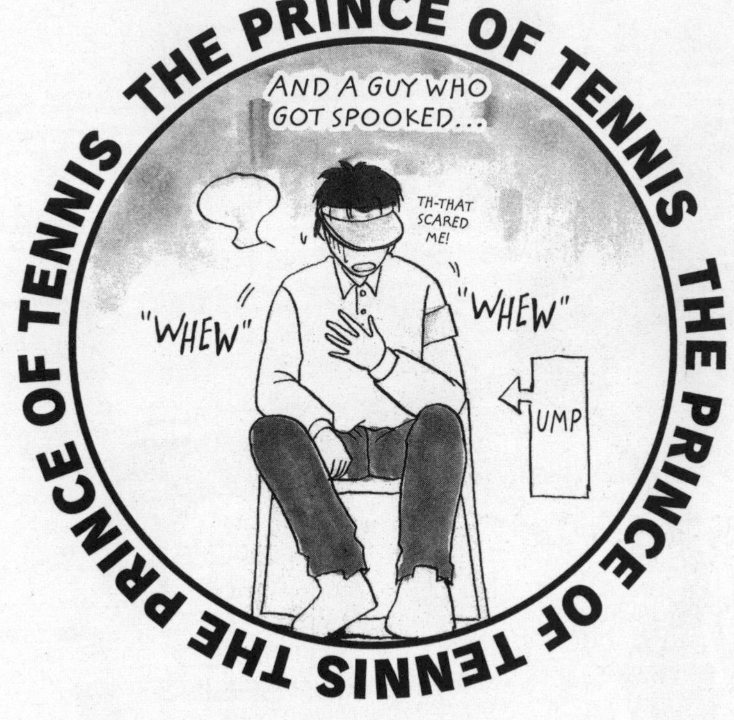
THE PRINCE OF TENNIS THE PRINCE OF TENNIS THE PRINCE OF TENNIS
AND A GUY WHO GOT SPOOKED...
TH-THAT SCARED ME!
"WHEW"
"WHEW"
UMP

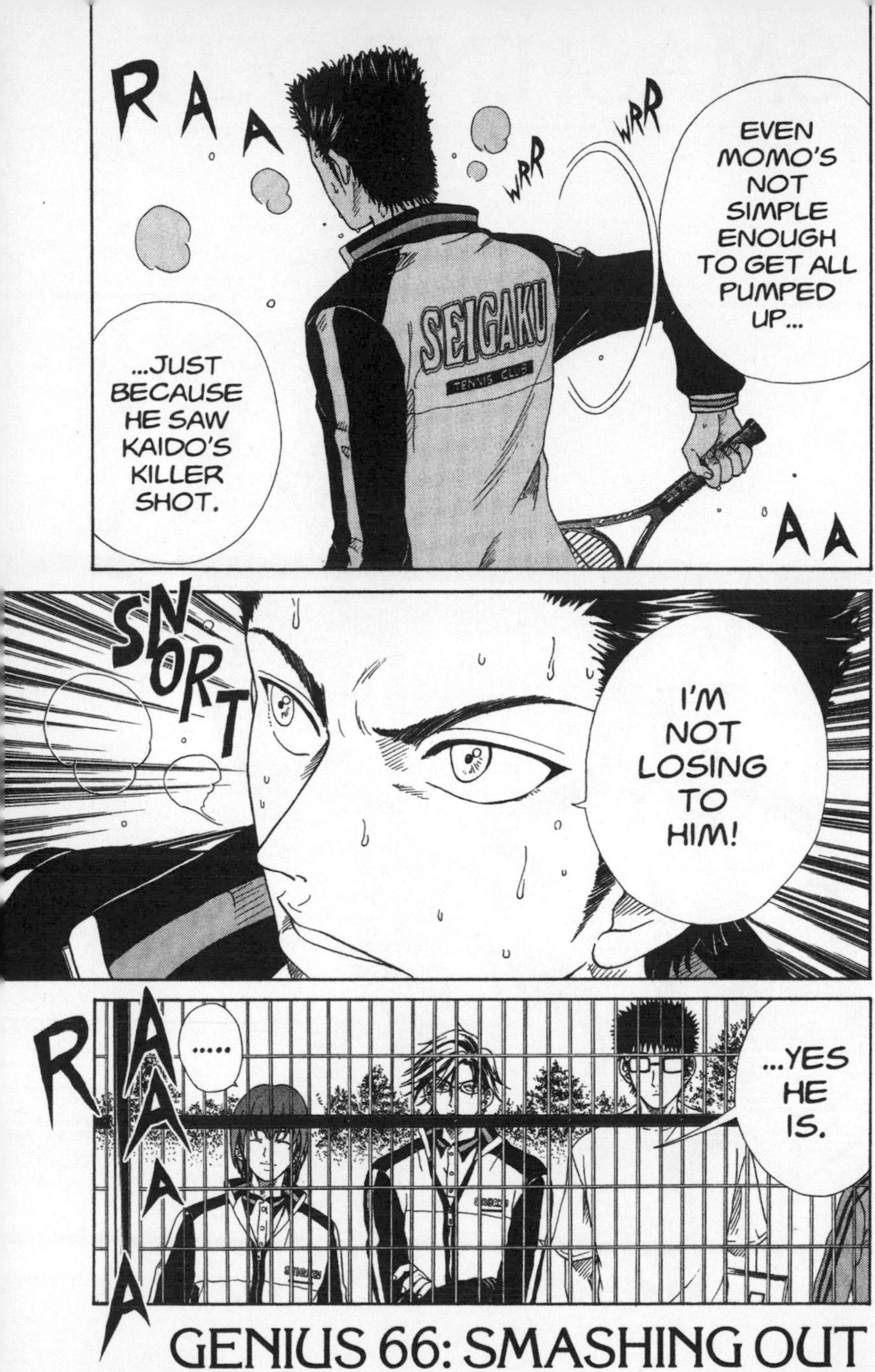
RAAA
WRR WRR
EVEN MOMO'S NOT SIMPLE ENOUGH TO GET ALL PUMPED UP...
...JUST BECAUSE HE SAW KAIDO'S KILLER SHOT.
AA
SNORT
I'M NOT LOSING TO HIM!
...YES HE IS.
......
RIAAAAA

GENIUS 66: SMASHING OUT

SMASHING OUT

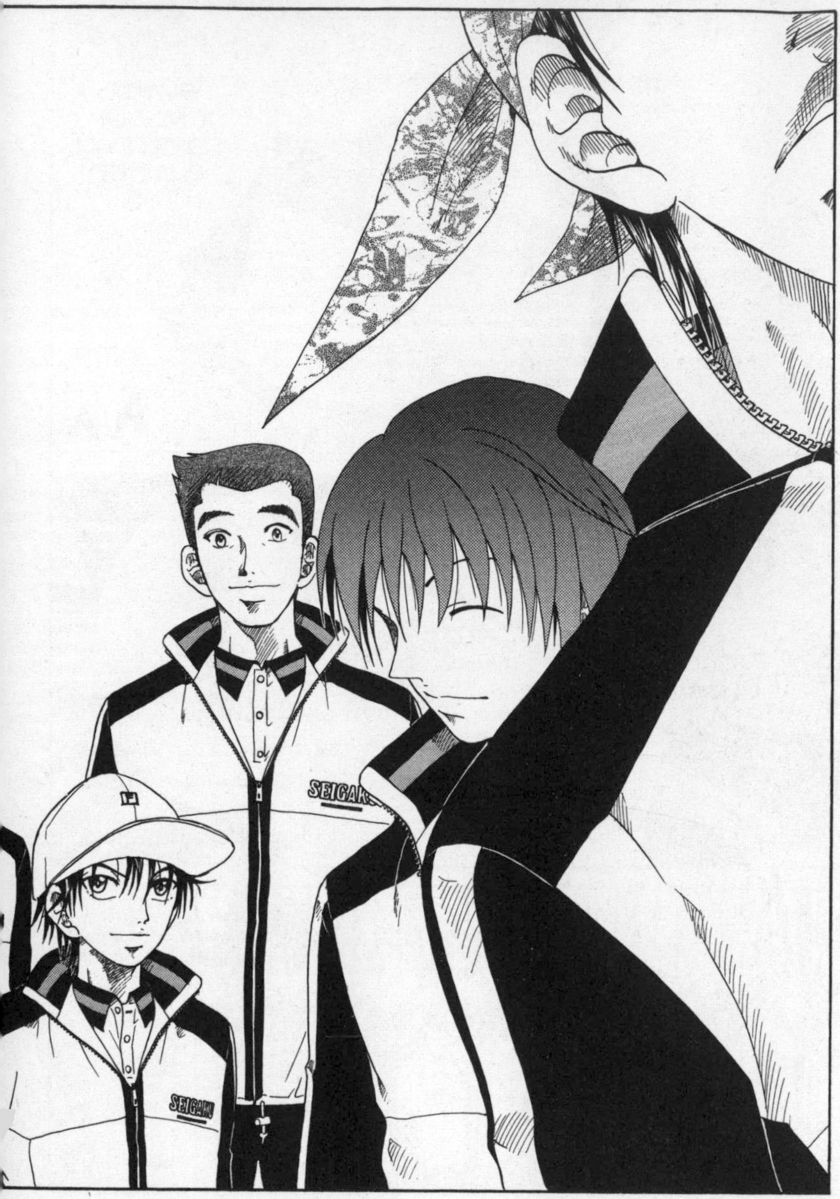
SEIGAKU

GENIUS 66:

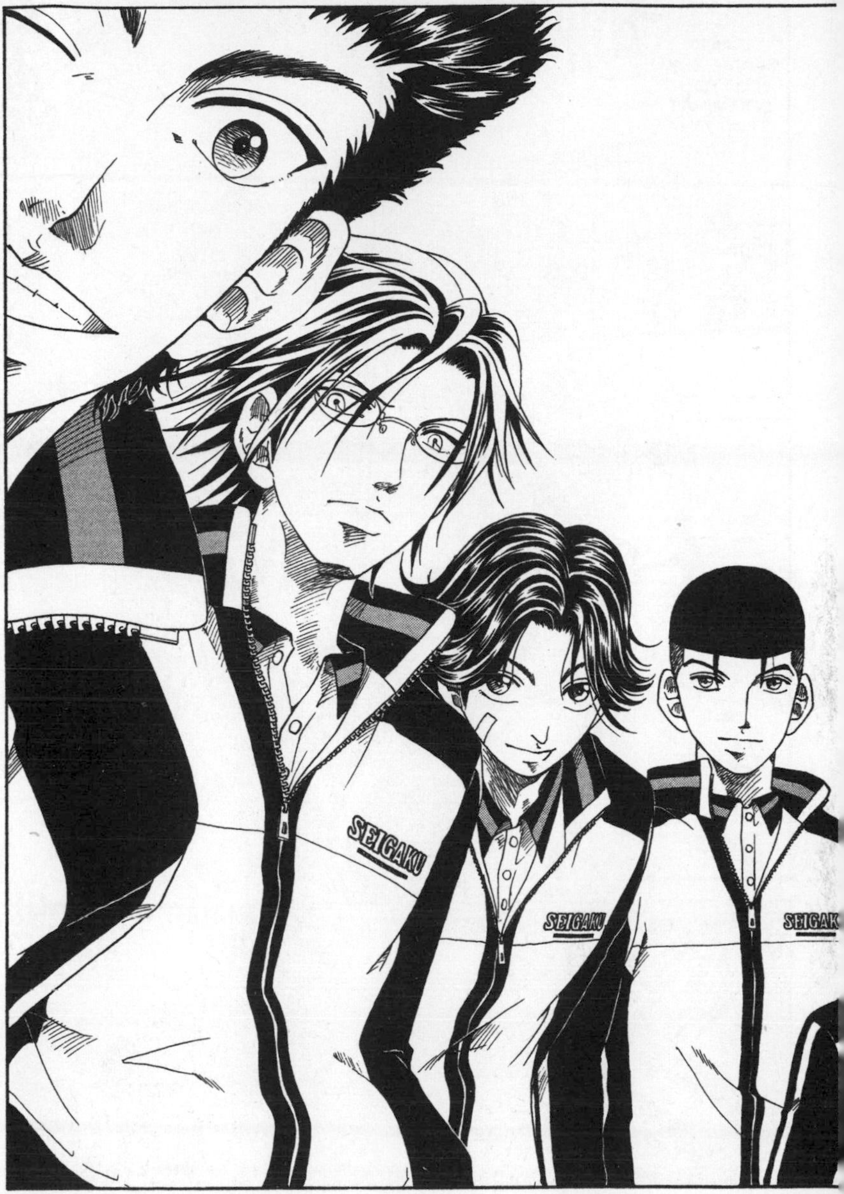
SEIGAKU
SEIGAKU
SEIGAK

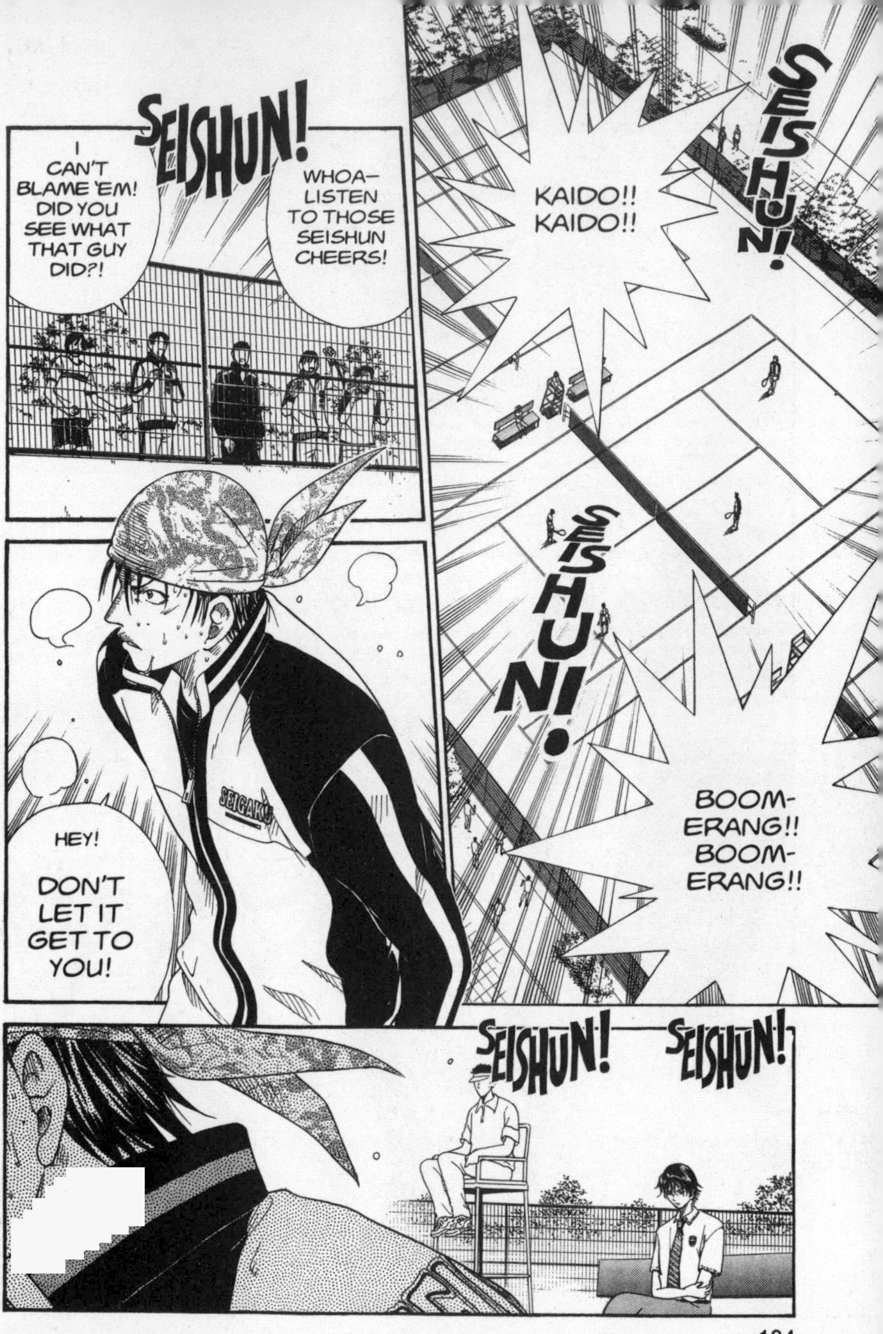
SEISHUN!
KAIDO!! KAIDO!!
SEISHUN!
BOOM-ERANG!! BOOM-ERANG!!
SEISHUN!
WHOA— LISTEN TO THOSE SEISHUN CHEERS!
I CAN'T BLAME 'EM! DID YOU SEE WHAT THAT GUY DID?!
HEY!
DON'T LET IT GET TO YOU!
SEISHUN!
SEISHUN!

READ THIS WAY

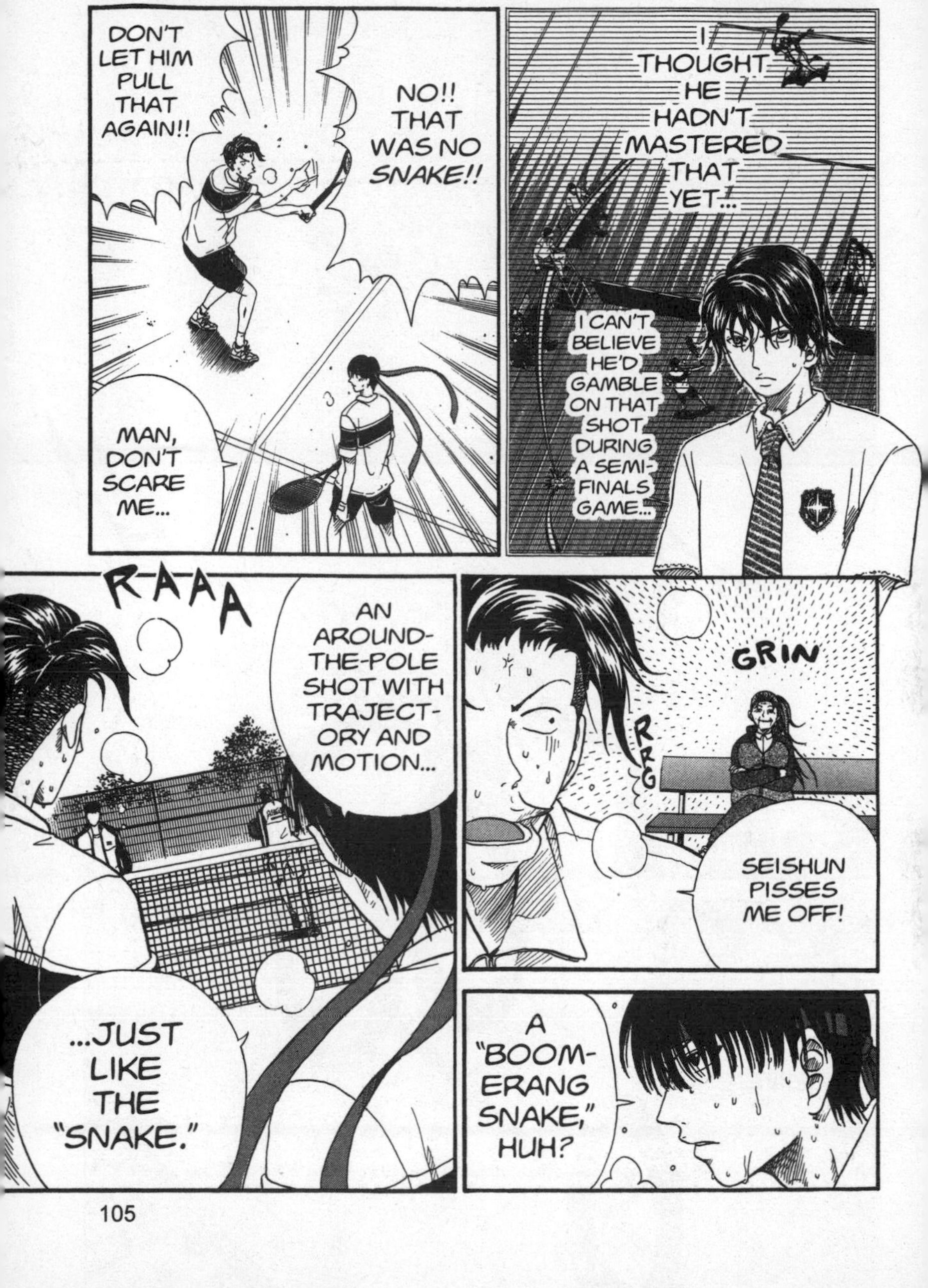
I THOUGHT HE HADN'T MASTERED THAT YET...
I CAN'T BELIEVE HE'D GAMBLE ON THAT SHOT DURING A SEMI-FINALS GAME...
NO!! THAT WAS NO SNAKE!!
DON'T LET HIM PULL THAT AGAIN!!
MAN, DON'T SCARE ME...
GRIN
RRG
SEISHUN PISSES ME OFF!
A "BOOM-ERANG SNAKE," HUH?
RAAA
AN AROUND-THE-POLE SHOT WITH TRAJECT-ORY AND MOTION...
...JUST LIKE THE "SNAKE."

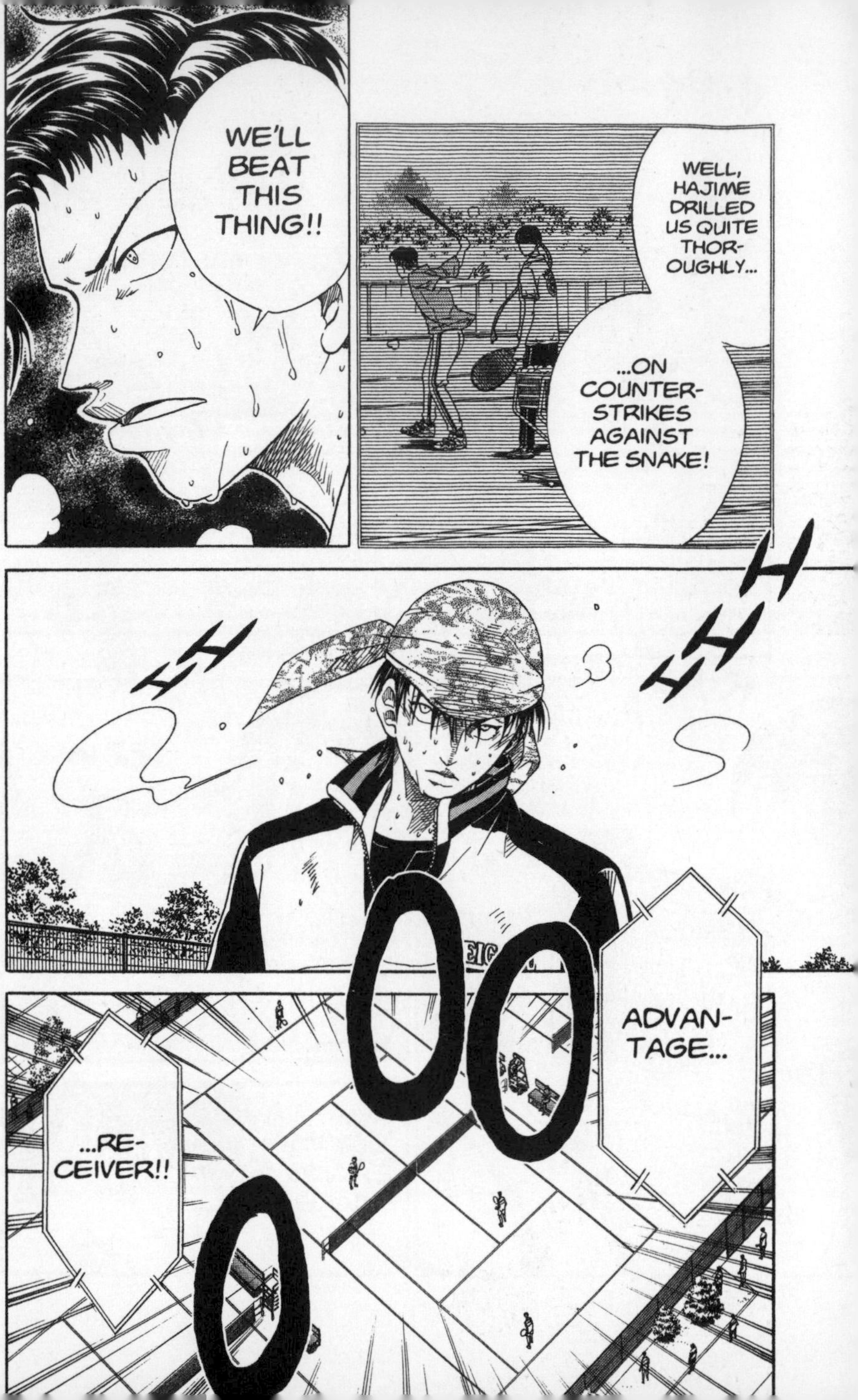
WELL, HAJIME DRILLED US QUITE THOR-OUGHLY...
...ON COUNTER-STRIKES AGAINST THE SNAKE!
WE'LL BEAT THIS THING!!
ADVAN-TAGE...
...RE-CEIVER!!

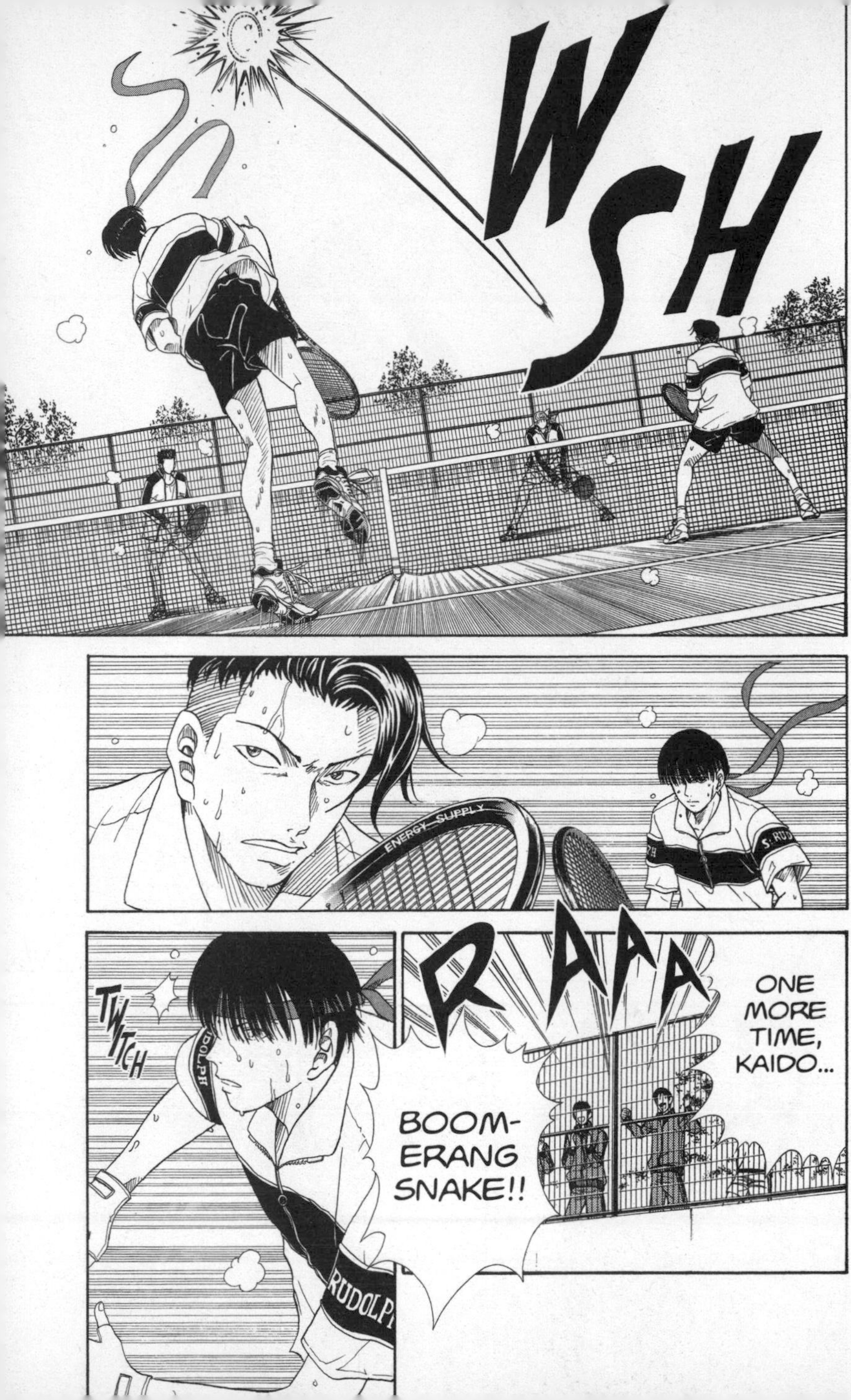
WSH
ONE MORE TIME, KAIDO...
RAAA
BOOM-ERANG SNAKE!!
TWITCH

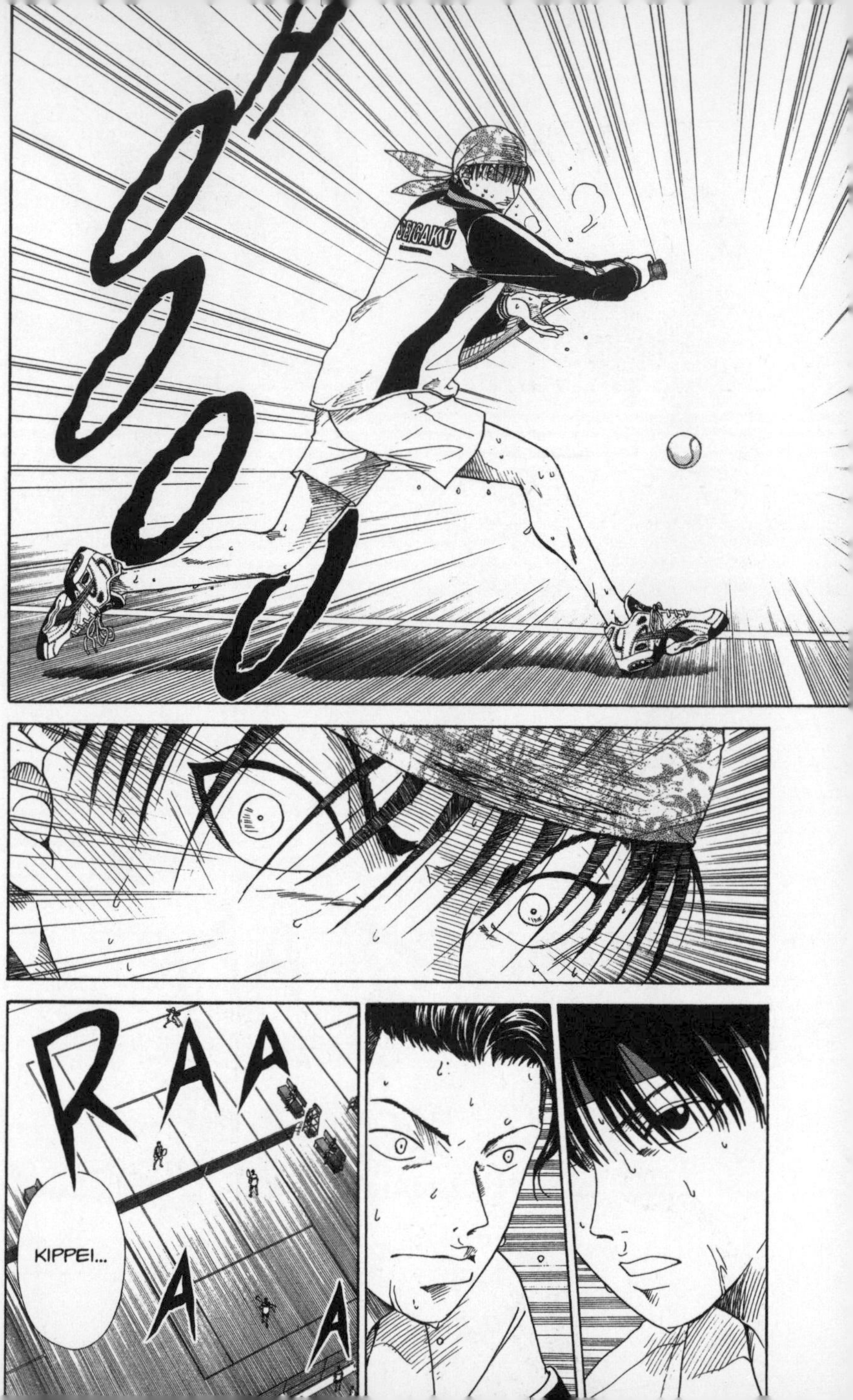
HOOOU
SEIGAKU
RAAAA
KIPPEI...

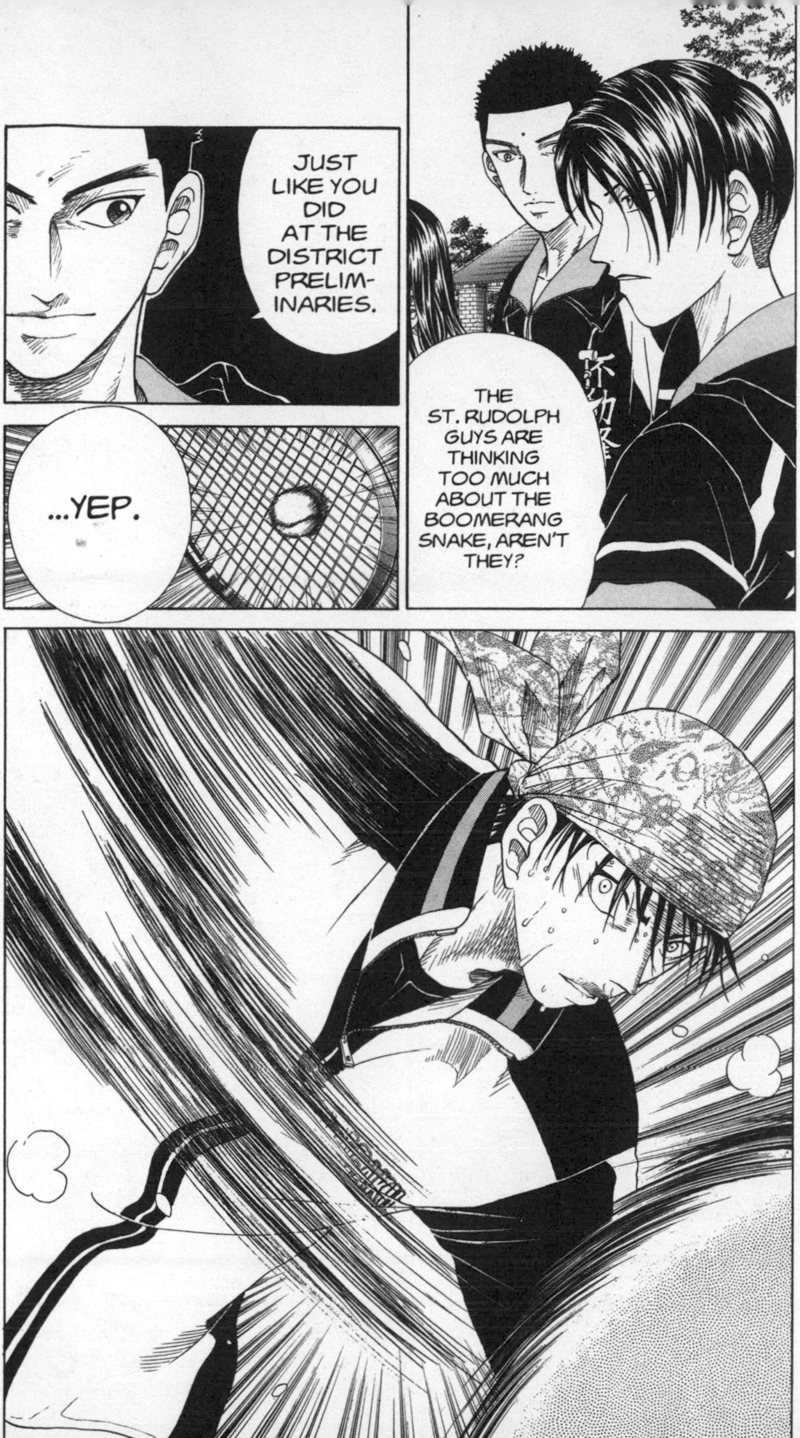
THE ST. RUDOLPH GUYS ARE THINKING TOO MUCH ABOUT THE BOOMERANG SNAKE, AREN'T THEY?
JUST LIKE YOU DID AT THE DISTRICT PRELIMINARIES.
...YEP.

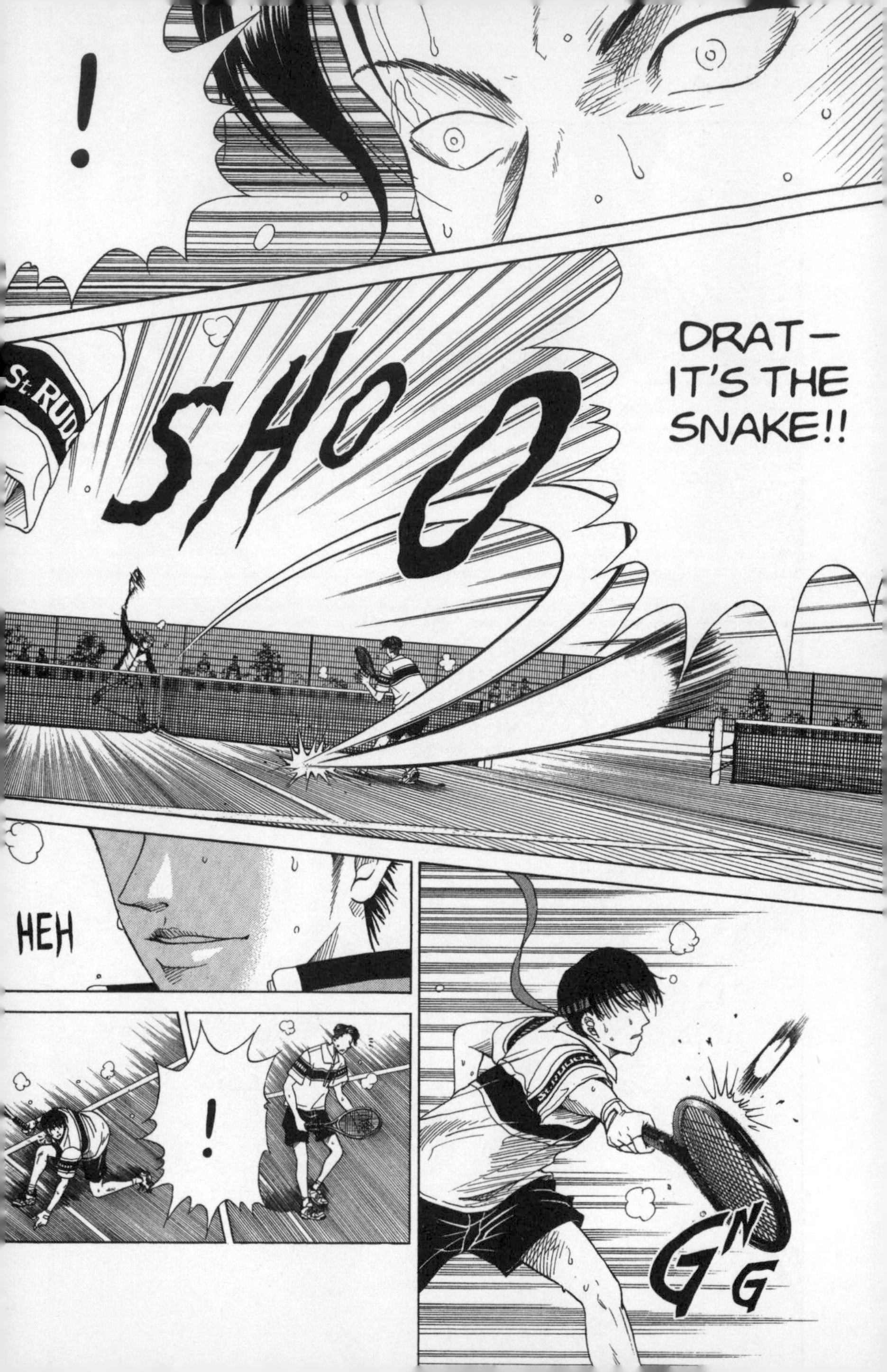
!
DRAT—
IT'S THE
SNAKE!!
SHOO
GNG
HEH
!

READ THIS WAY

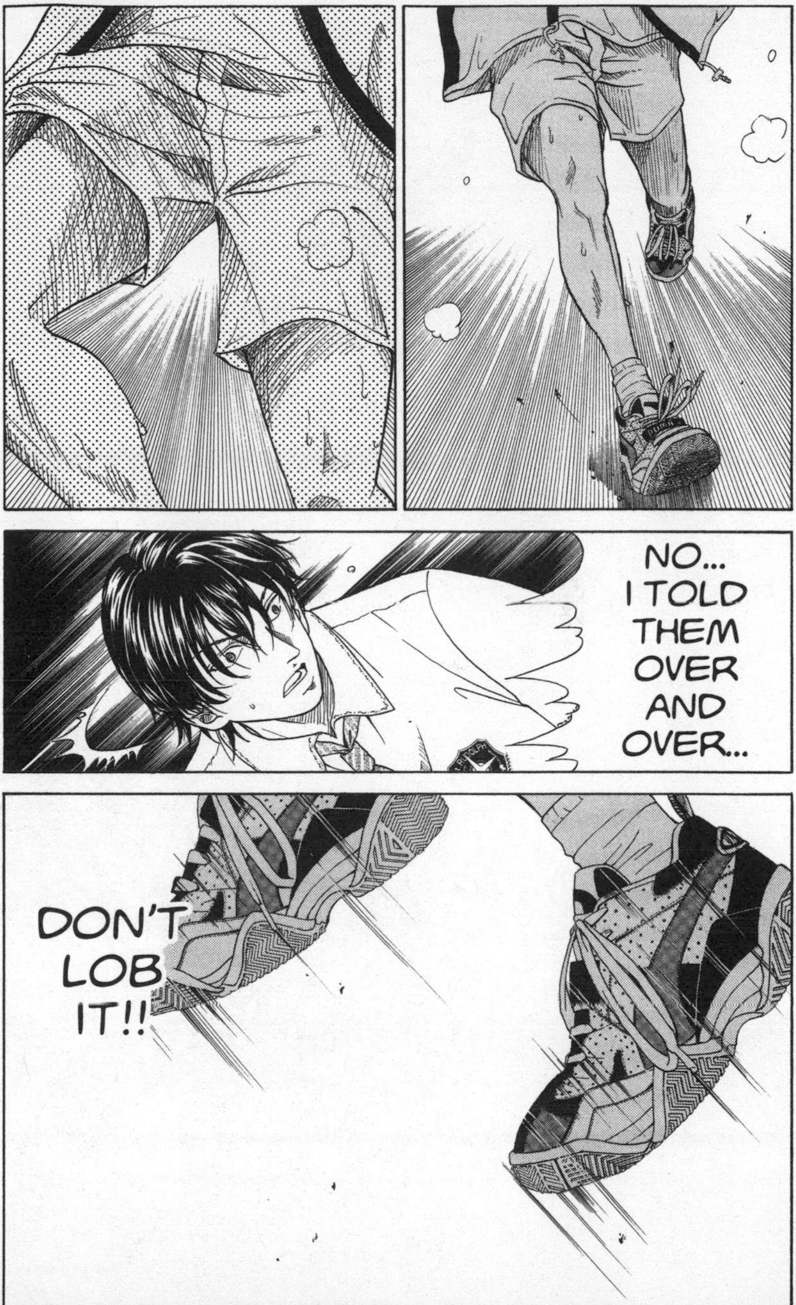
NO... I TOLD THEM OVER AND OVER...
DON'T LOB IT!!

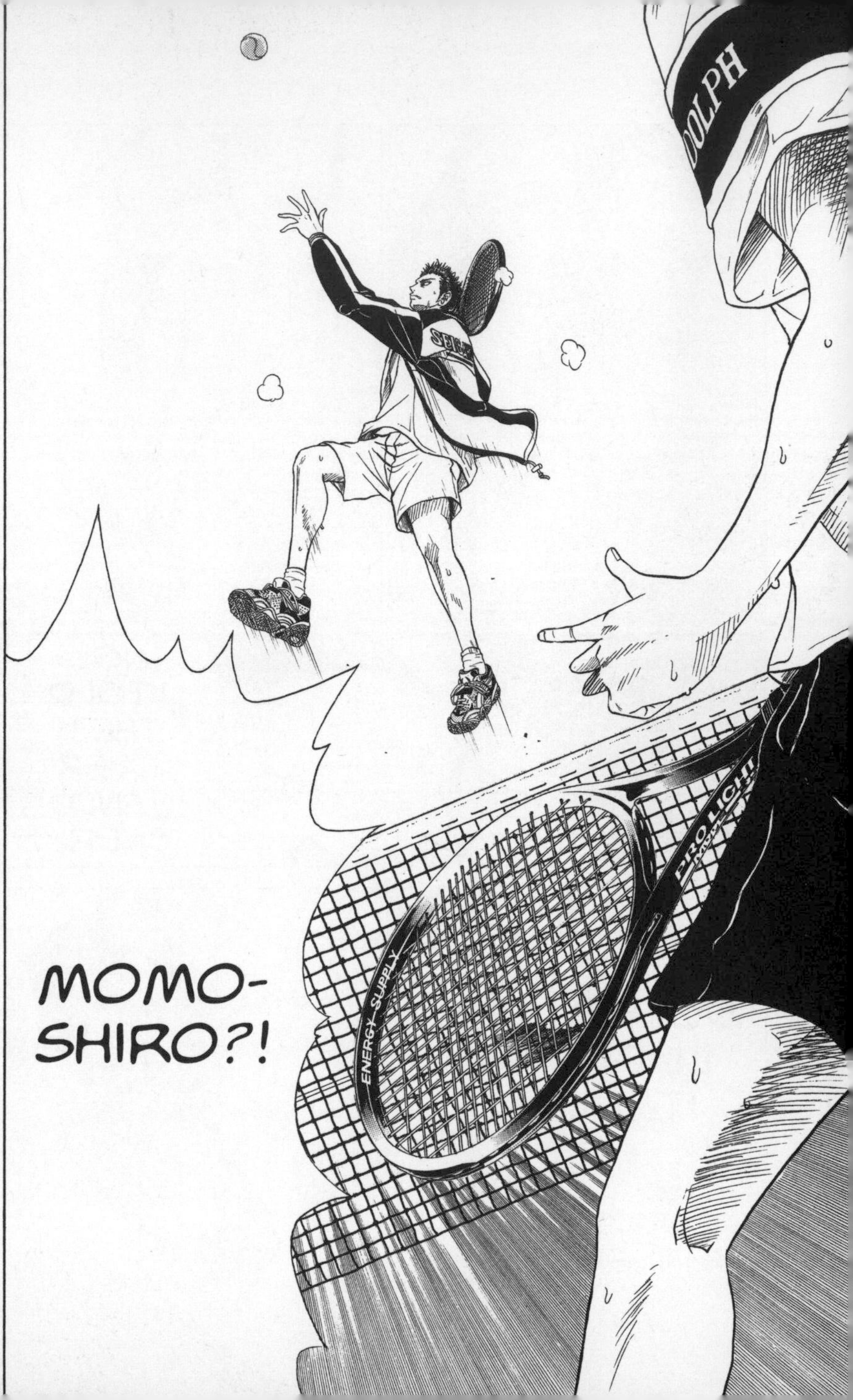
MOMO-SHIRO?!
DOLPH
ENERGY SUPPLY

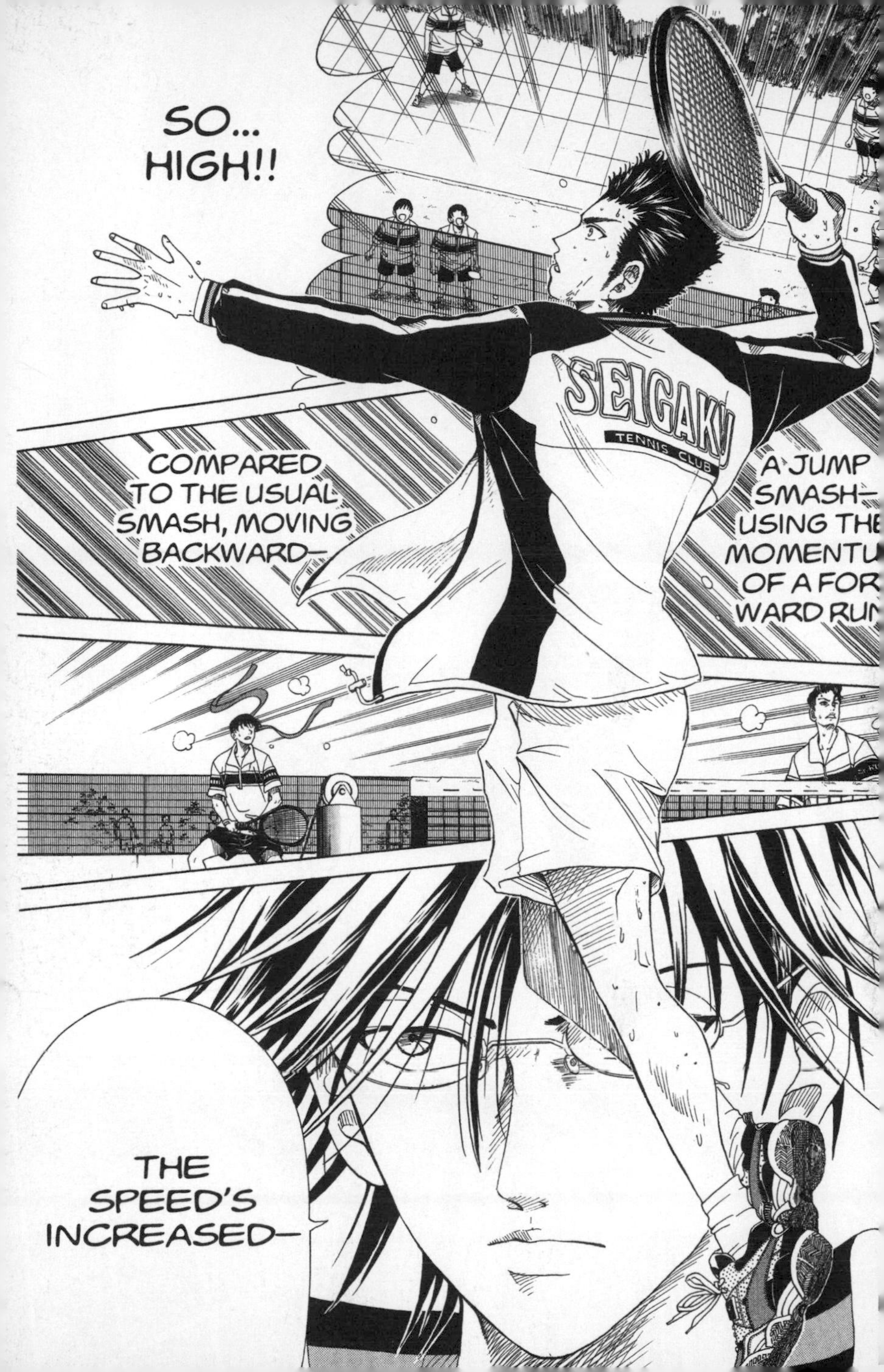
SO... HIGH!!
A JUMP SMASH— USING THE MOMENTU OF A FOR WARD RUN
COMPARED TO THE USUAL SMASH, MOVING BACKWARD—
THE SPEED'S INCREASED—

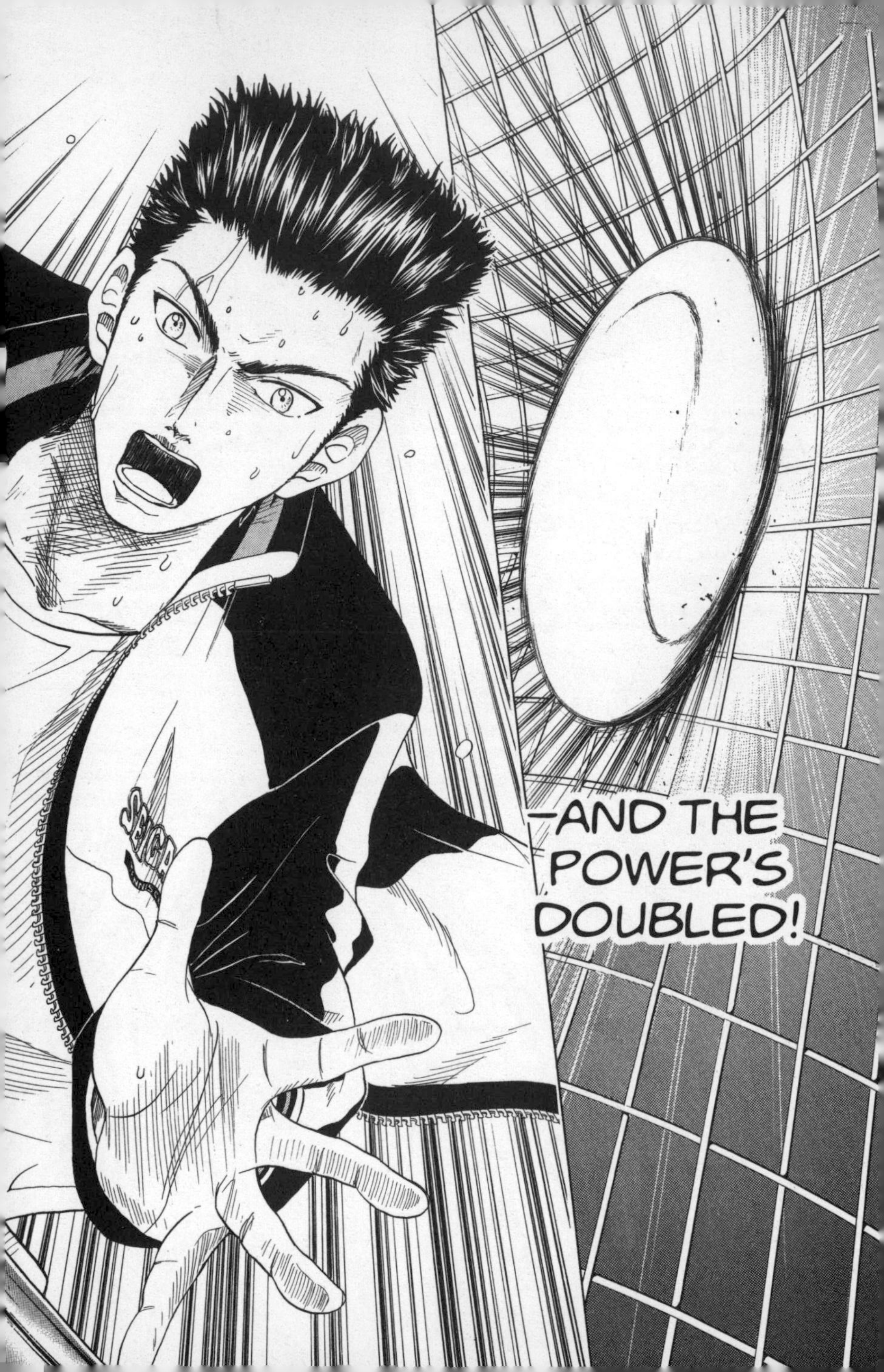
-AND THE POWER'S DOUBLED!

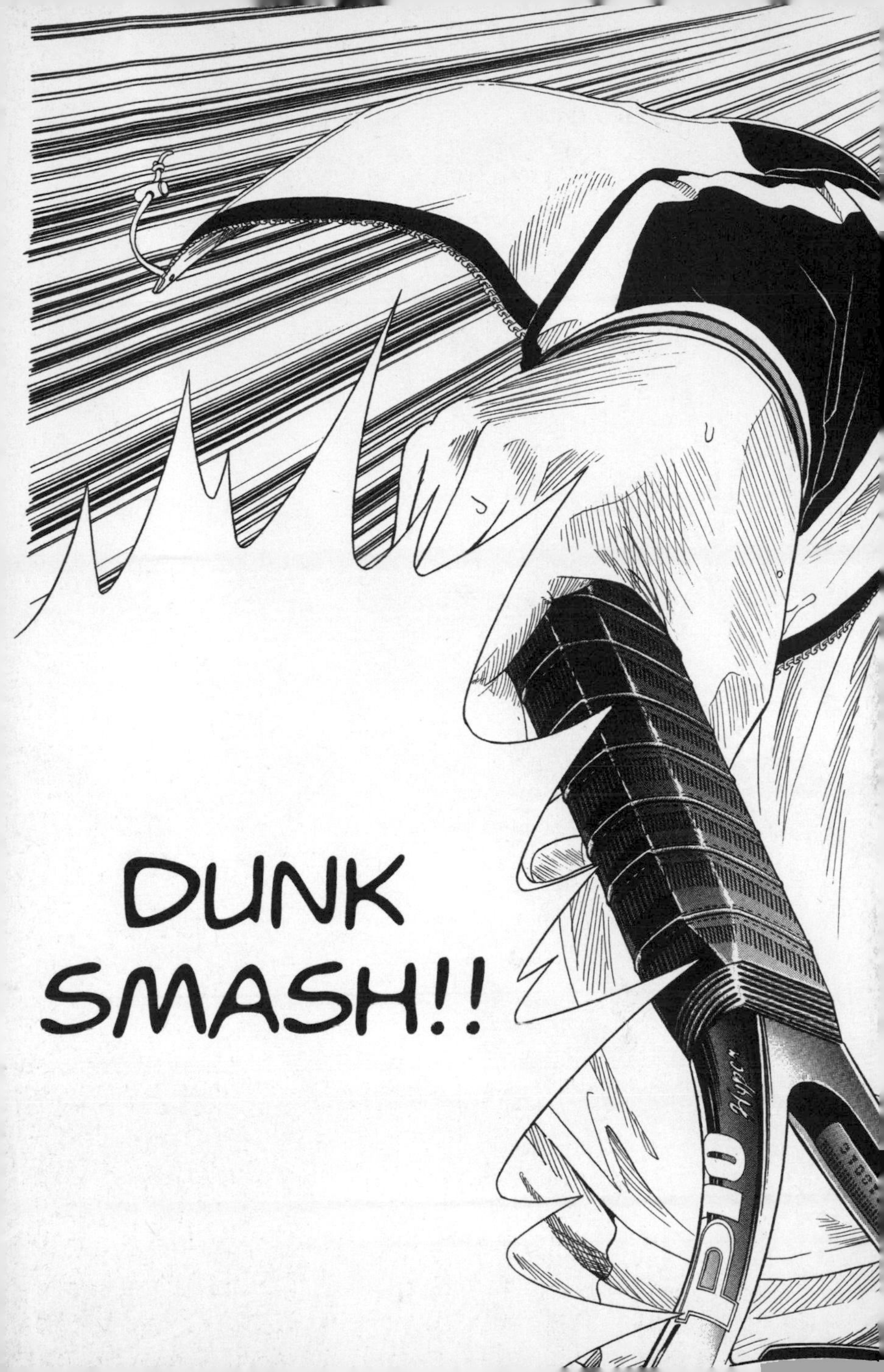
DUNK
SMASH!!

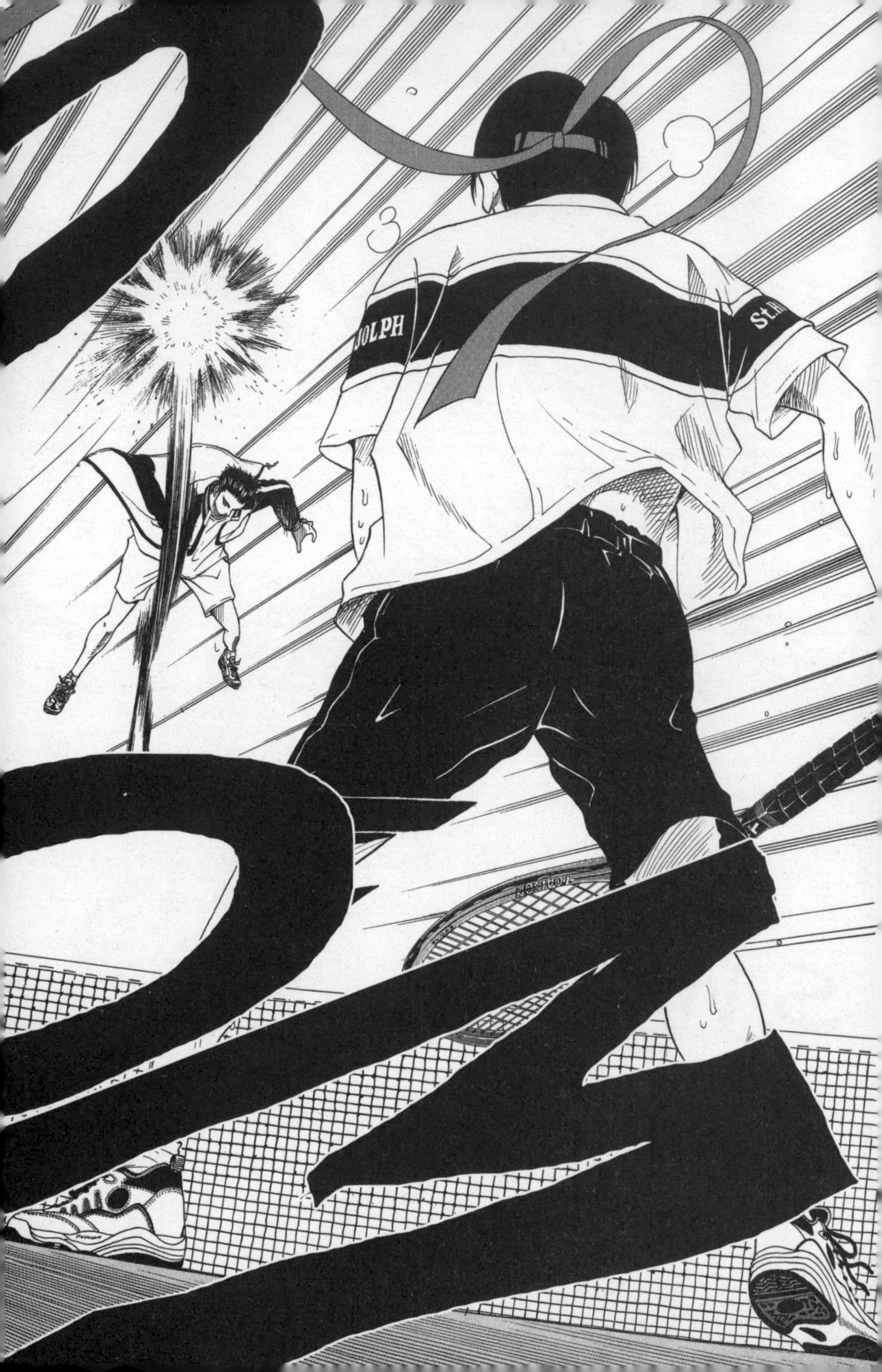

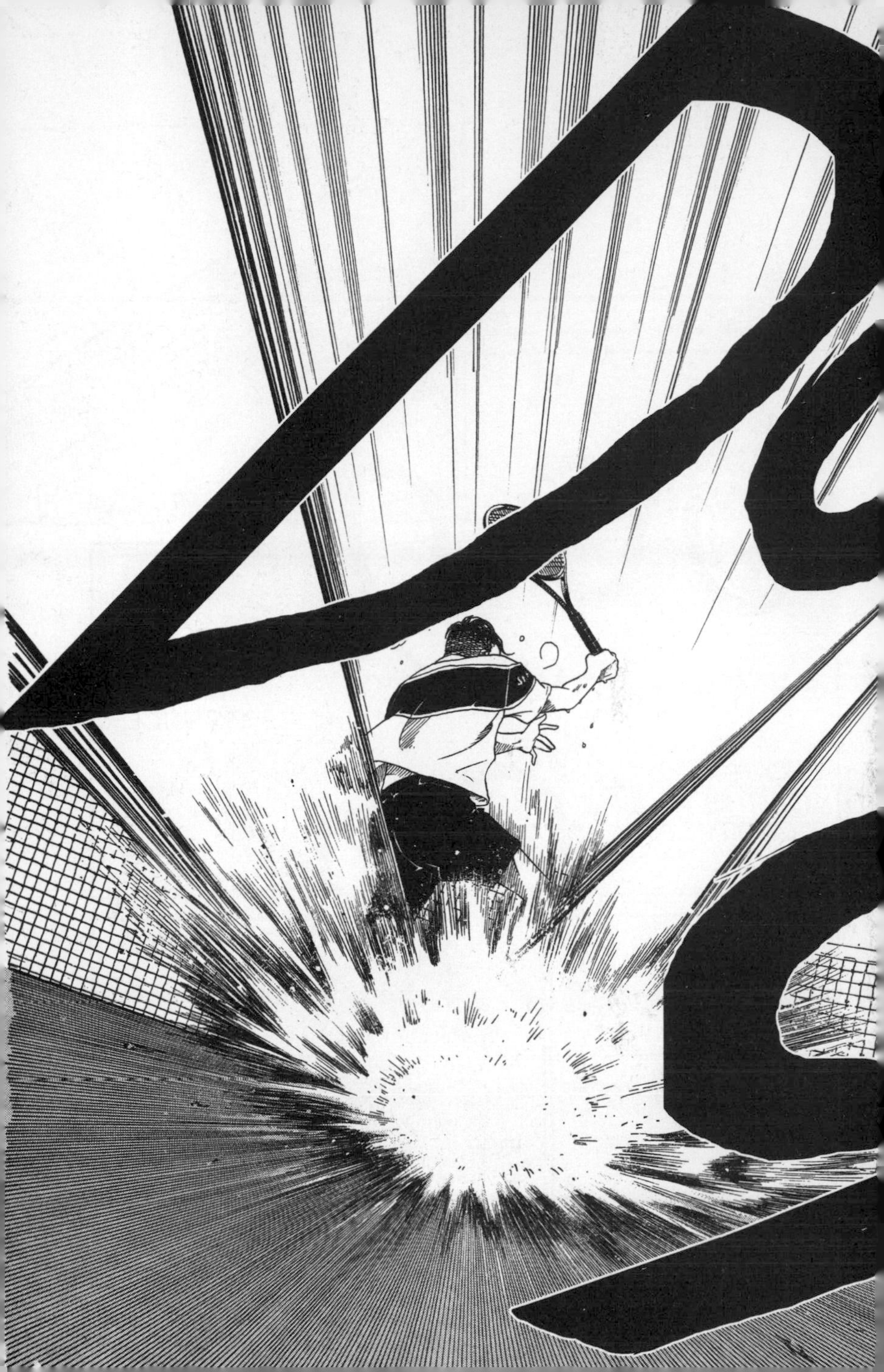

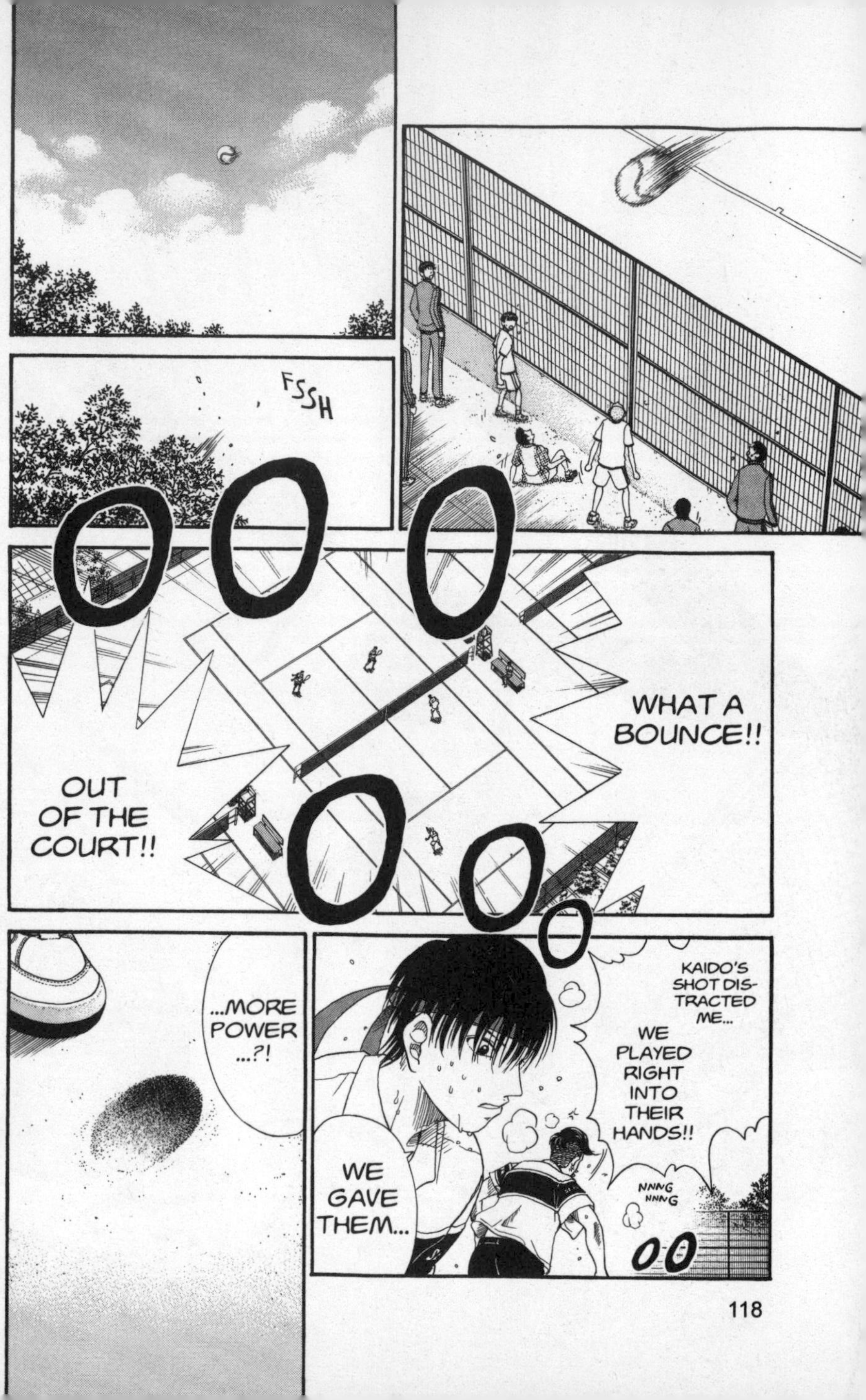
FSSH
OOOOOO
WHAT A BOUNCE!!
OUT OF THE COURT!!
KAIDO'S SHOT DIS-TRACTED ME...
WE PLAYED RIGHT INTO THEIR HANDS!!
WE GAVE THEM...
NNNG NNNG
0-0
...MORE POWER ...?!

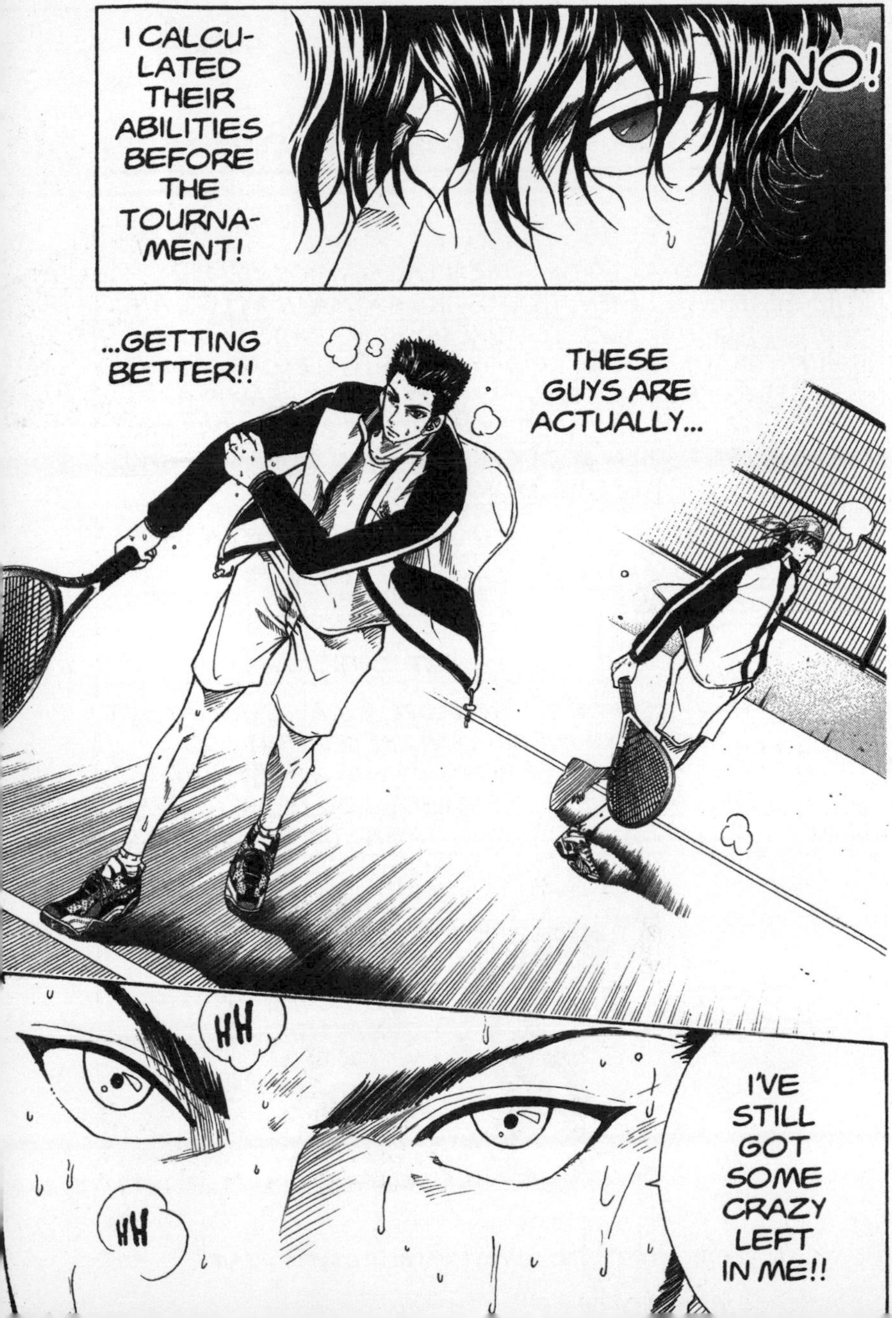
NO!
I CALCULATED THEIR ABILITIES BEFORE THE TOURNAMENT!
THESE GUYS ARE ACTUALLY...
...GETTING BETTER!!
I'VE STILL GOT SOME CRAZY LEFT IN ME!!
HH
HH

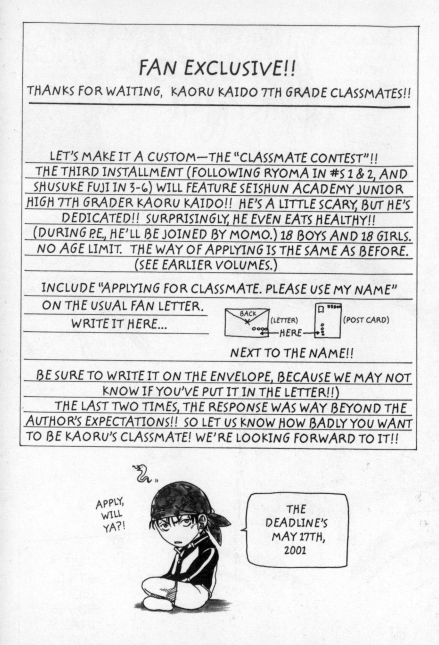

FAN EXCLUSIVE!!

THANKS FOR WAITING, KAORU KAIDO 7TH GRADE CLASSMATES!!

LET'S MAKE IT A CUSTOM—THE "CLASSMATE CONTEST"!! THE THIRD INSTALLMENT (FOLLOWING RYOMA IN #S 1 & 2, AND SHUSUKE FUJI IN 3-6) WILL FEATURE SEISHUN ACADEMY JUNIOR HIGH 7TH GRADER KAORU KAIDO!! HE'S A LITTLE SCARY, BUT HE'S DEDICATED!! SURPRISINGLY, HE EVEN EATS HEALTHY!! (DURING P.E., HE'LL BE JOINED BY MOMO.) 18 BOYS AND 18 GIRLS. NO AGE LIMIT. THE WAY OF APPLYING IS THE SAME AS BEFORE. (SEE EARLIER VOLUMES.)

INCLUDE "APPLYING FOR CLASSMATE. PLEASE USE MY NAME" ON THE USUAL FAN LETTER.

WRITE IT HERE...

BACK
(LETTER)
HERE
(POST CARD)

NEXT TO THE NAME!!

BE SURE TO WRITE IT ON THE ENVELOPE, BECAUSE WE MAY NOT KNOW IF YOU'VE PUT IT IN THE LETTER!!)

THE LAST TWO TIMES, THE RESPONSE WAS WAY BEYOND THE AUTHOR'S EXPECTATIONS!! SO LET US KNOW HOW BADLY YOU WANT TO BE KAORU'S CLASSMATE! WE'RE LOOKING FORWARD TO IT!!

APPLY, WILL YA?!
THE DEADLINE'S MAY 17TH, 2001

EDITOR'S NOTE: THIS CONTEST WAS HELD ONLY IN JAPAN.

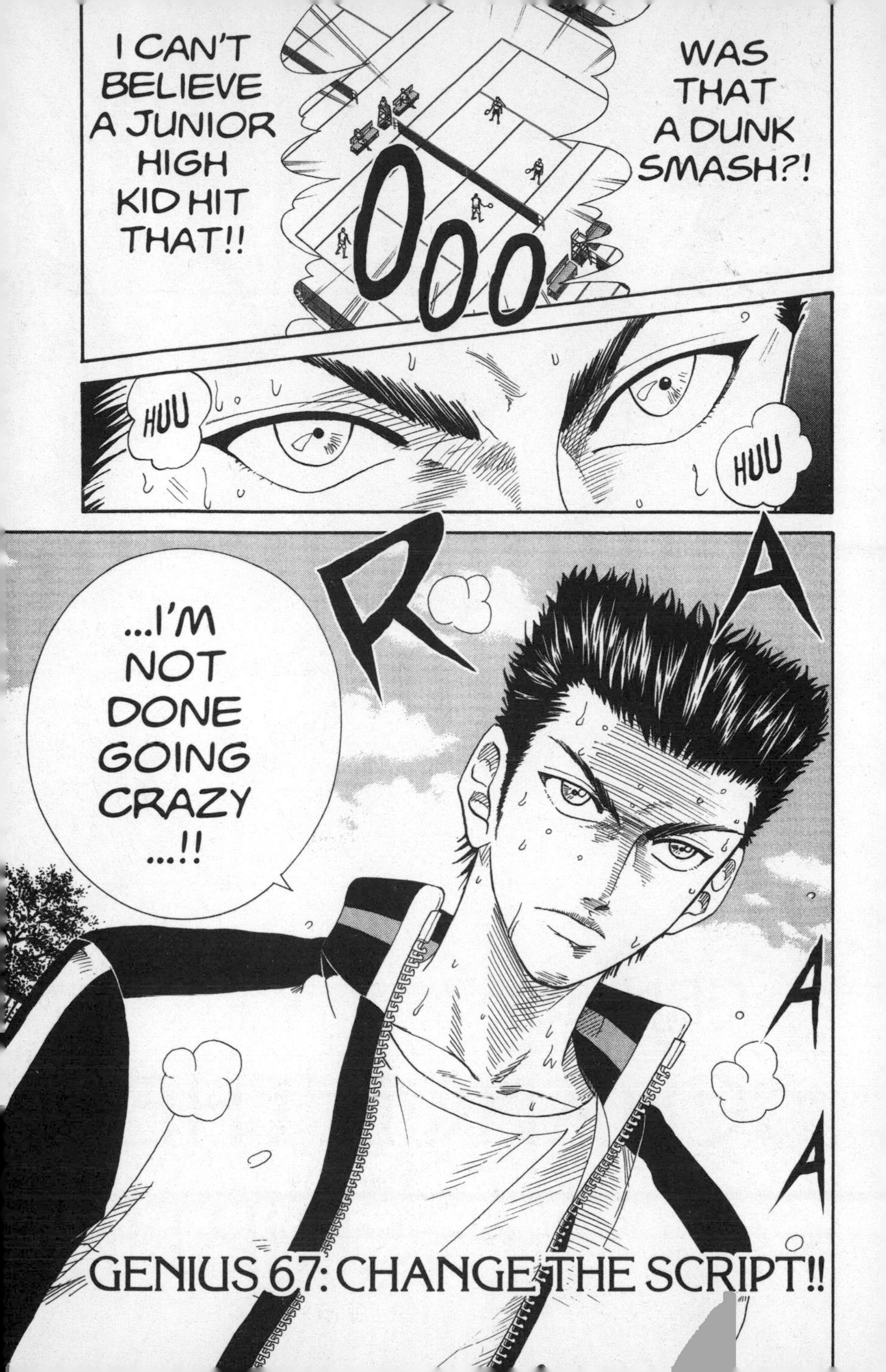
WAS THAT A DUNK SMASH?!
I CAN'T BELIEVE A JUNIOR HIGH KID HIT THAT!!
OOO
HUU
HUU
RAAAA
...I'M NOT DONE GOING CRAZY ...!!
GENIUS 67: CHANGE THE SCRIPT!!

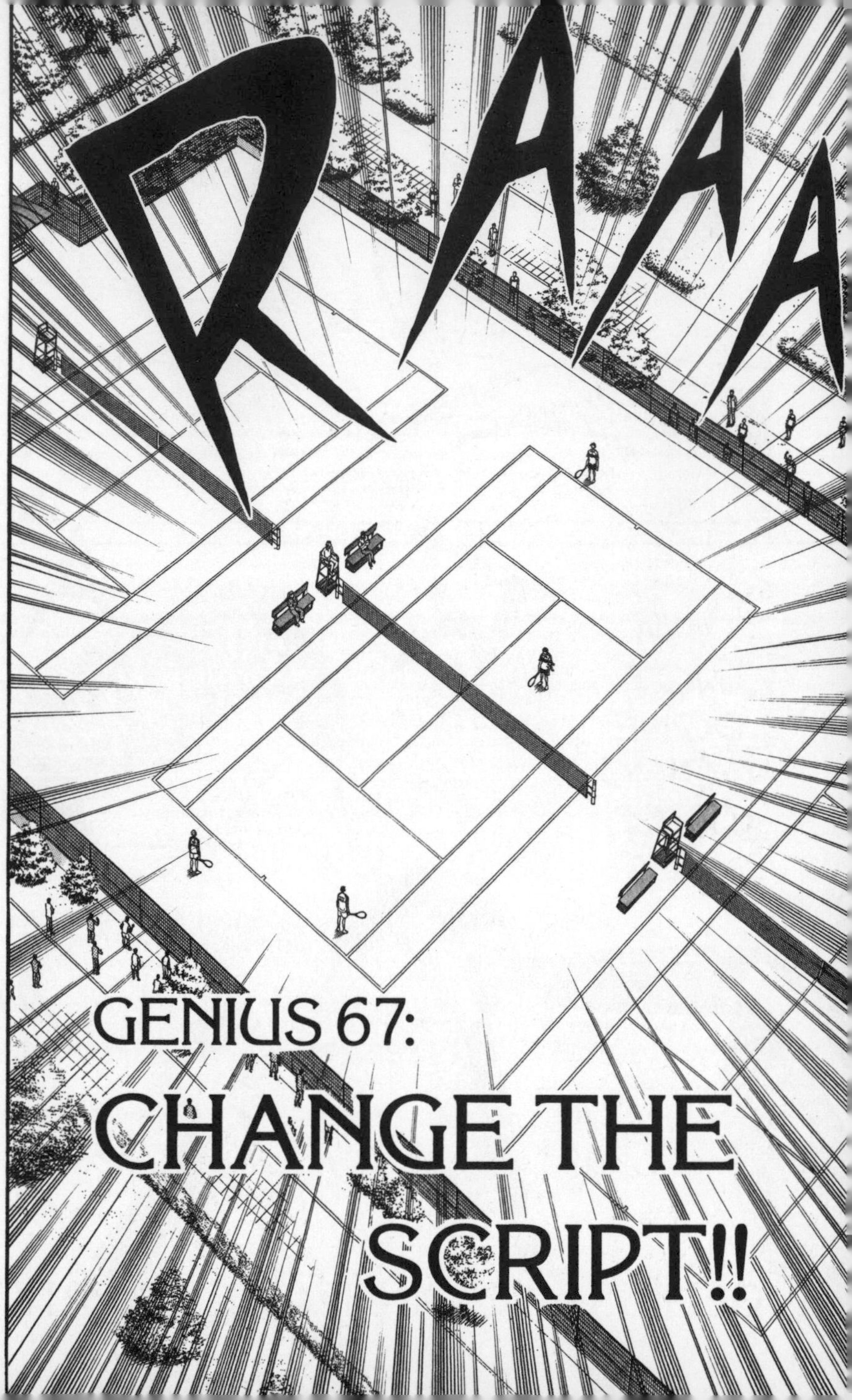
RAAA
GENIUS 67:
CHANGE THE SCRIPT!!

READ THIS WAY

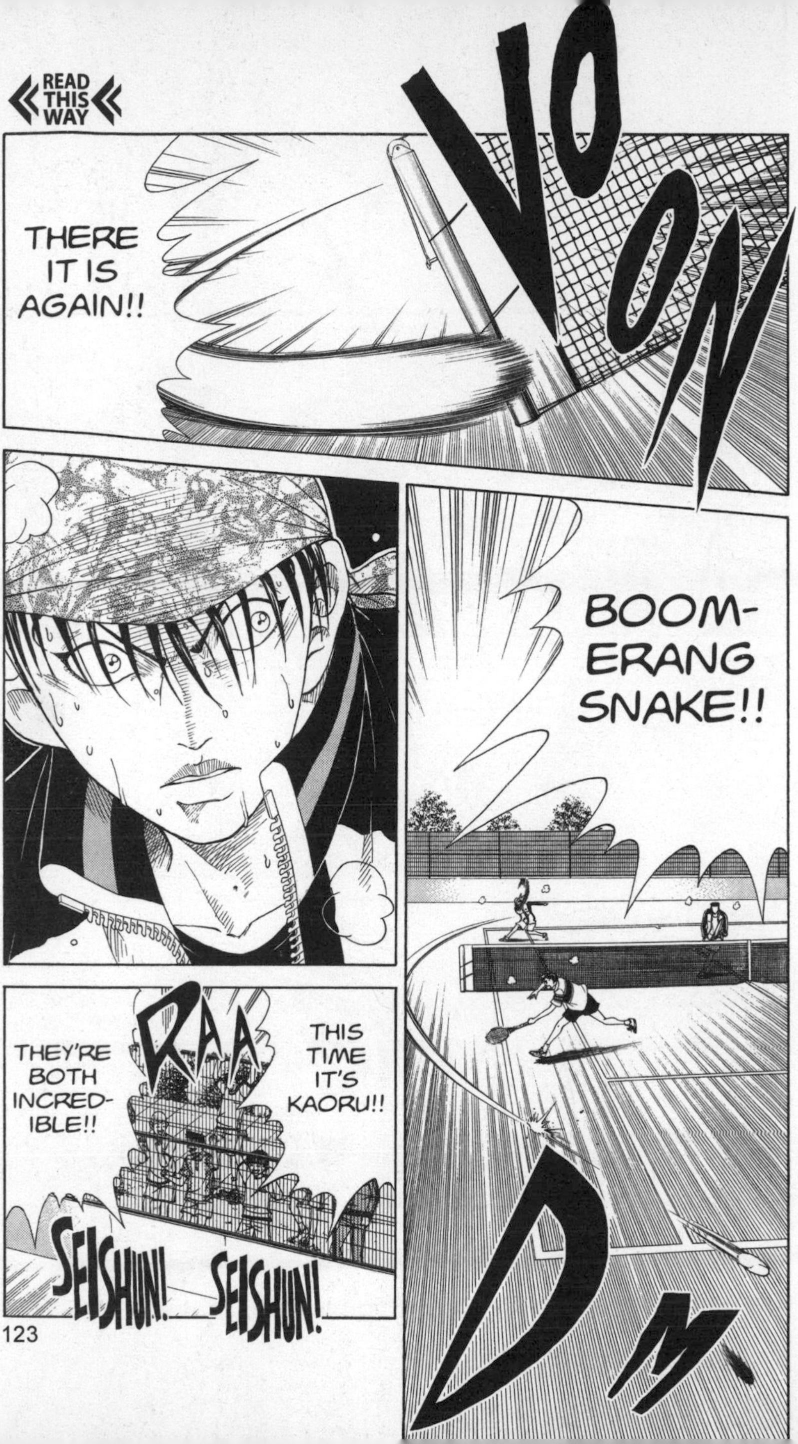
THERE IT IS AGAIN!!
VOON
BOOM-ERANG SNAKE!!
DM
THIS TIME IT'S KAORU!!
RAA
THEY'RE BOTH INCREDIBLE!!
SEISHUN! SEISHUN!

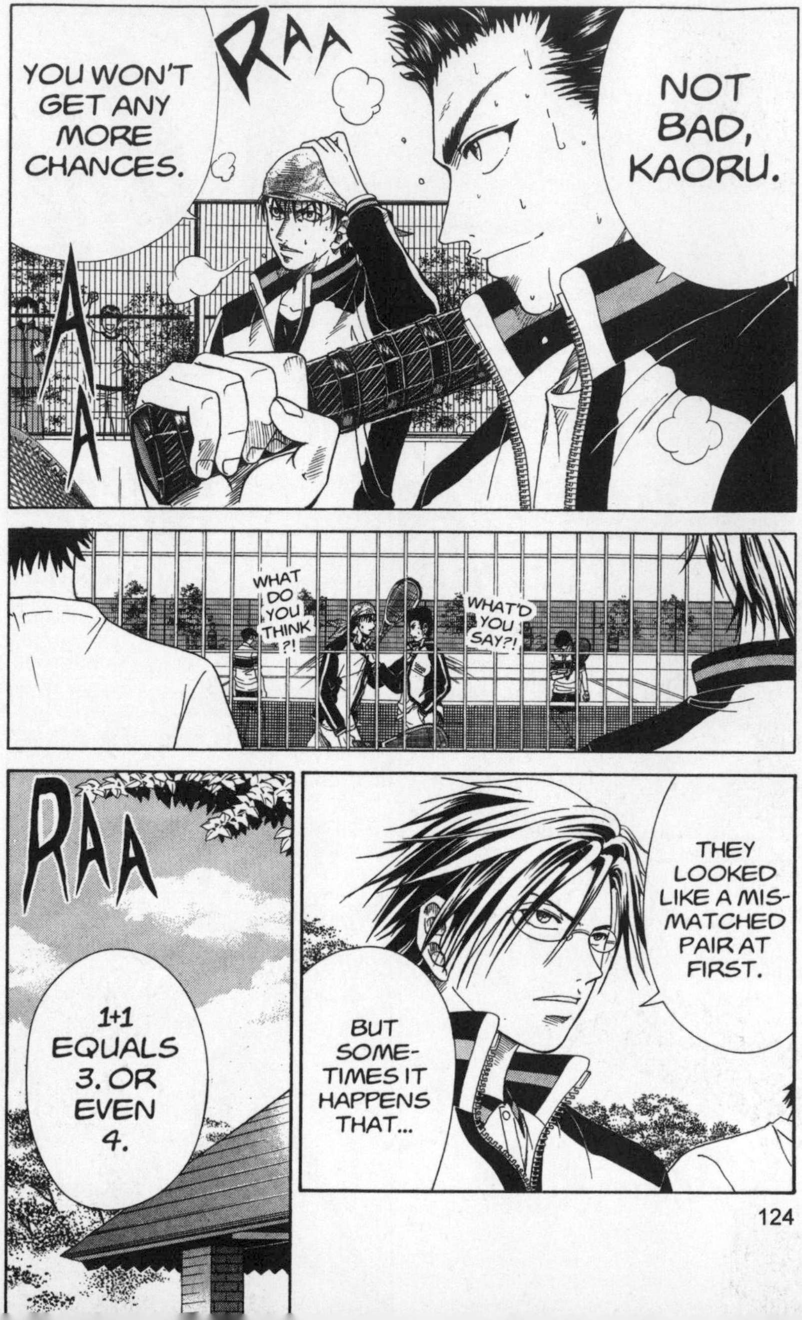
NOT BAD, KAORU.
RAA
YOU WON'T GET ANY MORE CHANCES.
AAA
WHAT'D YOU SAY?!
WHAT DO YOU THINK?!
THEY LOOKED LIKE A MIS-MATCHED PAIR AT FIRST.
BUT SOME-TIMES IT HAPPENS THAT...
RAA
1+1 EQUALS 3. OR EVEN 4.

READ THIS WAY

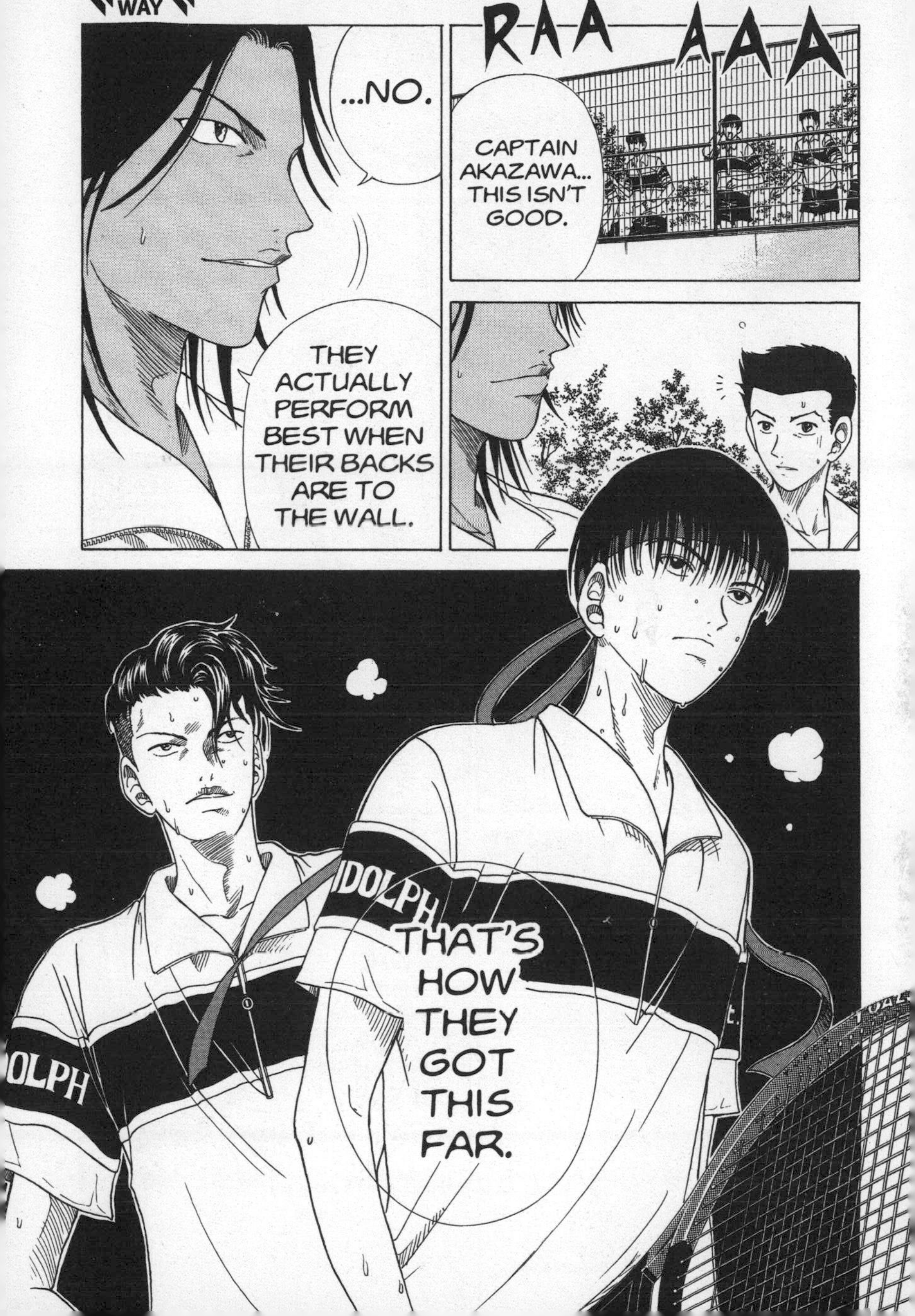
RAA AAA
CAPTAIN AKAZAWA... THIS ISN'T GOOD.
...NO.
THEY ACTUALLY PERFORM BEST WHEN THEIR BACKS ARE TO THE WALL.
THAT'S HOW THEY GOT THIS FAR.
IDOLPH
IDOLPH

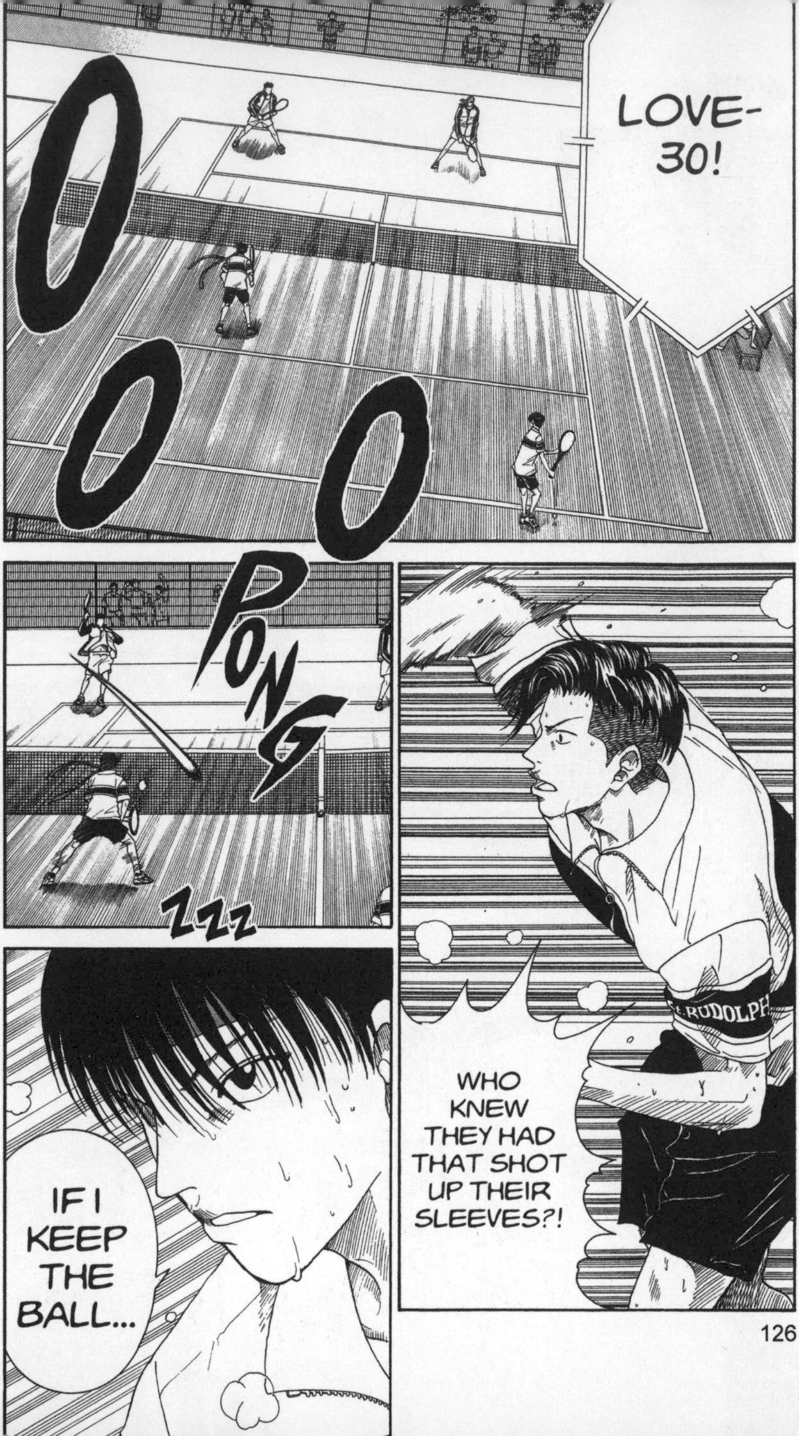
LOVE-30!
OOO
WHO KNEW THEY HAD THAT SHOT UP THEIR SLEEVES?!
ST. RUDOLPH
PONG
ZZZ
IF I KEEP THE BALL...

READ THIS WAY

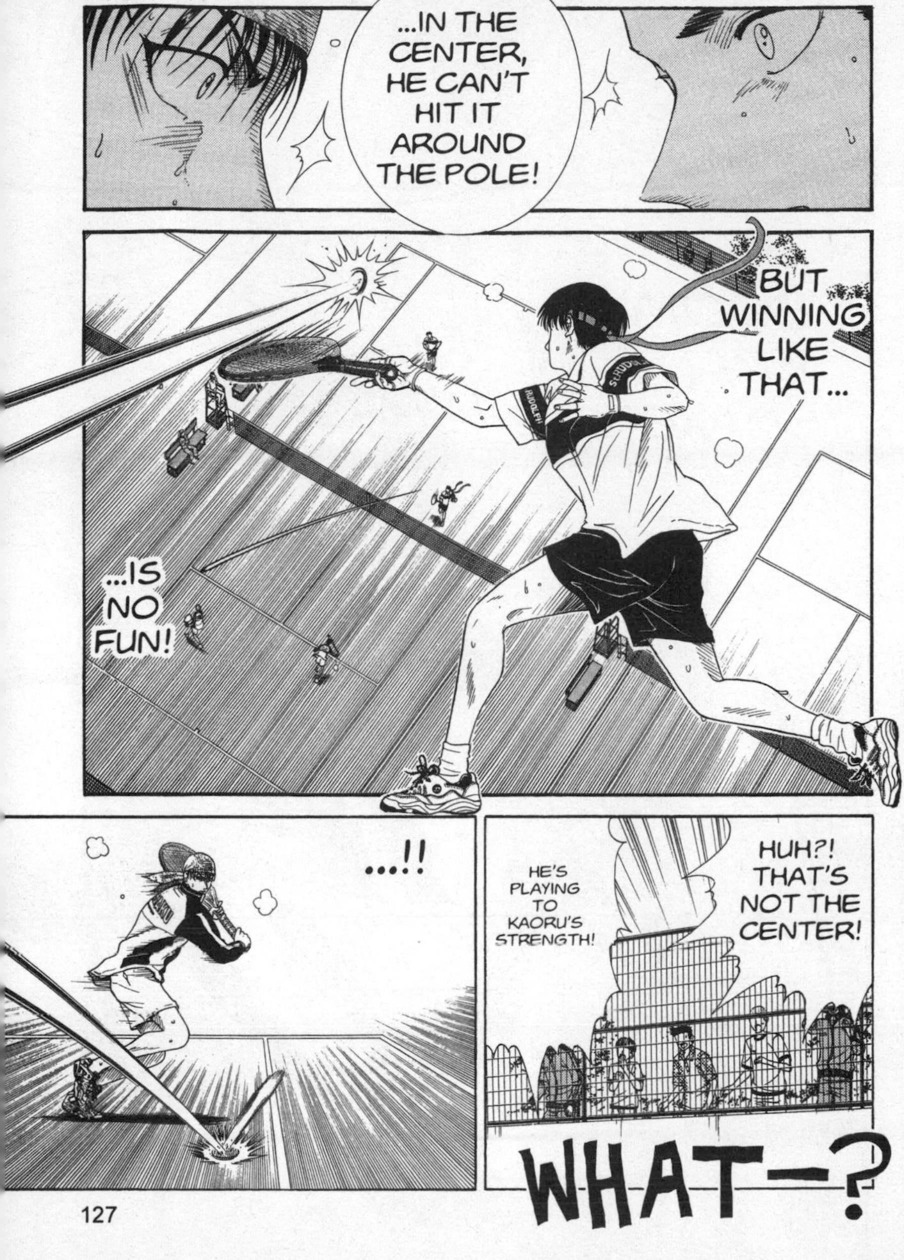
...IN THE CENTER, HE CAN'T HIT IT AROUND THE POLE!
BUT WINNING LIKE THAT...
...IS NO FUN!
HUH?! THAT'S NOT THE CENTER!
HE'S PLAYING TO KAORU'S STRENGTH!
WHAT—?
...!!

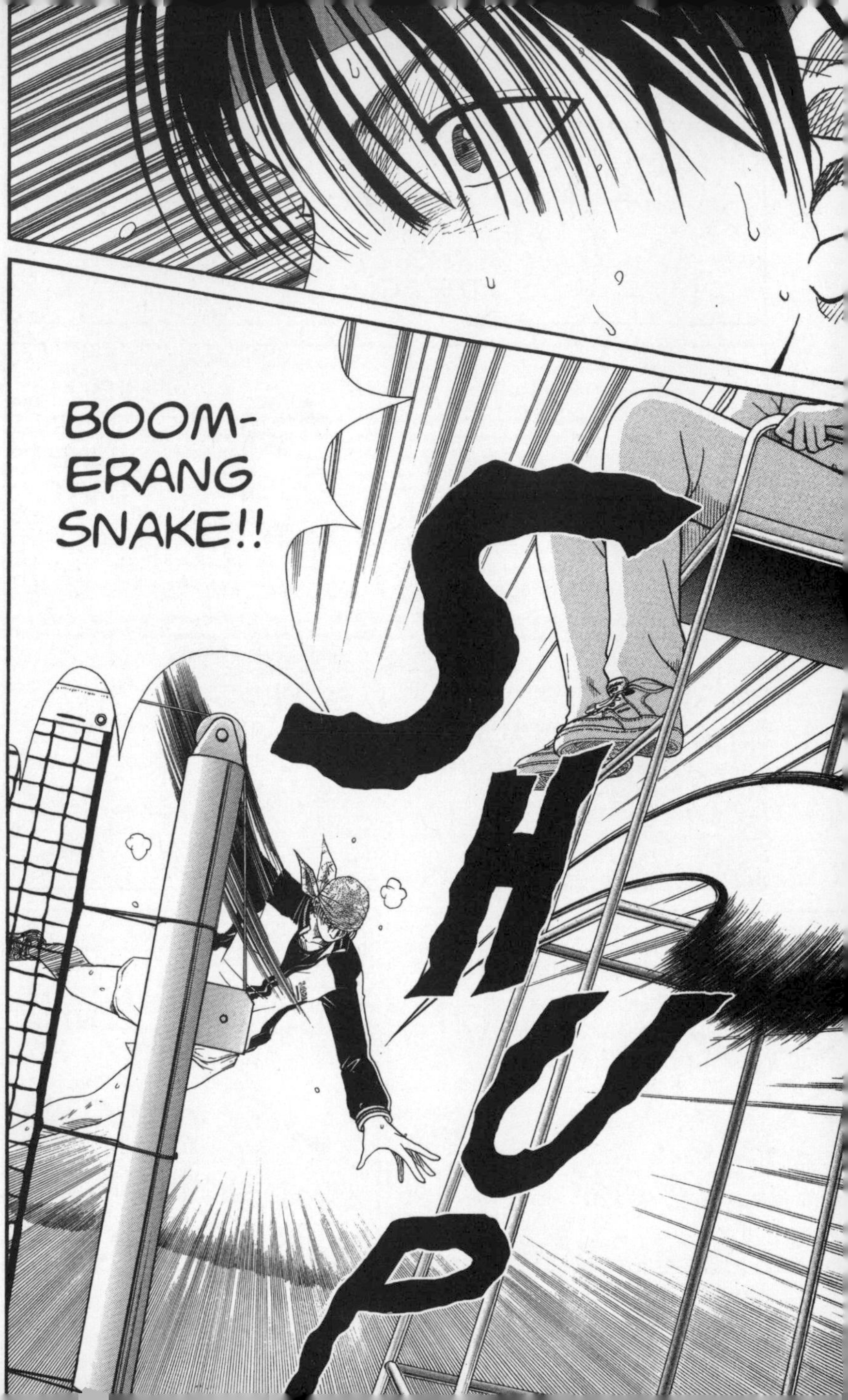
BOOM-
ERANG
SNAKE!!
SHUP

READ THIS WAY

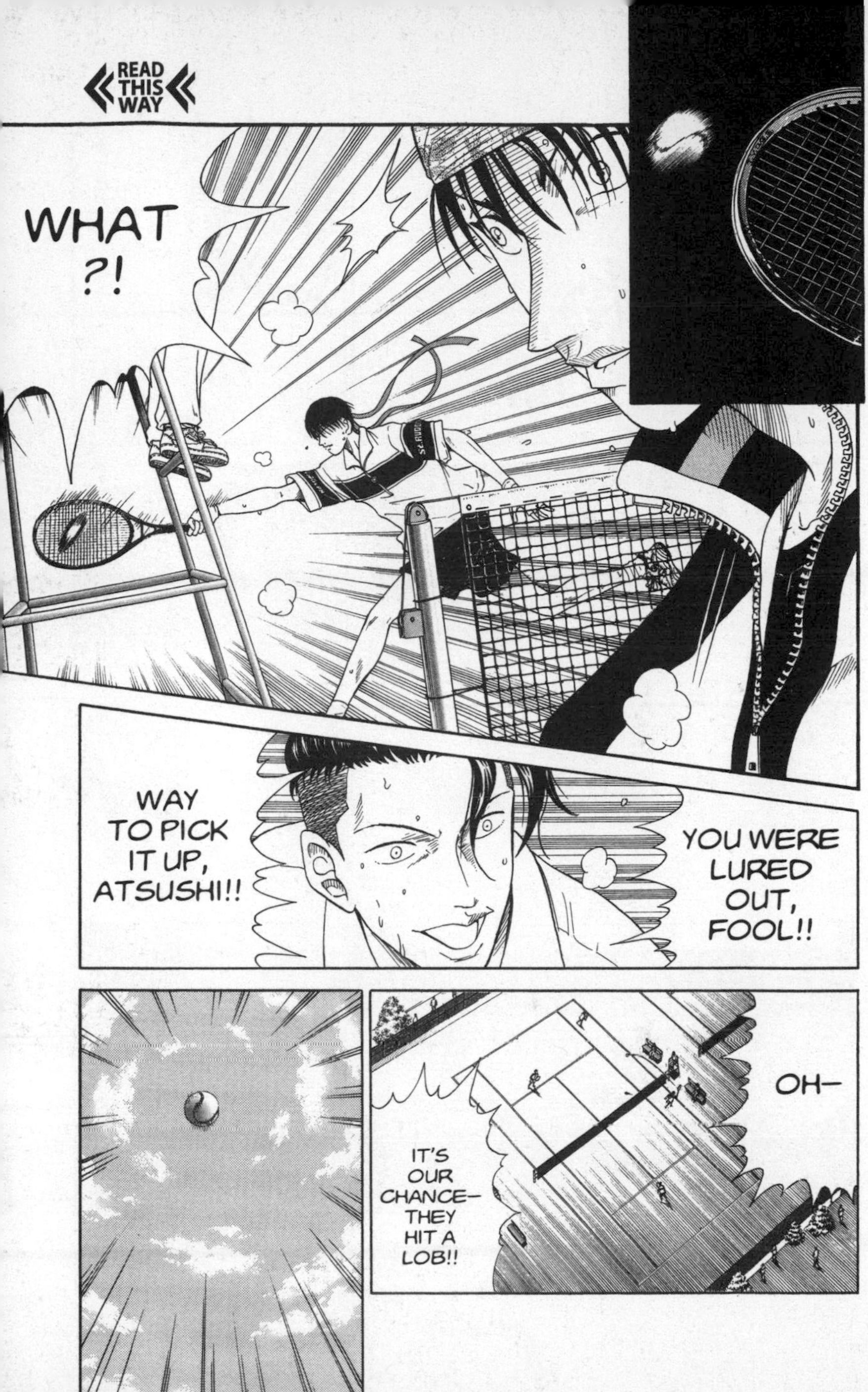

WHAT ?!
YOU WERE LURED OUT, FOOL!!
WAY TO PICK IT UP, ATSUSHI!!
OH—
IT'S OUR CHANCE— THEY HIT A LOB!!

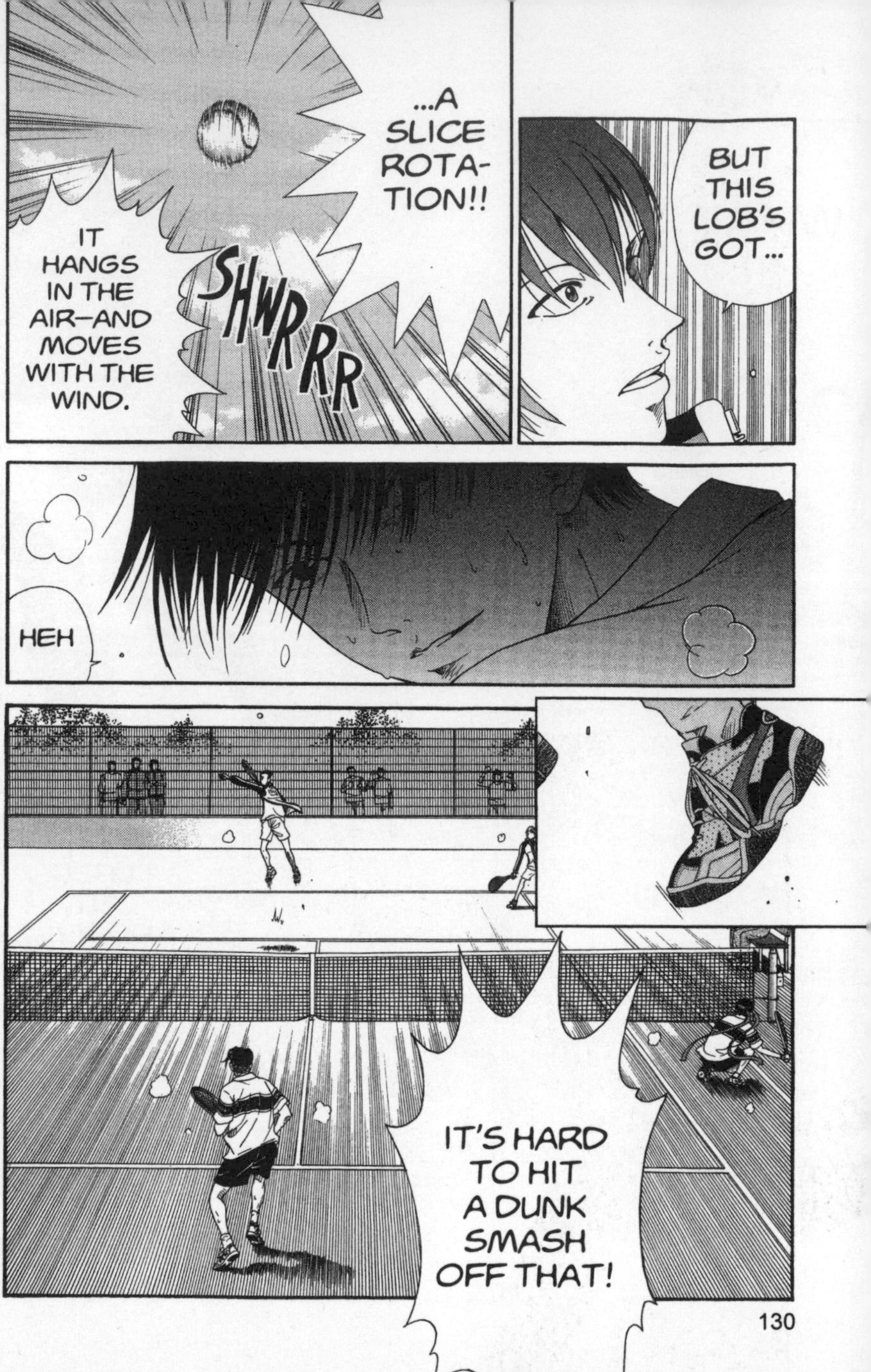
BUT THIS LOB'S GOT...
...A SLICE ROTATION!!
SHWRRRR
IT HANGS IN THE AIR—AND MOVES WITH THE WIND.
HEH
IT'S HARD TO HIT A DUNK SMASH OFF THAT!

READ THIS WAY

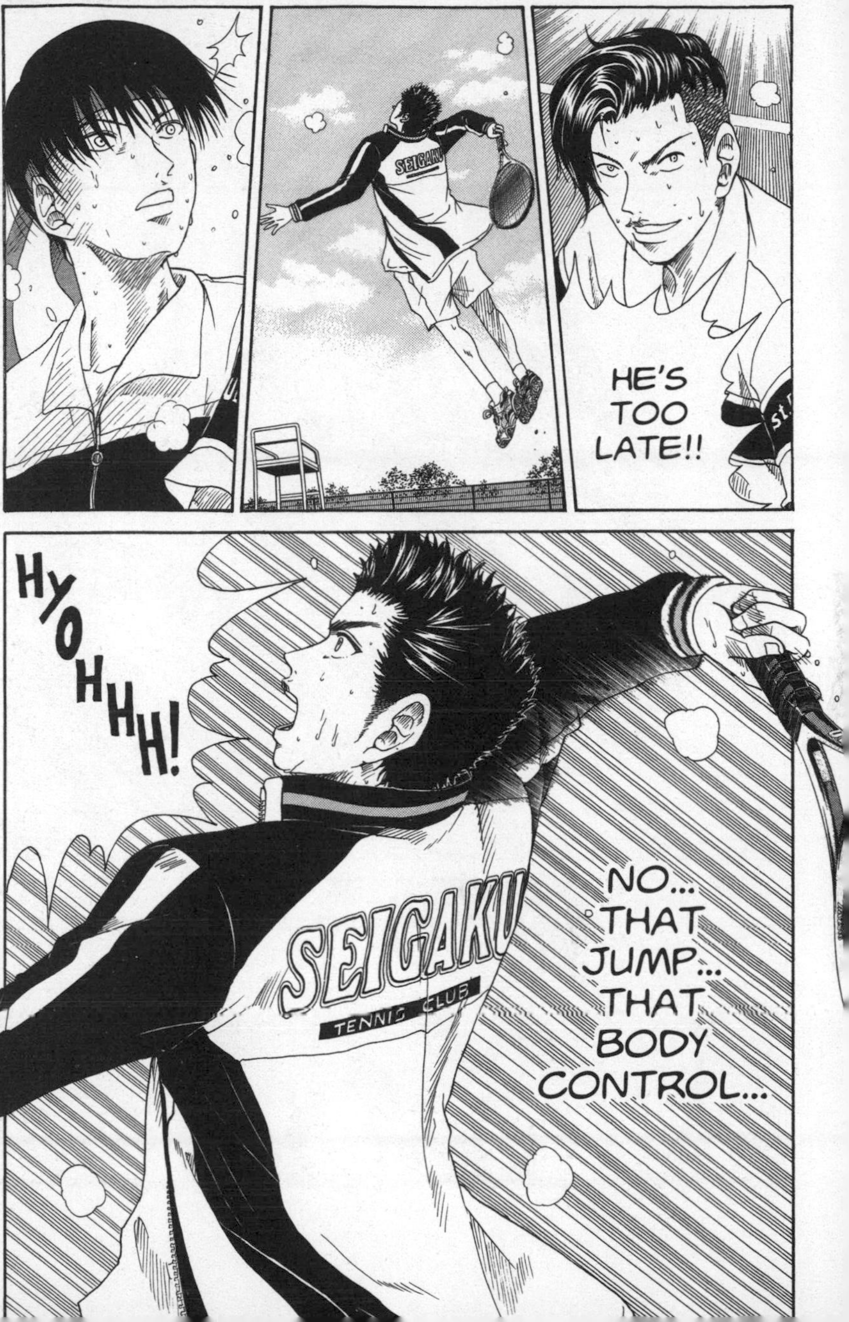

HE'S TOO LATE!!
NO... THAT JUMP... THAT BODY CONTROL...
HYOHHH!
SEIGAKU
TENNIS CLUB

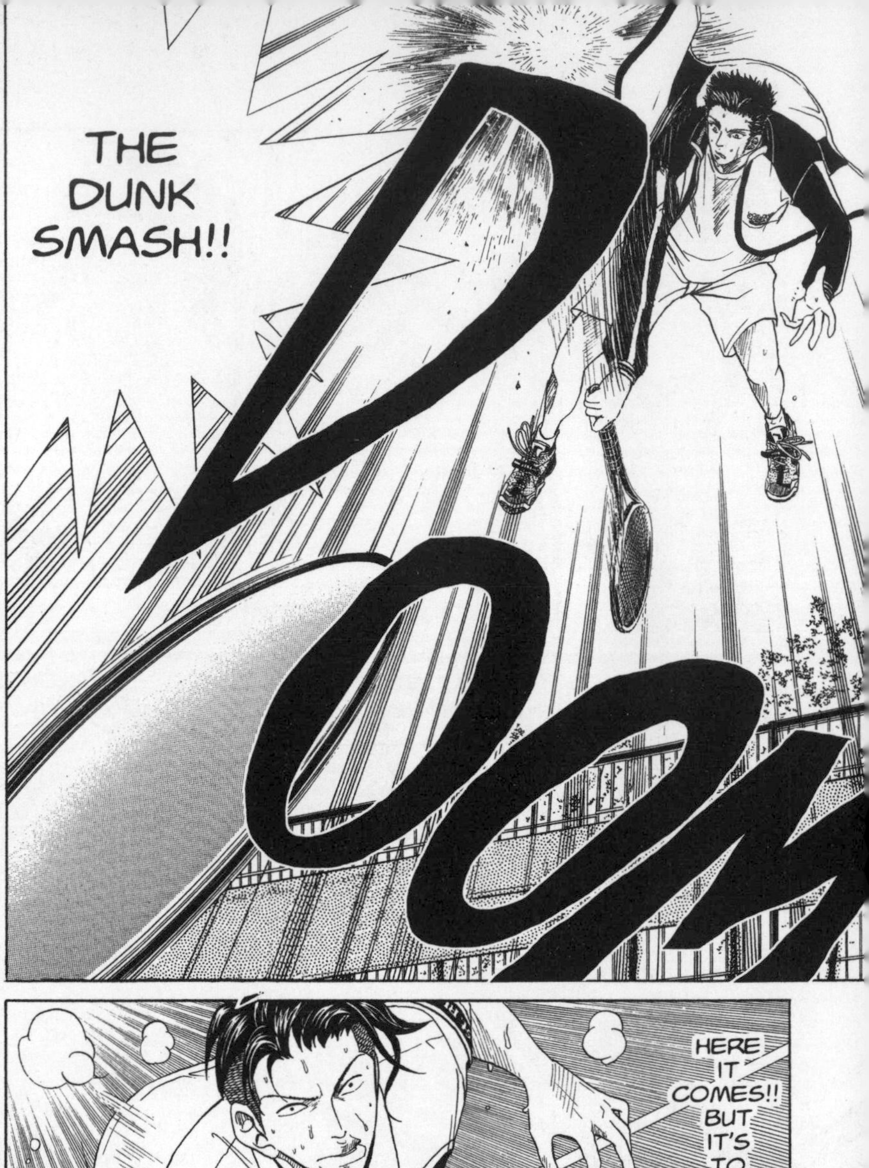
THE DUNK SMASH!!
DOOM
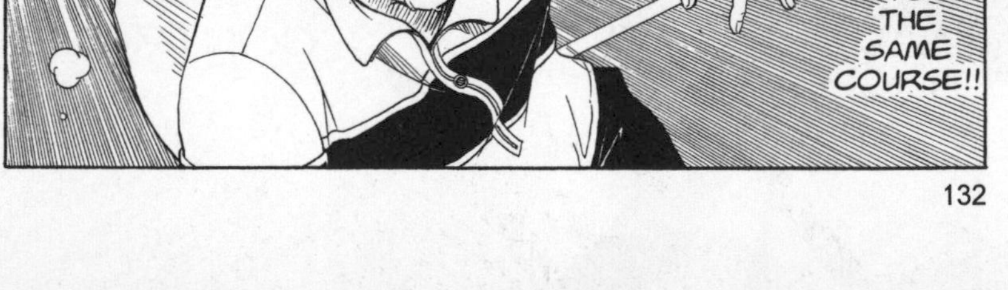
HERE IT COMES!! BUT IT'S TO THE SAME COURSE!!

READ THIS WAY

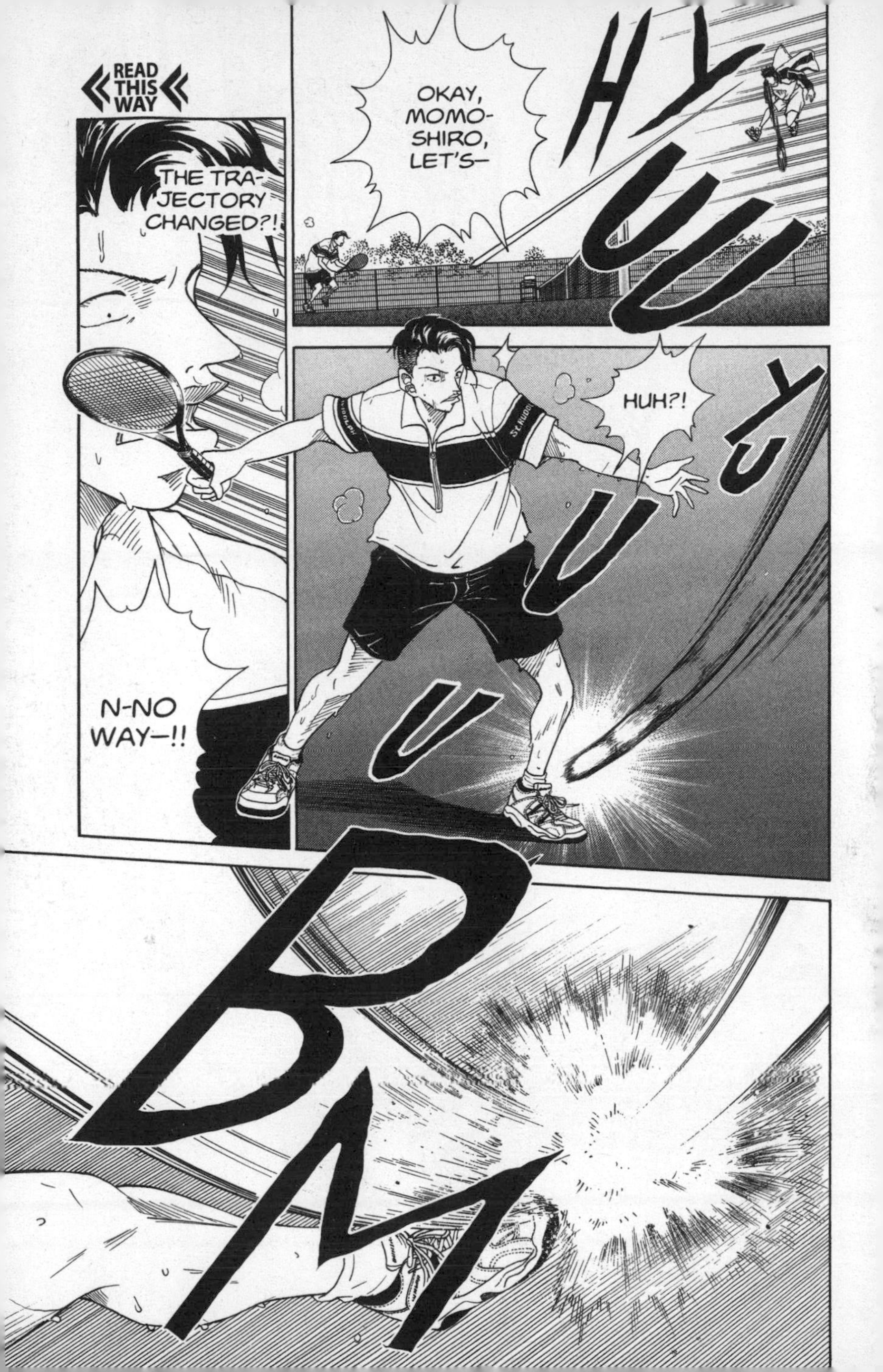
HYUUU
OKAY, MOMO-SHIRO, LET'S—
THE TRA-JECTORY CHANGED?!
YUUUU
HUH?!
N-NO WAY—!!
BAM

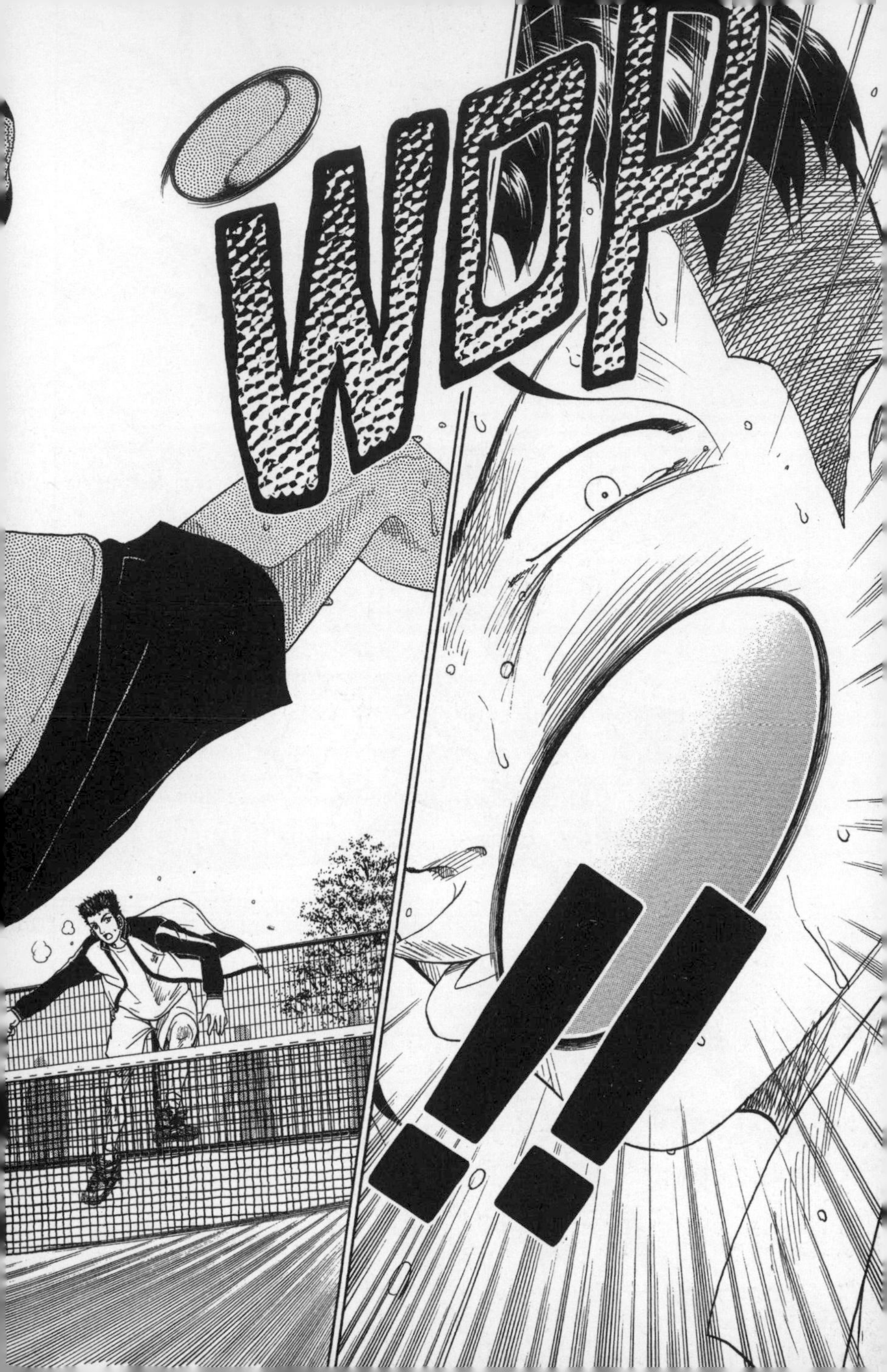

WOP
!!

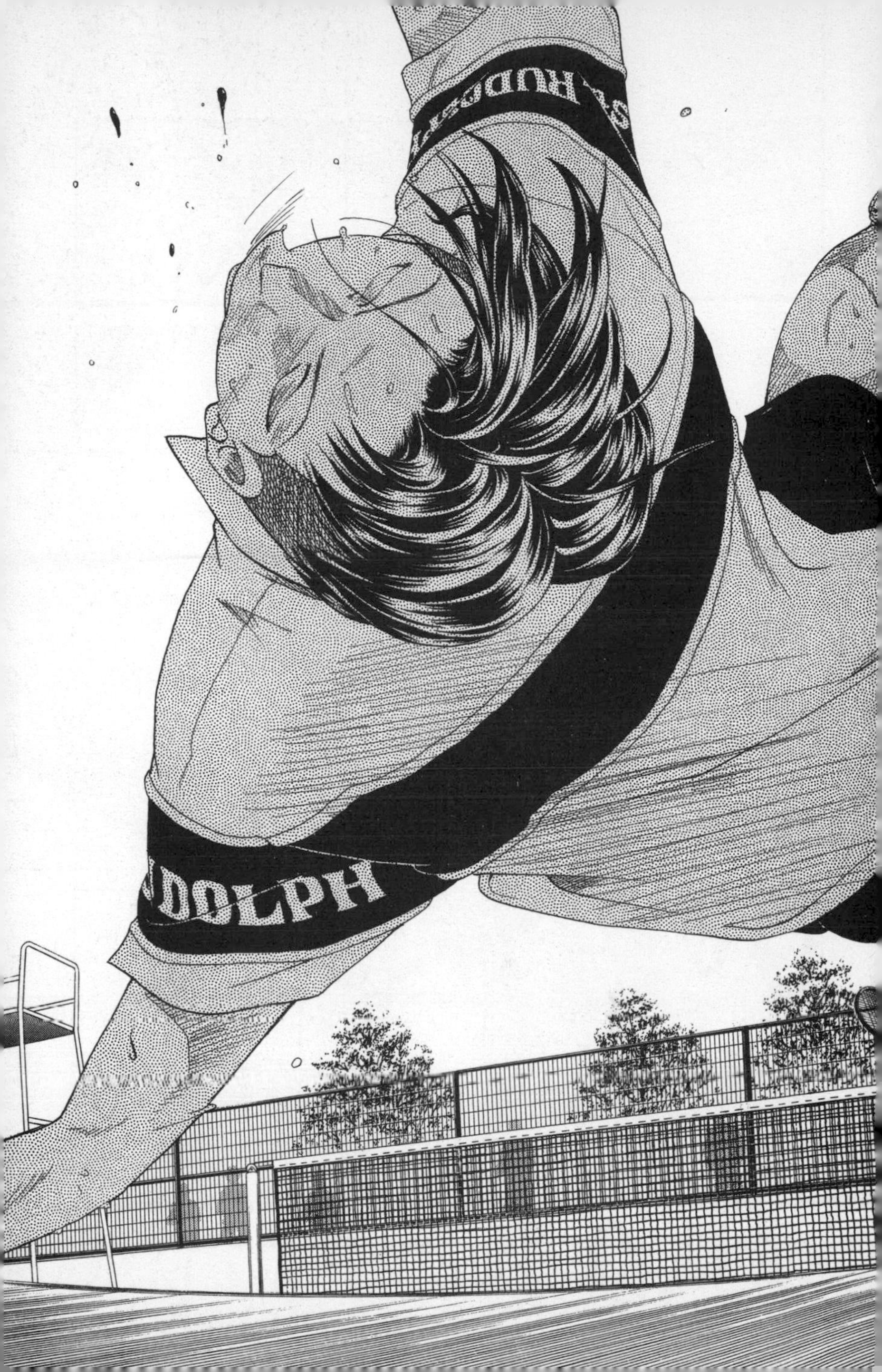
DOLPH

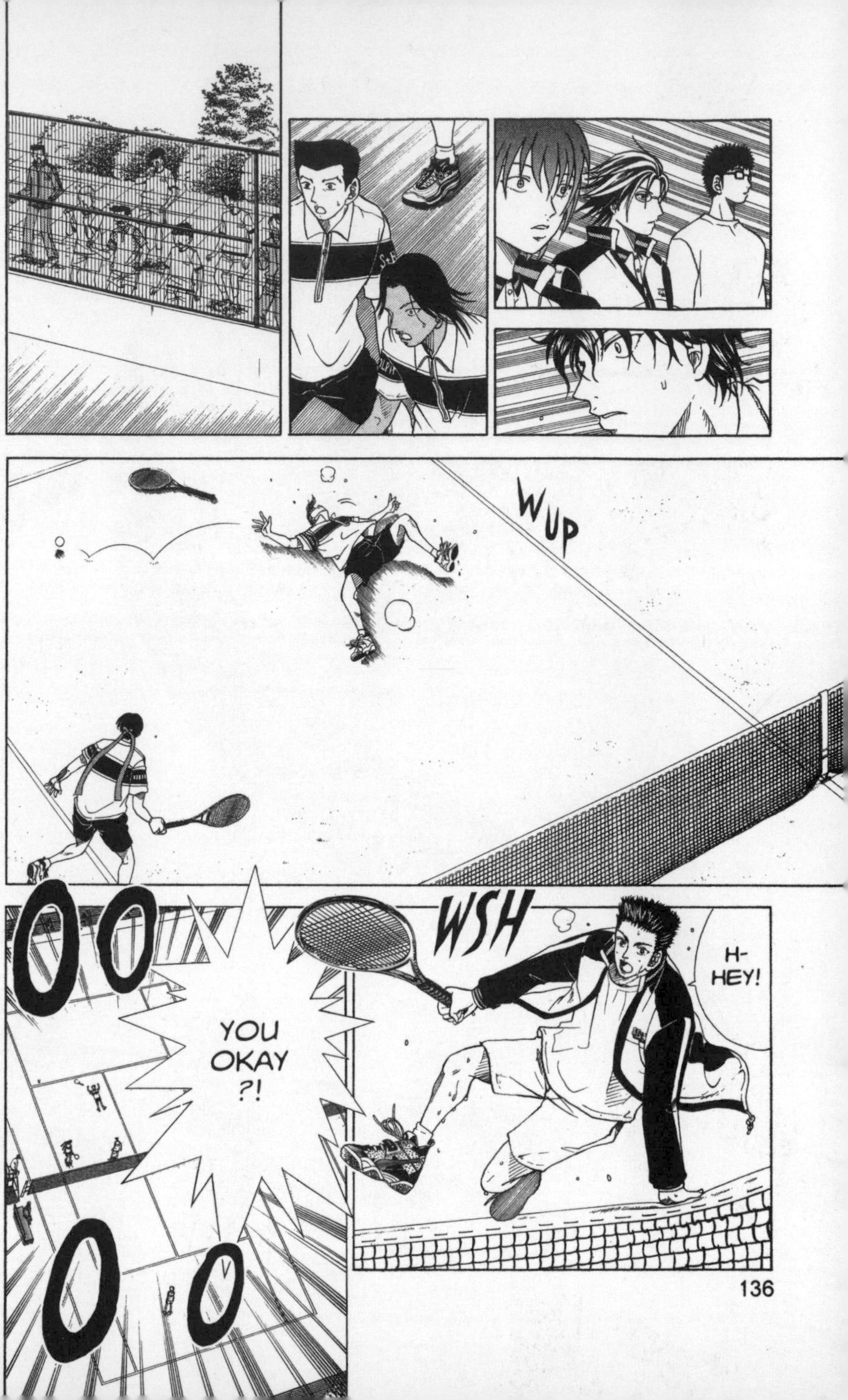
WUP
WSH
H-HEY!
OOOO
YOU OKAY ?!

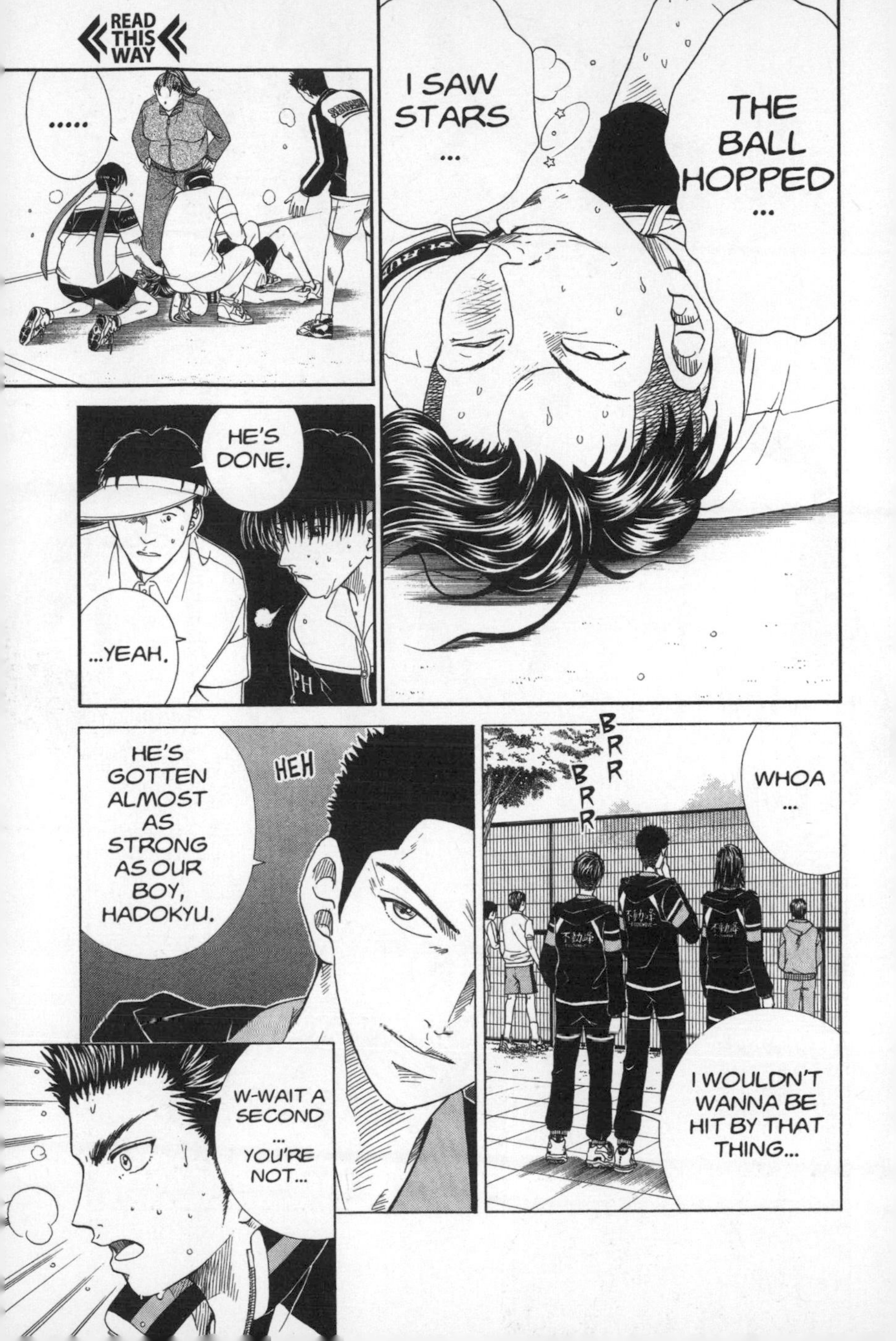
READ THIS WAY
THE BALL HOPPED ...
I SAW STARS ...
.....
HE'S DONE.
...YEAH.
BRRR BRRR
WHOA ...
I WOULDN'T WANNA BE HIT BY THAT THING...
HEH
HE'S GOTTEN ALMOST AS STRONG AS OUR BOY, HADOKYU.
W-WAIT A SECOND ... YOU'RE NOT...

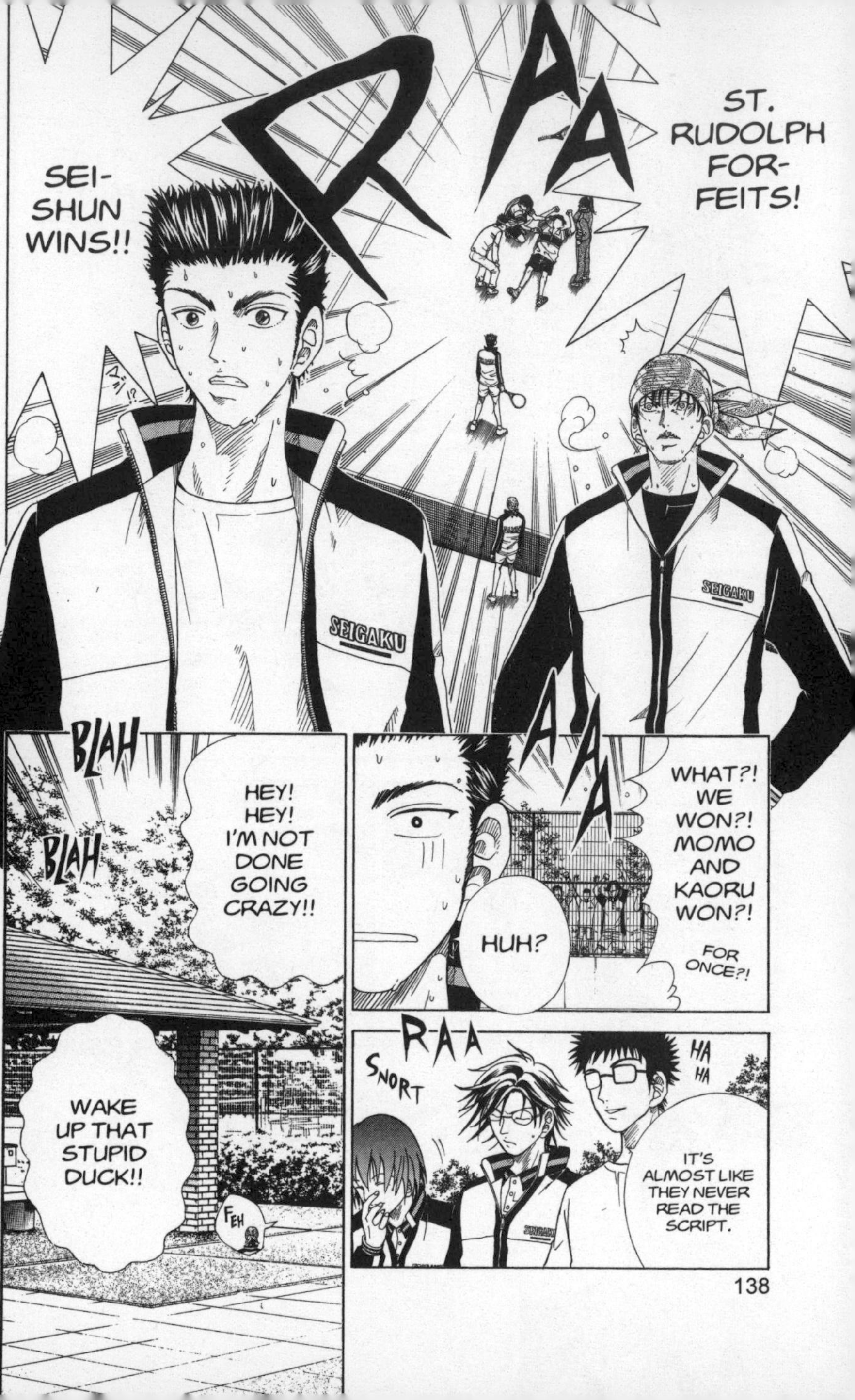
RAA
ST. RUDOLPH FOR-FEITS!
SEI-SHUN WINS!!
AAA
WHAT?! WE WON?! MOMO AND KAORU WON?!
FOR ONCE?!
HUH?
RAA
SNORT
HA HA
IT'S ALMOST LIKE THEY NEVER READ THE SCRIPT.
BLAH
BLAH
HEY! HEY! I'M NOT DONE GOING CRAZY!!
WAKE UP THAT STUPID DUCK!!
FEH

GENIUS 68: 1-1

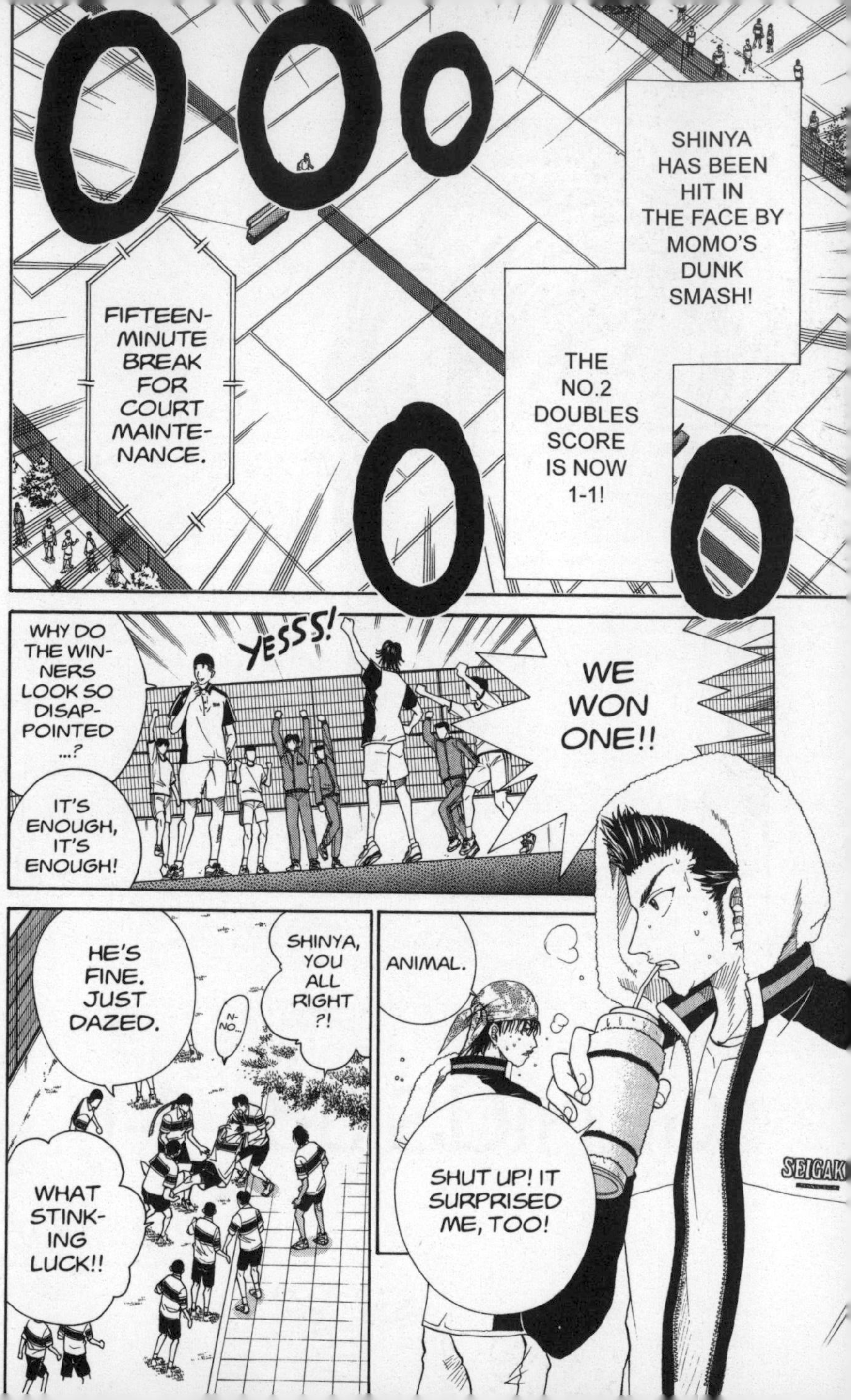
OOOOO
SHINYA HAS BEEN HIT IN THE FACE BY MOMO'S DUNK SMASH!
THE NO.2 DOUBLES SCORE IS NOW 1-1!
FIFTEEN-MINUTE BREAK FOR COURT MAINTENANCE.
WE WON ONE!!
YESSS!
WHY DO THE WINNERS LOOK SO DISAPPOINTED...?
IT'S ENOUGH, IT'S ENOUGH!
ANIMAL.
SHUT UP! IT SURPRISED ME, TOO!
SHINYA, YOU ALL RIGHT?!
N-NO...
HE'S FINE. JUST DAZED.
WHAT STINKING LUCK!!

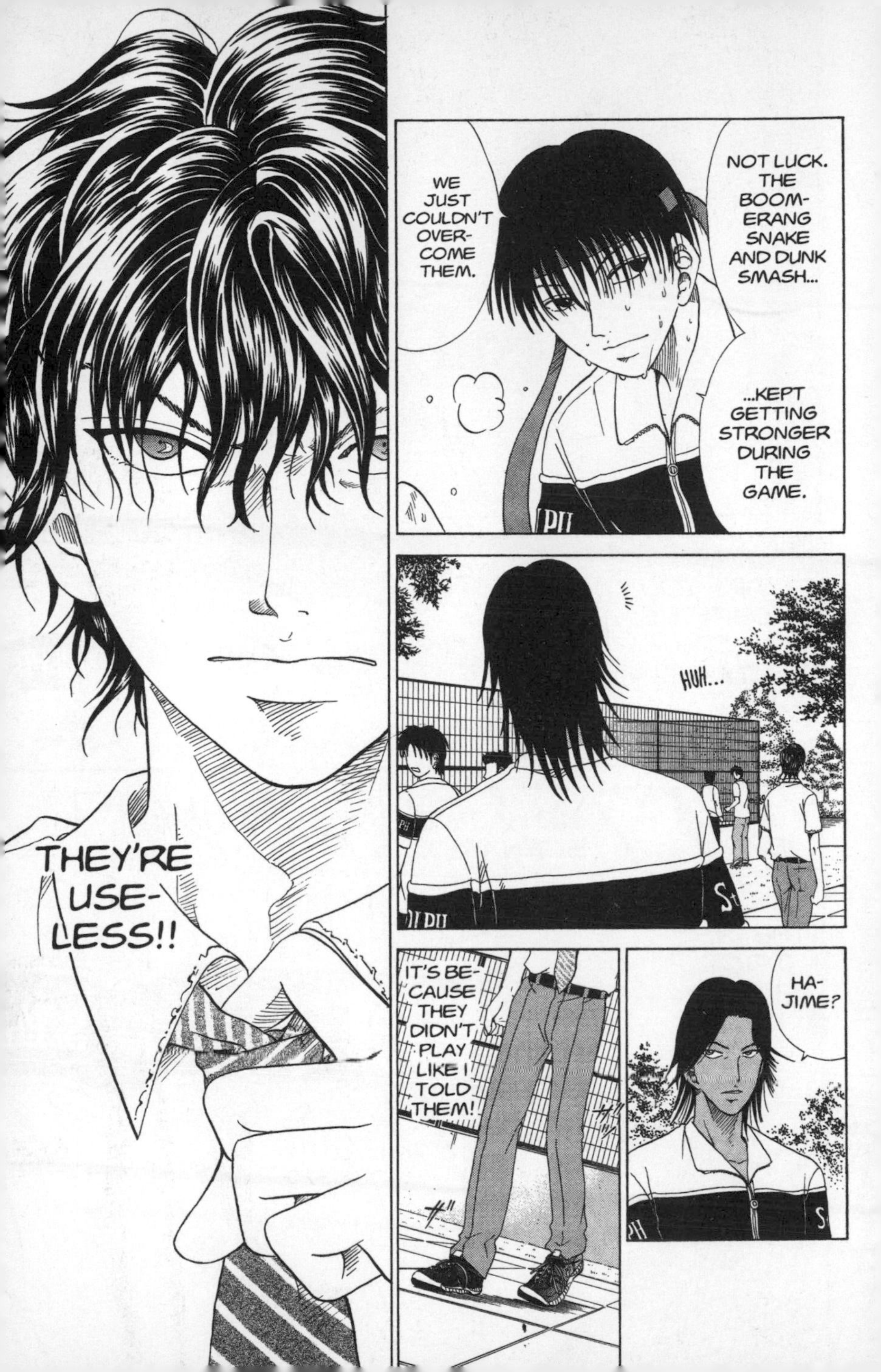
NOT LUCK. THE BOOMERANG SNAKE AND DUNK SMASH...
...KEPT GETTING STRONGER DURING THE GAME.
WE JUST COULDN'T OVERCOME THEM.
HUH...
HAJIME?
IT'S BECAUSE THEY DIDN'T PLAY LIKE I TOLD THEM!
THEY'RE USELESS!!

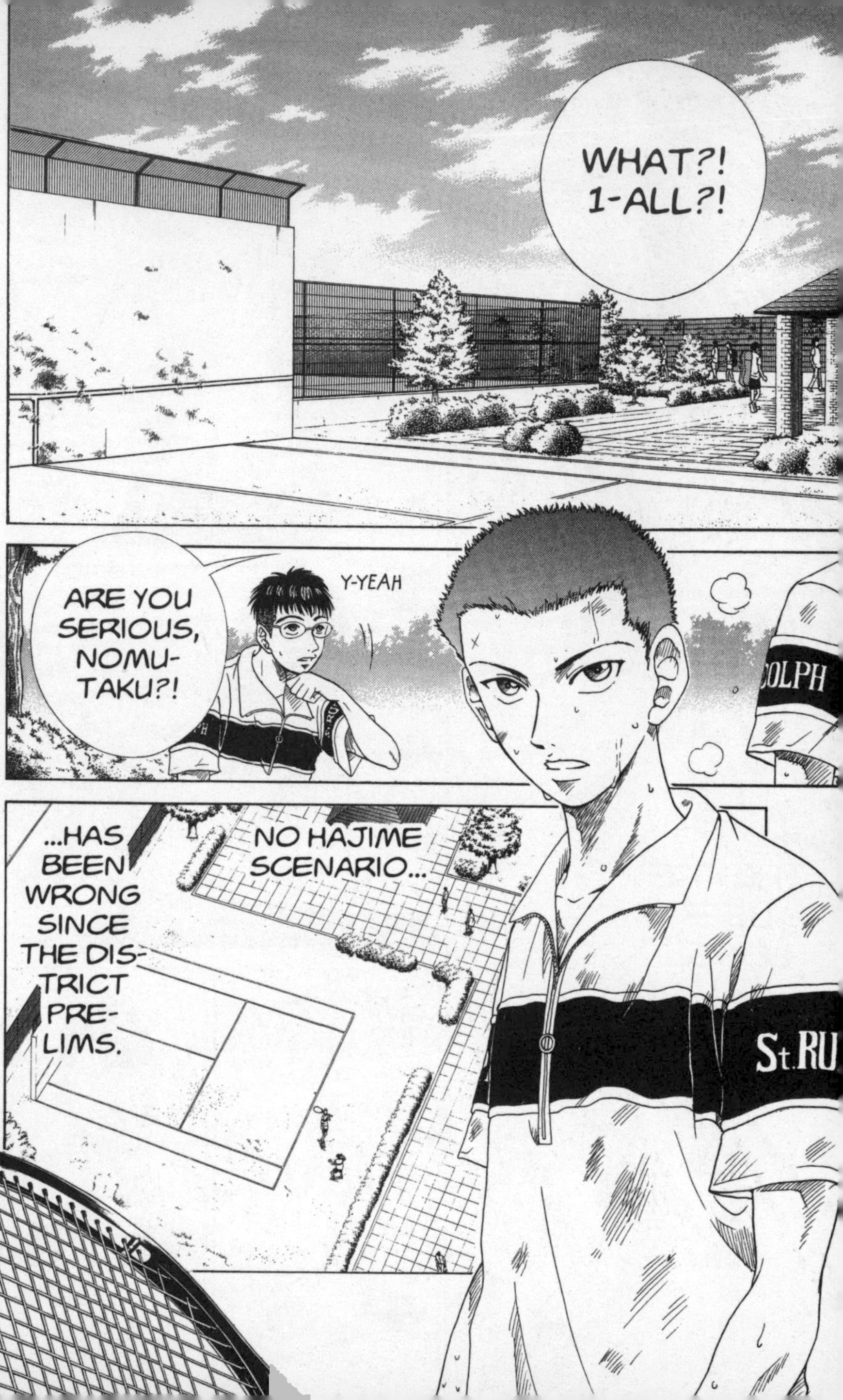
WHAT?! 1-ALL?!
ARE YOU SERIOUS, NOMU-TAKU?!
Y-YEAH
NO HAJIME SCENARIO...
...HAS BEEN WRONG SINCE THE DIS-TRICT PRE-LIMS.
St.RU
OLPH

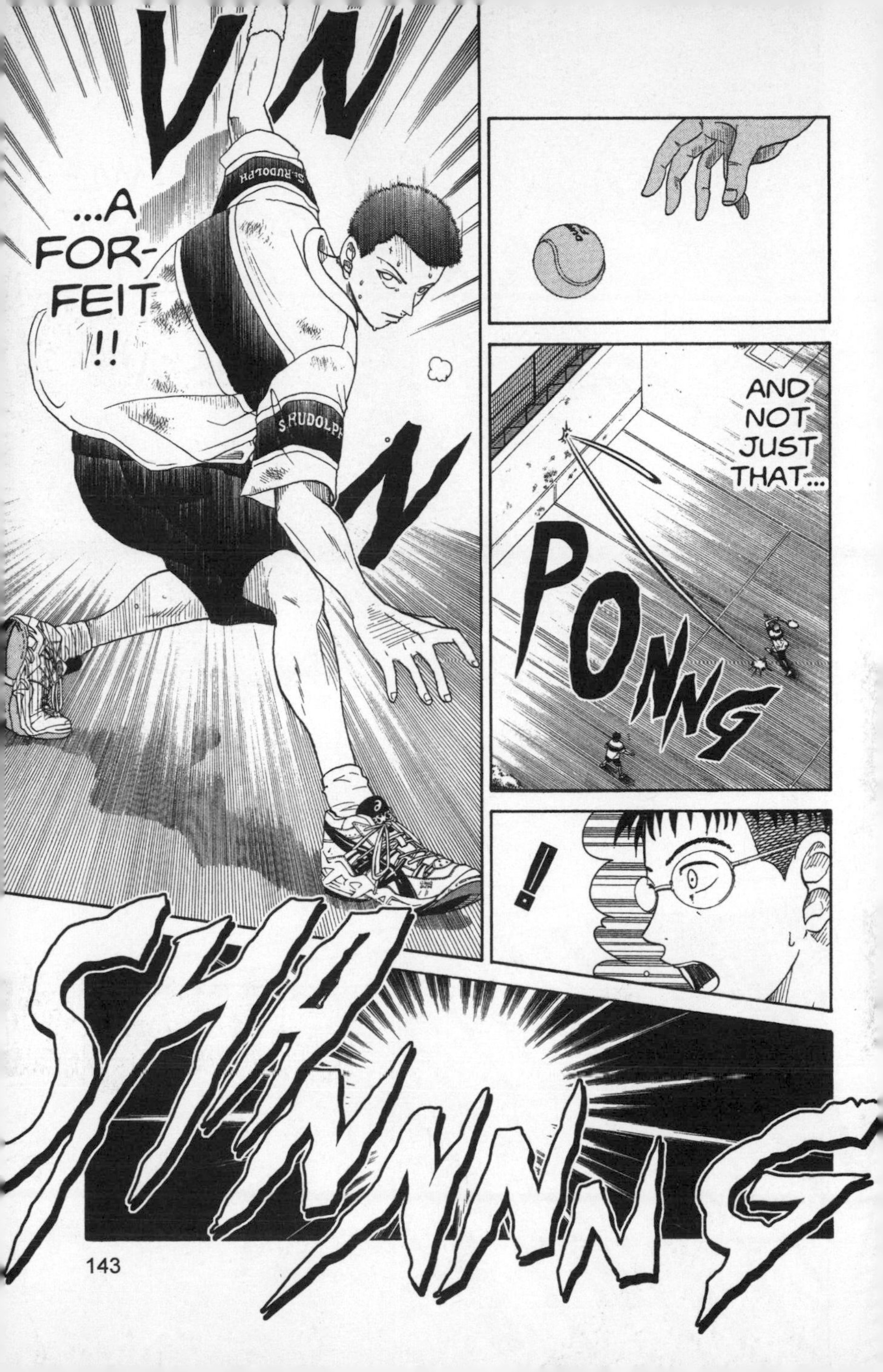
AND NOT JUST THAT...
PONNG
!
VN
...A FOR-FEIT!!
N
SHANNNG

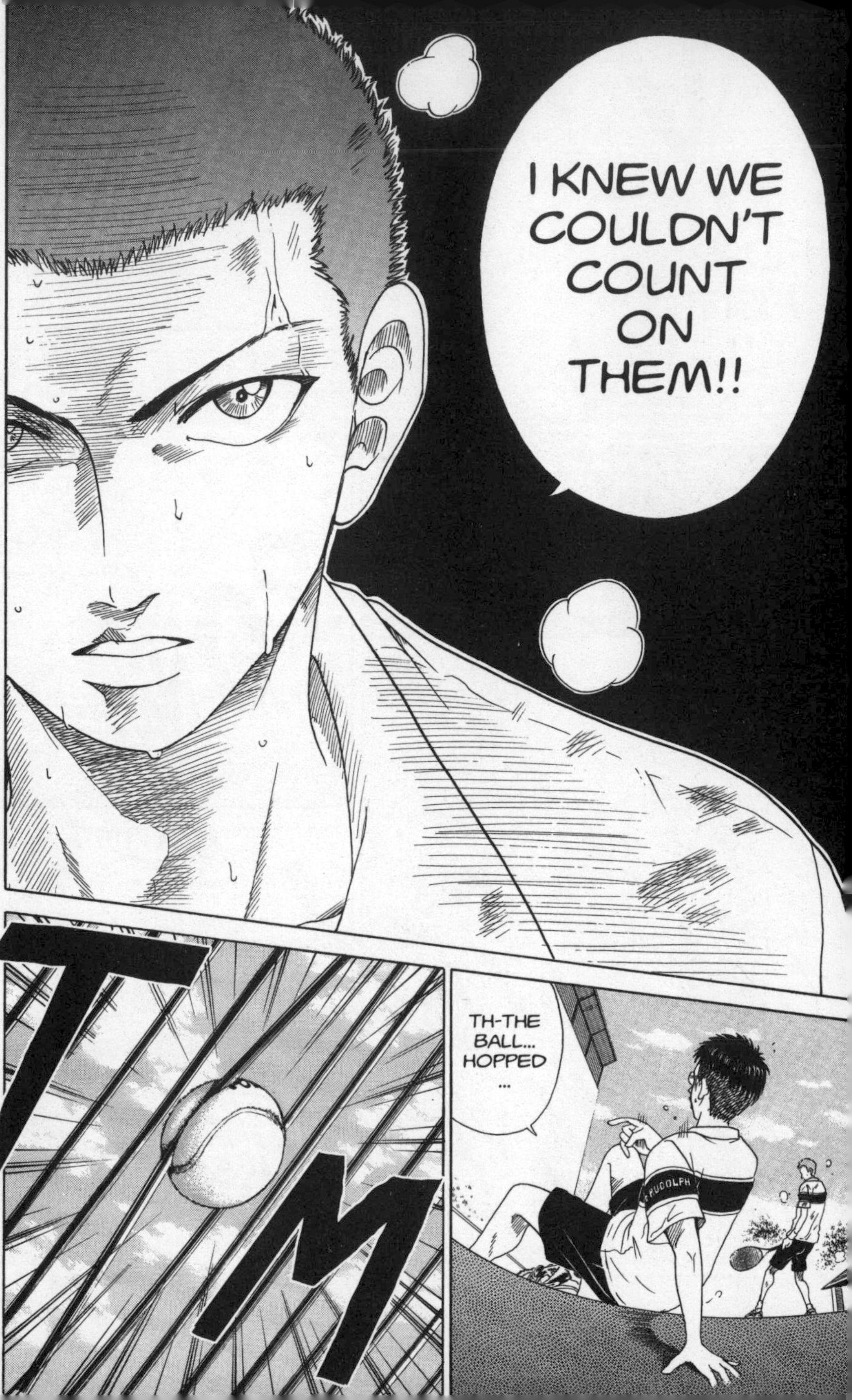
I KNEW WE COULDN'T COUNT ON THEM!!
TH-THE BALL... HOPPED ...
TM

READ THIS WAY

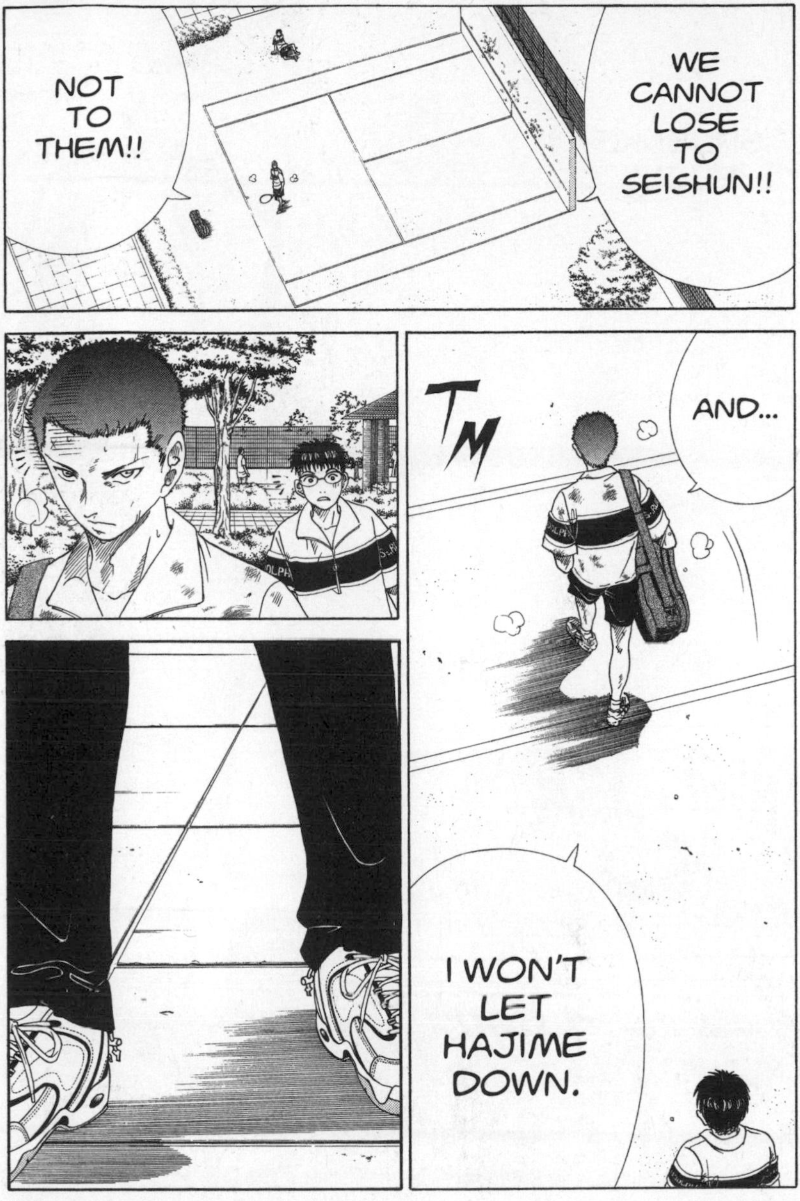

WE CANNOT LOSE TO SEISHUN!!
NOT TO THEM!!
AND...
TM
I WON'T LET HAJIME DOWN.

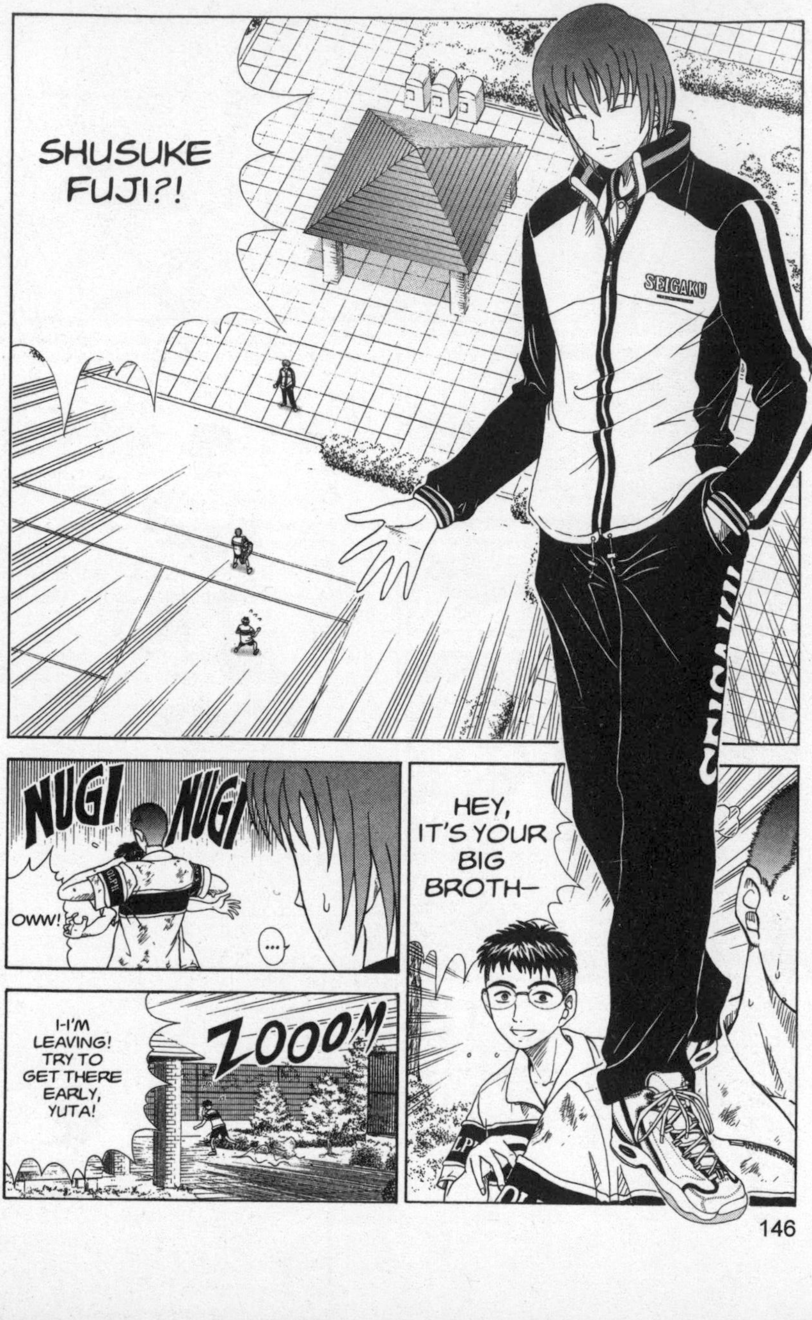
SHUSUKE FUJI?!
SEIGAKU
HEY, IT'S YOUR BIG BROTH—
NUGI NUGI
OWW!
...
I-I'M LEAVING! TRY TO GET THERE EARLY, YUTA!
ZOOOM

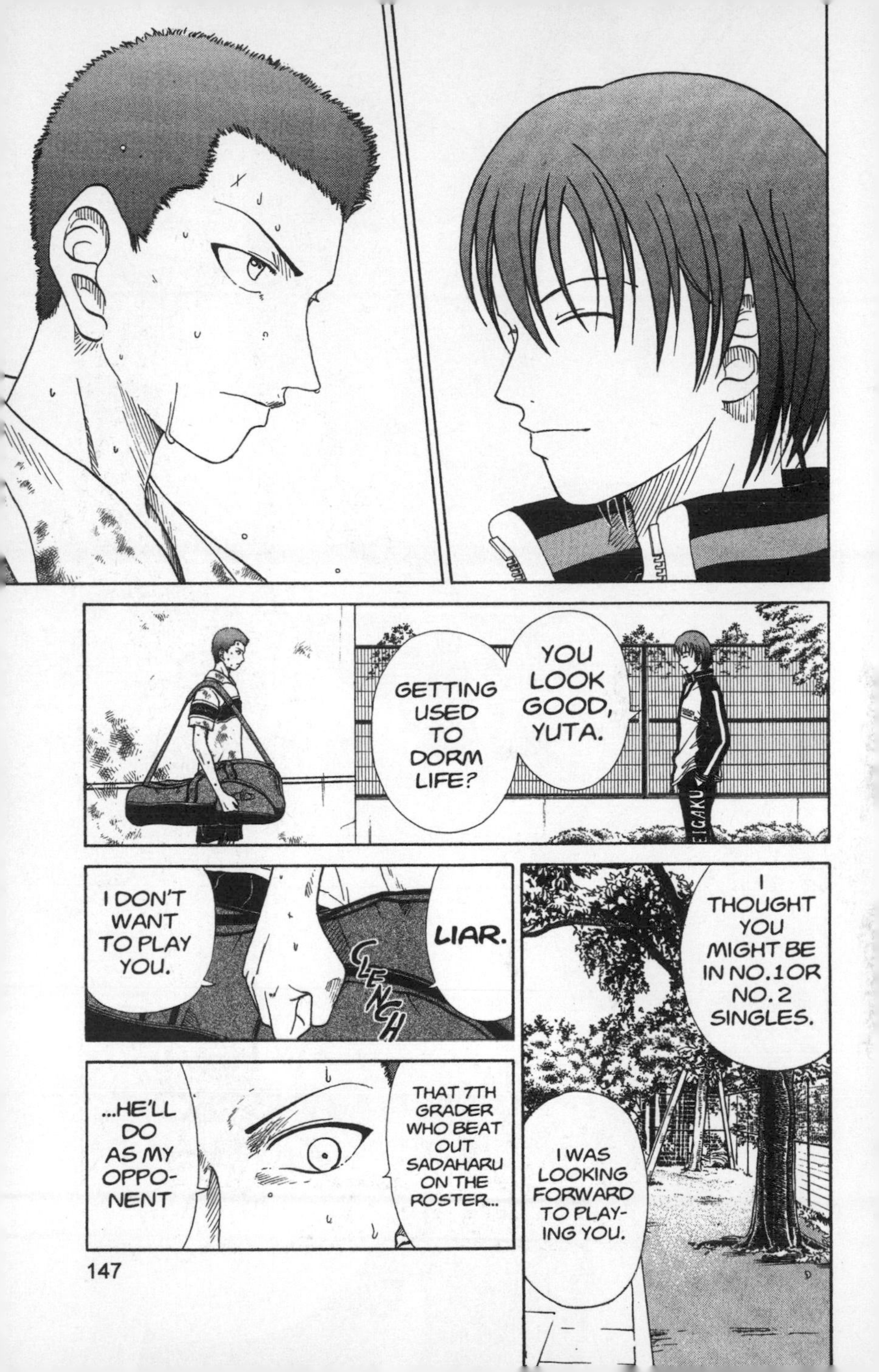
YOU LOOK GOOD, YUTA.
GETTING USED TO DORM LIFE?
I THOUGHT YOU MIGHT BE IN NO.1OR NO.2 SINGLES.
I WAS LOOKING FORWARD TO PLAYING YOU.
LIAR.
CLENCH
I DON'T WANT TO PLAY YOU.
THAT 7TH GRADER WHO BEAT OUT SADAHARU ON THE ROSTER...
...HE'LL DO AS MY OPPONENT

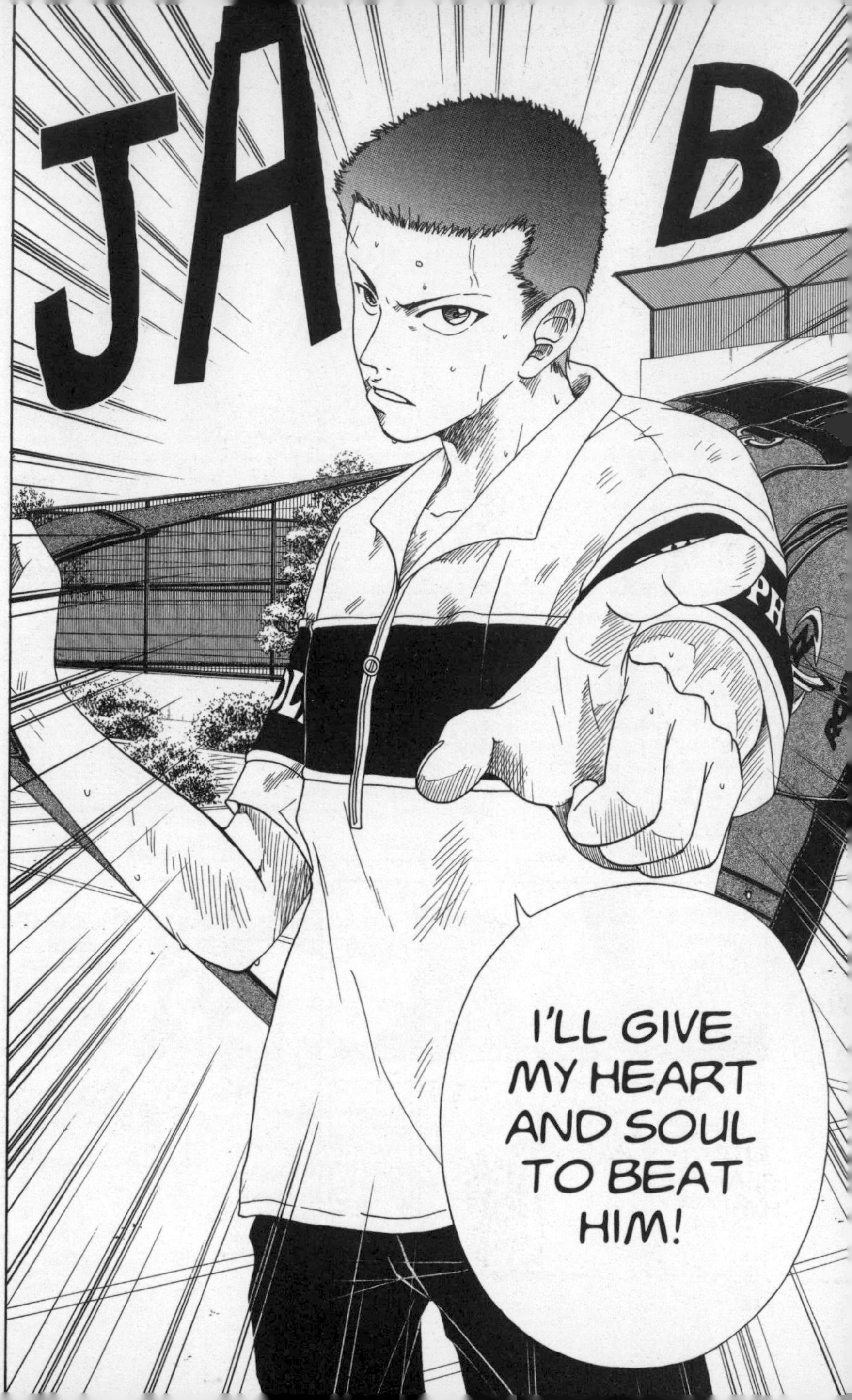
JAB
I'LL GIVE MY HEART AND SOUL TO BEAT HIM!

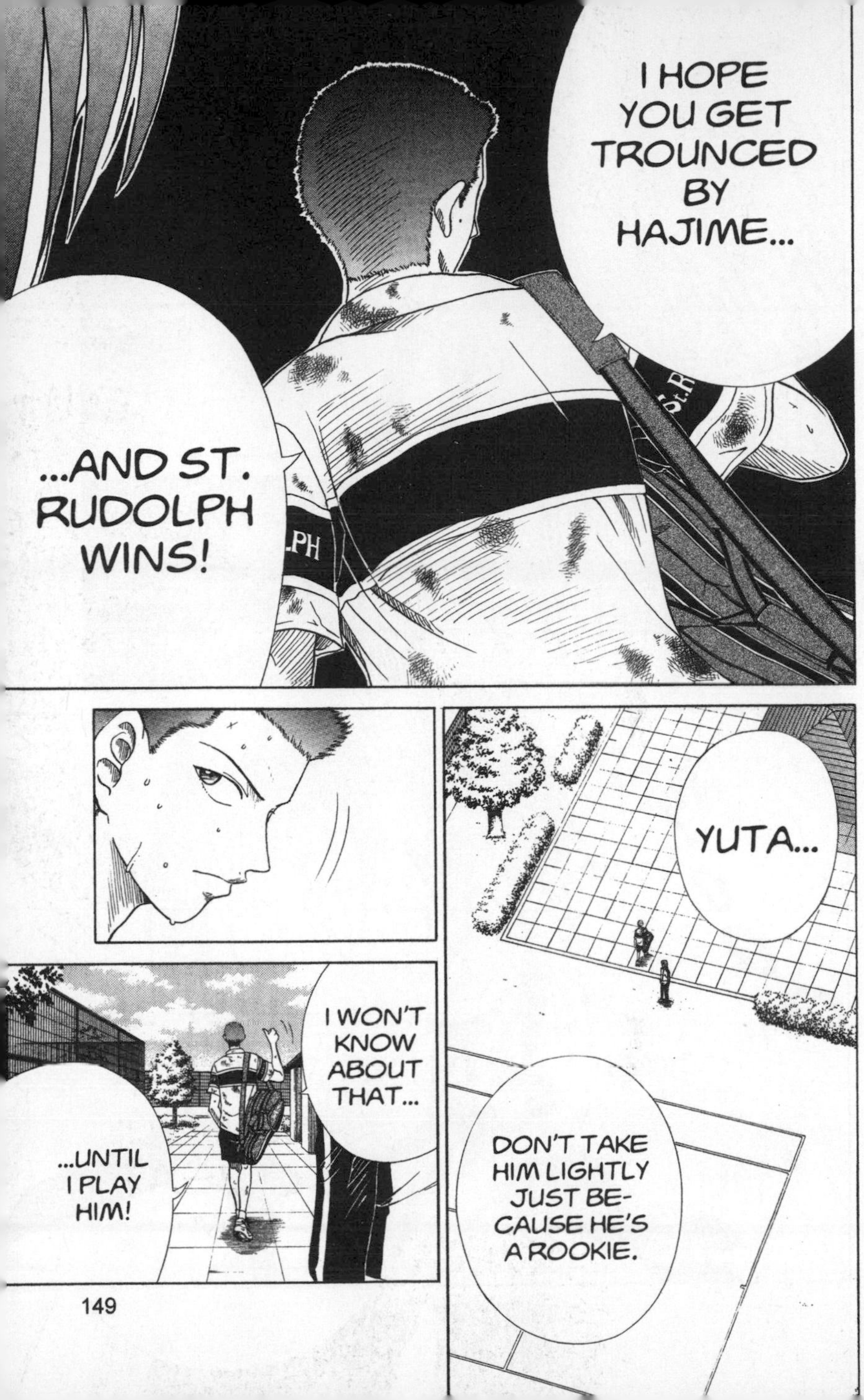
I HOPE YOU GET TROUNCED BY HAJIME...
...AND ST. RUDOLPH WINS!
YUTA...
DON'T TAKE HIM LIGHTLY JUST BE-CAUSE HE'S A ROOKIE.
I WON'T KNOW ABOUT THAT...
...UNTIL I PLAY HIM!

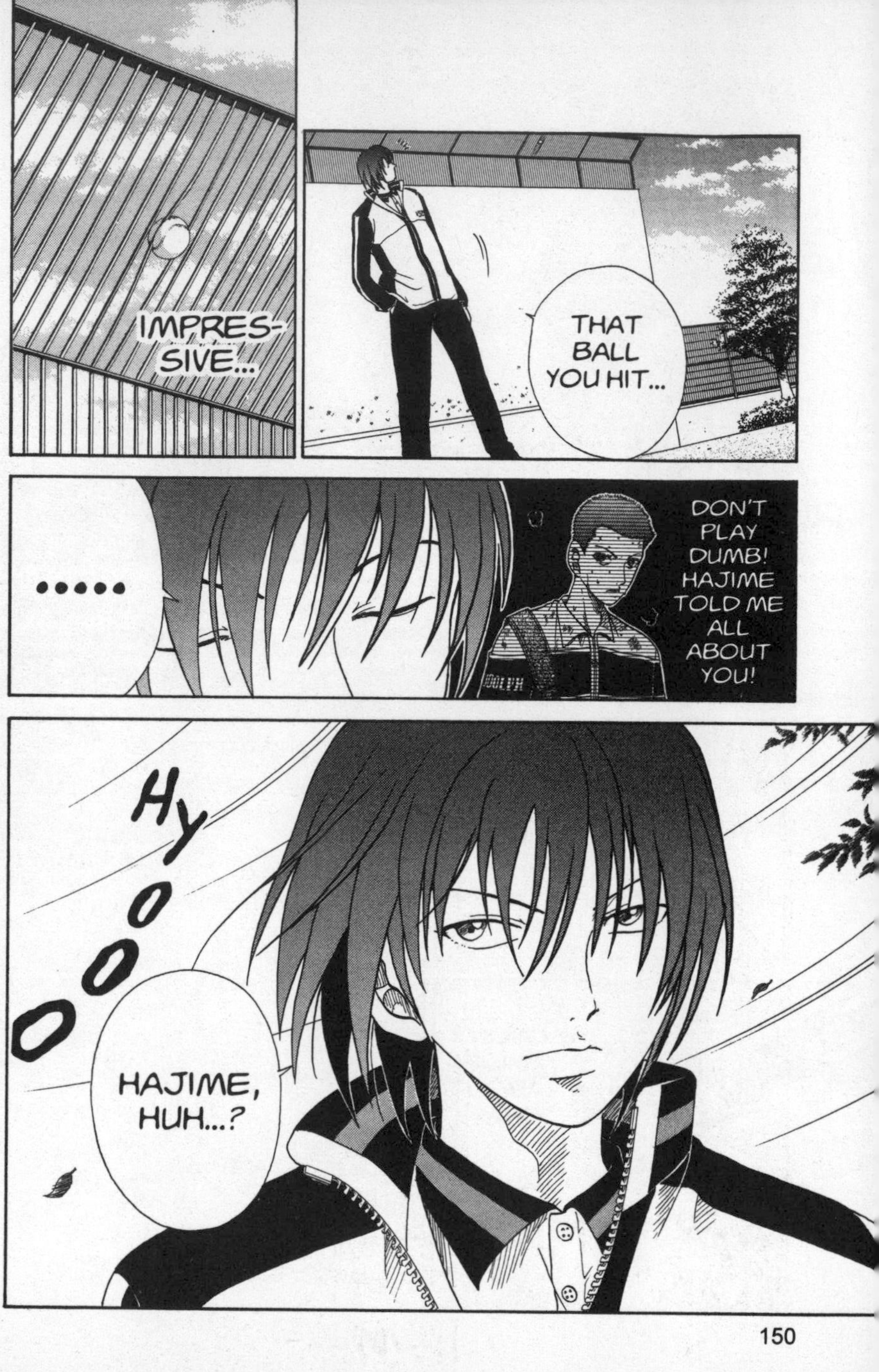
THAT BALL YOU HIT...
IMPRES-SIVE...
DON'T PLAY DUMB! HAJIME TOLD ME ALL ABOUT YOU!
.....
Hyoooo
HAJIME, HUH...?

READ THIS WAY

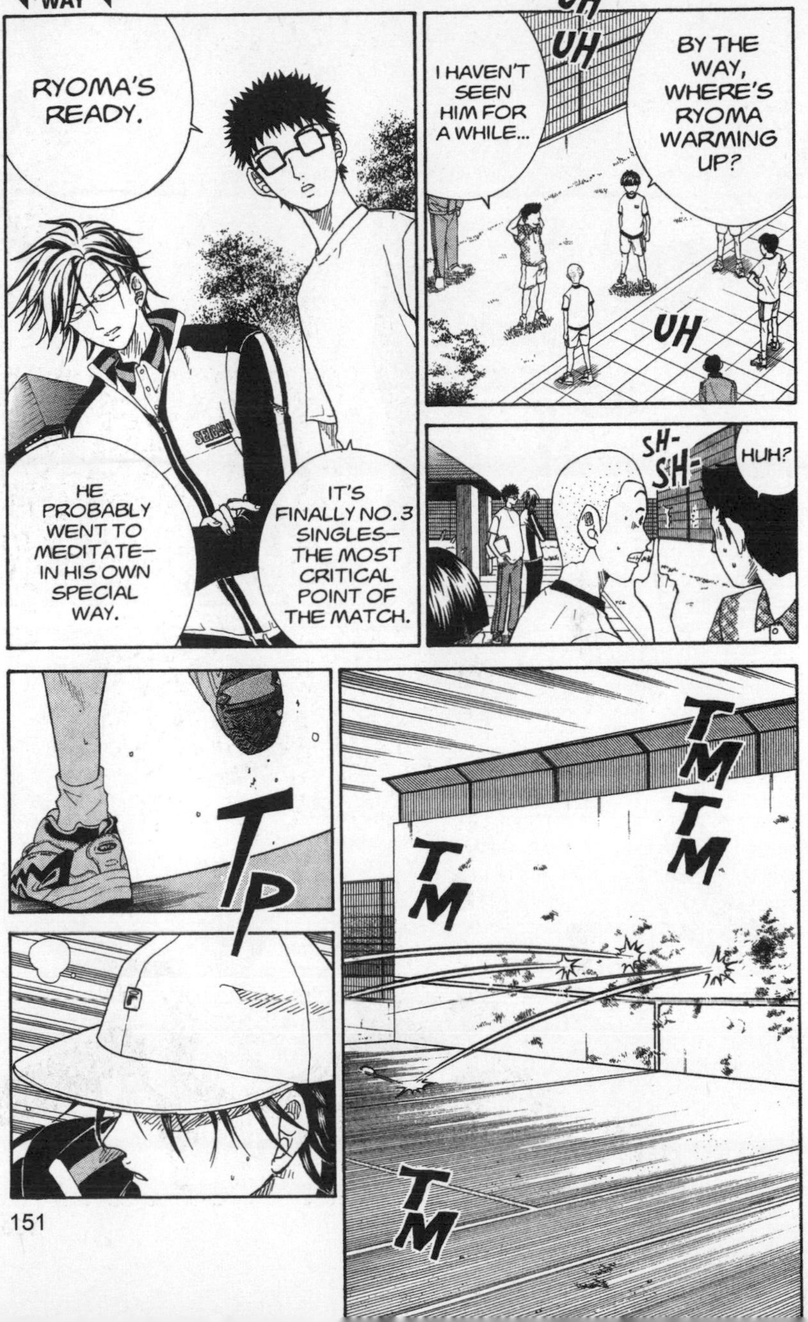
UH UH
BY THE WAY, WHERE'S RYOMA WARMING UP?
I HAVEN'T SEEN HIM FOR A WHILE...
UH
HUH?
SH- SH-
RYOMA'S READY.
IT'S FINALLY NO. 3 SINGLES— THE MOST CRITICAL POINT OF THE MATCH.
HE PROBABLY WENT TO MEDITATE— IN HIS OWN SPECIAL WAY.
TMTMTM
TM TM
TM TM
TP

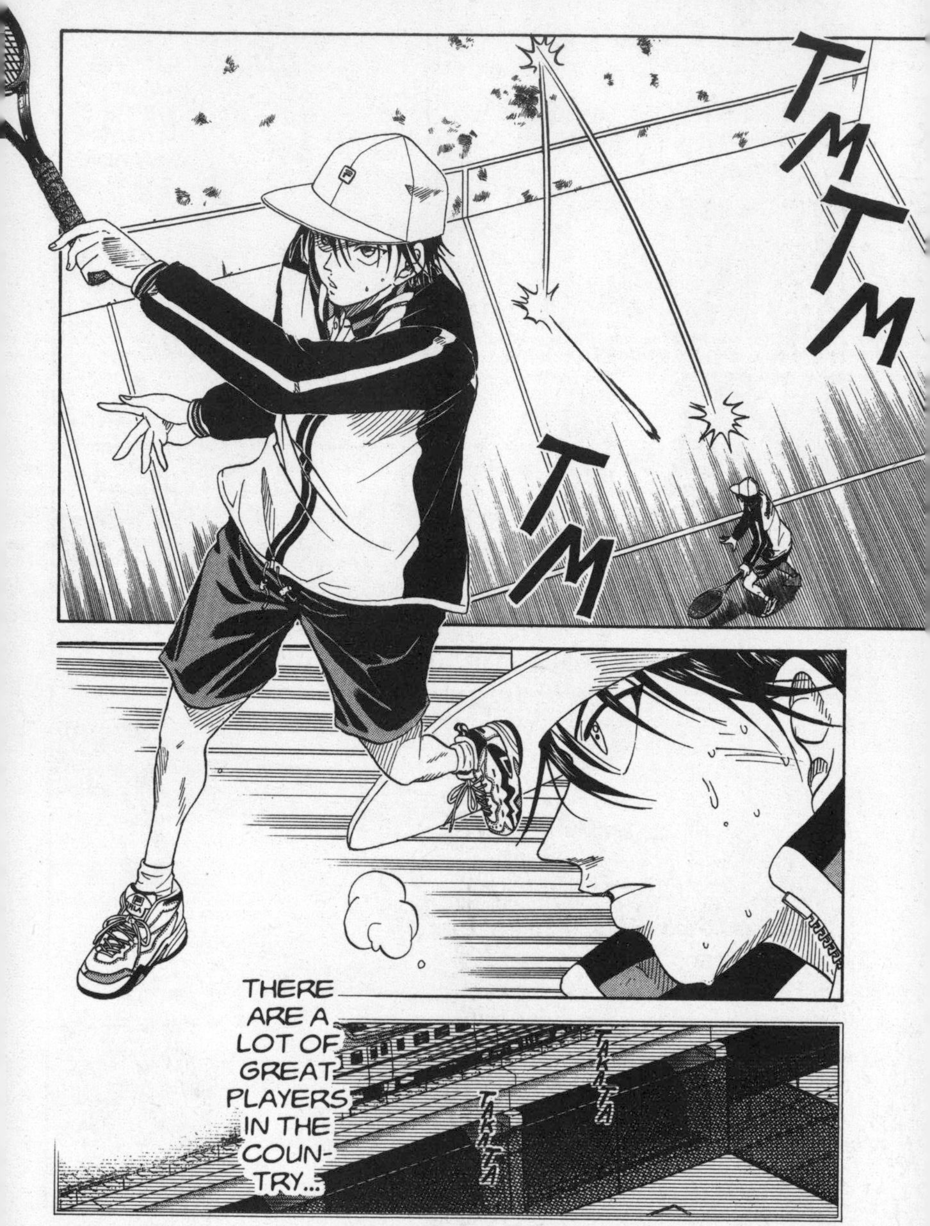
TMTM
TM
TAKATA
TAKATA
THERE ARE A LOT OF GREAT PLAYERS IN THE COUNTRY...

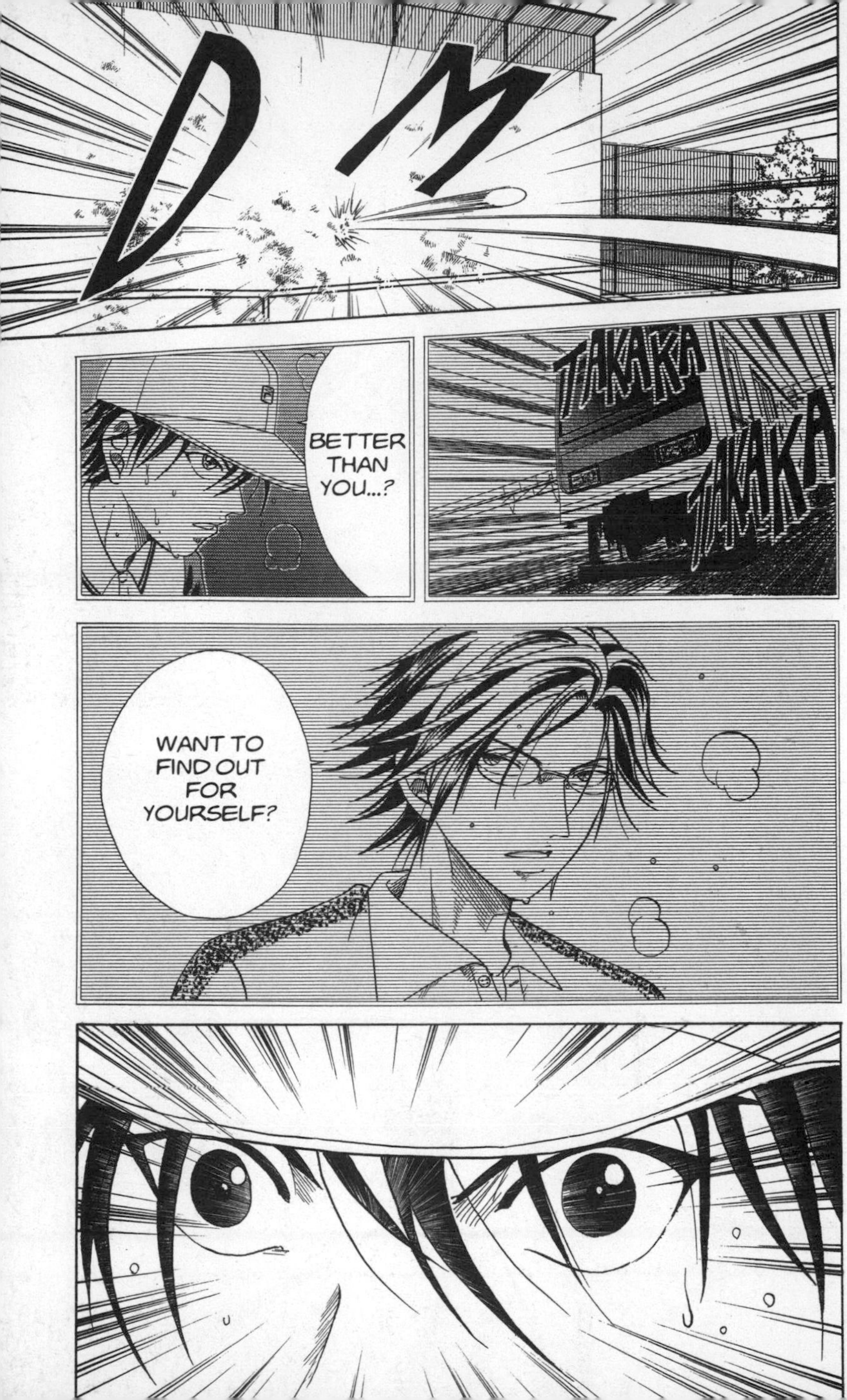
D M
TAKAKA
TAKAKA
BETTER THAN YOU...?
WANT TO FIND OUT FOR YOURSELF?

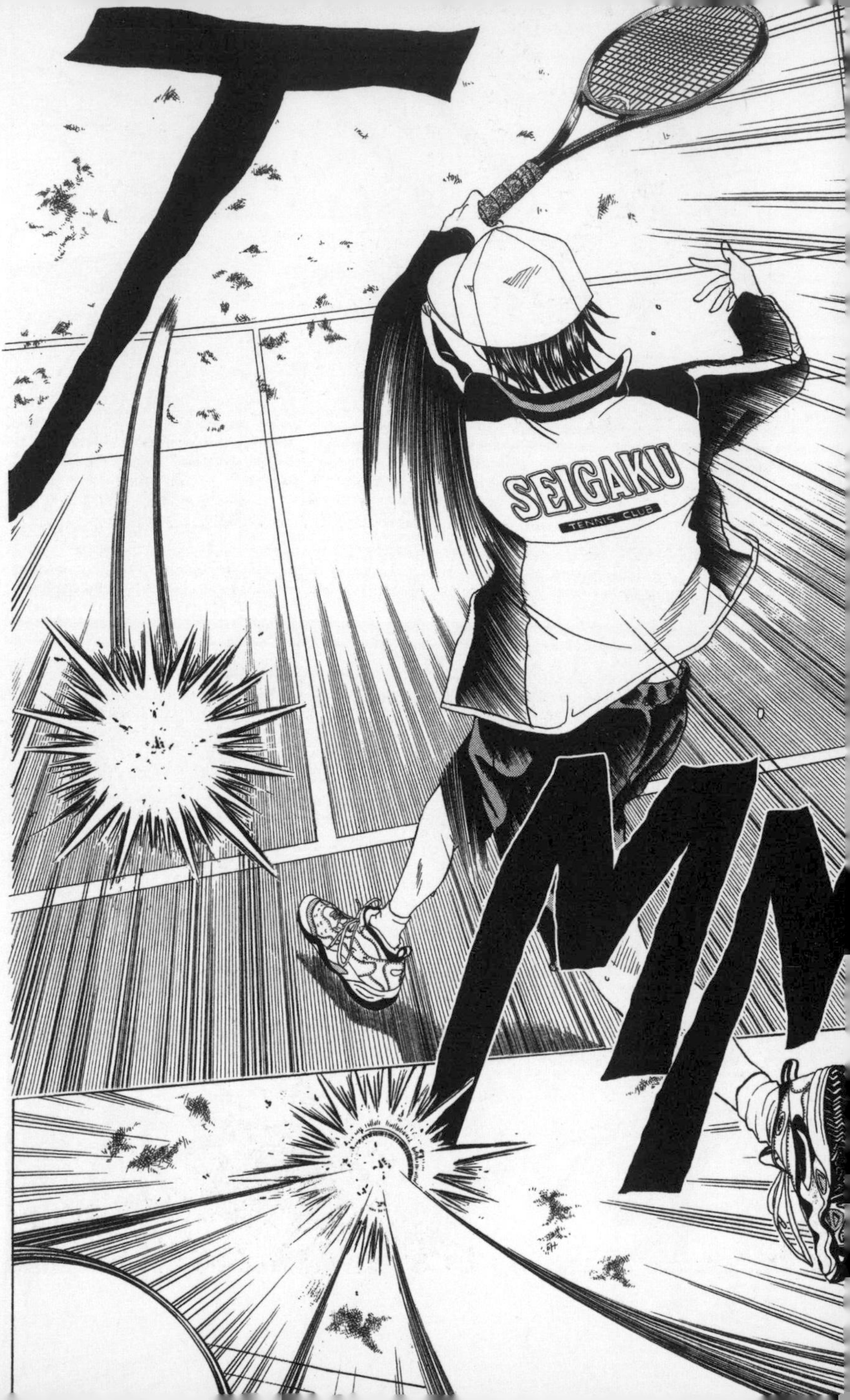
T
SEIGAKU
TENNIS CLUB
MM

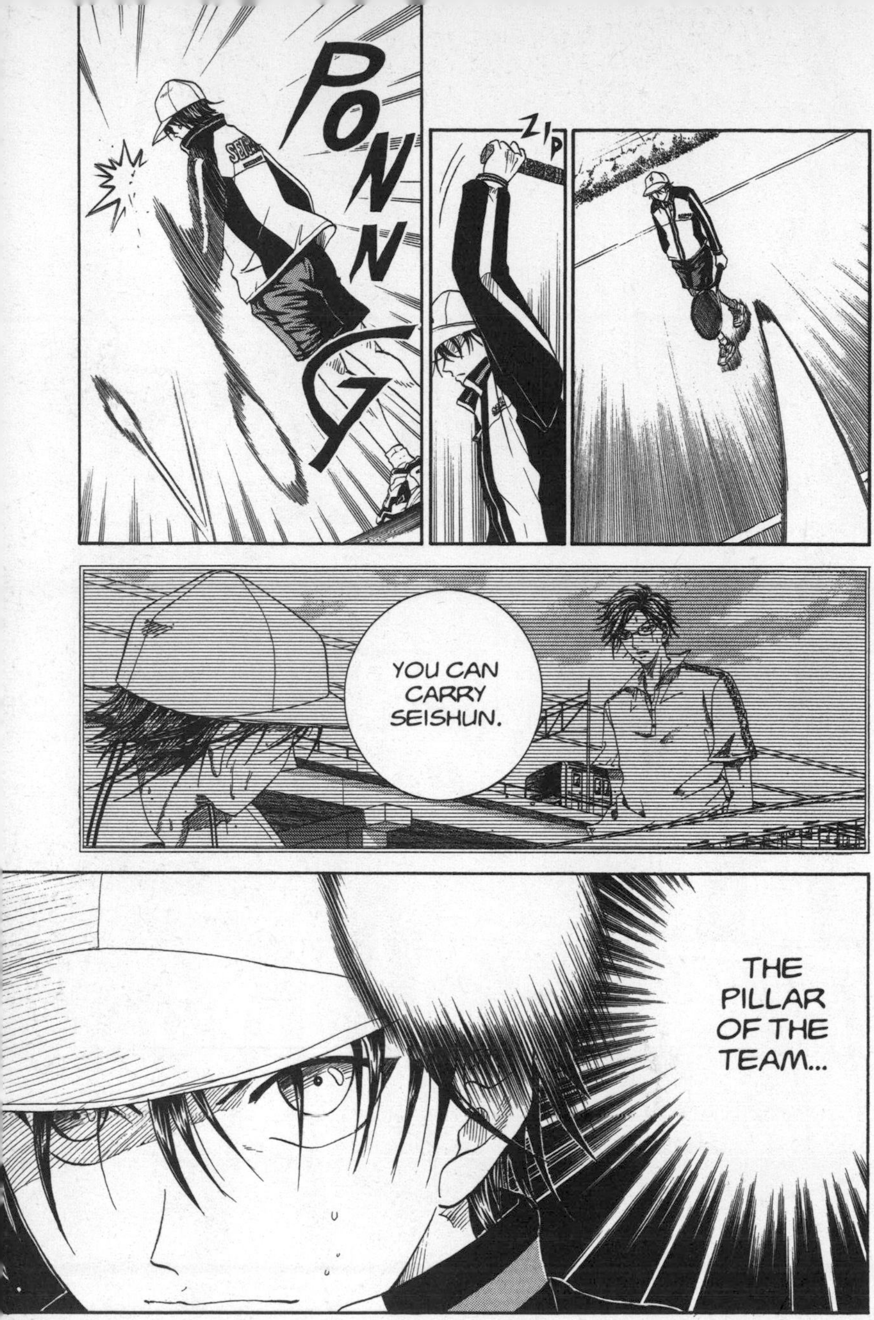
ZIP
PONNG
YOU CAN CARRY SEISHUN.
THE PILLAR OF THE TEAM...

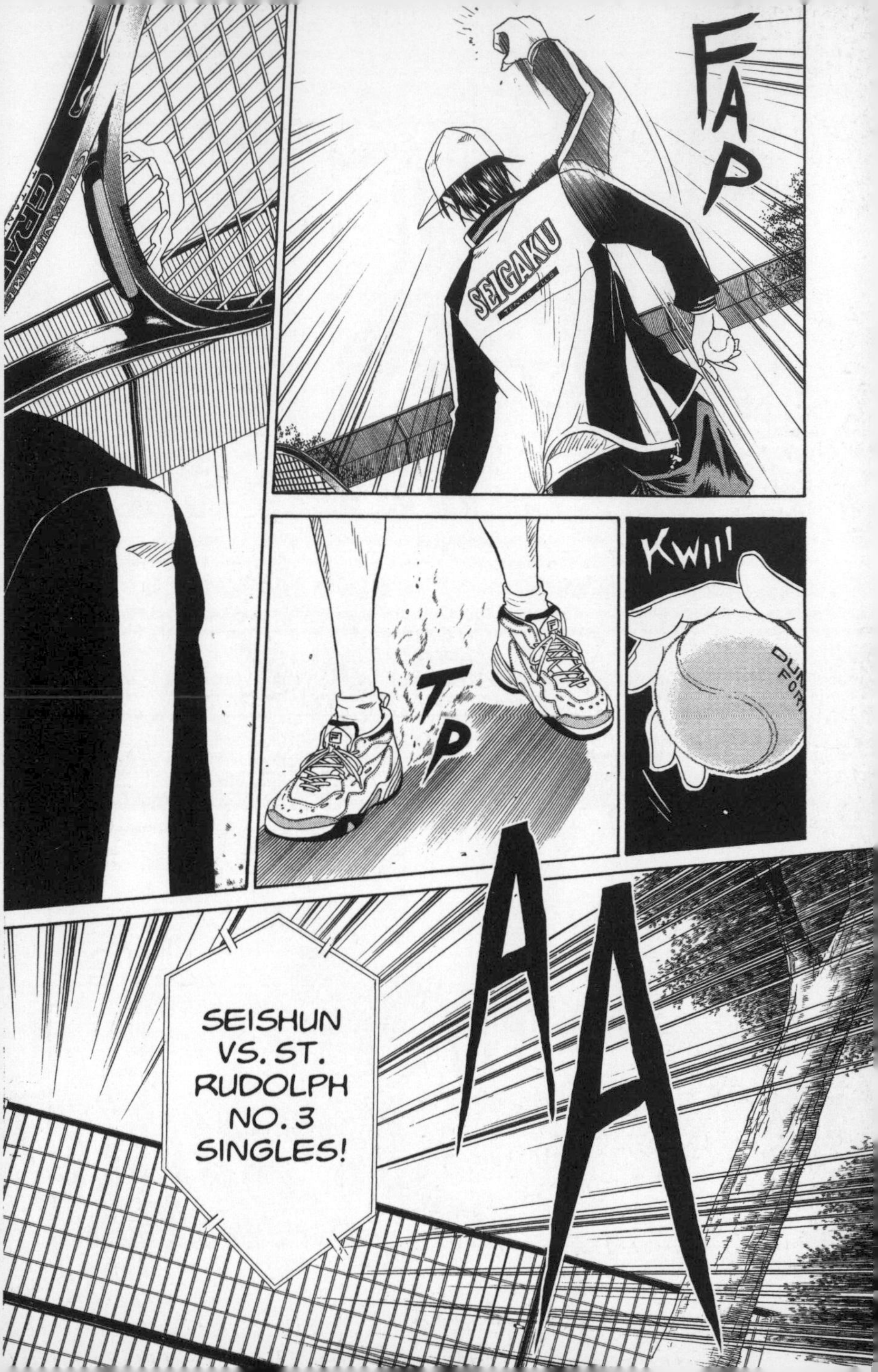
FAP
SEIGAKU
KWII'
TP
AA
SEISHUN VS. ST. RUDOLPH NO. 3 SINGLES!

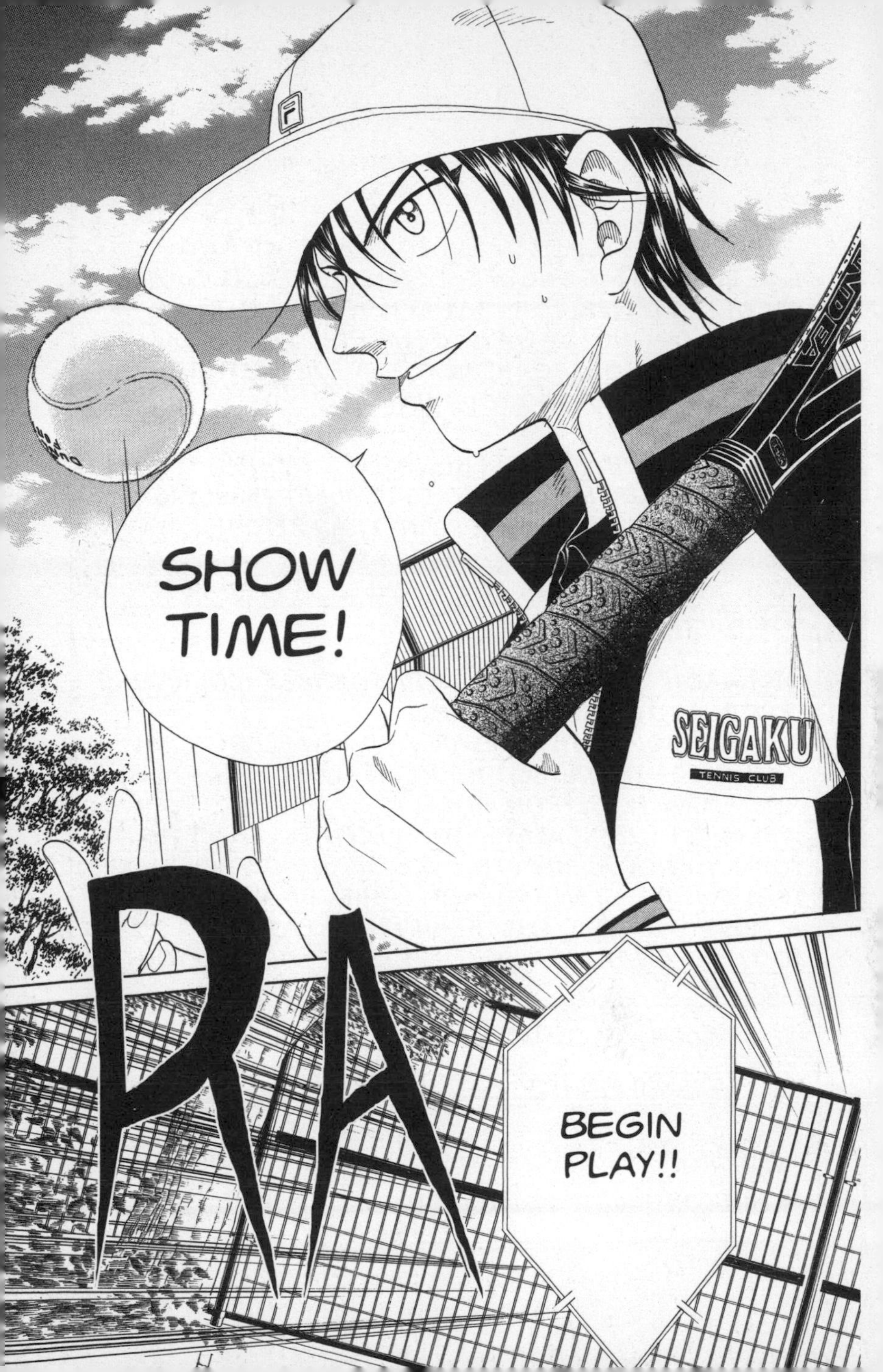
SHOW TIME!
SEIGAKU
TENNIS CLUB
BEGIN PLAY!!
PA

THANKS FOR READING PRINCE OF TENNIS VOL. 8!

IN THE LAST VOLUME, I INCLUDED A PANEL WITH NO PIC-
TURE IN IT DURING ONE OF THE GAME SEQUENCES. I GOT A
LOT OF FAN LETTERS FOR THAT—I'M VERY PLEASED! I'M
ALWAYS LOOKING FOR WAYS TO MAKE THE GAMES FLOW WELL
FROM ONE EPISODE TO THE NEXT. I TRIED ESPECIALLY HARD
THIS VOLUME. WHAT DO YOU THINK?

I'VE BEEN HAVING HEADACHES LATELY. I THOUGHT IT MIGHT
BE THE BAD AIR IN MY STUDIO, SO I BOUGHT THREE BIG
POTTED PLANTS. (THE LITTLE PLANT I HAD BEFORE
DIED...)
NOW THE STUDIO LOOKS LIKE A JUNGLE...BUT AM I GETTING
FEWER HEADACHES?

AS I WROTE BEFORE, I'M GRATEFUL FOR THE ENCOURAGING
LETTERS AND GIFTS YOU SEND ME.
LETTERS FROM BOTH REGULARS AND NEW READERS HAVE
INCREASED—IT'S THE BEST MEDICINE I COULD ASK FOR AS
MY STAMINA FLAGS FROM WORK!
THE GIFTS HAVE INCREASED TOO, RECENTLY. I CAN'T THANK
YOU GUYS ENOUGH. HEARTFELT GIFTS, HAND-DRAWN ILLUS-
TRATIONS, DOLLS, AND STICKERS... THEY'RE ALL GREAT!! I'M
ALMOST TEMPTED TO SELL THEM!! (BUT PLEASE DON'T SPEND
TOO MUCH ON THE GIFTS—I CHERISH JUST KNOWING YOU
SENT THEM.)

THE ST. RUDOLPH MATCH IS FINALLY ENTERING ITS SECOND
HALF! PLEASE STAY WITH IT FOR A LITTLE WHILE LONGER!

T. KONOMI!
2001.3.26

WELL THEN...
PLEASE CONTINUE TO SUPPORT PRINCE OF TENNIS AND RYOMA!!

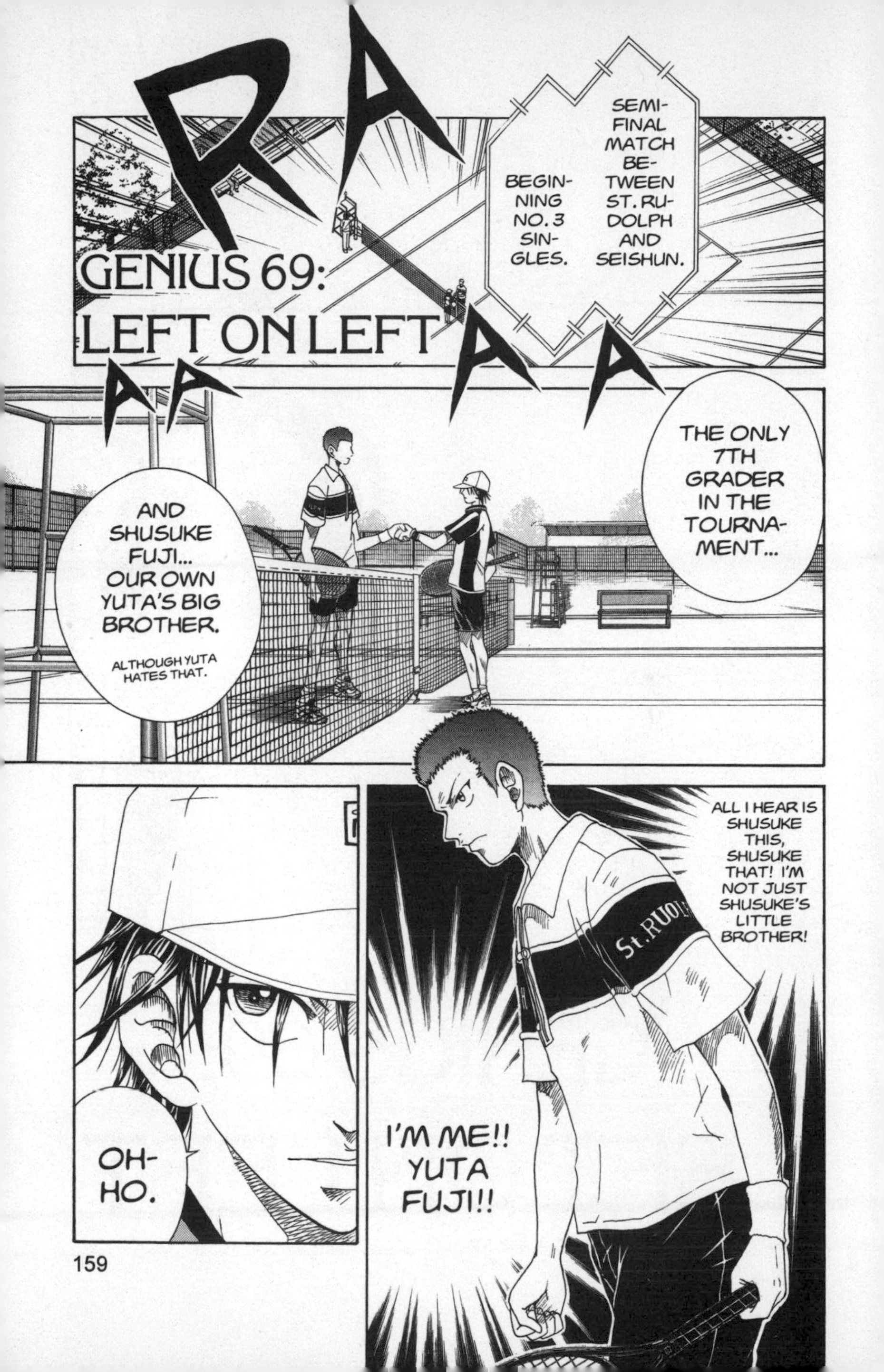

RAAAAA
GENIUS 69: LEFT ON LEFT
SEMI-FINAL MATCH BETWEEN ST. RUDOLPH AND SEISHUN.
BEGINNING NO. 3 SINGLES.
THE ONLY 7TH GRADER IN THE TOURNAMENT...
AND SHUSUKE FUJI... OUR OWN YUTA'S BIG BROTHER.
ALTHOUGH YUTA HATES THAT.
ALL I HEAR IS SHUSUKE THIS, SHUSUKE THAT! I'M NOT JUST SHUSUKE'S LITTLE BROTHER!
I'M ME!! YUTA FUJI!!
OH-HO.

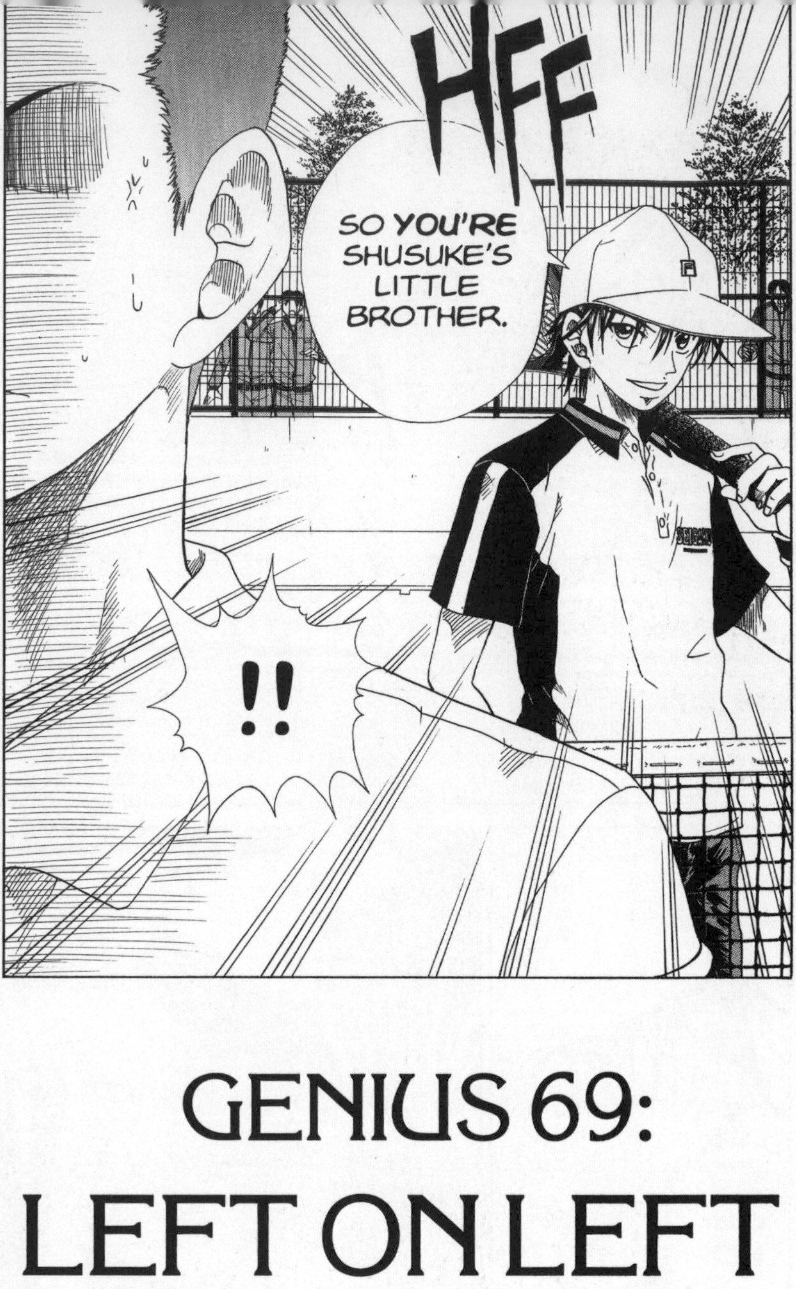
HFF
SO YOU'RE SHUSUKE'S LITTLE BROTHER.
!!

GENIUS 69:
LEFT ON LEFT

READ THIS WAY

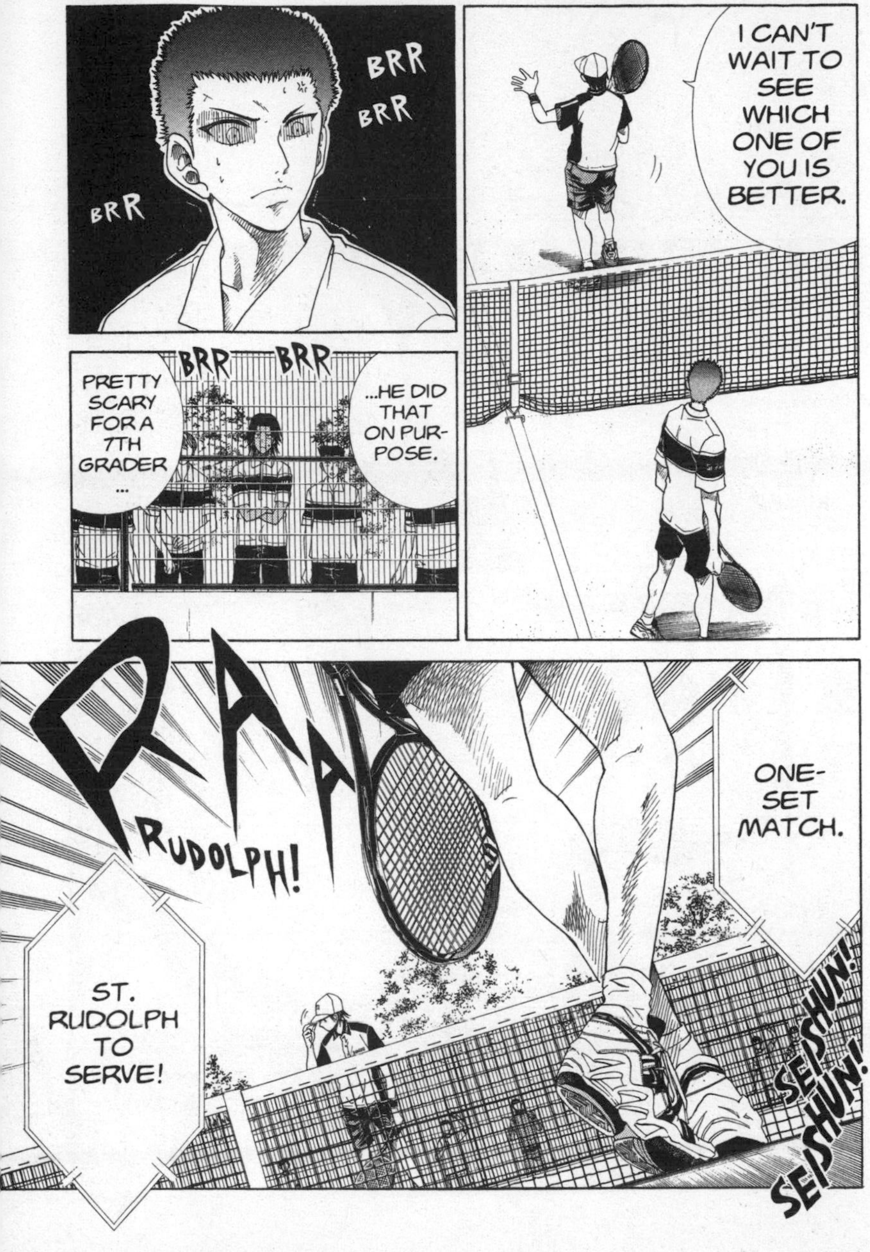

I CAN'T WAIT TO SEE WHICH ONE OF YOU IS BETTER.
BRR
BRR
BRR
...HE DID THAT ON PURPOSE.
BRR
BRR
PRETTY SCARY FOR A 7TH GRADER ...
ONE-SET MATCH.
SEISHUN!
SEISHUN!
RAA
RUDOLPH!
ST. RUDOLPH TO SERVE!

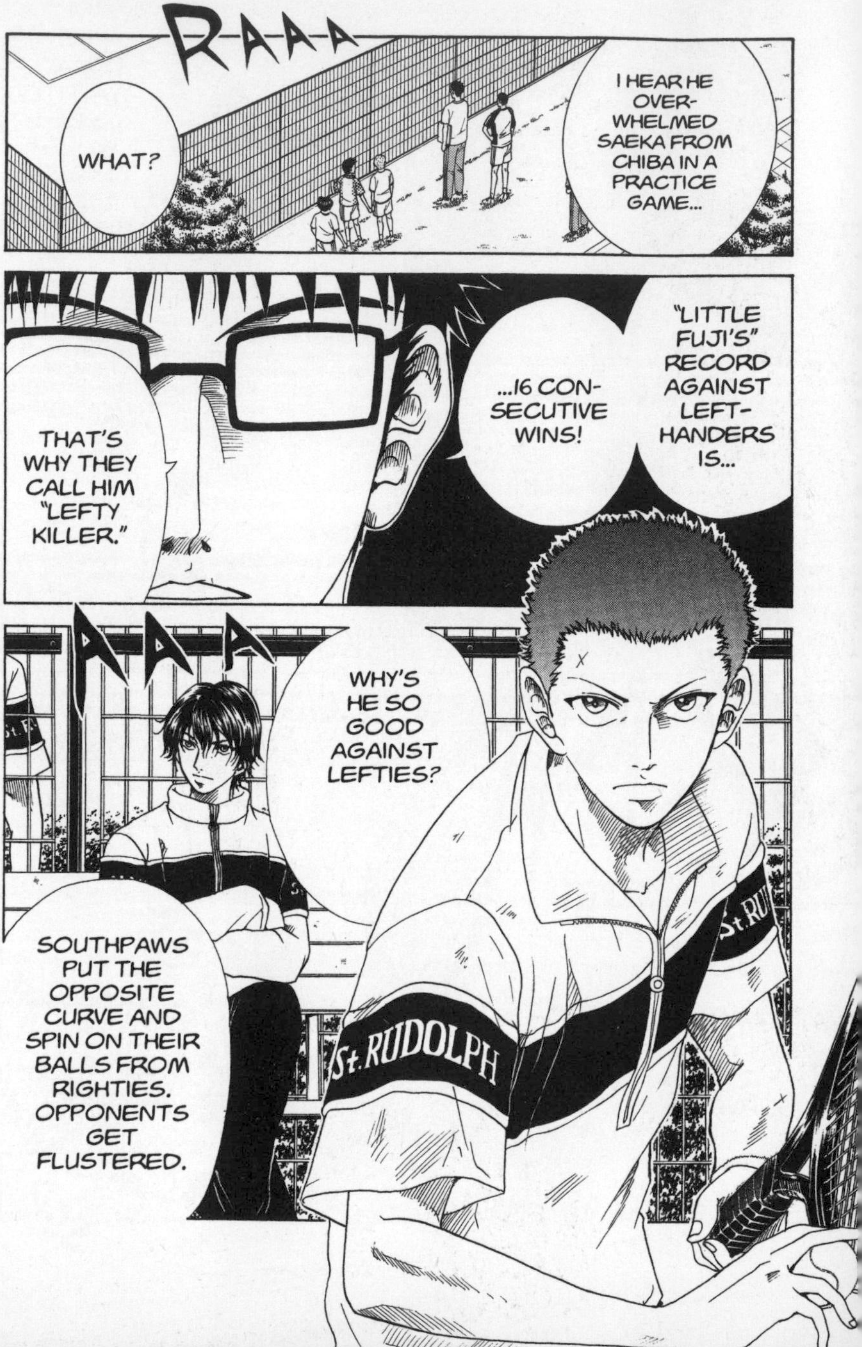
RAAA
I HEAR HE OVER-WHELMED SAEKA FROM CHIBA IN A PRACTICE GAME...
WHAT?
"LITTLE FUJI'S" RECORD AGAINST LEFT-HANDERS IS...
...16 CON-SECUTIVE WINS!
THAT'S WHY THEY CALL HIM "LEFTY KILLER."
AAA
WHY'S HE SO GOOD AGAINST LEFTIES?
SOUTHPAWS PUT THE OPPOSITE CURVE AND SPIN ON THEIR BALLS FROM RIGHTIES. OPPONENTS GET FLUSTERED.
St. RUDOLPH

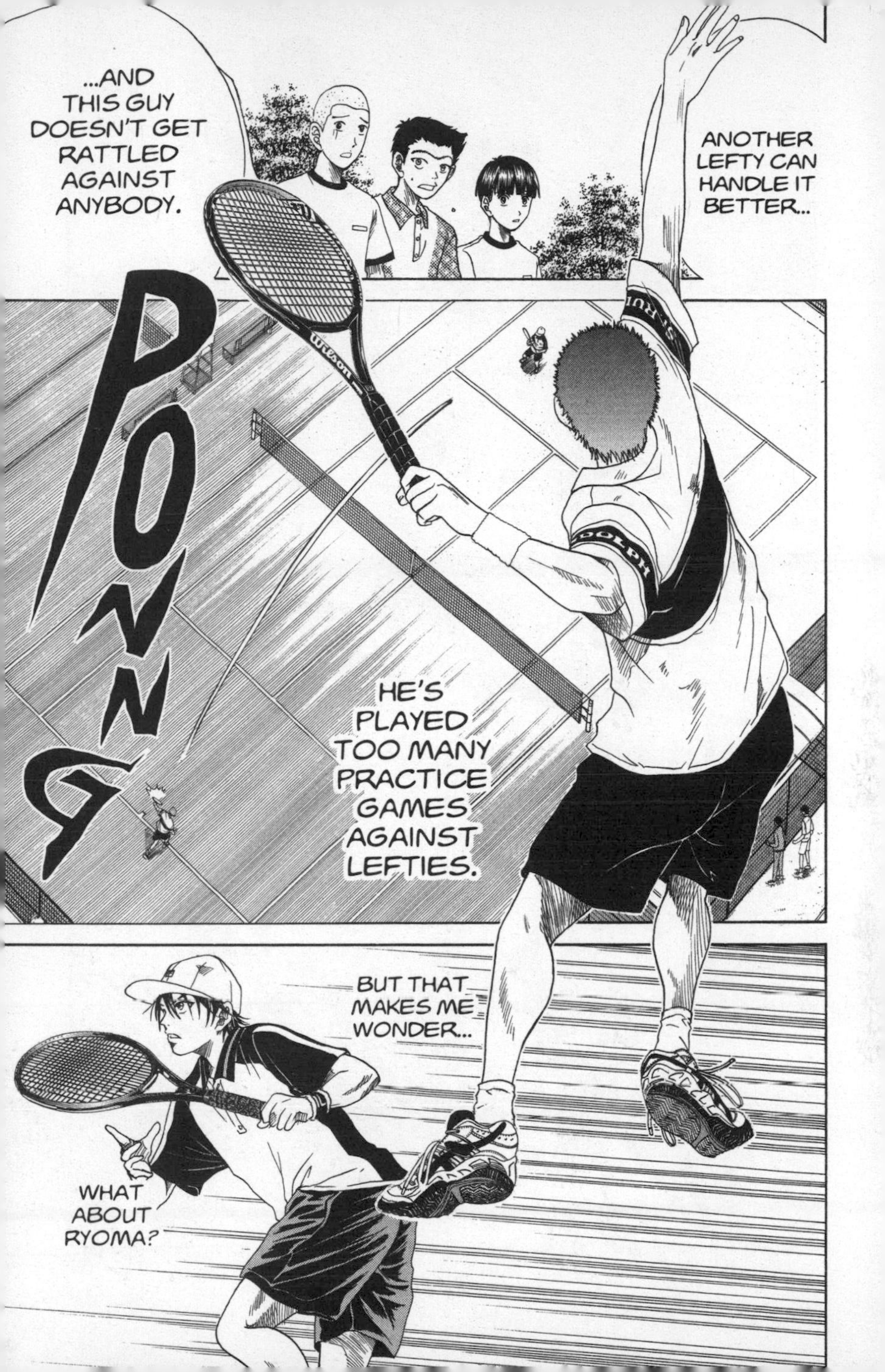
ANOTHER LEFTY CAN HANDLE IT BETTER...
...AND THIS GUY DOESN'T GET RATTLED AGAINST ANYBODY.
PONNG
HE'S PLAYED TOO MANY PRACTICE GAMES AGAINST LEFTIES.
BUT THAT MAKES ME WONDER...
WHAT ABOUT RYOMA?

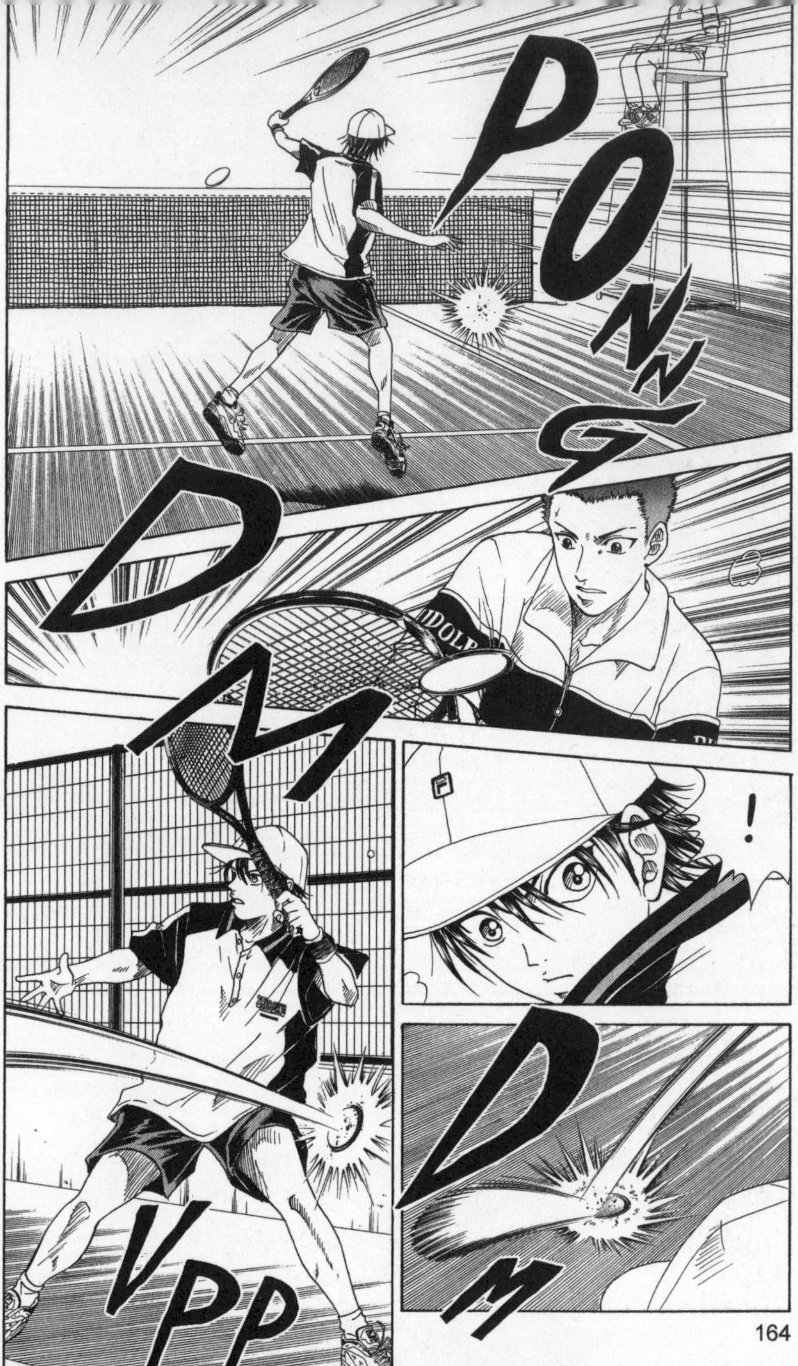
PONNG
DM
!
DDM
VPP

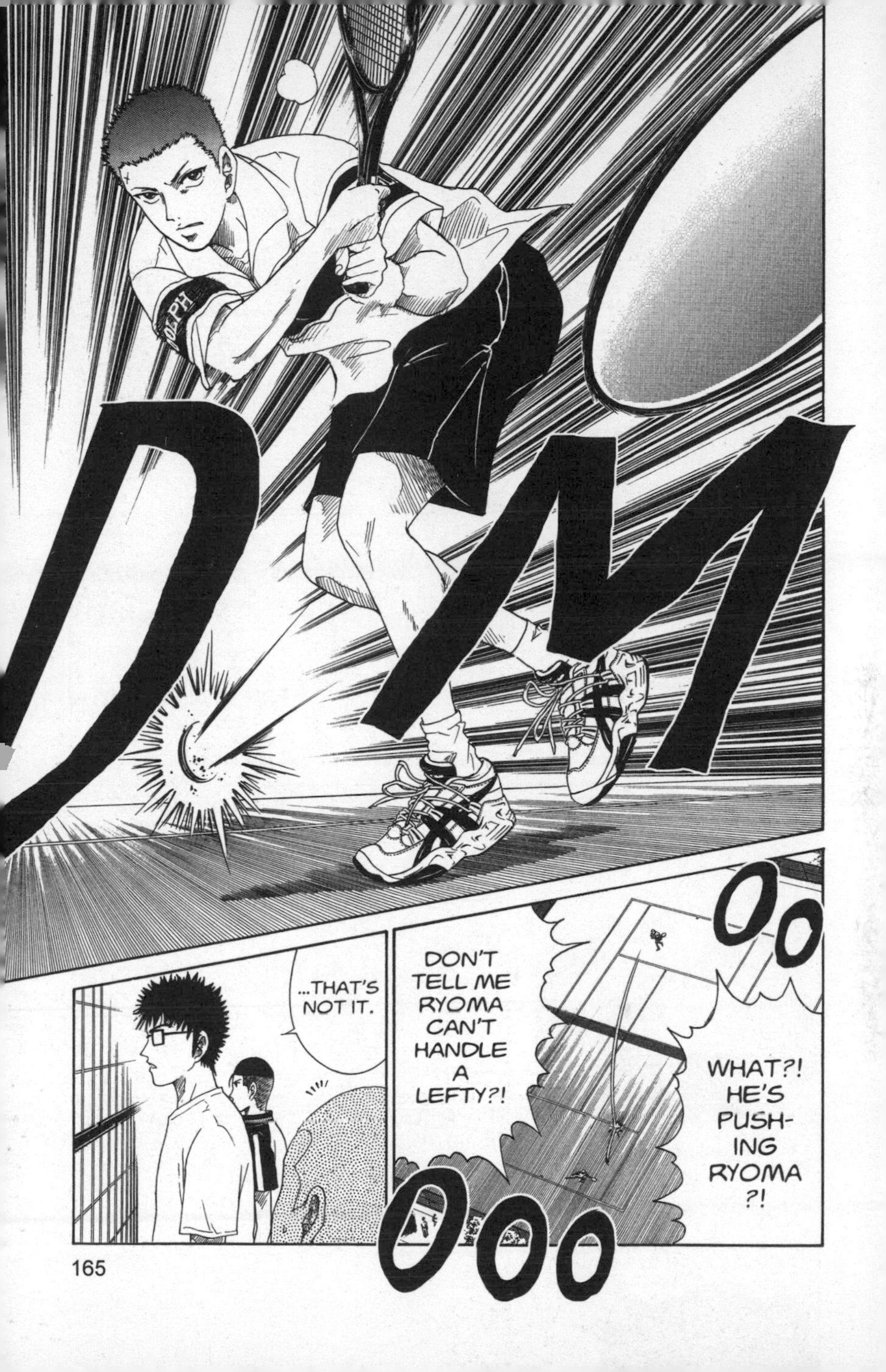
WHAT?! HE'S PUSHING RYOMA?!
DON'T TELL ME RYOMA CAN'T HANDLE A LEFTY?!
...THAT'S NOT IT.

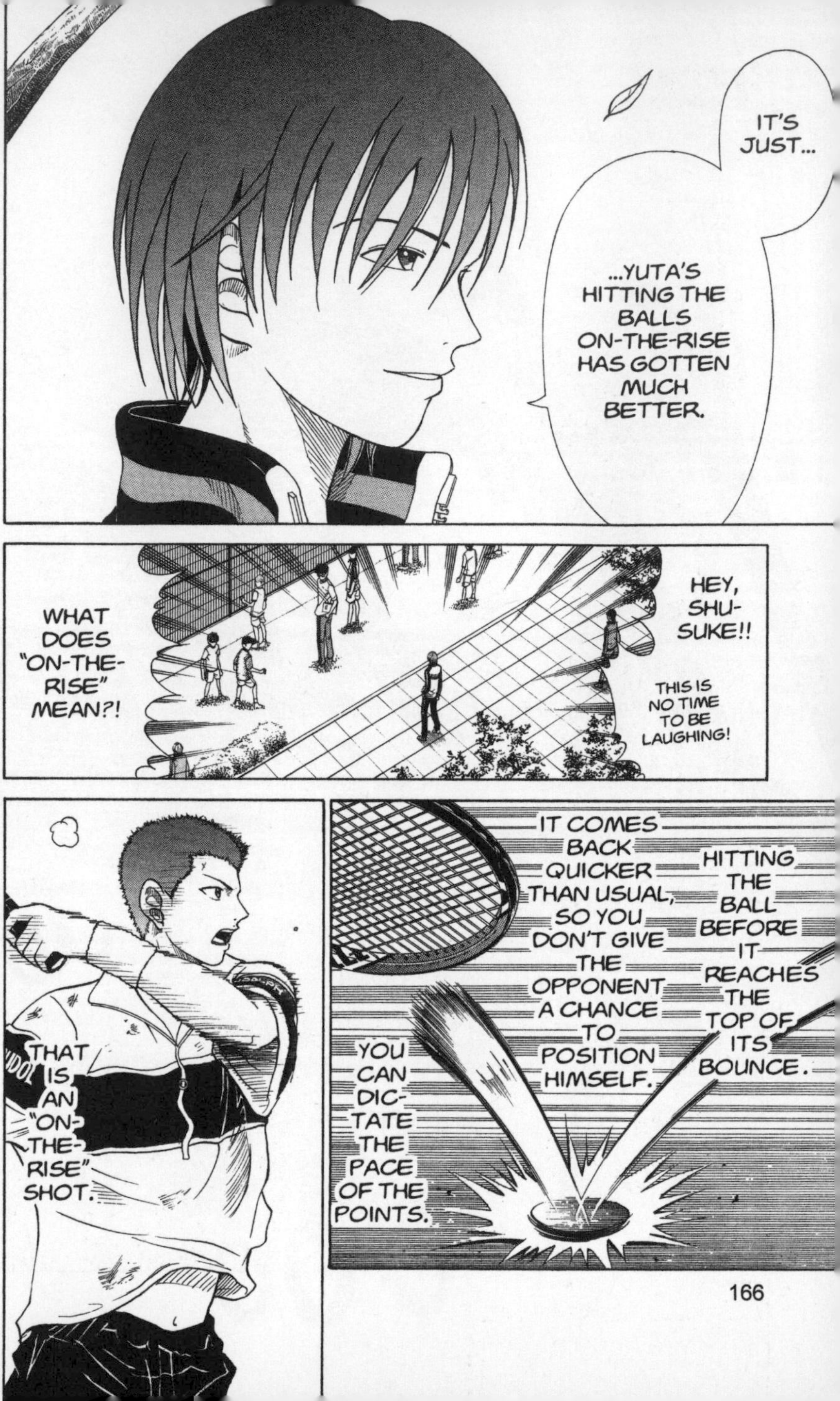
IT'S JUST...
...YUTA'S HITTING THE BALLS ON-THE-RISE HAS GOTTEN MUCH BETTER.
HEY, SHUSUKE!!
THIS IS NO TIME TO BE LAUGHING!
WHAT DOES "ON-THE-RISE" MEAN?!
HITTING THE BALL BEFORE IT REACHES THE TOP OF ITS BOUNCE.
IT COMES BACK QUICKER THAN USUAL, SO YOU DON'T GIVE THE OPPONENT A CHANCE TO POSITION HIMSELF.
YOU CAN DICTATE THE PACE OF THE POINTS.
THAT IS AN "ON-THE-RISE" SHOT.

READ THIS WAY

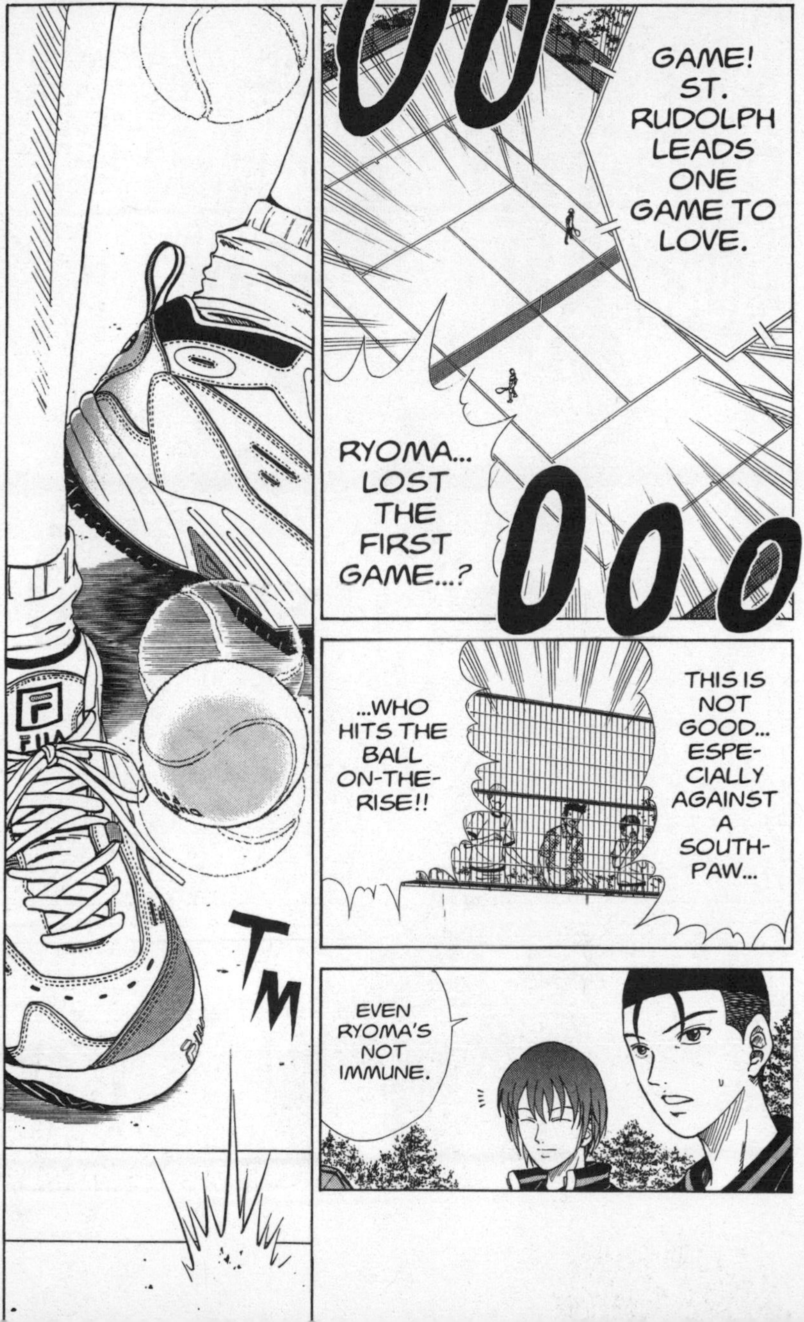
GAME! ST. RUDOLPH LEADS ONE GAME TO LOVE.
OO
RYOMA... LOST THE FIRST GAME...?
OOO
THIS IS NOT GOOD... ESPE-CIALLY AGAINST A SOUTH-PAW...
...WHO HITS THE BALL ON-THE-RISE!!
EVEN RYOMA'S NOT IMMUNE.
TM

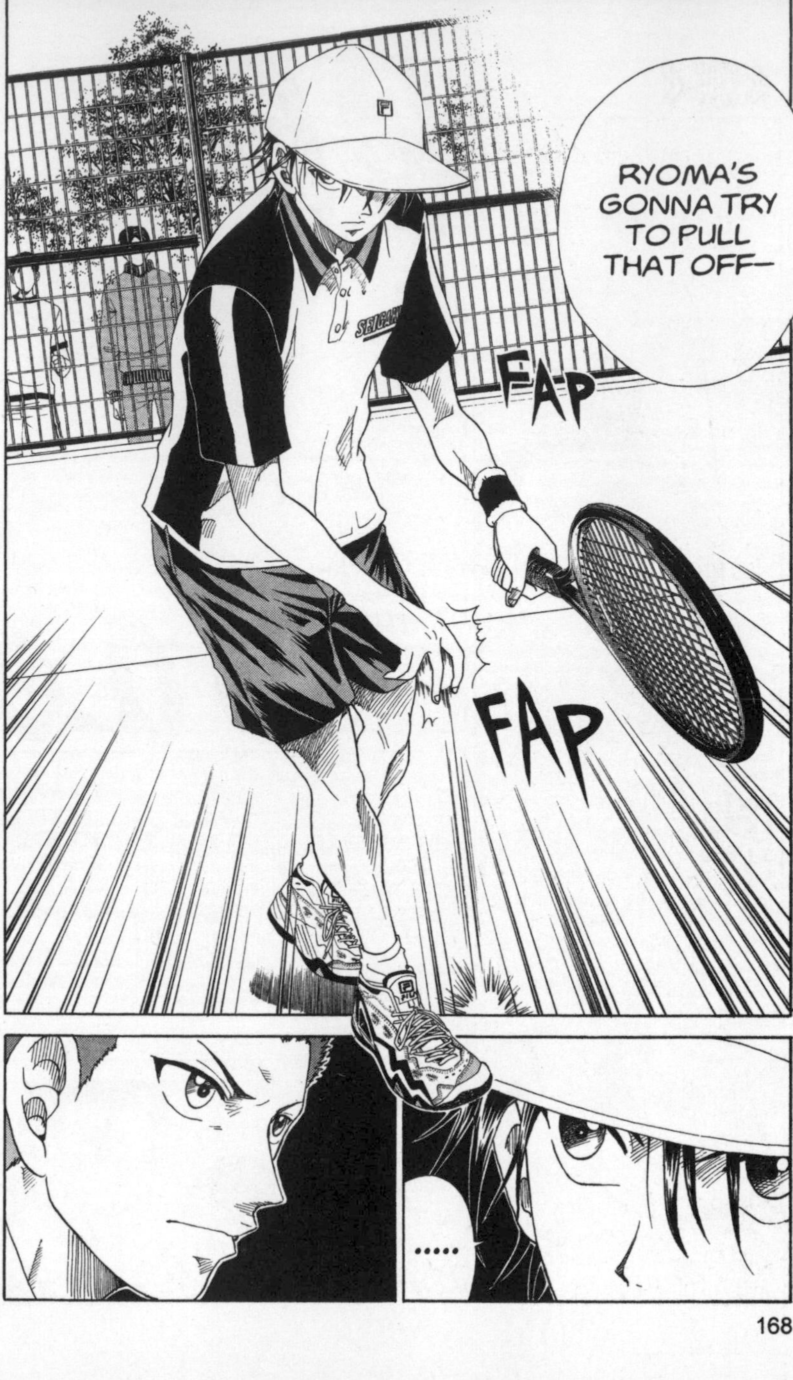
RYOMA'S GONNA TRY TO PULL THAT OFF—
FAP
FAP
.....

READ THIS WAY

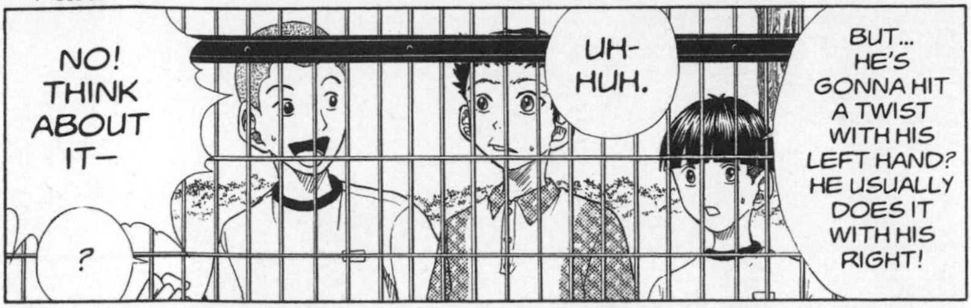
BUT... HE'S GONNA HIT A TWIST WITH HIS LEFT HAND? HE USUALLY DOES IT WITH HIS RIGHT!
UH-HUH.
NO! THINK ABOUT IT—
?

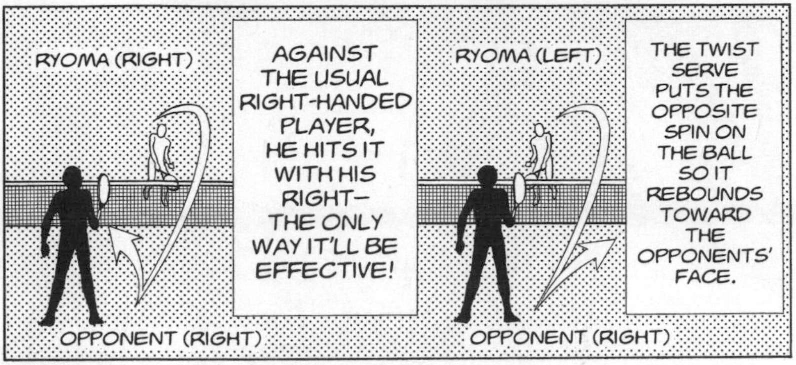
THE TWIST SERVE PUTS THE OPPOSITE SPIN ON THE BALL SO IT REBOUNDS TOWARD THE OPPONENTS' FACE.
RYOMA (LEFT)
OPPONENT (RIGHT)
AGAINST THE USUAL RIGHT-HANDED PLAYER, HE HITS IT WITH HIS RIGHT— THE ONLY WAY IT'LL BE EFFECTIVE!
RYOMA (RIGHT)
OPPONENT (RIGHT)

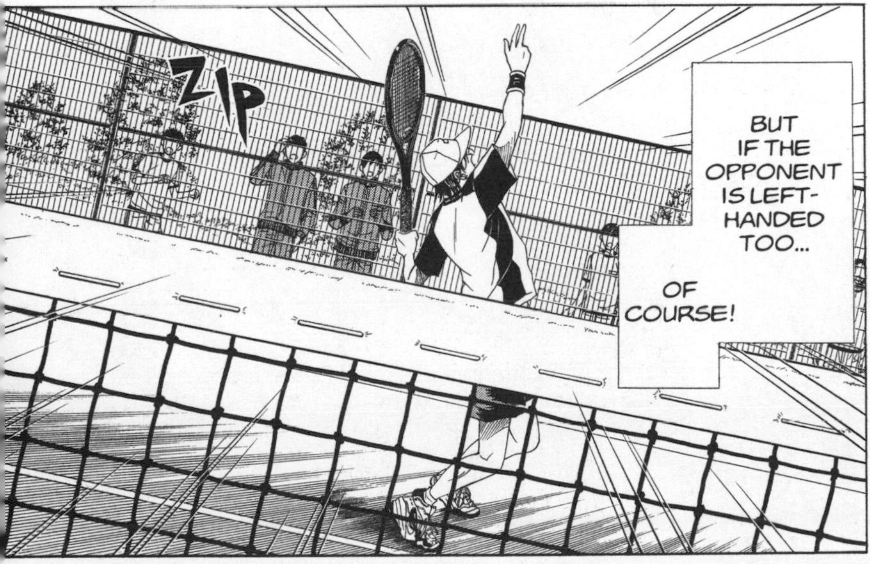
BUT IF THE OPPONENT IS LEFT-HANDED TOO...
OF COURSE!
ZIP

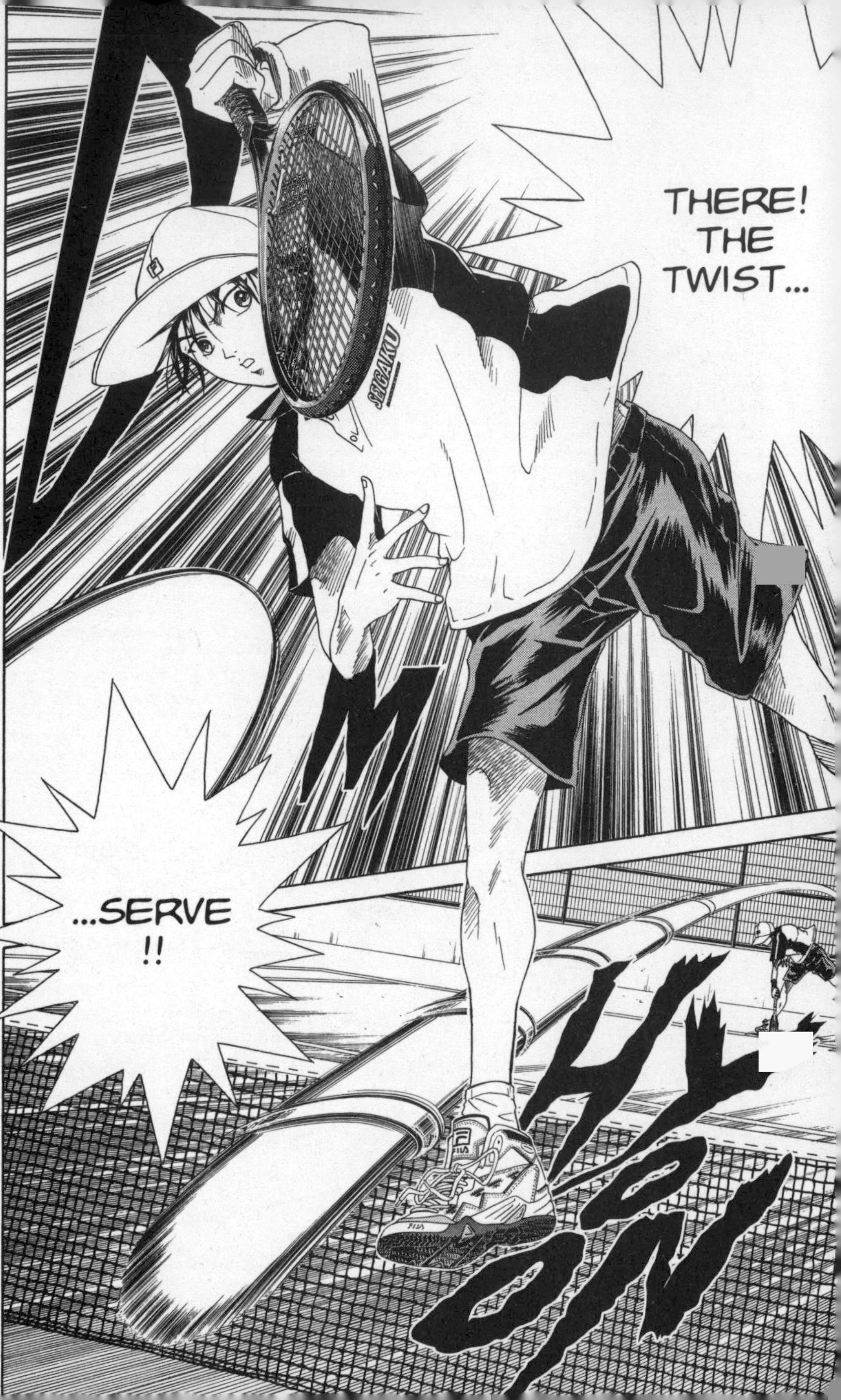
THERE! THE TWIST...
...SERVE !!

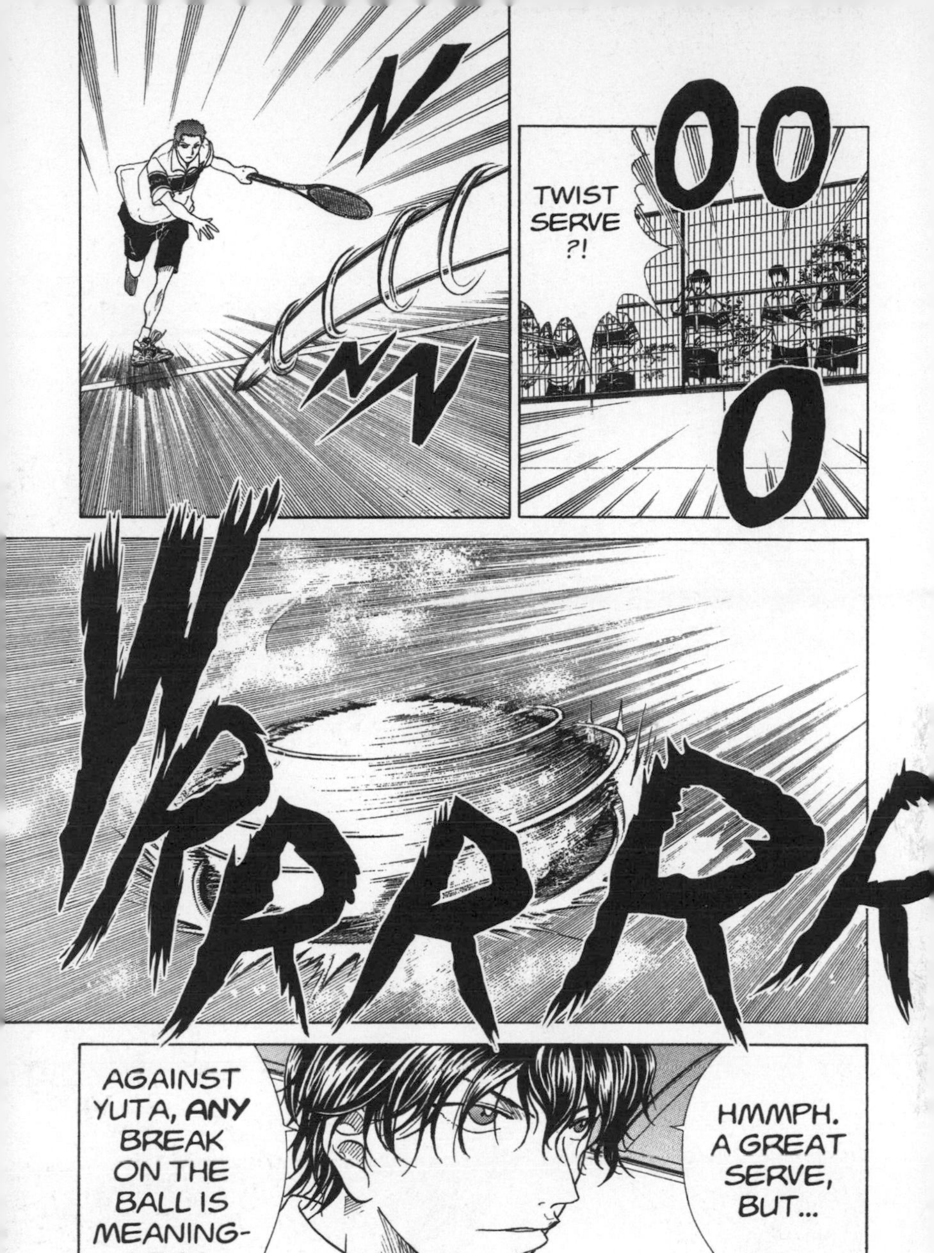
OOO
TWIST SERVE ?!
N
NN
WRRRK
HMMPH. A GREAT SERVE, BUT...
AGAINST YUTA, ANY BREAK ON THE BALL IS MEANINGLESS.

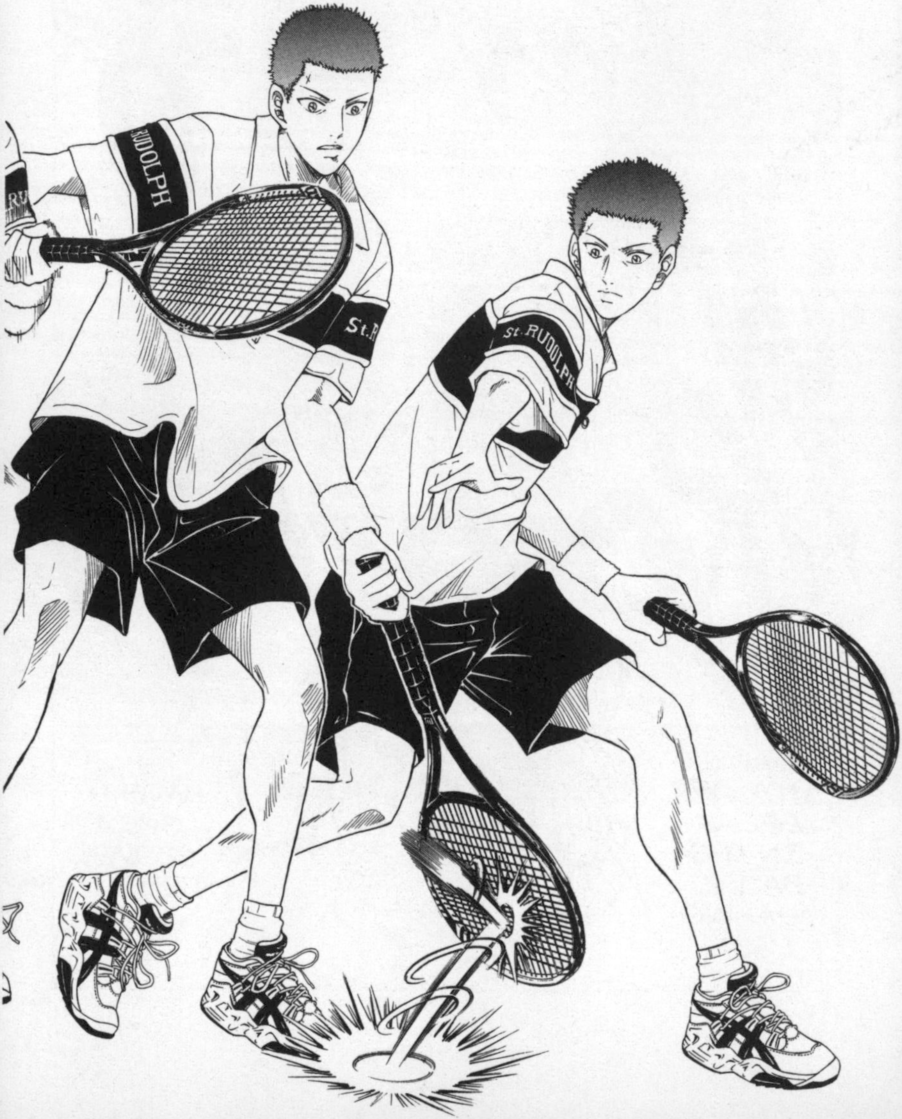
RUDOLPH
St.R
St.RUDOLPH

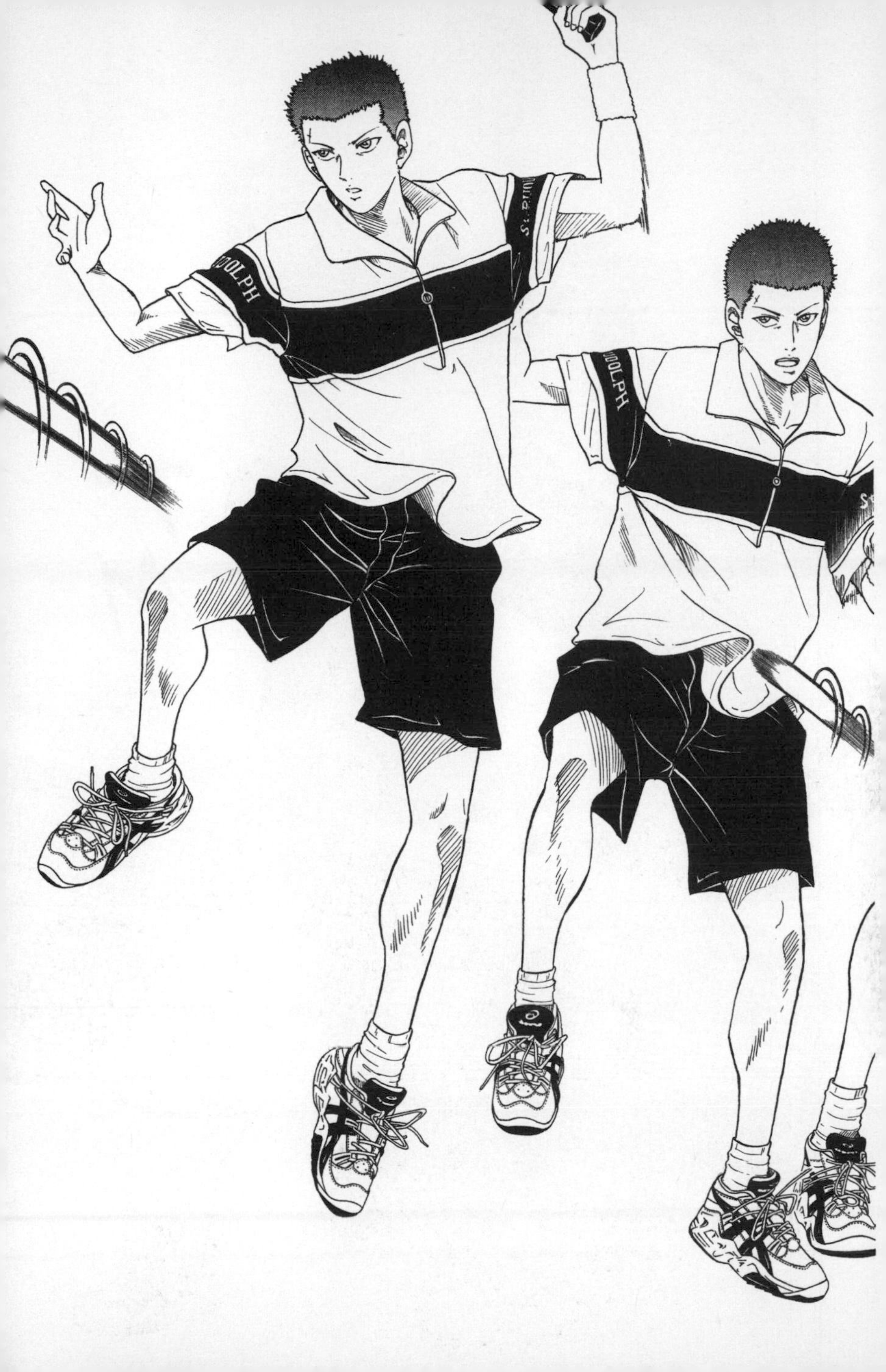

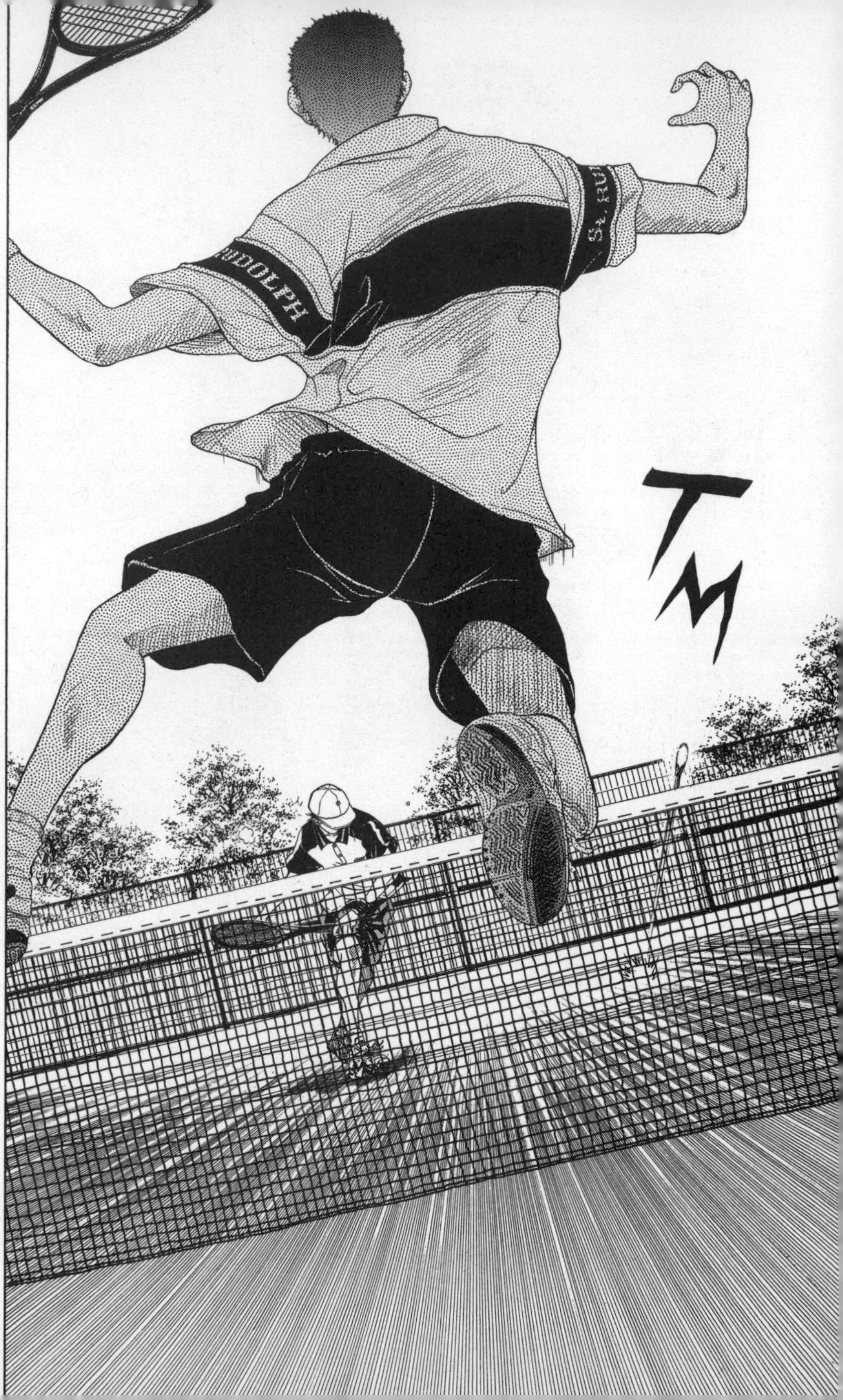
RUDOLPH
TM

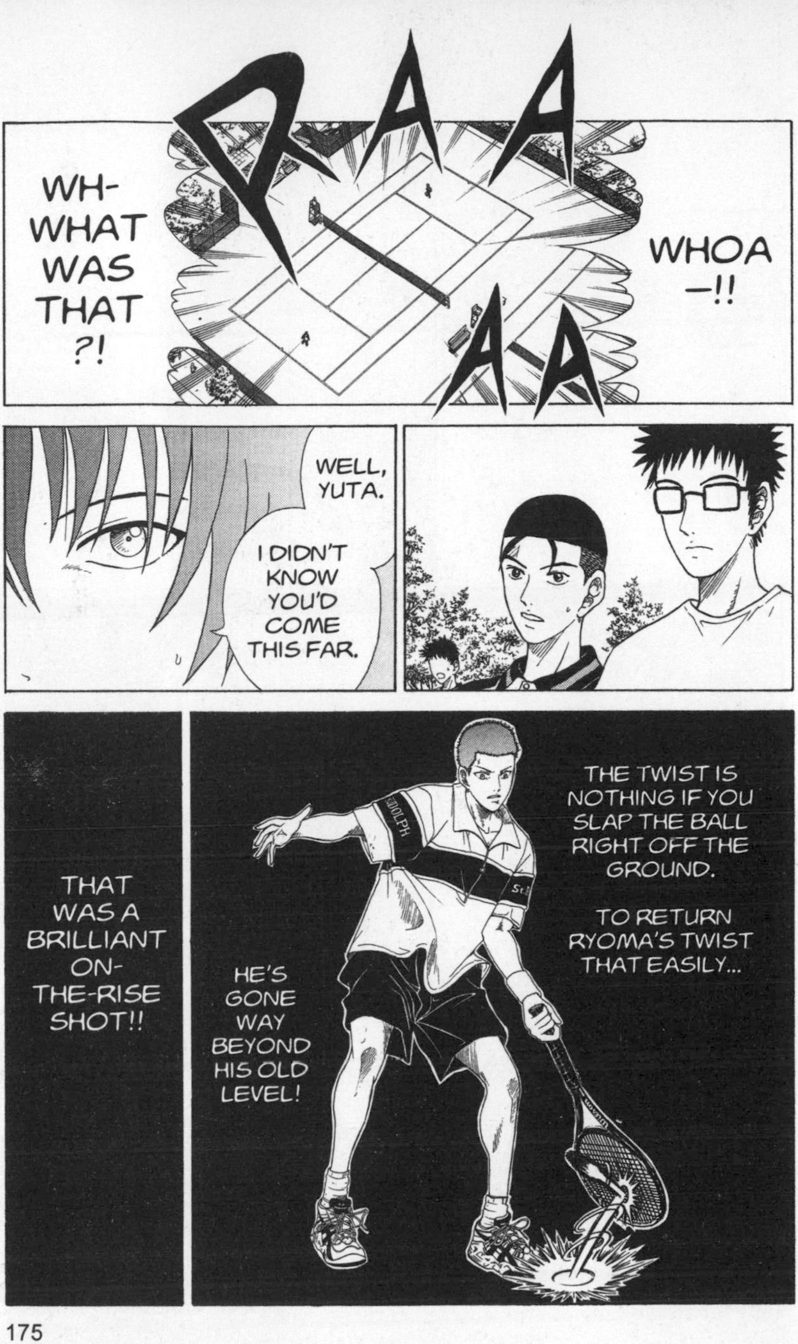
WHOA —!!
WH-WHAT WAS THAT ?!
WELL, YUTA.
I DIDN'T KNOW YOU'D COME THIS FAR.
THE TWIST IS NOTHING IF YOU SLAP THE BALL RIGHT OFF THE GROUND.
TO RETURN RYOMA'S TWIST THAT EASILY...
HE'S GONE WAY BEYOND HIS OLD LEVEL!
THAT WAS A BRILLIANT ON-THE-RISE SHOT!!

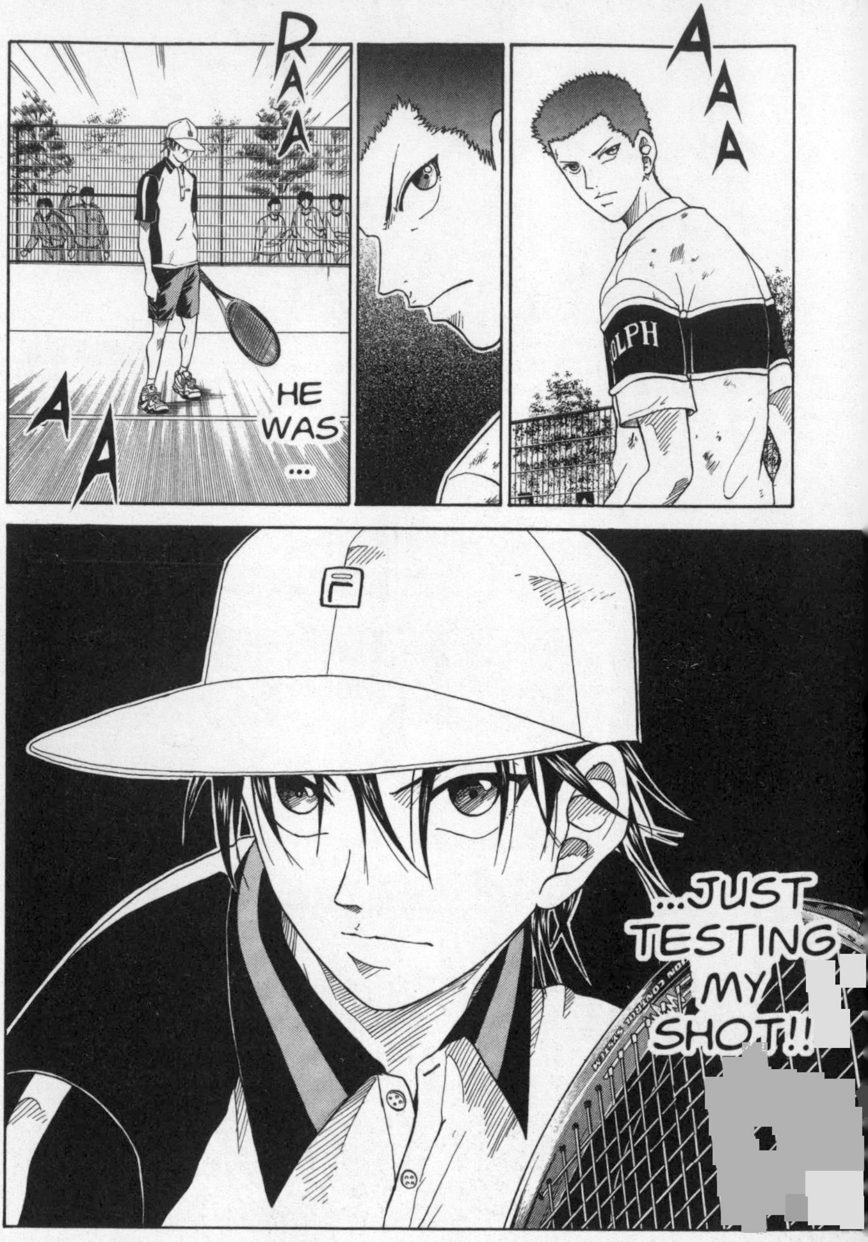
AAA
RAAA
HE WAS ...
AA
...JUST TESTING MY SHOT!!

TO BE CONTINUED...

In the Next Volume...

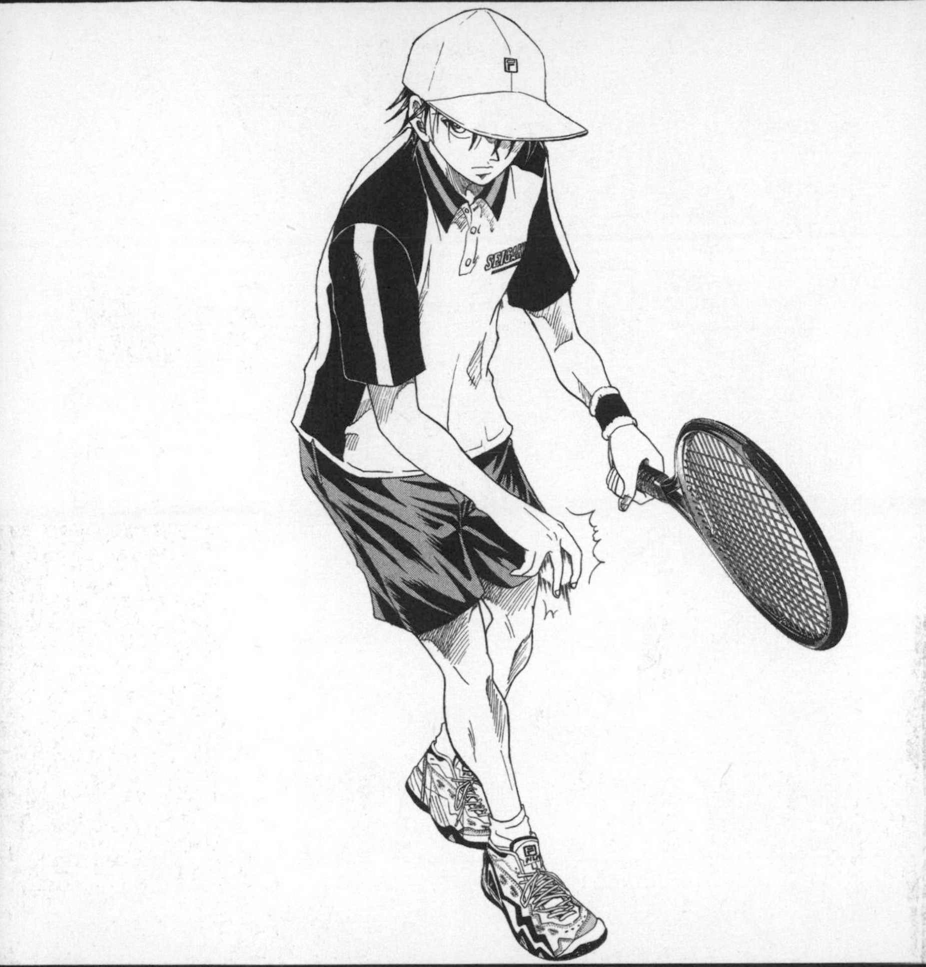

SEIGAKU

The wait is over! The highly charged match between The Prince of Tennis Ryoma Echizen and lefty killer Yuta is about to ignite. Per St. Rudolph's team manager Hajime's orders, Yuta must aim for Ryoma's previously injured left eye. Will Yuta execute this strategy, or will he try to beat Ryoma the old-fashioned way?

Available Now!

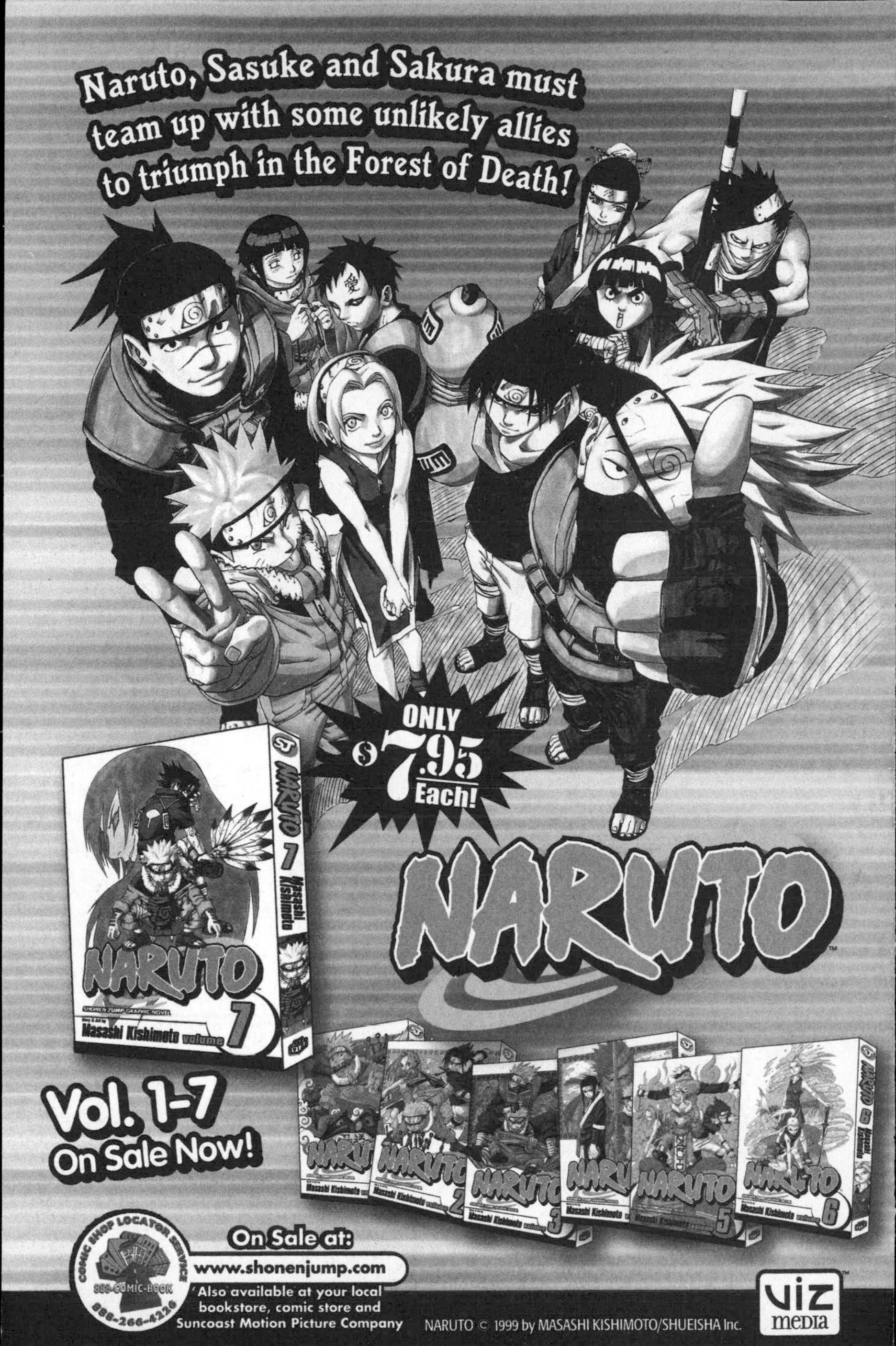
Naruto, Sasuke and Sakura must team up with some unlikely allies to triumph in the Forest of Death!
ONLY $7.95 Each!
NARUTO
Vol. 1-7 On Sale Now!
On Sale at:
www.shonenjump.com
Also available at your local bookstore, comic store and Suncoast Motion Picture Company
COMIC SHOP LOCATOR SERVICE
888-COMIC-BOOK
888-266-4226
NARUTO © 1999 by MASASHI KISHIMOTO/SHUEISHA Inc.
viz media

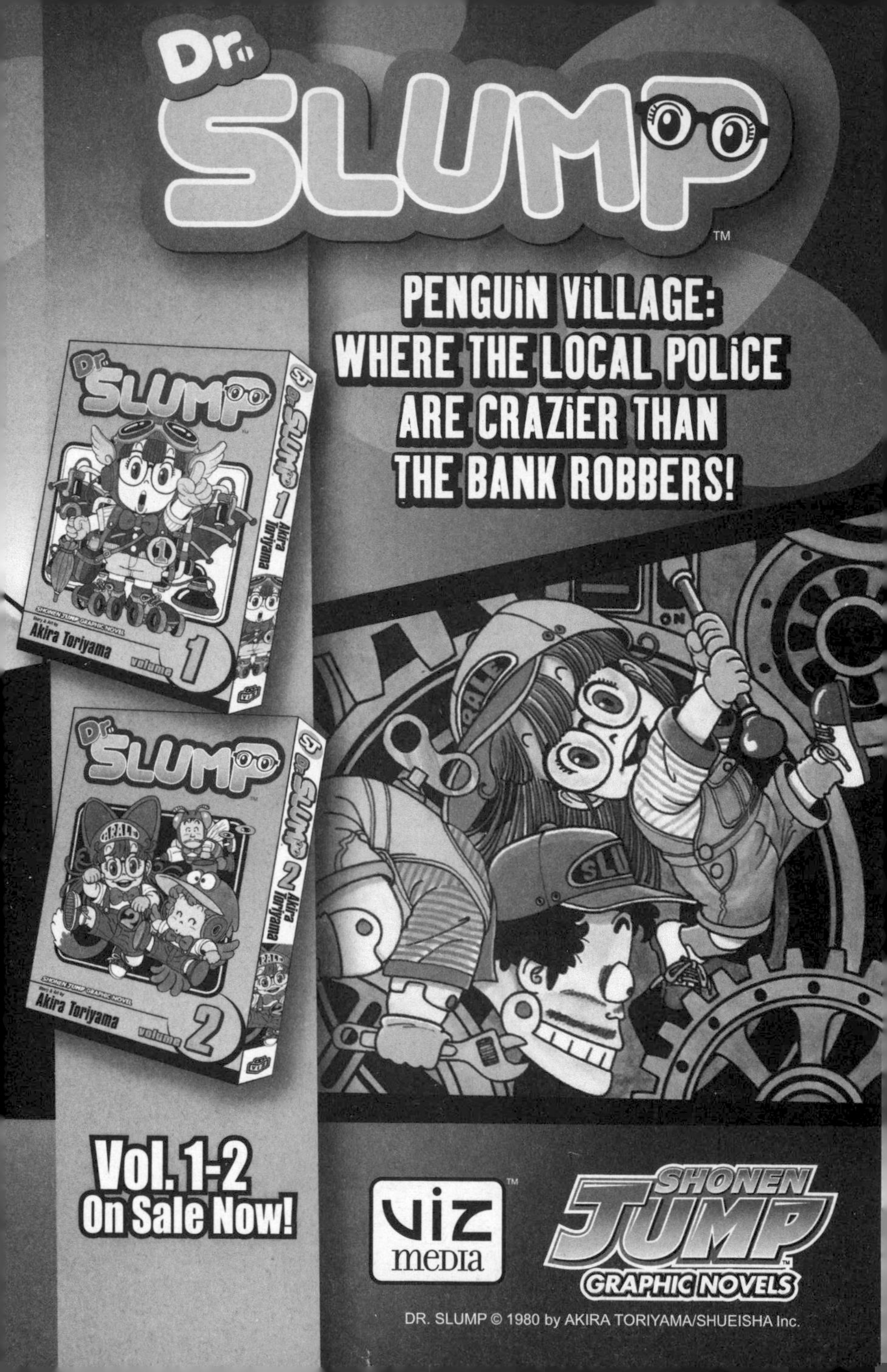
Dr. SLUMP™
PENGUIN VILLAGE:
WHERE THE LOCAL POLICE
ARE CRAZIER THAN
THE BANK ROBBERS!
Dr. SLUMP
Akira Toriyama
volume 1
Dr. SLUMP
Akira Toriyama
volume 2
Vol. 1-2
On Sale Now!
viz media™
SHONEN JUMP GRAPHIC NOVELS
DR. SLUMP © 1980 by AKIRA TORIYAMA/SHUEISHA Inc.